Business
Plans
Handbook

Business Plans

**A COMPILATION
OF BUSINESS
PLANS DEVELOPED
BY INDIVIDUALS
THROUGHOUT
NORTH AMERICA**

Handbook

VOLUME

37

**Kristin B. Mallegg,
Project Editor**

GALE
CENGAGE Learning

Farmington Hills, Mich • San Francisco • New York • Waterville, Maine
Meriden, Conn • Mason, Ohio • Chicago

GALE
CENGAGE Learning®

Business Plans Handbook, Volume 37

Project Editor: Kristin B. Mallegg

Content Developer: Michele P. LaMeau

Product Design: Jennifer Wahi

Composition and Electronic Prepress: Evi Seoud

Manufacturing: Rita Wimberley

For product information and technology assistance, contact us at
Gale Customer Support, 1-800-877-4253.
For permission to use material from this text or product,
submit all requests online at **www.cengage.com/permissions.**
Further permissions questions can be emailed to
permissionrequest@cengage.com

Gale, a part of Cengage Learning
27500 Drake Rd.
Farmington Hills, MI 48331-3535

ISBN-13: 978-1-4103-2820-5
1084-4473

Printed in Mexico
1 2 3 4 5 6 7 20 19 18 17 16

Contents

APPENDIXES

Highlights

Business Plans Handbook, Volume 37 (BPH-37) is a collection of business plans compiled by entrepreneurs seeking funding for small businesses throughout North America. For those looking for examples of how to approach, structure, and compose their own business plans, *BPH-37* presents 20 sample plans, including plans for the following businesses:

- 3-D Property Imaging Business
- Agricultural Drone Business
- Auto Appraiser
- Clothing Alterations and Tailoring
- Community-Supported Organic Farm
- Corporate Event Planning Business
- Specialty Coffee Roaster
- Tow Truck Operator
- Virtual Assistant
- Writing & Editing Business

FEATURES AND BENEFITS

BPH-37 offers many features not provided by other business planning references including:

- Twenty business plans, each of which represent an attempt at clarifying (for themselves and others) the reasons that the business should exist or expand and why a lender should fund the enterprise.
- Two fictional plans that are used by business counselors at a prominent small business development organization as examples for their clients. (You will find these in the Business Plan Template Appendix.)
- A directory section that includes listings for venture capital and finance companies, which specialize in funding start-up and second-stage small business ventures, and a comprehensive listing of Service Corps of Retired Executives (SCORE) offices. In addition, the Appendix also contains updated listings of all Small Business Development Centers (SBDCs); associations of interest to entrepreneurs; Small Business Administration (SBA) Regional Offices; and consultants specializing in small business planning and advice. It is strongly advised that you consult supporting organizations while planning your business, as they can provide a wealth of useful information.
- A Small Business Term Glossary to help you decipher the sometimes confusing terminology used by lenders and others in the financial and small business communities.
- A cumulative index, outlining each plan profiled in the complete *Business Plans Handbook* series.
- A Business Plan Template which serves as a model to help you construct your own business plan. This generic outline lists all the essential elements of a complete business plan and their

components, including the Summary, Business History and Industry Outlook, Market Examination, Competition, Marketing, Administration and Management, Financial Information, and other key sections. Use this guide as a starting point for compiling your plan.

- Extensive financial documentation required to solicit funding from small business lenders. You will find examples of Cash Flows, Balance Sheets, Income Projections, and other financial information included with the textual portions of the plan.

Introduction

Perhaps the most important aspect of business planning is simply doing it. More and more business owners are beginning to compile business plans even if they don't need a bank loan. Others discover the value of planning when they must provide a business plan for the bank. The sheer act of putting thoughts on paper seems to clarify priorities and provide focus. Sometimes business owners completely change strategies when compiling their plan, deciding on a different product mix or advertising scheme after finding that their assumptions were incorrect. This kind of healthy thinking and re-thinking via business planning is becoming the norm. The editors of *Business Plans Handbook, Volume 37 (BPH-37)* sincerely hope that this latest addition to the series is a helpful tool in the successful completion of your business plan, no matter what the reason for creating it.

This thirty-seventh volume, like each volume in the series, offers business plans created by real people. *BPH-37* provides 20 business plans. The business and personal names and addresses and general locations have been changed to protect the privacy of the plan authors.

NEW BUSINESS OPPORTUNITIES

As in other volumes in the series, *BPH-37* finds entrepreneurs engaged in a wide variety of creative endeavors. Examples include an Interior Design Company, a Microbrewery, and a Property Management Company. In addition, several other plans are provided, including a Document Shredding Business, a Fence Installation and Repair Company, Corporate Event Planning Business and a Cost Cutting Consulting Business, among others.

Comprehensive financial documentation has become increasingly important as today's entrepreneurs compete for the finite resources of business lenders. Our plans illustrate the financial data generally required of loan applicants, including Income Statements, Financial Projections, Cash Flows, and Balance Sheets.

ENHANCED APPENDIXES

In an effort to provide the most relevant and valuable information for our readers, we have updated the coverage of small business resources. For instance, you will find a directory section, which includes listings of all of the Service Corps of Retired Executives (SCORE) offices; an informative glossary, which includes small business terms; and a cumulative index, outlining each plan profiled in the complete *Business Plans Handbook* series. In addition we have updated the list of Small Business Development Centers (SBDCs); Small Business Administration Regional Offices; venture capital and finance companies, which specialize in funding start-up and second-stage small business enterprises; associations of interest to entrepreneurs; and consultants, specializing in small business advice and planning. For your reference, we have also reprinted the business plan template, which provides a comprehensive overview of the essential components of a business plan and two fictional plans used by small business counselors.

SERIES INFORMATION

If you already have the first thirty-six volumes of *BPH*, with this thirty-seventh volume, you will now have a collection of over 670 business plans (not including the updated plans); contact information for hundreds of organizations and agencies offering business expertise; a helpful business plan template; more than 1,500 citations to valuable small business development material; and a comprehensive glossary of terms to help the business planner navigate the sometimes confusing language of entrepreneurship.

ACKNOWLEDGEMENTS

The Editors wish to sincerely thank the contributors to *BPH-37*, including:

- Fran Fletcher
- Paul Greenland
- Claire Moore
- Zuzu Enterprises

COMMENTS WELCOME

Your comments on *Business Plans Handbook* are appreciated. Please direct all correspondence, suggestions for future volumes of *BPH*, and other recommendations to the following:

Managing Editor, Business Product
Business Plans Handbook
Gale, a part of Cengage Learning
27500 Drake Rd.
Farmington Hills, MI 48331-3535
Phone: (248)699-4253
Fax: (248)699-8052
Toll-Free: 800-357-GALE
E-mail: BusinessProducts@gale.com

3-D Property Imaging Business

SurroundSpace LLC

2563 Pinetree Rd.
Forrester, MA 01055

Paul Greenland

SurroundSpace LLC is a 3-D property imaging business based in Forrester, Massachusetts.

EXECUTIVE SUMMARY

SurroundSpace LLC is a 3-D property imaging business based in Forrester, Massachusetts. The company uses special cameras and imaging services from the Sunnyvale, California-based immersive media technology firm, Matterport (https://matterport.com), to produce interactive 3-D models of real spaces, including homes and commercial buildings. The company's virtual models provide facility managers, venue operators, interior designers, real estate agents, property owners, landlords, architects, and home improvement specialists with a unique tool to showcase or view properties and spaces for sale, rent, improvement and more. SurroundSpace is being established by Parker McKay, an entrepreneur with a property management background, and his wife, Jessica, who is a successful interior designer.

MARKET ANALYSIS

Although Matterport's immersive media technology was being used by companies like SurroundSpace throughout the world, the market for 3-D property imaging was still emerging in 2016. Significant opportunities existed to provide imaging of both residential and commercial spaces (e.g., homes, apartments, condominiums, commercial buildings, event venues, etc.).

Many service providers use Matterport's technology in the real estate market. While SurroundSpace will provide imaging services to realtors, the company will differentiate itself by focusing more heavily on venues and facilities (e.g., museums, convention centers, hospitals, art galleries, universities, etc.) and the interior design market. This approach will allow the business to capitalize on the skills and experience of its owners.

Because SurroundSpace charges customers by the square foot for its imaging services, large commercial spaces present the greatest opportunity for generating revenue. For example, a small medical clinic may span 10,000 square feet. A large outpatient cancer center may span approximately 65,000 feet. A typical shopping mall may be nearly 800,000 square feet, offering roughly 150 stores. An indoor sports complex with multiple basketball and volleyball courts can exceed 100,000 square feet.

SurroundSpace's owners have categorized their target markets as follows:

Primary Target Markets

- Interior Designers
- Venue Operators
- Architects
- Facility Managers
- Marketing Directors
- Home Improvement Specialists

Secondary Target Markets

- Landlords
- Property Owners
- Real Estate Agents

Geography

SurroundSpace is located in Forrester, Massachusetts, between the cities of Springfield and Worchester. In 2015 Forrester was home to 175,000 people. The business initially will concentrate on providing services within a 60-mile radius of Forrester. However, SurroundSpace will gradually expand its business to serve large customers (namely interior design firms and large venue operators) throughout the Eastern United States.

Following is a breakdown of prospects, by establishment type, in Forrester, Massachusetts, and in a 60-mile radius of Forrester.

Services:
- Amusement and Recreation Services 417/1,457
- Educational Services 556/1,755
- Health Services 1,648/5,423
- Hotels, Rooming Houses, Camps, and Other Lodging Places 77/284
- Museums, Art Galleries and Botanical and Zoological Gardens 33/124

Retail:
- Apparel and Accessory Stores 211/672
- Eating and Drinking Places 992/2,820
- Home Furniture, Furnishings and Equipment Stores 208/768
- Miscellaneous Retail 905/2,905

Real Estate:
- Real Estate Brokers 880/2,760

Competition

Currently, no other 3-D property imaging businesses are operating in or around Forrester. Several providers are located in the Boston area. SurroundSpace will capitalize on this opportunity by securing an early foothold in the local/regional market.

SERVICES

Overview

The 3-D property imaging services provided by SurroundSpace produce immersive digital representations of real spaces. These allow prospective customers or visitors to experience, tour, and interact with a space before visiting it physically. For example, an expectant mother may wish to see the birthing suites, nursery, and other areas of a local hospital from her tablet before deciding where to have her baby. A national association may wish to navigate the conference center and meeting rooms of a hotel before deciding where to host an annual conference. Families may wish to see the inside of a museum or local attraction while planning their vacation. Instead of a simple video clip or selection of photos, interior designers can now showcase their portfolios in new ways by offering interactive tours of the residential and commercial spaces they have designed.

Process

After connecting with a prospect, SurroundSpace's owners will meet with the potential customer to determine their specific goals, objectives, and expectations. The owners will require the potential customer to provide specific details regarding the number of square feet that will require imaging. Preferably, a floor plan can be provided. SurroundSpace also will require a brief property walkthrough with the customer, to gain a complete understanding of the project. Using details provided by the customer, a detailed time and cost estimate will be provided, based on a rate of $0.10 per square foot.

If the prospective customer accepts the estimate provided by SurroundSpace, the owners will arrange a date and time to perform the imaging using their Matterport equipment, which is simple to operate and does not require special lighting or intense training. Based on conversations with other providers, the owners anticipate that, on average, it will take approximately one hour to scan a 2,500-square-foot residential property. Compared to residential spaces, commercial facilities may involve the collection of a substantially larger number of images, and require a more significant amount of time. It is important that the imaging take place during a time when there is no movement in the room. In the case of commercial facilities, this may require imaging services to be provided after hours.

Once 360-degree views of all desired spaces have been obtained, SurroundSpace will upload scans to Matterport's cloud-based service, where they will be processed using special algorithms that result in a "Matterport Space" that customers can view privately or share on their Web sites. If desired, specific rooms, areas, or property features can be labeled/featured. Spaces can be navigated in a videogame-like fashion, as if one were actually in a space walking around, and also viewed in other ways, including a "dollhouse" mode.

OPERATIONS

Location

Although SurroundSpace easily could be operated as a home-based business, the company will lease space within a building currently used by Parker and Jessica McKay for their property management and interior design businesses.

Transportation

The McKays will purchase a 2012 Chevrolet Impala to use for their business at a cost of $9,438 (3.11% APR for 36 months/monthly payments of $262). They will purchase a second vehicle for approximately the same price during the second year of operations.

Business Structure

SurroundSpace is organized as a limited liability corporation in Massachusetts. This business structure provides owners with liability protection without the complexities associated with other types of business structures.

Equipment

The main equipment used by SurroundSpace is the Matterport Pro 3D Camera, which includes a wall charger, iPad app for capturing 3-D images, and a quick-release plate. To avoid potential service disruption in the event of equipment damage or malfunction, the business will purchase two cameras at a cost of $4,500 each. Additionally, the owners will purchase two Apple iPad's capable of running the Matterport 3D Capture App, as well as two tripods and two protective camera carrying cases.

Total equipment cost: $15,000

Legal

SurroundSpace's owners used a popular online document service to obtain standard business agreements for use with their customers. Additionally, they have secured an appropriate level of business liability coverage through their insurance agent (policy available upon request).

PERSONNEL

SurroundSpace is being established by Parker McKay, an entrepreneur with a property management background, and his wife, Jessica, a successful interior designer. Parker, who will serve as president of SurroundSpace, is the owner of Westwood Property Management Inc., which owns and manages 14 residential rental properties and three commercial office buildings in Forrester. Jessica, who will serve as vice president, is the owner of Jessica McKay Design LLC, an interior design practice that she has operated for seven years since receiving a diploma in residential planning from the Trenton Institute of Design. The McKays will be solely responsible for performing imaging services during the first year of operation, but will add additional staff beginning in the second year.

Professional & Advisory Support

SurroundSpace has retained Smith & Tanner, a local accounting firm, to assist with bookkeeping and tax preparation. The company also has established a business checking account with Forrester Community Bank, including a merchant account for accepting credit card payments. SurroundSpace will use a hosted version of a popular accounting software application to simplify bookkeeping and financial management.

GROWTH STRATEGY

Parker and Jessica McKay have established the following growth targets for SurroundSpace.

Year One: Image approximately 1.5 million square feet of space. Generate net profit of $25,931 on revenue of $150,000.

Year Two: Image approximately 3 million square feet of space. Generate net profit of $110,212 on revenue of $300,000. Add one full-time staff person to support growth, along with two additional camera packages and one additional vehicle.

Year Three: Image approximately 4.5 million square feet of space. Generate net profit of $197,484 on revenue of $450,000. Add one full-time staff person to support growth, along with two additional camera packages.

The following table shows a detailed breakdown of the average square footage SurroundSpace is projected to scan during its first three years of operations:

Average weekly square footage	2016	2017	2018
Residential	5,000	10,000	15,000
Commercial	25,000	50,000	75,000
Total	**30,000**	**60,000**	**90,000**

Average annual square footage	2016	2017	2018
Residential	250,000	500,000	750,000
Commercial	1,250,000	2,500,000	3,750,000
Total	**1,500,000**	**3,000,000**	**4,500,000**

MARKETING & SALES

The following marketing tactics will be used to promote SurroundSpace and grow the business:

1. A high-impact Web site that showcases SurroundSpace's 3-D property imaging capabilities and includes customer testimonials, contact information, and links to the business' social media channels.

2. A multi-faceted social media marketing presence, including Facebook, Twitter, LinkedIn, Instagram, and YouTube, that provides multiple ways to connect with the business' target markets.

3. An Allied Membership in the International Association of Venue Managers (IAVM), a professional organization for managers and executives from amphitheaters, stadiums, arenas, auditoriums, exhibit halls, convention centers, performing arts centers, and more. The IAVM is organized into seven regions. SurroundSpace will focus on marketing to members in Region 1, which includes Massachusetts. More information is available at: www.iavm.org.

4. An Industry Partner membership in the American Society of Interior Designers, allowing the business to target local and regional interior designers. The association, which is "the oldest, largest and leading professional organization for interior designers," provides Industry Partner members with opportunities to reach members in a variety of ways, including the use of mailing lists and an online directory listing. More information is available at: www.asid.org.

5. Membership in the Forrester Chamber of Commerce, providing an opportunity to build relationships and gain exposure among area business leaders, property owners, and decision-makers.

6. Quarterly postcard mailings to key prospects in the categories listed in the Market Analysis section of this plan (obtained from a business directory at the Forrester Public Library). The owners will use a local mail shop to prepare and send the mailings, saving them valuable time.

7. At least five sales calls per week to key prospects in Forrester and the surrounding region.

8. A Public relations strategy that involves working with customers' PR staff to use 3-D property imaging in connection with news coverage about their facilities.

9. Exhibition and networking at regional and national trade shows.

10. Professional stationery (business cards, envelopes, letterhead, etc.).

FINANCIAL ANALYSIS

	2016	2017	2018
Projected annual revenue	**$150,000**	**$300,000**	**$450,000**
Expenses			
Salaries	$ 75,000	$125,000	$175,000
Office lease	$ 3,600	$ 3,600	$ 3,600
Payroll tax	$ 11,250	$ 18,750	$ 26,250
Books & subscriptions	$ 250	$ 250	$ 250
Vehicle loans	$ 3,144	$ 6,288	$ 6,266
Insurance	$ 1,000	$ 1,100	$ 1,200
Equipment	$ 15,000	$ 15,000	$ 15,000
Memberships	$ 750	$ 750	$ 750
Office supplies	$ 565	$ 565	$ 565
Telecommunications	$ 510	$ 510	$ 510
Legal & regulatory	$ 500	$ 325	$ 325
Accounting	$ 1,100	$ 1,100	$ 1,100
Postage	$ 450	$ 500	$ 550
Internet	$ 950	$ 1,050	$ 1,150
Marketing	$ 10,000	$ 15,000	$ 20,000
Total expenses	**$124,069**	**$189,788**	**$252,516**
Net profit	**$ 25,931**	**$110,212**	**$197,484**

Agricultural Drone Business

Skyview Farm Analysis Inc.

65 Foster Ave.
Bridgeview, IA 50455

Paul Greenland

Skyview Farm Analysis Inc. is a specialized provider of aerial imagery and analysis for the agriculture industry.

EXECUTIVE SUMMARY

Skyview Farm Analysis Inc. is a specialized provider of aerial imagery and analysis for the agriculture industry. The business uses an aerial drone (quad copter) to survey farm fields accurately and efficiently, providing farmers with Normalized Difference Vegetation Index (NDVI) data that can be used to quickly gauge the health of their crops. Skyview Farm Analysis' services are substantially faster (reducing days of work to hours) and more highly detailed than traditional crop scouting methods, and far more cost effective than alternatives such as the use of manned aircraft or satellite imagery. The business is being established by the father-and-son team of Budd and Jake Williamson. Budd is a retired third-generation Iowa farmer. Jake is a technology-minded college student with an entrepreneurial spirit. Jake's knowledge of technology, coupled with his father's farming experience, has enabled the Williamsons to establish a cutting-edge business with tremendous growth potential.

INDUSTRY ANALYSIS

Devices popularly known as "drones," unmanned aerial vehicles (UAVs), unmanned aircraft systems (UAS), or remotely-piloted aircraft (RPA), typically are quad copters that feature an autopilot and corresponding software, along with physical components such as GPS modules, pressure sensors, gyros, accelerometers, magnetometers, and cameras. Their use has increased significantly in a wide range of industries and industry segments, including agriculture, cinematography, surveying, real estate, mapping, energy (oil and gas), insurance (claims processing), property management and inspection, weddings, conservation, and powerline/utility management. By capturing video footage and still images, and utilizing specialized accessories, drones can be used for a variety of applications. These include inspection, analysis, data collection, evaluation, observation, and monitoring/surveillance.

Federal Aviation Administration

The main government agency overseeing the use of drones in the United States is the Federal Aviation Administration (FAA), whose mission is "to provide the safest, most efficient aerospace system in the world." According to the FAA, the introduction of unmanned aircraft systems has presented the agency with a variety of challenges. Therefore, the FAA has taken "an incremental approach to safe UAS integration."

The latest information from the FAA regarding the commercial and recreational use of drones, including details regarding registration, regulations and policies, publications, and temporary flight restrictions, is available at: https://www.faa.gov/uas.

Additionally, several industry organizations have emerged to serve the drone market. These include the Association for Unmanned Vehicle Systems International (AUVSI) and the Academy of Model Aeronautics (AMA).

Association for Unmanned Vehicle Systems International

AUVSI bills itself as "the world's largest nonprofit organization devoted exclusively to advancing the unmanned systems and robotics community." The organization's base of approximately 7,500 members includes individuals from the academic sector, as well as both government and industry. It provides members with industry data, a magazine, daily news updates, and more. Additional details are available at: http://www.auvsi.org.

Academy of Model Aeronautics

Based in Muncie, Indiana, the Academy of Model Aeronautics "is a world-class association of modelers organized for the purpose of promotion, development, education, advancement, and safeguarding of modeling activities. The Academy provides leadership, organization, competition, communication, protection, representation, recognition, education, and scientific/technical development to modelers." Although the organization is geared toward the recreational segment, including model airplane clubs, it includes approximately 175,000 members and is open to anyone interested in the subject of model aviation. More information is available at: http://www.modelaircraft.org.

Industry Safety

In conjunction with the FAA, the AUVSI and the AMA have developed an educational campaign called "Know Before You Fly" to promote safe and responsible drone use. The campaign includes useful information, which is available at: http://knowbeforeyoufly.org.

MARKET ANALYSIS

According to data from the market research and consulting company, Radiant Insights Inc., the drone market was estimated at $6.8 billion in 2016 and was expected to reach $36.9 billion by 2022. The firm's report, "Drone Market Shares, Strategies, and Forecasts, Worldwide, 2016 to 2022," provides detailed information regarding several market segments, including agriculture, photography, and videography.

Studies have been conducted to demonstrate the return-on-investment for drone use in agriculture. For example, in 2015 the American Farm Bureau, in conjunction with Informa Economics and Drone as a Service, developed an ROI calculator that demonstrates the return-on-investment for different types of crops, including wheat ($2.30 per acre), soybeans ($2.60 per acre), and corn ($12 per acre).

In addition to public safety, many industry observers agree that agriculture is among the industry segments with the greatest potential for drones. This is because farmers require a significant amount of data regarding the status of their crops on a frequent basis. As the global population increases, farmers are being tasked with producing crops more efficiently, more cost effectively, and with less labor. In addition to traditional crop surveying, other agricultural applications include livestock monitoring.

Some estimates indicate that the average U.S. farm is approximately 420 acres. According to the Census of Agriculture, U.S. Department of Agriculture and U.S. Census Bureau, the state of Iowa had approximately 88,000 farms in 2012. The Williamsons will target their services to farms in Buchanan (1,075 farms), Delaware (1,382 farms), and Linn (1,402 farms) Counties.

SERVICES

Skyview Farm Analysis provides farmers with aerial crop scouting services using specially equipped aerial drones. Traditional visual and multispectral imagery (e.g., infrared) provides insight regarding things like soil moisture, crop health/disease, and crop stress. The resulting NDVI data allows farmers to be more targeted and precise when watering and using pesticides, fungicides, and other crop applications, resulting in significant potential savings, higher crop yields, and reduced environmental impact. Some estimates indicate that farmers can reduce their use of herbicides and pesticides by roughly 40-50 percent via "precision farming." Another main advantage is time savings. Manual crop scouting can take days, depending on a farm's size, yet does not yield the same depth of insight provided by drone analysis. Drones also can be used to monitor for things such as weather damage, drainage system performance, and problems with irrigation systems.

Although farmers are free to choose when they wish to use aerial drone analysis, the Williamsons will recommend aerial scouting at least three times per season:

- Planting

- Mid-season

- Harvest time

Agriculture is a seasonal business. Considering that Skyview Farm Analysis is located in Iowa, the owners anticipate that they will provide the majority of their services between April and October (for approximately 30 weeks).

Process

All services begin with an initial consultation (on-site and/or via phone), during which the owners will gain a complete understanding of the farmer's specific needs. This information will be used to provide a detailed time and cost estimate based on the number of acres that need to be surveyed. Skyview Farm Analysis charges $5 per acre for aerial crop scouting.

Once the customer has signed off on the estimate, Skyview Farm Analysis' partners will be on-site, at a mutually agreed-upon date and time, to perform the actual aerial survey. Although both partners are capable of operating the drone, Budd Williamson typically will interact with the client (if they are present), while Jake oversees drone operations.

Following the aerial survey, Skyview Farm Analysis will provide customers with a secure online link to the NDVI data, allowing them to gauge the health of their vegetation. In addition to providing a visual representation of their acreage, the NDVI data also can be imported into a variety of different farm management software applications. Customers have access to their data for inspection/download for a period of 30 days, after which they will be provided with a fee-based option for long-term storage.

Ancillary Services

In addition to aerial crop scouting, Skyview Farm Analysis also provides optional cloud-based data storage for its customers at a rate of $.20 per acre. The Williamsons have secured storage space through a third-party, which they can mark up, providing them with a reasonable profit (and a source of passive income).

Consulting

If desired, Budd Williamson will provide customers with a detailed analysis of their data in the form of a written report that includes visual depictions of their acreage (compiled with "stitched" images), specific recommendations, as well as one hour of discussion. As with aerial scouting, this service is provided at a rate of $5 per acre.

OPERATIONS

Business Structure

Skyview Farm Analysis is organized as an S Corporation in the state of Iowa. This business structure will allow the owners to receive half of their revenue in the form of salary, while taking the rest as quarterly profits that are not subject to Social Security and Medicare taxes. Additionally, the corporation provides the owners with a certain level of liability protection.

Equipment

The equipment used by Skyview Farm Analysis is simple to operate. The company's drone is a high-end quad copter equipped with specialized sensors (e.g., thermal/infrared), and can simply be "thrown" into the air when commencing a flight. The drone will then follow a pre-programmed route and perform the specified analysis before returning to its point of origin. Data can be stored on-board or uploaded directly to the cloud. A variety of drones and accessories are available to drone operators. While cheaper systems cost as low as $1,000, higher quality packages (including data processing solutions) are more expensive. The Williamsons invested approximately $10,000 in their equipment. The owners will ensure their equipment against damage, and also maintain an inventory of spare parts, extra batteries, and other accessories.

Legal

Skyview Farm Analysis has received a grant of exemption in accordance with Section 333 and a civil Certificate of Waiver or Authorization from the Federal Aviation Administration, allowing the business to use its drone commercially. More information regarding this required commercial certification is available at: http://www.faa.gov/uas/civil_operations. In addition, the Williamsons have obtained an appropriate level of liability insurance for their business in partnership with their insurance agent.

PERSONNEL

Skyview Farm Analysis is being established by the father-and-son team of Budd and Jake Williamson.

Budd Williamson

Budd is a retired third-generation Iowa farmer. Along with his wife, Betsy, Budd operated on a 650-acre farm that was in his family for more than 100 years. Upon retirement, Budd sold the farm, but retained several adjacent acres, including his family home. Budd is well-known throughout the community, having served on the Buchanan County Board and is a long-time member of the Iowa Farmers Union.

Jake Williamson

Jake is a technology-minded college student with an entrepreneurial spirit. While pursuing a computer programming degree, Jake has obtained certificates in both Web and mobile application development, allowing him to earn an income and gain valuable experience while pursuing his degree. His knowledge of technology, coupled with his father's farming experience, has enabled the Williamsons to establish a cutting-edge business with tremendous growth potential.

To familiarize themselves with the use of drones, the Williamsons first purchased a very inexpensive unit, providing them with a low-risk means of mastering the basics of maneuverability and camera operation. This was incredibly useful, since neither Budd nor Jake had experience flying remote aircraft or with photography/videography. After mastering the basics, the Williamsons then found a one-day training course that helped them to refine their skills and techniques. Ultimately, the owners were comfortable investing in the more expensive equipment required for their operation.

GROWTH STRATEGY

According to the Census of Agriculture, U.S. Department of Agriculture and U.S. Census Bureau, the state of Iowa had approximately 88,000 farms in 2012. The Williamsons will target their services to farms in Buchanan, Delaware, and Linn Counties, which are collectively home to more than 3,800 farms:

- Buchanan (1,075)

- Delaware (1,382)

- Linn (1,402)

The business will target farms with an average size of 400 acres, resulting in the following average charges:

- Aerial scouting: $2,000

- Cloud-based data storage: $80

- Consulting: $2,000

Based on an informal survey of area farmers, the owners estimate that 65 percent of customers will use aerial drone scouting three times per season, while 25 percent will use the service twice per season, and 10 percent will use it only once per season. Additionally, 75 percent of customers will likely take advantage of Skyview Farm Analysis' optional cloud data storage service. Finally, 55 percent are expected to take advantage of the business' consulting services.

The owners anticipate that revenue will break down as follows during the first three years of operations:

Service	2016	2017	2018
One aerial scout	6	9	12
Two aerial scouts	15	23	30
Three aerial scouts	39	58	78
Consulting	33	50	66
Data storage	45	68	90

Additionally, the Williamsons have established the following annual goals:

Year One: Focus on building awareness of Skyview Farm Analysis in the counties of Buchanan, Delaware, and Linn. Develop a base of 60 customers. Generate net profit of $133,300 on revenue of $376,600.

Year Two: Continue to increase visibility of Skyview Farm Analysis in the local three-county area. Increase the business' network of customers to 90. Generate net profit of $170,420 on revenue of $463,440.

Year Three: Maintain awareness of the business in the local market. Increase Skyview Farm Analysis' customer base to 120. Develop a strategy for expansion into nearby Benson and Jones Counties, including the purchase of additional equipment and hiring two seasonal employees. Generate net income of $312,500 on revenue of $761,200.

MARKETING & SALES

Skyview Farm Analysis has developed a marketing plan that includes the following primary tactics:

1. A high-quality, color brochure describing the benefits of drone-based crop scouting and precision farming.

2. Membership in the Bridgeview Chamber of Commerce.

3. Periodic presentations to local agricultural groups.

4. Placemat advertising at local diners frequented by farmers in Buchanan, Delaware, and Linn Counties.

5. Pre-season and mid-season direct mailings to all farmers in Buchanan, Delaware, and Linn Counties. The mailing list will be obtained from a reputable list broker, and mailings will be managed by a mail house in Davenport, Iowa.

6. A public relations strategy that involves guest columns and/or news stories in both free and subscription-based newspapers distributed throughout Buchanan, Delaware, and Linn Counties.

7. A Web site with complete details about Skyview Farm Analysis, including profiles of the owners, details of the services provided, and sample video and imagery.

8. Exhibition and networking at regional and state agricultural shows/exhibitions.

9. Professional stationery (business cards, envelopes, letterhead, etc.) featuring the Skyview Farm Analysis name.

10. Digital advertising on the Web, sites of leading farm journals, targeting subscribers in the business' market area.

FINANCIAL ANALYSIS

	2016	2017	2018
Revenue			
One aerial scout	$ 13,000	$ 18,000	$ 34,000
Two aerial scouts	$ 60,000	$ 92,000	$120,000
Three aerial scouts	$234,000	$348,000	$468,000
Consulting	$ 66,000	$100,000	$132,000
Data storage	$ 3,600	$ 5,440	$ 7,200
Total revenue	**$376,600**	**$463,440**	**$761,200**
Expenses			
Salary	$188,300	$231,720	$380,600
Payroll tax	$ 12,000	$ 18,000	$ 24,000
Equipment	$ 15,000	$ 15,000	$ 15,000
Mileage	$ 1,750	$ 2,000	$ 2,250
Data storage	$ 1,500	$ 2,000	$ 2,500
Office supplies	$ 750	$ 750	$ 750
Telecommunications	$ 1,200	$ 1,200	$ 1,200
Legal & regulatory	$ 1,000	$ 500	$ 500
Accounting	$ 800	$ 850	$ 900
Internet	$ 1,000	$ 1,000	$ 1,000
Marketing	$ 20,000	$ 20,000	$ 20,000
Total expenses	**$243,300**	**$293,020**	**$448,700**
Net profit	**$133,300**	**$170,420**	**$312,500**

Auto Appraiser
Abe's Auto Appraisals, Inc.

120 East Vernon St.
Roseville, CA 95678

Claire Moore

Abe's Auto Appraisals, Inc. (AAAI) is an independent automobile appraisal service for owners of classic automobiles, specialty vehicles, motorcycles and recreational vehicles. We specialize in providing comprehensive pre-purchase inspections, market value appraisals and damage estimates for classic, vintage, and custom automobiles, motorcycles and recreational vehicles along with contemporary exotic and high-performance vehicles. We offer a range of options to suit any budget, from virtual appraisals to complete, on-site physical inspections, test drives, and evaluations.

EXECUTIVE SUMMARY

Abe's Auto Appraisals, Inc. (AAAI) is an independent automobile appraisal service for owners of classic automobiles, specialty vehicles, motorcycles and recreational vehicles. We specialize in providing comprehensive pre-purchase inspections, market value appraisals and damage estimates for classic, vintage, and custom automobiles, motorcycles and recreational vehicles along with contemporary exotic and high-performance vehicles.

We offer a range of options to suit any budget, from virtual appraisals to complete, on-site physical inspections, test drives, and evaluations.

AAAI operates as a California corporation that is wholly owned by Abe Vernon, a licensed and certified automobile appraiser with over 25 years' experience in the automotive repair field.

The home office is located in Roseville, California and services are offered throughout the Western United States.

Keys to Success
- The vast experience of Abe Vernon in auto repairs and valuation.
- We provide personalized service to USAAP (Uniform Standards for Automotive Appraisal Procedures) standards, which means acceptance by insurance companies, courts, charities and the IRS.
- We utilize the latest software solutions for conducting appraisals and managing clients.
- We specialize in the unusual type of vehicle such as a Pro-Street 55 Shoebox or a one-off vintage Ferrari.
- We endeavor to produce the most accurate and impartial Evaluation Reports possible, consistent with accepted industry standards.

OBJECTIVES

The objectives for the first three years of operation include:

- To develop relationships that make a positive difference in our clients' lives.
- To uphold the highest standards of integrity in all our actions.
- To increase revenues by at least 12% per year.
- To scale the business growth over the next five years to include additional appraisal staff.

MISSION STATEMENT

Abe's Auto Appraisals will provide timely and comprehensive professional valuations to help owners and potential owners of specialty vehicles to protect their investments and assist insurers and other interested parties to establish a fair and equitable value.

FINANCING

Mr. Nelson will be providing the startup financing of $23,350 out of his own funds. The business does not require any outside financing at this time.

COMPANY SUMMARY

AAAI is a service company that provides appraisals of autos, classic automobiles, motorcycles and recreational vehicles. We specialize in specialty vehicles. Clients who will employ our services will include individuals, businesses, insurers, attorneys, and estates.

Our appraisal services are designed to enable our clients to negotiate the best deal when buying or selling a vehicle, settling legal and insurance disputes, justifying charitable contributions and providing a valuation for an estate.

Company Ownership

AAAI is a California corporation wholly owned by Abe Nelson.

STARTUP SUMMARY

AAAI has incurred the following start-up costs:

List of equipment needed for startup

Item	Estimated cost
Computer/printer/copier/scanner/fax	$1,500
Digital camera	$ 500
Telephone/cell phone	$ 700
Storage/filing/shelving	$ 150
Adding machine	$ 25
Paper shredder	$ 50
Desk/table/chair/lamp	$ 255
Software: MS Office	$ 120
	$3,300

Requirements

Start-up expenses

Licenses	$ 150
Supplies	$ 150
Advertising/cards/brochures	$ 750
Web site development	$ 1,000
Legal fees incorporation	$ 1,500
Travel during training	$ 2,500
Training/certification	$ 8,500
Total start-up expenses	**$14,550**

Startup funding

Cash required	$ 5,500
Startup assets to fund	$ 3,300
Startup expenses to fund	$14,550
Total funding required	**$23,350**

SERVICES

Our vision for AAAI is to provide auto appraisal services to individuals, businesses, insurers, attorneys, and estates. Our clients benefit from a compliant auto appraisal when buying or selling a vehicle, settling legal and insurance disputes, justifying charitable contributions and providing a valuation for an estate.

The most common reason for an appraisal is for insurance purposes. Published value guides such as Kelly Blue Book and the NADA guides from National Appraisal Guides, Inc. and J.D. Power are often insufficient in determining the value of a classic or custom car that has had significant upgrades and additions.

In order to establish accurate value, especially after an accident has caused loss or damage, there must be adequate documentation that proves every facet of the conversion work that had been done.

The Need for Appraisal Services

- *Diminished value:* assessing the loss in value from a collision

- *Insurance Coverage:* accurate valuation is essential to determining the appropriate amount of insurance coverage

- *Total loss:* a comprehensive valuation that takes all circumstances and conditions into account

- *Pre-purchase:* when securing an auto loan an appraisal may be required by the lender

- *Lease return:* at the end of a lease the lessee must pay for the cost of what would be considered beyond normal wear and tear. An independent appraisal can assist in negotiating an equitable settlement.

- *Classic car coverage:* accurate valuation is essential to determining the appropriate amount of insurance coverage

- *Bankruptcy:* when completing bankruptcy forms it is necessary to provide the value of each item of personal property

- *Estate taxes:* an accurate valuation of property that is part of estate is necessary to establish gain or loss if the property is sold

- *Charitable donations:* the IRS requires a professional appraisal when the value of a donated vehicle exceeds $5,000

Steps in completing an appraisal include:

1. Thorough examination of the vehicle, its equipment and condition

2. Examination of service records and documented vehicle history

3. Test drive, if possible

4. Research of the sales history of similar vehicles

5. Compilation of findings and photos into a multi-page report

Our fee for a typical auto appraisal starts at $250. Additional charges apply if travel is required. Owners of exotic or classic cars and those who own a vehicle for investment or business purposes are advised to conduct an appraisal every three years.

Types of Appraisals

We will perform the following appraisal services

- *Virtual Appraisal:* A professional review and opinion of a specific vehicle's current value range based only on information provided by the client. No physical inspection.

- *Estimated Current Market Value:* A detailed overview, assessment and market valuation for contemporary or vintage vehicles based on comparison of subject vehicle against current local market vehicles for sale or recently sold. Takes into account adjustments for specific model, option accessory, condition, mileage, modifications, guide book references, auction results, historical data and other factors. Physical inspection is optional.

- *Pre-purchase Inspection/Actual Market Value Appraisal:* A complete physical inspection by certified technicians and appraiser. The deliverable is documentation to support market value for the specific vehicle. Can include road test, evaluation of options, equipment, accessories, modifications and local market comps.

Each of our detailed appraisals includes a state-of-the-art report that entails a full, bumper-to-bumper field inspection of each vehicle by an ASE-certified Inspector, verification of VIN number and a careful analysis of the cosmetic and mechanical condition, where possible. Accompanying the visual inspection is a full complement of digital photographs to verify the observations made.

MANAGEMENT SUMMARY

The company is owned and managed by Abe Nelson. The home office is located in Abe's residence in Roseville, California.

After working on cars for fun as a teenager, Abe paid for his bachelor's degree in Business by buying, fixing and selling old and classic cars. After graduation Abe worked in sales and service for a Toyota dealership in Sacramento, California.

Abe became an Automotive Service Excellence Certified Master Mechanic (ASE) in 1989. Although California does not require that car mechanics possess certification, Abe knew that employment was more likely if he had earned ASE certification which requires the following:

- California work experience in either parts or service—2 years

- On-the-job training from auto dealers

- Auto collision and repair training

- Successfully passing ASE certification exams

Over the next 25 years Abe eventually owned and operated his own automobile service (Abe's Auto Service) facility providing repairs, inspections, estimates and leasing services. It was during his tenure as a shop owner/operator that Abe gained approval for Toyota and Acura appraisals and approval to complete lease termination appraisals for Honda Finance.

Abe also developed an avid interest in antique, classic, muscle and custom cars. Over the years he has been an active member of several car clubs including:

- BMW Car Club
- Classic Car Club of America
- Vintage Car Club
- Antique Automobile Club of America
- The Stutz Club
- DKW Club of America

With an eye toward specialization in auto appraisal Abe joined the Bureau of Certified Auto Appraisers and after a course of study successfully passed the Bureau of Certified Auto Appraisers—Independent Appraiser Certification Program (IACP).

As a member of the Bureau of Certified Auto Appraiser IACP Mr. Nelson receives access to useful valuation guides that provide important information necessary to complete each appraisal effectively. Abe is also a member of the International Automotive Appraisers Association (IAAA) and The American Society of Certified Auto Appraisers (ASCAA).

In 2015 Abe sold Abe's Auto Service to his son Jon Nelson and began the process of starting AAAI. For the next five years Abe will receive payments from the sale of his business to Jon. This income stream will enable Abe to devote his time and effort into developing AAAI into a profit-making enterprise.

Their collaboration will continue with the sharing of services when an auto appraisal requires a physical inspection by a certified mechanic. Abe will "sub" the inspection to the auto service shop which is equipped with state-of-the-art technology and certified mechanics to complete a thorough inspection.

MARKET ANALYSIS

Vehicle appraisals are beneficial when there is a change in ownership of that vehicle. Change of ownership occurs upon sale, death of owner, donation of the vehicle to charity, return of a lease vehicle or loss of use due to accident or other casualty.

As opposed to a vehicle inspection, an appraisal can assess valuation more accurately because it takes into account more factors that can affect total value. Therefore an appraisal is usually recommended for a vehicle with a value over $5,000.

When a client requests a pre-purchase inspection and actual value appraisal, we will oversee then entire process. The physical inspection will be performed by certified mechanics at Abe's Auto Service and Abe will complete the appraisal and complete all documentation.

Those who can benefit from vehicle appraisal services include prospective purchasers of a high-value, classic, custom or specialty vehicle and anyone in the following situations:

- Collector
- Insurance dispute
- Legal disputes including bankruptcy or divorce

- Estates

- Vehicle financing

Furthermore, we focus our services to the following vehicle types:

- *Classic car:* typically a car built between 1925 and 1948 and is maintained with its original design and specifications.

- *Antique vehicles:* a designation by the state which qualifies for a special license plate; typically a car over 45 years old and is maintained according to its original specifications.

- *Vintage car:* generally made between 1919 and 1930; may or may not have modifications beyond original specifications.

- *Custom show cars:* a car that has been modified as to alter its performance and make it more stylish.

- *Stock car or motorcycle:* modified for racing.

- *Pro-Street:* a car that has been customized for racing but is still street-legal.

- *Recreational vehicles—RVs*

We will also offer expert witness service to law firms whose clients are involved in disputes such as divorce, estate settlement, purchase agreements or fraud. Expert witness fees are a standard $250.00 per hour, with a four hour minimum.

We will target owners and prospective owners of these specialty vehicles. Our message is that we can help them to save money and establish the true market value of their vehicle through our comprehensive appraisal backed by powerful documentation.

According to the Hagerty Group, which sells classic car insurance, there are about 5 million collector cars in the U.S. Roughly 58 percent are owned by people over the age of 50 with the median age being 56 years.

These collectors see their hobby as preserving the craftsmanship of a bygone era. But the demographic of owners is changing in the following ways:

- Older owners are scaling down their collections as they approach age 70.

- Younger, Gen X and Y owners are more interested in the "restomod" where an older car's guts are replaced with something newer.

- Interest is growing in Europe although there is an increased interest in repatriating their own automotive heritage.

The Classic Car Club of America states that 71 percent of its members are between 45 and 74 years of age. Other characteristics of members include:

- 91.3 percent are male

- Net worth ranges from $1 million to $5 million

- Travel nationally one or more times a year

- 32.9% travel abroad one or more times a year

- 84% have computers, email and Internet

- 80.2% own one or more Full Classic® Cars; 64% own 1 to 3 Full Classics

TARGET MARKET STRATEGY

The key to marketing success is to focus our dollars and our efforts on reaching our target market. Unlike other types of businesses, we won't get much benefit from mass marketing efforts. We will reach our target market by being visible in venues where they congregate such as car clubs, car events and car dealerships that specialize in classic and specialty vehicles.

These enthusiasts understand that prices on specialty vehicles range from five to seven figures. An accurate appraisal is crucial because even a beautifully restored car can have serious mechanical problems that can alter its value.

We will employ the following strategies:

- *Web site:* Our web site will include information about our background and qualifications, our services, our contact information and a contact form submission process that allows the prospect to request more information.

- *Car clubs:* Car clubs such as the Classic Car Club of America can reach thousands of avid car collectors. Their publications and web sites are ideal vehicles for reaching this audience. Advertising packages can include print and web exposure and opportunities at club events. Directory listings are also available in a club's resource directory listing.

- *Events:* Attendance at events such as the Main Street Reunion Car Show in Napa, California presents an opportunity to connect with our target market and present the features and benefits of our services.

- *Web advertising:* Pay-per-click (PPC) ads through Google AdWords will allow us to set a budget limit while focusing on reaching our niche.

- *Yellow Pages:* Our ad will contain our name and contact information where more information can be obtained.

COMPETITIVE EDGE

Our competitive edge is our years of experience, our professional approach and the resources at our disposal. We not only offer pre-purchase inspections, we offer thorough and comprehensive appraisals for a number of situations and can provide repair services through our connection with Abe's Auto Service.

- Personalized service and quality

- Timeliness and accuracy

- Dedicated, loyal and trusted appraiser

- Vast experience in automobile service and valuation

- Focus on specialty vehicles

Sales Strategy

Our sales strategy will be grounded in communicating the value that we can provide to our clients in verifying the market value appraisals and damage estimates for classic, vintage, and custom automobiles, motorcycles and recreational vehicles along with contemporary exotic and high-performance vehicles.

PERSONNEL PLAN

Abe's Auto Appraisal, Inc. will be a one-person operation for the next three- to -five years. In year three we anticipate hiring a part-time secretary/bookkeeper who will perform duties related to billing, collections and customer relations management.

Personnel plan	Year 1	Year 2	Year 3
Owner	$0	$12,000	$12,000
Office staff	0	0	$ 6,000
Total people	**1**	**1**	**2**
Total payroll	**$0**	**$12,000**	**$18,000**

MILESTONES

Building a solid foundation is critical to business success. We will have several milestones in our first year.

Milestone	End date	Budget
Business plan completion	November 1, 2015	$ 0
Complete web site	December 1, 2015	$ 1,000
Begin advertising campaign	January 15, 2016	$10,800
Begin Abe's salary	January 1, 2017	$12,000
Profitability	December 1, 2016	
Hire part-time office staff	February 1, 2017	$ 6,000

FINANCIAL PLAN

Pro forma profit and loss

	Year 1	Year 2	Year 3
Revenues			
Appraisal fees	$25,000	$50,000	$65,000
Pre-purchase inspection fees	$ 7,500	$ 8,000	$12,000
Expert witness fees	$ 0	$ 2,000	$ 6,000
Total revenues	**$32,500**	**$60,000**	**$83,000**
Expenses			
Advertising	$10,800	$10,800	$12,000
Payroll	$ 0	$12,000	$18,000
Depreciation	$ 100	$ 100	$ 100
Phone/Internet	$ 640	$ 960	$ 960
Insurance: liability/life/disability	$ 350	$ 350	$ 400
Payroll taxes	$ 0	$ 1,200	$ 1,800
Professional dues/memberships	$ 650	$ 650	$ 650
Inspection sub fee	$ 6,525	$ 6,960	$10,440
Office supplies	$ 400	$ 450	$ 550
Auto: lease, gas, oil, repair, insurance	$ 8,000	$ 9,600	$11,000
Software subscription: appraisal	$ 1,750	$ 1,750	$ 1,750
Legal/accounting	$ 800	$ 1,000	$ 1,000
Travel	$ 1,500	$ 2,500	$ 3,800
Other expenses	$ 400	$ 600	$ 800
Total operating expenses	**$31,915**	**$48,920**	**$63,250**
Profit before interest and taxes	$ 585	$11,080	$19,750
Taxes incurred	$ 88	$ 1,662	$ 2,963
Net profit	**$ 497**	**$ 9,418**	**$16,788**
Net profit/sales	**2%**	**16%**	**20%**

Projected balance sheet

Assets	Year 1	Year 2	Year 3
Cash in bank	$5,000	$7,708	$21,258
Other current assets			
Total current assets	**$5,000**	**$7,708**	**$21,258**
Fixed assets			
Office furniture & equipment	$2,850	$2,850	$ 2,850
Misc equipment			
Less: depreciation	($ 570)	($1,140)	($ 1,710)
Total assets	**$7,280**	**$9,418**	**$22,398**
Liabilities			
Current liabilities			
Accounts payable	$ —	$ —	
Current maturities loan			
Total current liabilities	**$ —**	**$ —**	
Long term liabilities loan			
Total liabilities	**$ —**	**$ —**	
Paid-in capital	$6,783	$6,783	$ 6,783
Retained earnings			
Earnings	497	9,418	16,788
Total capital	**497**	**9,418**	**16,788**
Total liabilities & equity	**$7,280**	**$9,418**	**$22,398**

Clothing Alterations and Tailoring
Fiona's Alterations and Embroidery

514 Cypress Pond Road
Broxton, GA 31519

Fran Fletcher

Fiona's Alterations and Embroidery is a home-based business in Broxton, Georgia specializing in formalwear alterations and embroidery services. Mrs. Fairchild has been altering dresses for family and friends for many years. She made the decision to quit her job as a bank teller and open Fiona's Alterations and Embroidery when she started getting so many requests that she was having to turn many people away.

BUSINESS OVERVIEW

Fiona's Alterations and Embroidery is a home-based business in Broxton, Georgia specializing in formalwear alterations and embroidery services. Mrs. Fairchild has been altering dresses for family and friends for many years. She made the decision to quit her job as a bank teller and open Fiona's Alterations and Embroidery when she started getting so many requests that she was having to turn many people away.

In addition to alterations, Mrs. Fairchild will provide embroidery services. Embroidery is very popular in the area. From sports jerseys to baby gifts, there is currently a high demand for these items.

The closest alteration competitor is located 60 miles from Broxton at a bridal shop in Valdosta, Georgia. However, there are several other individuals and businesses who offer embroidery services in the area. Fiona's embroidery will set itself apart from those businesses by offering a faster turnaround time with appointments for "embroider while you wait."

Mrs. Fairchild has converted a spare bedroom in her home into a sewing/fitting room. Start-up costs include purchasing an embroidery machine and some pieces needed to make dress fittings easier.

The target market for Fiona's Alterations and Embroidery will be anyone who needs alterations made to their formalwear. This includes brides, bridal parties, pageant participants, and girls who need alterations made to their prom and homecoming dresses.

Fiona's Alterations and Embroidery will use its marketing ideas to boost business. Ongoing advertising will include:

- Partnering with local dress shops to perform alterations for their customers.

- Utilizing social media for advertising, showcasing work, and announcing dates/times for "Embroider while you wait."

The owner of Fiona's Alterations and Embroidery wishes to obtain financing in the form of a business loan or line of credit in the amount of $6,310, which will cover the start-up costs and expenses for the first three months. According to the estimated expenses vs. income, Fiona's Alterations and Embroidery will be able to pay back the small loan within three years.

COMPANY DESCRIPTION

Location

Fiona's Alterations and Embroidery is located at Mrs. Fairchild's home at 514 Cypress Pond Road in Broxton, Georgia. The spare bedroom has been transformed into a sewing/fitting room.

Hours of Operation

Hours vary. Customers will be required to call for an appointment to drop off dresses and for final fittings.

Personnel

Fiona Fairchild (owner)

Mrs. Fairchild has been sewing since she was a teenager. Her aunt taught her how to make and alter clothing. She has been altering dresses as a side business for some time. Mrs. Fairchild's specialty is altering formal dresses and wedding gowns.

Mrs. Fairchild will be the sole proprietor and will provide all services at this time.

Products and Services

Services
- Alterations
- Embroidery

Products
- Caps
- Bags
- Baby items
- Towels
- Blankets

MARKET ANALYSIS

Industry Overview

The owner believes that dress alterations is becoming a lost art. It is becoming increasingly difficult to find someone that has the skills to alter beaded and sequined gowns. Usually, the best place to find someone to alter formalwear is at the store where it is purchased, which is not always convenient if purchased online or far from home. Formal dresses can have a hefty price tag and the buyer shouldn't trust the alterations to just anyone. Mrs. Fairchild has been turning people away because she didn't have the time to meet the demand, so there should be plenty of customers to grow her business.

Embroidery is very popular in the area and is currently in high demand.

Target Market

The target market for Fiona's Alterations and Embroidery are girls and women of all ages who need alteration services. Brides, bridal parties, pageant participants, and girls going to prom and homecoming will all be included in the targeted group.

Competition

There are currently no other seamstresses in the immediate area offering formalwear alterations. The closest competition is 60 miles from Fiona's Alterations and Embroidery at a bridal shop called Dreamy Dresses in Valdosta, Georgia. Alterations are only offered for dresses bought at Dreamy Dresses.

There are several other individuals and businesses who offer embroidery services in the area. Most individuals and retail businesses offering embroidery services offer a two-week turnaround time, with rush orders incurring an additional fee. Fiona's embroidery will set itself apart from the competition by offering appointments for "embroider while you wait."

GROWTH STRATEGY

The overall strategy of Fiona's Alterations and Embroidery is to earn a reputation for quality and timely dress alterations and embroidery at an affordable price. Mrs. Fairchild already has an established customer base that will grow quickly as word gets around that she is working full time.

Sales and Marketing

Ongoing advertising/marketing will include:

- Partnering with local dress shops to offer alterations for their customers
- Utilizing social media for advertising, showcasing work, and announcing dates/times for "Embroider while you wait"
- Old fashioned word-of-mouth referrals

FINANCIAL ANALYSIS

Start-up Costs

Start-up costs will be minimal. Mrs. Fairchild has turned the spare bedroom of her home into her sewing and fitting room. Purchasing an embroidery machine will be the largest expense.

She plans to purchase the following:

- Large full-length mirror
- Pedestal
- Screen
- Embroidery machine
- Clothing racks
- Miscellaneous items to embroider, i.e. baby bibs, blankets, onesies, caps, shirts
- Three chairs

Start-up costs

Embroidery machine	$1,000
Large full length mirror	$ 200
Pedestal	$1,000
Screen	$ 200
Clothing racks	$ 200
Chairs	$ 300
Misc items to embroider	$ 500
Sewing accessories	$ 300
Business license	$ 100
Initial advertising	$ 100
Legal/accounting fees	$1,000
Total	**$4,900**

Estimated Monthly Expenses

Generally, the cost of monthly expenses is fixed.

Mrs. Fairchild's salary will vary. She will be paid whatever she makes after paying her monthly expenses.

Monthly expenses

Loan repayment	$200
Electricity	$200
Phone/Internet	$ 50
Advertising	$ 20
Total	**$470**

Estimated Monthly Income

The owner expects a high volume of appointments from the start. The owner thinks her marketing strategy will keep the momentum going in subsequent months and years.

Price Schedule

Prices for alteration services

Wedding dresses	$150
Formal dresses—floor length	$100
Formal dresses—short	$ 75
Formal dresses—top only (no embellishment)	$ 50
Formal dresses—top only (embellished)	$ 75

Prices for embroidery services

Baby items

Blanket	$10
Bib	$ 5
Onesie	$ 5

Apparel

Dress	$10
Cap	$ 8
Shirt	$12

Miscellaneous

Towel	$12
Umbrella	$10
Handbag	$10
Luggage	$12
Backpack	$12

Profit/Loss

Mrs. Fairchild conservatively estimates that she will alter three dresses per week and will embroider five items per week for the first month and business will steadily increase as word spreads about her business. The company will also see increases during spring and summer with wedding parties and before prom and homecoming seasons. Mrs. Fairchild will eventually max out in the number of dresses she is able to alter by herself. At this time, she has no plans of expanding or hiring help.

Monthly profit/loss

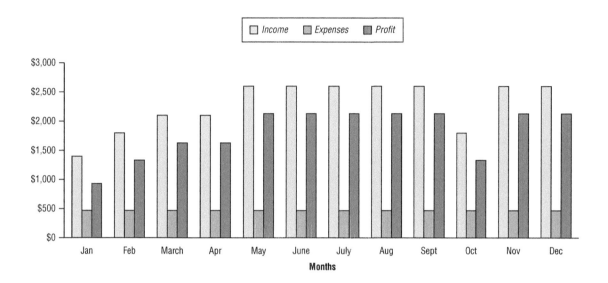

Estimated yearly profits

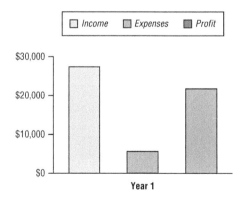

Financing

Fiona's Alterations and Embroidery wishes to obtain financing in the form of a business loan or line of credit in the amount of $6,310, which will cover the start-up costs and expenses for the first three months. According to the estimated expenses vs. income, Fiona's Alterations and Embroidery will be able to pay back the loan within three years.

Loan repayment plan

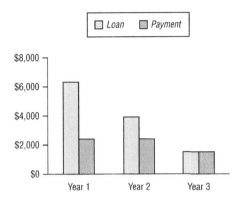

Community-Supported Organic Farm

Earth Connection Farms Inc.

Rural Route 6
Baldwin Hills, WI 63329

Paul Greenland

Earth Connection Farms Inc. provides healthy, locally-grown organic vegetables and products in the Milwaukee, Wisconsin area.

EXECUTIVE SUMMARY

When Mark Jacobson inherited 20 acres of Wisconsin farmland, along with a farmhouse and several barns and outbuildings, from the estate of his grandfather, he was ready for a major life change. After 15 years as human resources professional, Mark was ready to leave the corporate world and rediscover the strong connection he once had with nature. Growing up, Mark spent many a summer working on his grandparents' farm, which once spanned about 400 acres. Although most of the land was sold to a larger farming operation many years ago, his grandfather had continued to live on the remaining 20-acre property.

After relocating with his family from New Jersey to Wisconsin, Mark has decided to invest a portion of his personal savings, along with a modest financial inheritance from his grandfather, to establish an organic farm using a community-supported agriculture (CSA) model. Earth Connection Farms Inc. will provide healthy, locally-grown organic vegetables and products in the Milwaukee, Wisconsin area.

In addition to providing his family with a source of food and economic sustenance, Mark's objective is to grow the organic farm into a profitable enterprise. His plans for accomplishing this are outlined in the following business plan.

INDUSTRY ANALYSIS

Industry Snapshot

Organic farming is one of the fastest-growing areas of agriculture, driven by the demand for healthy food. According to information released by the Organic Trade Association (OTA) in 2016, the United States is home to approximately 22,000 certified organic farms. This number increased by 12 percent from 2014 to 2015, marking the strongest industry growth seen since 2008. Organic farms are a key element of the larger organic products retail market, which the OTA reports is valued at approximately $39 billion in the United States alone.

29

Associations

The OTA, which includes approximately 8,500 organic businesses among its members, is one of the industry's leading advocates for farmers, distributors, retailers, growers, shippers, processors, and more. More information is available at: http://www.ota.com. Other leading national organizations include the non-profit Ecological Farming Association (http://eco-farm.org), whose mission is "to nurture safe, healthy, just, and ecologically sustainable farms, food systems, and communities by bringing people together for education, alliance building, advocacy, and celebration." Finally, organic farmers also have access to state and regional organizations. One example is the Spring Valley, Wisconsin-based Midwest Organic & Sustainable Education Service (MOSES) (https://mosesorganic.org), a non-profit organization that "promotes organic and sustainable agriculture by providing the education, resources and expertise farmers need to succeed."

Government Organizations

Through its National Organic Program, the U.S. Department of Agriculture's Agricultural Marketing Service (AMS) oversees and enforces standards for organically-produced agricultural products in the United States. More information about the Organic Certification process is available by reading the document, "What is Organic Certification?" (http://www.ams.usda.gov/sites/default/files/media/What%20is%20Organic%20Certification.pdf).

At the government level, another useful organization is the USDA Rural Business-Cooperative Service (USDA-RBS), which seeks "to enhance the quality of life for all rural Americans by providing leadership in building competitive businesses including cooperatives that can build sustainable economic communities. RBS objectives are to invest its financial resources and technical assistance in businesses and communities, and to build partnerships that leverage public and private resources to stimulate rural economic activity." More information is available at: http://www.rd.usda.gov/about-rd/agencies/rural-business-cooperative-service.

MARKET ANALYSIS

Earth Connection Farms is located on 20 acres of land in Baldwin Hills, Wisconsin. The farm is within a 30-minute drive of Milwaukee and the surrounding suburbs, providing the owners with a sizable market and the ability to charge higher prices than organic farms operating in smaller or mid-sized markets.

The Jacobsons will begin operations with no brand recognition, requiring them to invest heavily in marketing initiatives to generate awareness among potential customers in the Milwaukee area.

Several established competitors already operate in Baldwin Hills and similar nearby farming communities, including:

1. Bruce Hardwicke Farms Inc.

2. Gaston Organics LLC

3. Right Way Gardens

SERVICES

Earth Connection Farms will employ a farmer-managed, community-supported agriculture model, in which members of the community will purchase full or half-shares of the expected harvest in advance, either by cash or check. This approach will enable the Jacobsons to distribute both the risks and rewards associated with their operation.

Share Prices

- *Full Share:* $450 (typically feeds 3-5 people)

- *Half-Share:* $225 (typically feeds 1-3 people)

Based on the needs of the community and other factors, the Jacobsons plan to sell some or all of the following types of vegetables:

- Asparagus

- Bell Peppers

- Broccoli

- Cabbage

- Carrots

- Cauliflower

- Celery

- Cucumber

- Eggplant

- Green Beans

- Hot Peppers

- Kale

- Leeks

- Lettuce

- Okra

- Onions

- Pumpkins

- Radish

- Spinach

- Sugar Snap Peas

- Summer Squash

- Sweet Peppers

- Sweetcorn

- Tomatoes

- Winter Squash

Shareholders can receive their vegetables on a regular (typically weekly) basis in two ways: (1) by pickup at Earth Connections Farms or (2) by pickup at a convenient location in downtown Milwaukee. The Jacobsons will notify shareholders when their vegetables are available for pickup. In the future, the Jacobsons may add a home or office delivery service for an extra fee. Additionally, based on regional expansion, they may add suburban pickup locations as well.

OPERATIONS

Location

Earth Connection Farms' is situated on 20 acres of land on Rural Route 6 in Baldwin Hills, Wisconsin. The property has a strong cropping history, with excellent soil quality. It offers the Jacobsons plenty of flat, tillable land for their organic farming operation. The property also has adequate access to fresh water and a 5,000-square-foot pack house that provides 250 square feet of packing space per acre.

The Jacobsons will operate their farm with the following equipment:

Power Equipment & Implements

- 160 HP Tractor
- 150 HP Tractor
- Two Rototillers
- Spading Machine
- Seeder
- Plows
- Discs

Hand Tools

- Rakes
- Shovels
- Hoes
- Digging Forks
- Hand Spades

Office Equipment

- Computer
- Telephone
- Filing Cabinet
- Desk

LEGAL

The owners have incorporated their business in partnership with a local attorney and registered with the Wisconsin Department of Financial Institutions and the Wisconsin Department of Revenue. A health permit has been obtained from Morrison County. In addition, the Jacobsons have obtained a general liability policy. Finally, Organic Certification for Earth Connection Farms has been obtained in the crops category, in accordance with the National Organic Program, which is overseen by the U.S. Department of Agriculture's Agricultural Marketing Service.

PERSONNEL

Considering that the equivalent of approximately one full-time worker is needed per acre of land, the Jacobson's will staff their farm (a seasonal business) as follows:

1. *Mark Jacobson, President* ($35,000 salary): Mark will focus on the business management aspects of the Jacobson farm (including CSA membership management, record keeping, and personnel management), drawing upon his human resources background. Additionally, he will assume responsibility for maintenance and repair issues.

2. *Andrea Jacobson, Vice President* ($14,125): Andrea will concentrate on marketing and sales, capitalizing on her background as the assistant manager of a supermarket.

3. *Laura Jacobson, Lead Farmhand* ($10,000): Laura, who learned a great deal about agriculture from her father, will work in partnership with her father to play a lead role in crop production issues (e.g., planting, pest management, etc.).

4. *Steve Jacobson, Seasonal Farmhand* ($6,000): Steve will work as a farmhand, learning the ropes of the family farming business from his family, and assisting his father with construction and repair issues.

5. Seasonal Farmhand ($4,000)

6. Seasonal Farmhand ($4,000)

Total first-year labor costs: $73,125

GROWTH STRATEGY

Year One: Begin operations by farming 5 acres of land. Host a fall festival, with a pumpkin patch and corn maze, to attract the public. Generate net income of $28,125 on projected gross revenue of $112,500.

Year Two: Double farming to 10 acres and introduce a modest range of retail items from local craftspeople for sale (honey, candles, soaps, craft items, and baked goods). In addition to the fall festival, host a summer festival featuring cold beverages, delicious food, live entertainment, and a petting zoo. Generate net income of $56,250 on projected gross revenue of $225,000.

Year Three: Expand farming to 15 acres. Begin offering organic farming and gardening classes to the public, along with occasional guest presentations from dietitians and nutritionists on healthy eating. Generate net income of $84,375 on projected gross revenue of $337,500.

Future Options: Based on Earth Connection Farms' success during its initial three years, the Jacobsons may consider selling their vegetables at nearby farmers' markets and offering a berry picking area.

MARKETING & SALES

Earth Connection Farms will employ the following main tactics to market the business:

- Web site with information about the Jacobsons, products offered (e.g., examples of typical vegetables offered to shareholders throughout the season), share prices, location, payment options, etc.

- Search Engine Optimization

- Soliciting Positive Online Reviews

- A listing on the online database, LocalHarvest.org.

- Advertising on select local/regional Web sites.

- *Early Bird Discounts:* Earth Connection Farms will give customers a 15 percent discount for purchasing their share by the end of January, prior to the upcoming growing season.

- *Referral Program*: Earth Connection Farms will reward existing shareholders with free vegetables in exchange for each new member that they refer.

- *Public relations:* The Jacobsons will contact local television and print media, as well as industry publications, to promote their story as a health-focused, family-owned business.

- *Contests:* Earth Connection Farms will sponsor a contest with public and private schools in Milwaukee to offer three lucky families a free CSA membership.

- *Direct Marketing:* Mailings to nutritionists, dietitians, and vegetarian groups in the Milwaukee area, in an effort to spread awareness and word-of-mouth among health-conscious populations.

- Colorful flyers with key details about Earth Connection Farms.

- Social Media Marketing (Facebook, Twitter, & Instagram)

FINANCIAL ANALYSIS

Startup Costs

According to figures from Iowa State University's extension office, startup costs for a five-acre mixed vegetable farm total approximately $100,000. A sizable portion of this amount ($40,000) is required to purchase the land, while about $20,000 is needed to buy a tractor. Related implements cost another $5,000, while miscellaneous tools cost $10,000. Finally, the cost of building a shed or packing station can total approximately $25,000.

The Jacobsons are fortunate in that they will not need to purchase any of these things. In addition to 20 acres of land, and the house where the family will live, the Jacobson farm includes two full-size barns, three steel outbuildings, several small sheds, two tractors (capable of farming all 20 acres if needed), and a generous supply of tools and implements. Mark Jacobson will use the majority of his $45,000 investment to pay the salaries of six seasonal (e.g., 20 weeks) employees, purchase seeds, and market the business.

Financing

The Jacobsons will invest $45,000 (from personal savings, along with a modest financial inheritance from Mark Jacobson's grandfather) to establish their organic farm. However, if needed, other sources of funding are available, including state and local agriculture programs, as well as microloans from the U.S. Department of Agriculture.

First-Year Snapshot

Using a community-supported agricultural model, the Jacobsons anticipate that they will be able to receive a share price of $450 per acre. This figure varies from market to market, with farms in close proximity to urban areas commanding higher share prices. With each acre accommodating 50 shares, the Jacobsons are anticipating gross revenue of $22,250 per acre during the farm's first year of operations (total revenue of $112,500). With anticipated labor costs of $73,125 and another $11,250 required for seeds and operational expenses, this will result in an estimated net profit of $28,125. The owners will invest the majority of these profits back into the business, to support the aforementioned growth strategy.

Projected Revenue & Expenses

Based on the growth strategy developed for their farm, the Jacobsons are anticipating the following revenue and expenses for their first three years of operations:

	2016	2017	2018
Revenue	$112,500	$225,000	$337,500
Expenses			
Labor	$ 73,125	$146,250	$219,375
Other	$ 11,250	$ 22,500	$ 33,750
Total	$ 84,375	$168,750	$253,125
Net income	$ 28,125	$ 56,250	$ 84,375

A full set of pro forma financial statements have been prepared by the Jacobsons' accountant and are available upon request.

SWOT ANALYSIS

Strengths: The Jacobsons are able to begin a new business with a minimal investment and will benefit from Mark Jacobson's past farming experience.

Weaknesses: Several established competitors already operate in the local market, and Earth Connection Farms will begin operations with no brand recognition.

Opportunities: Nationwide, there is strong and growing demand for healthy food options, especially organic vegetables.

Threats: Farming not only is a risky and physically intense/exhausting enterprise, crops can be impacted by unpredictable conditions, including the weather.

Corporate Event Planning Business

Impact Events, Inc.

2555 Gateway Oaks Drive, Ste. 200
Sacramento, CA 94232

Claire Moore

Impact Events, Inc. works with clients to produce and manage events. We plan to exceed client expectations by handling the details required to produce a memorable and effective event. We will specialize in several event types such as: sales meetings, incentive programs, retreats and gala dinners. In our first three years of operation we will concentrate our efforts on events to be held in Northern California and Northern Nevada.

EXECUTIVE SUMMARY

Impact Events, Inc. works with clients to produce and manage events. We plan to exceed client expectations by handling the details required to produce a memorable and effective event. We will specialize in several event types such as: sales meetings, incentive programs, retreats and gala dinners.

In our first three years of operation we will concentrate our efforts on events to be held in Northern California and Northern Nevada.

Our services will include: pre-planning, vendor management, staffing, entertainment, speaker management, budget and accounting, lodging, transportation and more. We will focus our efforts on serving corporations, associations, government agencies and nonprofit organizations.

We are a boutique event planning company. At Impact Events, we first start our work with understanding your goals. We give every client the attention they need regardless of the size or complexity of their event or meeting. We embrace client input. We assign a dedicated account manager to every event. The account manager acts as the sole point of contact with the client. We offer our service on a menu basis. Thus, our open-line budget policy allows our clients to pick and choose the services they need and pay for what they need.

Impact Events, Inc. is structured as a California corporation. Its principle shareholders are Joan Elkin, Robert Short and Kim Spenser. All three owners are certified meeting planners. Together they possess over 55 years of experience in the meeting industry.

Our board of advisors includes executives from major hotels and event venues in Northern California.

The company headquarters is located in a commercial office space in Sacramento, California.

MISSION

At Impact Events our mission is to create events that will have measurable impact and return on investment for our clients. We will exhibit the utmost professionalism in creating and managing our clients' events from small gatherings of 20 people up to conventions for thousands.

We strive to provide affordable meeting and event planning services that are environmentally friendly and that generate a reasonable profit for our company.

OBJECTIVES

In order to ensure our success we have identified several objectives that will be the focus of our planning and activities.

- Create and employ systems that optimize our clients' investment and our profitability.
- Achieve profitability by year two.
- Ensure that our staff and partners are compensated fairly and according to their contributions.
- Our team of experienced planners and producers will build crucial and beneficial relationships with sponsors, community partners, venue managers, destination marketing organizations, vendors and presenters.

KEYS TO SUCCESS

Key factors in our success are based firmly in our personnel and our work ethic. We have fostered strategic relationships with a team of experienced and proven artists, engineers, planners and producers.

- We are committed to elevating our clients' brands with flawless productions and measurable ROI.
- Our team of artists, engineers, planners and producers will achieve an energetic and unique experience for our clients.
- We will maintain seamless, behind-the-scenes collaborations between internal and external event team members.
- We will use the latest technology to provide the entire team with a collaborative platform where event goals, plans, budgets, action items and materials are available 24/7 to streamline the entire event management process.

COMPANY SUMMARY

Impact Events was born from the desire and talents of three passionate event planners who wanted to make their own mark on the industry. Our founders Joan Elkin, Robert Short and Kim Spenser have acquired an extraordinary track record and an impressive catalog of business relationships with planners, artists, speakers, vendors and site managers.

Heeding the call of a growing economy along with the affordable home and office prices Joan Elkin and Robert Short migrated to the Sacramento area in search of opportunity. The three founders became acquainted through professional networking events and gradually developed the dream that has manifested as Impact Events.

The greater Sacramento area is an ideal location to launch their enterprise because it offers both business opportunity as well as a desirable quality of life.

According to Sacramento County, the area now has the fifth fastest private sector job growth in U.S. metropolitan cities. At least 17 companies from the Sacramento region show up on Inc. magazine's annual list of the 5,000 fastest-growing privately held companies in the U.S.

Major employers in the Sacramento area include:

- Aeroject International, Inc.

- Delta Dental

- Intel Corporation

Other reasons for Impact Events and thousands of other businesses to call Sacramento home include:

- It is one of the most affordable areas in the state for both homes and office spaces.

- There are 15,000 acres of parks.

- It is the third fastest growing metro area in California.

- Sacramento is home to Sacramento International Airport, light rail, buses and bike lanes.

- There are abundant shovel-ready sites for development.

As companies establish themselves and grow in Sacramento they will need to have access to professional event planning services. We aim to become the go-to providers for their event planning needs.

Our services are not limited to the Sacramento area. Joan Elkin and Robert Short have strong ties to businesses in the Bay Area and in Reno/Tahoe. They will continue to foster these relationships in order to build our client list and expand our reach.

COMPANY OWNERSHIP

Impact Events is established as a California corporation headquartered in Sacramento, California. The company shareholders are its founders Joan Elkin, Robert Short and Kim Spenser. Together the owners have over 55 years' experience in professional corporate event planning and management.

START UP SUMMARY

Anticipated and incurred startup costs include legal costs for incorporation, contract creation and liability management, branding and marketing, rent, office supplies, furniture and equipment.

All funding has been contributed by the founders/shareholders and we do not anticipate the need for outside funding at this time. While the owners wish to remain debt-free they recognize that as expansion of the business becomes a reality, debt or outside investment could be an option.

Startup expenses

Rent	$ 4,300
Furniture/equipment	$ 5,500
Office/stationery	$ 500
Licenses and taxes	$ 350
Web design	$ 1,250
Advertising/promotion	$ 2,000
Legal fees	$ 2,500
Accounting	$ 1,200
Insurance	$ 450
Utilities deposits	$ 400
Miscellaneous	$ 500
Total	**$18,950**

COMPANY LOCATION & FACILITIES

Our needs are small and manageable as we require only enough office space to house management, support staff, storage and a meeting room. We have secured an office space in the Natomas area of Sacramento which is conveniently located near shops, restaurants, and the Sacramento International Airport. We are minutes away from downtown Sacramento.

Our office is just off of Highway 80 which extends west into San Francisco and east all the way to Reno. This location will allow us to both reach out and be reached easily by clients from downtown Sacramento and areas as far as Roseville and Auburn in Placer County.

We recognize that many of our potential clients are located along the Highway 50 corridor which extends from Sacramento through Rancho Cordova and El Dorado Hills to Folsom. Key businesses along Highway 50 include Intel and Vision Service Plan (VSP). In anticipation of developing clients in this geographic area we have made a shared rental arrangement for an office facility on an as-needed basis where we can meet with clients.

Eventually we plan to open a second permanent office in the Rancho Cordova area in order to better serve our clientele who are based along Highway 50.

MANAGEMENT TEAM

Our team of management professionals has a combined total of 55 years of experience in hospitality, tourism, travel, event services and business.

Joan Elkin began her career with a degree in Hospitality Business from the Michigan State University, School of Hospitality Business. The program includes two levels of internship of 400 hours each. Her second internship took her to New York where she assisted in all events taking place at Ralph Wilson Stadium and First Niagara Center including Buffalo Bills home games, concerts and special events. This experience led to a permanent post in event management for All Access Sports & Events Marketing, an event management firm with a sports focus.

During her fifteen year tenure with All Access, Joan gained valuable experience in all aspects of event management and promotion along with creating a catalog of valuable contacts and resources.

Robert Short earned a degree in Hospitality Management from San Jose State University. His career experience began in the restaurant and hotel industry where he worked for several years and eventually rose to Director of Catering and Convention Services for Hyatt San Jose.

Later Robert took a post as meeting planner for California State Association of Counties where he earned his "stripes" as well as his CMP (Certified Meeting Professional) from the Convention Industry Council (CIC).

Kim Spenser earned her CMP in 2006. Kim gained her wealth of experience with Smith Moore Associates, a management company in Sacramento specializing in administration, accounting, meeting planning, strategic planning and communications services for nonprofit associations.

First as an account manager Kim was responsible for meetings, events, member relations, and managing client web sites. Eventually Kim earned the responsibility for managing client administration and budget development, planning and execution of meetings and conferences including site selection, on-site management, hotel relations, program development, sponsorship generation and financial tracking.

SERVICES

For corporate events held in the Sacramento area we have created strategic alliances with several exclusive partners and suppliers who are prepared to offer our clients an unforgettable experience. Our list of contractors includes caterers, audio/visual companies, speakers, graphic artists, printers, photographers, limousine companies, tour companies, security services, equipment supply, and language translators including sign language interpreters.

Pre-Planning Services

- Site Selection / RFP—Starting with your event ideas, we will search for the best location and prices for the event. From there we will request proposals from the most suitable venues.

- Contract Negotiations—After selecting a property, we will negotiate the best possible pricing and terms for the event.

- Budget—We can assist with projecting costs and with maintaining records throughout the planning process and event.

Planning & Preparing

- Event registration and support services including online registration.

- Multilingual staffing and guides.

- Food & Beverage Management—We can secure and work with your event caterer to create the ideal menu based on the event and theme, project costs, coordinate tastings, etc.

- Trade Show—We coordinate, create & manage trade show floor plans, booth placement, security, equipment & supply rentals, approvals, shipping and delivery.

- Event Schedule—We can create and manage agendas, timelines, individualized attendee schedules, etc.

- VIPS / Guests—We can assist with VIPs, guests, corporate gifts & amenities, special requests, etc.

- Event Materials—We can create informational packets, provide instructions & coordinate shipping, create badges, manage giveaways, etc.

Event Management

- On-site Event Management—Act as liaison between venue & client to manage meeting space, streamline the event registration process, food & beverage, audio visual & other in-house suppliers.

- Off-site Event Management—Whether it's a VIP dinner or a large closing night event, we will handle everything from venue contracts, food & beverage planning, ground transportation, entertainment, decor, and activities.

Wrap-Up

- Post Event Services—Event evaluation, surveys, final review of invoices and budget reconciliation.

We have also developed a working relationship with a number of venues that offer a unique experience to their customers. The list includes:

- *SkyZone:* a low-impact, healthy fun workout on trampolines

- *iFlyWorld:* groups up to 100 can experience indoor skydiving

- *Go Kart Racer*: meeting rooms, gourmet catering, arcade, racing and more

- *Thunder Valley Casino Resort, Red Hawk Casino, Cash Creek Casino:* casino games

- *GolfLand Sunsplash:* fast cars, mini golf, an arcade and laser tag and a waterslide park.

MARKET ANALYSIS

As of June 2014 there were 256 convention centers in the U.S. California has the largest number with 23 locations. In 2012 some 1.83 million meetings were held in the U.S. The majority of these were corporate or business meetings. An estimated 113 million people attended those meetings, 61 million attended conventions, conferences and congresses and 27 million visited trade shows.

Direct spending on meeting related activities approached $300 billion dollars in the U.S. in 2012. The cost of a meeting increased by 2.5 percent per person in North America in 2015.

According to *Successful Meetings* magazine several trends for 2016 have been identified.

These trends include:

- A desire for new types of venues for corporate gatherings such as private villas, casinos and theme parks.

- Use of unique decor to brand the event.

- A focus on attendee engagement with live feeds, video conferencing, audience participation, on-site bloggers and event apps.

- Use of high-tech such as GPS event locator and navigation assistance, information kiosks, on-demand video feeds, on-the-spot surveys and contests.

- The event as community where the event begins with pre-registration and social media is a key element for building community and creating excitement.

- Sustainable and green: examples include serving of locally produced food, glass bottles instead of plastic, energy efficient lights and "green" decor.

MARKET SEGMENTATION

We have identified several groups that will be the focus of our marketing efforts. These groups include:

- Corporations

- Associations

- Non-profits

- Government agencies

The types of meetings of interest to these groups differs somewhat and so we have provided a more thorough description below. Our definitions come from the Convention Industry Council (CIC) 2011 report "The Economic Significance of Meetings to the U.S. Economy."

Corporations:

Corporate events typically occur during the business week. Typical corporate events include the following:

- *Seminar:* A lecture/dialog allowing participants to share experiences in a particular field under guidance of an expert discussion leader.

- *Incentive event:* A reward event intended to showcase persons who meet or exceed sales or production goals.

- *Business meeting:* A business-oriented meeting usually hosed by a corporation, in which participants represent the same company, corporate group or client/provider relationships. Also a gathering of employees or representatives of a commercial organization. Usually attendance is required and travel, room and most meal expenses are paid by the organization.

- *Conference:* Participatory meeting designed for discussion, fact-finding, problem solving and consultation. Conferences are usually held for a short period of time with specific objectives.

Associations and Trade Groups:

Typical events include the following:

- *Conference/Convention/Congress:* An event where the primary activity of the attendee is to attend educational sessions, participate in meetings/discussions, socialize, or attend other organized events Peak convention demand typically occurs in the spring and fall.

- *Trade show/Business exhibition:* An exhibition of products and/or services held for members of a common industry. The primary activity of attendees is visiting exhibits on the show floor. These events focus primarily on business-to-business relationships but part of the event may also be open to the public.

Non-profit Organizations:

Events can include board meetings, auctions, raffles, and themed fundraisers. We can assist with helping to secure the venue, audio/visual, catering consultation, registration and on-site management. SMERFE (social, military, ethnic, religious, fraternal, and educational) groups are typically price-sensitive and tend to meet on weekends and/or during the summer months or holiday season, when greater discounts are usually available.

Government Agencies:

Events can include seminars, incentives, meetings and conferences.

As the capital of California, Sacramento is home to our governor, the legislature and a number of state agencies. We intend to invest efforts on developing this segment of the market due to its proximity but we do not consider it to be a "cash cow" as government agencies are prone to fluctuations in budgetary availability. We have also found that the current trend for government meetings is on the decline.

According to Meetings Outlook's 2015 winter edition the meeting industry showed signs of stabilization throughout 2014. Organizations' budgets have been rising steadily and are predicted to continue.

Our research indicates that the market segment with the most potential is the corporate market. In order to reach this market we will continue to build on our existing network of contacts and satisfied customers from our previous contracts.

MARKETING STRATEGY

Experience has taught us how to quickly identify the key decision makers at a large corporation. We also understand how to approach these people and demonstrate the value of our services. Our technique for closing the sale is based on the idea that the client will gain a positive return on investment (ROI) from engaging our event managing services.

We have a knack for finding the road less traveled when it comes to approaching a potential client. For example, when pitching ideas for an incentive award event we once approached the head of the customer service department at a large corporation. While others might have thought that the human resources department would be the logical choice, our pitch was based on the idea that happy employees treat customers better. This leads to as much as an 85% increase in corporate profitability.

High-level executives are charged with keeping the company profitable and increasing the value of the company's stock to its shareholders. They are more than happy to hear about products and services that will legitimately help them achieve these goals.

One way we stay on top of mind with corporate decision makers is to use Google alerts help us keep an eye on relevant press releases and news articles about our target clients. This helps us to create pitches that are timely and poised to get a positive response.

We have also found that a way to gain credibility with a potential client is with a referral from a vendor they already work with. Therefore we will continue our strategy of identifying and working with vendors who have existing contracts with our ideal client and who provide complementary but non-competing services.

We have also assembled an advisory board that includes key executives at venue sites, hotels and other service provider companies. This places us in an optimal position in approaching clients and in our ability to schedule our events according to our clients' preferences.

We will also build our brand and credibility by gaining visibility as experts in our industry. This will be accomplished by speaking at events, writing articles for magazines and blogs and our own web site and blog. We will target publications, blogs and events that aim at reaching our key demographic of corporate decision-makers.

Milestone

Milestone	End date	Budget
Business plan completion	November 1, 2015	$ 1,000
Complete web site	December 1, 2015	$ 1,500
Begin advertising campaign	November 15, 2015	$ 3,000
Secure office location	January 1, 2016	$18,000
Profitability	December 31, 2016	
Hire part-time office staff	March 1, 2016	$12,000

PERSONNEL PLAN

In the first three- to five years of operations we will be building up our internal support staff. Because Impact Events is a corporation, payroll estimates include data for both the owners and office staff.

Direct cost figures on our projected profit/loss statement include costs of subcontractors who will assist us on managing events.

Personnel plan	Year 1	Year 2	Year 3
Owners	$60,000	$65,000	$100,000
Office staff	$20,000	$25,000	$ 35,000
Total people	**4**	**4**	**5**
Total payroll	**$80,000**	**$90,000**	**$135,000**

FINANCIAL PLAN

Pro forma profit and loss

	Year 1	Year 2	Year 3
Sales	$145,000	$195,000	$265,000
Direct costs of sales	$ 26,100	$ 35,100	$ 47,700
Gross margin	$118,900	$159,900	$217,300
Gross margin %	82%	82%	82%
Expenses			
Advertising	$ 2,500	$ 2,500	$ 2,000
Payroll	$ 80,000	$ 90,000	$135,000
Payroll taxes	$ 8,000	$ 9,000	$ 13,500
Employee benefits	$ 4,000	$ 4,500	$ 6,750
Rent	$ 18,000	$ 18,000	$ 18,000
Utilities	$ 1,500	$ 1,500	$ 1,500
Depreciation	$ 550	$ 550	$ 550
Phone/Internet	$ 640	$ 960	$ 960
Insurance	$ 1,650	$ 1,650	$ 1,650
Web site fees	$ 250	$ 250	$ 250
Web site maintenance	$ 400	$ 400	$ 400
Software/app subscriptions	$ 1,800	$ 1,800	$ 1,800
Professional dues/memberships	$ 750	$ 750	$ 750
Office supplies	$ 200	$ 250	$ 300
Auto	$ 2,000	$ 2,200	$ 2,400
Travel	$ 575	$ 600	$ 850
Other expenses	$ 400	$ 600	$ 800
Total operating expenses	**$123,215**	**$135,510**	**$187,460**
Net profit before interest/taxes	**($ 4,315)**	**$ 24,390**	**$ 29,840**
Taxes	$ 0	$ 3,659	$ 4,476
Net profit/sales	**−3%**	**13%**	**11%**

Pro forma balance sheet

Assets	Year 1	Year 2	Year 3
Current assets			
Cash	$ 6,535	$37,490	$33,990
Accounts receivable	$14,200	$12,500	$22,000
Other current assets	$ 0	$ 0	$ 0
Total current assets	**$20,735**	**$49,990**	**$55,990**
Long-term assets			
Long-term assets	$ 5,500	$ 5,500	$ 5,500
Accumulated depreciation	($ 550)	($ 1,100)	($ 1,650)
Total long-term assets	**$ 4,950**	**$ 4,400**	**$ 3,850**
Total assets	**$25,685**	**$54,390**	**$59,840**
Liabilities and capital			
Current liabilities			
Accounts payable	$ 0	$ 0	$ 0
Other current liabilities	$ 0	$ 0	$ 0
Subtotal current liabilities	**$ 0**	**$ 0**	**$ 0**
Long-term liabilities	$ 0	$ 0	$ 0
Total liabilities	**$ 0**	**$ 0**	**$ 0**
Paid in capital	$30,000	$30,000	$30,000
Earnings	($ 4,315)	$24,390	$29,840
Total capital	**$25,685**	**$54,390**	**$59,840**
Total liabilities and capital	**$25,685**	**$54,390**	**$59,840**

Cost-Cutting Consulting Business

Cost Reduction Consultants Inc.

3250 Madeleine Dr., Suite 3
Mason Hills, KY 33952

Paul Greenland

Cost Reduction Consultants Inc. is an independent consulting practice with one important focus: helping small and medium-sized business owners achieve a low-cost position.

EXECUTIVE SUMMARY

Saving money is important to individuals and businesses alike. No one likes to pay more for a product or service than absolutely necessary. Following a 15-year career with a leading national firm, Bill Peterson has decided to establish his own independent consulting practice with one important focus: helping small and medium-sized business owners achieve a low-cost position.

In his previous role, Bill worked on large teams that helped global organizations (including many Fortune 100 companies) to identify cost-reduction opportunities, research potential alternatives and solutions, develop effective strategies, and oversee the execution of those strategies. Using his knowledge, skills, and experience, he will take this very same approach to help small and medium-sized businesses improve their bottom lines through cost reduction and containment. This will free up valuable resources that can be used for other things, such as debt reduction, marketing, new business development, and expansion. Based on his experience, Bill knows that most organizations can achieve cost reductions of at least 10 percent, and in some cases, 35 percent or more.

INDUSTRY ANALYSIS

According to data from the U.S. Bureau of Labor Statistics, approximately 758,000 management consultants were employed in 2014. By 2024, an additional 103,400 positions are expected to develop within the industry, fueled by an above-average growth rate of 14 percent. Median annual pay for management consultants was $80,880 in 2014. One of the key factors driving growth was the need for businesses to control costs and improve efficiency. Approximately one of every five management consultants is self-employed.

A key professional association serving the management consulting industry is the Institute of Management Consultants USA (https://imcusa.site-ym.com), whose mission is "to promote excellence and ethics in management consulting through certification, education, and professional resources." The association offers a number of membership levels, including Affiliate, Professional, Young Professional, Student, Guest, and Firm, each with a different level of benefits.

MARKET ANALYSIS

Many management consultants specialize in specific industries and/or types of consulting work. Cost Reduction Consultants will focus on small and medium-sized businesses with annual revenues between $15 million and $65 million in the manufacturing, retail, and services sectors. Initially, Cost Reduction Consultants will concentrate on serving businesses in a 150-mile radius of Mason Hills, Kentucky. Using data from a leading information service, Bill Peterson has determined that the number of qualified prospects in his target market breaks down as follows:

Manufacturing

- Apparel, Finished Products from Fabrics & Similar Materials (23)
- Chemicals and Allied Products (28)
- Electronic, Electrical Equipment & Components, except Computer Equipment (36)
- Fabricated Metal Products, Except Machinery & Transport Equipment (34)
- Food and Kindred Products (20)
- Furniture and Fixtures (25)
- Industrial and Commercial Machinery and Computer Equipment (35)
- Leather and Leather Products (31)
- Lumber and Wood Products, Except Furniture (24)
- Miscellaneous Manufacturing Industries (39)
- Paper and Allied Products (26)
- Petroleum Refining and Related Industries (29)
- Primary Metal Industries (33)
- Printing, Publishing and Allied Industries (27)
- Rubber and Miscellaneous Plastic Products (30)
- Stone, Clay, Glass, and Concrete Products (32)
- Textile Mill Products (22)
- Tobacco Products (21)
- Transportation Equipment (37)

Retail

- Apparel and Accessory Stores (142)
- Automotive Dealers and Gasoline Service Stations (375)
- Building Martials, Hardware, Garden Supply & Mobile Home Dealers (125)
- Eating and Drinking Places (58)
- Food Stores (246)
- General Merchandise Stores (94)
- Home Furniture, Furnishings and Equipment Stores (187)
- Miscellaneous Retail (647)

Services

- Amusement and Recreation Services (79)

- Automotive Repair, Services and Parking (75)

- Business Services (295)

- Educational Services (117)

- Engineering, Accounting, Research, Management & Related Svcs (123)

- Health Services (80)

- Hotels, Rooming Houses, Camps, and Other Lodging Places (70)

- Legal Services (81)

- Membership Organizations (86)

- Miscellaneous Repair Services (140)

- Motion Pictures (78)

- Museums, Art Galleries and Botanical and Zoological Gardens (39)

- Personal Services (293)

- Services, Not Elsewhere Classified (89)

- Social Services (83)

SERVICES

Cost Reduction Consultants has one important focus: helping small and medium-sized business owners achieve a low-cost position. To accomplish this, Bill Peterson will work with his clients to:

1.) Identify cost-reduction opportunities. This step typically will involve taking a deeper dive into the client's operations, in order to gather detailed information about existing methods and processes. Bill Peterson will spend time on-site, making observations, analyzing data, speaking with employees, and taking detailed notes.

2.) Research potential alternatives and solutions. In this phase of the process, Bill will identify a range of potential cost-savings options based on the information gathered in the previous step.

3.) Develop effective strategies. Following conversations with his client about potential options, Bill will then recommend specific cost-reduction strategies, which may involve organizational and/or personnel changes, the adoption of new methods and systems, etc. Final recommendations will be provided to clients in the form of a written report and an oral presentation.

4.) Oversee strategy execution. Finally, for clients that need comprehensive assistance, Bill Peterson will assist with the implementation of the aforementioned cost-reduction strategies, providing hands-on assistance and oversight.

5.) Review & adjustment. After a pre-determined time period, Bill will confer with his clients to ensure that the recommended strategies are working as planned. If changes and adjustments are needed, Bill will work with his clients on an hourly basis if his expertise is needed.

Businesses can find numerous opportunities to reduce costs and improve their bottom lines. While some areas may be specific to a particular organization or industry, others are relevant to businesses of all types. Some examples include:

- Materials Management (purchasing more cost-effective packaging materials, janitorial supplies, office supplies, raw materials, parts, etc.)

- Energy/Utilities (installing LED light bulbs and programmable thermostats; negotiating more competitive waste disposal contracts; taking advantage of rebates; installing more energy-efficient equipment, etc.)

- Insurance (switching agencies and insurance companies, putting policies out for competitive bids, etc.)

- Marketing & Advertising (seeking promotional tactics that offer greater impact at a lower cost, negotiating more competitive advertising rates with newspapers, online sites, television stations, radio stations, etc.)

- Transportation/freight (negotiating more competitive shipping rates; changing to more cost-effective freight/logistics providers, etc.)

- Waste Reduction (implementing more efficient manufacturing/production processes)

- Office Machines (purchasing more energy-efficient equipment; negotiating more competitive leases for copy machines, etc.)

- Billing Errors (identifying erroneous charges and/or overcharges and correcting them, etc.)

- Human Resources Administration (negotiating more competitive health insurance contracts, outsourcing administrative functions that can be automated by national providers, etc.)

- Rent/Leasing (moving to less expensive quarters, negotiating lower lease rates at existing facilities, etc.)

Based on his experience, Bill knows that most organizations can achieve cost reductions of at least 10 percent, and in some cases, 35 percent or more. This will enable his clients to free up valuable resources that can be used for a wide range of other purposes, including:

- Debt Reduction

- Marketing

- New Business Development

- Expansion

- Research and Development

- Capital Expenditures

- Additional Employees

- Educational Programs

- Business Travel

Process

Cost Reduction Consultants will begin all client relationships with a discovery process, focused on understanding the customer's business model, operations, challenges, strategies, and competitive landscape. Once Bill Peterson has a solid understanding of these things, he will provide his client with a time and cost estimate based on their specific goals and needs. Some clients may only need assistance identifying cost-reduction opportunities, while others may want a consultant to oversee the entire process, through strategy execution.

Fees

Some consultants charge hourly rates of $185 or more, with the highest rates typically found in major Metropolitan areas and coastal regions. Because Bill's focus is small and medium-sized businesses in Kentucky, he will base his estimates on an hourly rate of $100 per hour, so that his services are always within reach of the target market.

OPERATIONS

To reduce overhead, Bill Peterson will operate his new consulting practice from a home office. Fortunately, he is located near major interstate highways and airports, providing him with quick access to local, regional, and national clients. One attractive aspect of a management consulting practice is minimal overhead. In addition to operating the business from his home, Bill's main expenses will be a laptop computer, a tablet computer, a portable projector, marketing, and office supplies. He has secured an inexpensive toll-free phone number for his consulting practice, which is programmed to ring on his personal cell phone. This presents a professional image to prospective clients and allows anyone to call him for free, regardless of their location. Finally, Bill has secured a business liability policy from his insurance agent.

PERSONNEL

Bill Peterson, CMC, President

During a 15-year career with a leading national consulting firm, Bill Peterson worked on large teams that helped global organizations (including many Fortune 100 companies) identify cost-reduction opportunities, research potential alternatives and solutions, develop effective strategies, and oversee the execution of those strategies. Using his knowledge, skills, and experience, he will take this very same approach to help small and medium-sized businesses improve their bottom lines through cost reduction and containment. Bill holds an undergraduate business degree from the University of Kentucky, and a Master's in Business Administration from Northwestern University. In addition, he holds the Certified Management Consultant (CMC) credential from the Institute of Management Consultants USA.

Bill has all of the important qualities and skills necessary for success as a management consultant. In addition to a keen analytical mind, Bill has exceptional written and oral communication skills. He is extremely organized and thorough, and does an exceptional job keeping his clients up-to-date regarding the status of projects. Importantly, Bill is an effective time manager and problem solver who is ethical in his dealings with others. Rounding it all out, Bill is a people person who can get along with just about anyone, including demanding, cost-conscious business owners.

GROWTH STRATEGY

Bill Peterson has developed a thoughtful growth strategy for Cost Reduction Consultants. Understanding that he will need to devote uncompensated time to run his new practice (e.g., for administrative and marketing-related tasks), Peterson has identified what he feels are realistic and conservative targets for billable hours during the consultancy's first three years of operations. These projections are based on 50 work weeks annually:

Year One: Achieve an average of 20 billable hours per week. Break even on revenue of $100,000 and draw an annual salary of $75,000. Concentrate on serving businesses in a 150-mile radius of Mason Hills, Kentucky.

Year Two: Generate a net profit of $31,435 on revenue of $125,000 and draw an annual salary of $85,000. Began expanding regionally, serving clients in Kentucky, Illinois, Ohio, West Virginia, Tennessee, and Missouri.

Year Three: Generate net profit of $20,200 on revenue of $150,000 and draw an annual salary of $95,000. Begin considering the expansion of the practice to include a second management consultant, based on organic and geographic growth.

MARKETING & SALES

Bill Peterson has identified key marketing tactics to help Cost Reduction Consultants grow, including:

1. A Web site with complete details about Cost Reduction Consultants and a robust testimonial section with brief case studies from satisfied customers.

2. The use of social media channels, including LinkedIn, to network with potential customers, as well as professional peers within the management consulting field.

3. A media relations strategy focused on expert columns that Bill Peterson will submit to local and regional business publications.

4. Printed collateral describing the consultancy. A high-quality, four-color panel card will be developed. It will include a brief bio of Bill Peterson, testimonials from satisfied customers, and powerful examples of the potential return-on-investment that customers can expect from using Cost Reduction Consultants.

5. A targeted, quarterly direct mail campaign, consisting of a brief letter of introduction, the aforementioned panel card, and Bill Peterson's business card. Peterson will work with a national mailing list broker to obtain a list of companies outlined in the Marketing Analysis section of this plan. He will work with a local mail service to manage this ongoing campaign, the objective of which is to produce a steady stream of qualified prospects.

6. Periodic presentations at business conferences attended by prospects in key industries such as retail, manufacturing, etc.

FINANCIAL ANALYSIS

Following is a breakdown of projected revenue, expenses, and net income for Cost Reduction Consultants' first three years of operations. Additional financial projections are available upon request.

Revenue	2016	2017	2018
Total revenue	**$100,000**	**$125,000**	**$150,000**
Expenses			
Salary	$ 75,000	$ 85,000	$ 95,000
Payroll tax	$ 11,250	$ 12,750	$ 14,250
Insurance	$ 500	$ 550	$ 600
Accounting & legal	$ 750	$ 750	$ 750
Office supplies	$ 500	$ 600	$ 700
Equipment	$ 2,000	$ 1,500	$ 1,500
Marketing & advertising	$ 4,500	$ 5,500	$ 6,500
Telecommunications & Internet	$ 1,250	$ 1,250	$ 1,250
Professional development	$ 500	$ 1,500	$ 2,000
Unreimbursed travel	$ 2,500	$ 3,500	$ 4,500
Donations & contributions	$ 500	$ 1,500	$ 2,000
Subscriptions & dues	$ 250	$ 250	$ 250
Misc.	$ 500	$ 500	$ 500
Total expenses	**$100,000**	**$109,850**	**$129,800**
Net income	**$ 0**	**$ 31,435**	**$ 20,200**

Document Shredding Business

Shred Right Enterprises Inc.

56912 Marietta Parkway
Chalmers, MN 56703

Paul Greenland

Shred Right Enterprises Inc. provides on- and off-site shredding and disposal of confidential and non-confidential documents, film, and magnetic media.

EXECUTIVE SUMMARY

Shred Right Enterprises Inc. provides on- and off-site shredding and disposal of confidential and non-confidential documents, film, and magnetic media. The company, which operates in a $4 billion North American industry, is being established by brothers Tim and Ted Morton, who have backgrounds in information privacy and transportation, respectively, along with an entrepreneurial spirit. The Mortons have developed the following business plan, which details their strategy for growing Shred Right Enterprises into a highly profitable operation with the potential for regional expansion. The owners are funding the business with their own money, which they expect to fully recoup during the third year of operations.

INDUSTRY ANALYSIS

According to an independent market analysis conducted by Stericycle Inc., in 2015 the North American secure information destruction services market was worth $4 billion. Industry players enjoy representation by the National Association for Information Destruction Inc. (NAID) (http://www.naidonline.org), a trade association that has a mission "to promote the information destruction industry and the standards and ethics of its member companies." NAID benefits its members with a quarterly professional journal called *NAIDnews,* a semi-monthly newsletter called *NAIDDirect,* as well as the NAID AAA Certification Program and the Certified Secure Destruction Specialist Accreditation Program. The association hosts a two-day comprehensive training program called Shred School at locations throughout the country.

In addition, the industry also is covered by trade publications such as *Storage & Destruction Business* (http://www.sdbmagazine.com) and *Security & Shredding Storage News* (http://www.securityshred dingnews.com), whose readers include document shredding and product construction contractors.

One of the key drivers of the document shredding industry is regulatory compliance. Companies (especially in the healthcare and financial sectors) face significant fines if they are found liable for breaching confidential information. Examples of related legislation include, but are not limited to:

- The Privacy Act of 1974

- The Health Insurance Portability and Accountability Act of 1996 (HIPAA)

- The Fair and Accurate Credit Transactions Act (FACTA)

In 2015 more than half of states were evaluating security breach-related notification laws. That year, the federal government proposed new privacy legislation in the form of the Consumer Privacy Bill of Rights Act. Similar legislation exists in Canada, such as the Personal Information Protection and Electronic Documents Act (PIPEDA).

In this climate, the need to destroy paper documents, as well as magnetic media, has become more pressing than ever before. Smaller organizations are especially vulnerable. According to Shred-it's *2015 State of the Information Security Industry* report, only 46 percent of small businesses owners have confidential data storage and disposal protocols in place, compared to 63 percent of senior executives running large organizations.

MARKET ANALYSIS

A wide range of businesses and organizations require secure document destruction services. Shred Right Enterprises has identified the following types of organizations as key prospects in its local market:

- Accountants

- Architects

- Banks/Financial Institutions

- Churches/Religious Organizations

- Colleges and Universities

- Counselors Offices

- Dental Offices

- Engineering Firms

- Foundations

- Hospitals

- Independent Physician Practices

- Insurance Companies

- Law Offices

- Manufacturers

- Medical Centers

- Mental Health Facilities

- Mortgage Companies

- Nonprofit Agencies

- Pharmaceutical Companies

- Public Administration Facilities

- Real Estate Offices

- School Districts

- Software Developers

Because Shred Right Enterprises is new to the market and the industry, the company will focus on providing exceptional customer service to smaller and medium-sized organizations, which as previously mentioned, often lag behind larger organizations in the management and disposal of confidential information. As the business' capacity and reputation grows, it will pursue larger customers.

Competition

Document shredding is a highly fragmented industry. In addition to national players such as Stericycle, the industry includes many smaller competitors. Although there are several competitors in the local market, the Morton Brothers have determined that there is ample room for competition, with demand for document shredding and information destruction exceeding the supply of available vendors. A list of Shred Right Enterprises' key primary and secondary competitors is available upon request.

SERVICES

Shred Right Enterprises Inc. provides on- and off-site shredding and disposal of confidential and non-confidential documents, film, and magnetic media, including:

- Computer Tape

- Credit Cards

- Microfiche

- Microfilm

- Paper Documents (e.g., job applications, credit applications, medical records, legal documents, financial records, tax documents, credit card receipts, etc.)

- Photographs

- Videotape

- X-ray film

The company offers a wide variety of service options to its customers, including:

1. *On-site service:* Shred Right Enterprises' mobile unit will come directly to the customer's location and perform on-site document/media destruction. Customers will be provided with the ability to witness the destruction via video monitor, and will be provided with a certificate of destruction upon completion. On-site service provides customers with the assurance and peace of mind that their sensitive material has been destroyed.

2. *Off-site service:* Shred Right Enterprises will come directly to the customer's location, remove designated items, transport them to the company's facility, and perform the destruction. Off-site service may be more convenient for customers who wish to avoid noise, or any potential operational disruptions caused by having a third-party working on-site at their facility.

In either case, commodity materials will then be transported to a recycling facility for resale.

In addition, Shred Right Enterprises offers both one-time and recurring service options. For recurring customers, the company will provide recycling containers/bins to the customer at no charge, based on their specific situation/specifications.

Fees

Although it is difficult to provide specific rates, due to the considerable variability from job to job (e.g., time, disposal volume, fuel, mileage, etc.), Shred Right Enterprises estimates that, on average, its rates will break down as follows per visit, considering a minimum charge in each category and typical customer shredding volume:

- One-Time Cleanout: $150-$250

- Recurring Service: $75-$175

OPERATIONS

Location

Shred Right Enterprises has identified affordable warehouse space that is adjacent to a major recycling center, which will allow the company to minimize its post-destruction transportation costs. The facility will allow the business to begin with a relatively small footprint and expand floor space based on growth.

Hours of Operations

Shred Right Enterprises typically will maintain regular business hours from 8 AM to 5 PM, Monday through Friday. Exceptions will be made for shredding events/drives, which may be held on weekends. In addition, the business will make staff available to meet the needs of customers with special disposal projects that require the destruction of large amounts of paper or magnetic media.

Liability

Shred Right Enterprises has secured an appropriate level of liability insurance coverage. This policy is available for review upon request.

PERSONNEL

Shred Right Enterprises has developed a personnel plan for its first five years of operations. The business anticipates having the following positions:

- President (Tim Morton)—Will focus on administration and sales/new business development, capitalizing on his prior management experience in the information technology industry.

- Disposal Manager (Ted Morton)—Will focus on ensuring equipment maintenance/operations, and the supervision of disposal staff, relying on his background as an operations supervisor with a local trucking company.

- Disposal Staff—Will handle all document/media destruction.

- Administrative Assistant—Will handle customer service, invoicing, accounts payable, filing, etc.

	2016	2017	2018	2019	2020
President	$ 45,000	$ 46,125	$ 47,278	$ 48,460	$ 49,672
Disposal manager	$ 35,000	$ 35,875	$ 36,772	$ 37,691	$ 38,633
Administrative assistant	$ 25,000	$ 25,625	$ 26,265	$ 26,923	$ 27,595
Disposal associate	$ 18,000	$ 18,450	$ 18,911	$ 19,384	$ 19,869
Disposal associate	$ 18,000	$ 18,450	$ 18,911	$ 19,384	$ 19,869
Disposal associate	$ 0	$ 18,000	$ 18,450	$ 18,911	$ 19,384
Disposal associate	$ 0	$ 18,000	$ 18,450	$ 18,911	$ 19,384
Disposal associate	$ 0	$ 0	$ 18,000	$ 18,450	$ 18,911
Disposal associate	$ 0	$ 0	$ 18,000	$ 18,450	$ 18,911
Disposal associate	$ 0	$ 0	$ 0	$ 18,000	$ 18,450
Disposal associate	$ 0	$ 0	$ 0	$ 18,000	$ 18,450
Total	$141,000	$180,525	$221,037	$262,564	$269,128

Professional & Advisory Support

Shred Right Enterprises has established a commercial checking account with Minnesota Community Bank, including a merchant account for accepting credit card payments. In addition, the owners will utilize Johnson Tax Service for accounting and tax preparation.

GROWTH STRATEGY

Year One: Begin operations with a single shredder, operating from a fixed/permanent location.

Year Two: Expand operations through the addition of a mobile shredding unit. Begin emphasizing magnetic media destruction services in marketing efforts.

Year Three: Increase capacity through the addition of a second on-site shredder. Begin pursuing larger accounts and emphasizing high-volume, off-site document destruction services.

Year Four: Add two additional mobile units to operations.

Year Five: Begin marketing/offering shredding events at area organizations. Add an additional mobile unit to operations. Develop growth and expansion strategy for years 5-10. Begin exploring the addition of floor space at existing location, or opening a second facility in a nearby regional market. Consider the need for additional staff and mobile units, based on market demand.

MARKETING & SALES

A marketing plan has been developed for Shred Right Enterprises that includes these main tactics:

1. *Social Media:* Guests will be able to follow Shred Right Enterprises on Facebook, Twitter, YouTube, and LinkedIn. These channels will provide the business with several platforms for connecting with prospective customers.

2. *Blog:* Tim Morton will write a monthly blog about information security and destruction topics.

3. *Guest Column:* In addition to his blog, Tim Morton also will attempt to write a regular monthly guest column for local and regional news outlets.

4. *Web Site:* Shred Right Enterprises will develop a Web site that includes a tool for scheduling online pickups. Additionally, the site will include information about the Morton Brothers, services offered, terms and conditions, certifications, and liability coverage (to alleviate concerns about the proper disposal of confidential information).

5. *Direct Marketing:* Shred Right Enterprises will produce a two-panel brochure that will accompany a letter of introduction to local companies in the target market. The brochure will discuss the potential risks and consequences of improper document management and disposal (e.g., government fines and penalties) and how Shred Right Enterprises can be an effective partner in minimizing these risks. During the first year of operations, the Mortons will send direct mailings to key prospects on a monthly basis. In conjunction with their administrative assistant, they will make follow-up phone calls to increase response rates.

6. *Print & Online Advertising:* Shred Right Enterprises will run a regular print and online advertisement in *Wexford County Business*, a regional business publication. Additionally, the business also will advertise in *Chalmers Commerce Monthly*, a monthly publication produced by the local Chamber of Commerce.

7. *Event Marketing:* Shred Right Enterprises will sponsor public shredding events in partnership with local and regional organizations. Additionally, the business also will exhibit at local and regional business trade shows.

8. *Advertising Specialties:* Shred Right Enterprises will distribute premium items such as pens, note-pads, and magnetic business cards when exhibiting at trade shows, in order to remain visible with potential customers.

FINANCIAL ANALYSIS

Startup Costs

The owners will provide $75,000 from personal savings to fund the startup of Shred Right Enterprises, including $25,000 needed to purchase their first on-site shredding machine. Tim Morton will contribute $50,000 to the business, while Ted will contribute $25,000. The brothers will base their stock ownership percentages according to these initial investments. The addition of mobile units beginning in year two will result in a per-unit cost of approximately $50,000 ($25,000 equipment/$25,000 vehicle). After initially breaking even during the first two years of operations, the owners are anticipating significant profitability beginning in year three, which will allow them to recoup their initial startup investments.

Financial Projections

Shred Right Enterprises has prepared a complete set of pro forma financial statements, which are available upon request. The following table provides an overview of key projections during the first five years of operations:

	2016	2017	2018	2019	2020
Total	**$250,000**	**$325,000**	**$550,000**	**$650,000**	**$685,000**
Expenses					
Salary	$141,000	$180,525	$221,037	$262,564	$269,128
Payroll taxes	$ 21,150	$ 27,079	$ 33,156	$ 39,385	$ 40,369
Insurance	$ 2,500	$ 3,250	$ 6,500	$ 7,500	$ 7,850
Accounting & legal	$ 1,200	$ 1,400	$ 1,600	$ 1,800	$ 2,000
Office supplies	$ 500	$ 600	$ 700	$ 800	$ 900
Equipment	$ 5,000	$ 25,000	$ 25,000	$ 50,000	$ 25,000
Marketing & advertising	$ 7,500	$ 9,750	$ 19,500	$ 22,500	$ 23,550
Telecommunications & Internet	$ 1,100	$ 1,100	$ 1,100	$ 1,100	$ 1,100
Facility lease	$ 25,000	$ 25,000	$ 25,000	$ 25,000	$ 25,000
Maintenance & repair	$ 1,000	$ 2,000	$ 3,000	$ 4,000	$ 4,000
Utilities	$ 15,000	$ 23,000	$ 52,000	$ 60,000	$ 62,800
Vehicles	$ 5,000	$ 25,000	$ 0	$ 50,000	$ 25,000
Misc.	$ 500	$ 600	$ 700	$ 800	$ 900
Total expenses	**$226,450**	**$324,304**	**$389,293**	**$525,449**	**$487,597**
Net income	**$ 23,550**	**$ 696**	**$160,707**	**$124,551**	**$197,403**

Fence Installation and Repair Company

Fortress Fence Company

7555 Central Ave.
Macon, GA 31212

Fran Fletcher

Fortress Fence Company is a fence installation and repair business located in Macon, Georgia. It is owned and operated by cousins Jackson and Parker Richardson.

EXECUTIVE SUMMARY

Fortress Fence Company is a fence installation and repair business located in Macon, Georgia. It is centrally located in the heart of Georgia, which makes jobs all over the state easily accessible.

Fortress Fence Company is owned and operated by cousins Jackson and Parker Richardson. Jackson has several years of experience in general construction and fence installation. Parker brings his business knowledge to the enterprise, and together they will bid on projects to help ensure the success of Fortress fence Company.

The owners install a variety of fence types, including:

- Chain link
- Privacy
- Wrought iron
- Vinyl
- Metal
- Picket
- Farm
- Wood

According to the Bureau of Labor Statistics, jobs in the fence installation industry are expected to increase 16% over the next decade. Fortress Fence Company's location in central Georgia will enable it to bid on projects all over the state.

Fortress Fence Company will target the following market categories:

- Municipalities, Department of Defense, State prisons
- Commercial
- Residential

The overall strategy of the company is to obtain government and commercial contracts. The owners plan to bid on government contracts in Georgia, including local, state, and federal. In addition to government contracts, the owners will also bid on commercial jobs, including fencing for cemeteries, rail yards, etc. The company will also become affiliated with commercial construction and landscaping companies in the area. Fortress Fence Company will strive to achieve strong financial growth during the first two years of operation. The company plans to accomplish its goal by getting a reputation for producing quality work.

The owners would like to take out a business line of credit for the amount needed to cover the start-up costs and the three months' operating expenses. This loan would be in the amount of $125,850 and would be paid back within six years.

COMPANY DESCRIPTION

Location
Fortress Fence Company is located in Macon, Georgia. It is centrally located in middle Georgia, which makes all areas of the state easily accessible.

Hours of Operations
Monday through Friday, 7 AM—6 PM

Closed Saturday and Sunday

Personnel

Jackson Richardson (Co-owner)
Jackson is a natural when it comes to building things. He worked in general construction for two years and with a local fence company for three years, so he knows the business. Jackson will bid, plan, and oversee all projects.

Parker Richardson (Co-owner)
Parker has an A.S. in Business Administration. He worked in general construction for three years. He will manage work crews and perform accounting duties.

Fence Installation Technicians
Two full time employees will be hired to help with fence installation upon start-up. As demand for services increases, more employees will be hired.

Services

Fence Installation
- Chain link
- Privacy
- Wrought iron
- Vinyl
- Metal
- Picket
- Farm
- Wood

Fence repair
- All types of fences

MARKET ANALYSIS

Industry Overview

According to the Bureau of Labor Statistics, jobs in the fence installation industry are expected to increase 16% over the next decade.

Fortress Fence Company's location in central Georgia will make it easy to bid on projects all over the state. The area around Macon is experiencing economic growth in the business and private sectors. Therefore, the fence industry is expected to follow.

Target Market

Fortress Fence Company will target the following market categories:

*   Municipalities, Department of Defense, State prisons

*   Commercial

*   Residential

Competition

There are currently three other fence companies in Macon, Georgia. Two of the competitors specialize, and one company installs all types of fencing.

1.   Atlas Fence Company, 5458 Peach Street, Macon, Georgia—Chain link fence installation

2.   A-1 Fence, 6554 Garrison Circle, Macon, Georgia—All types of fence installation

3.   Jarrett's Fence Company, 8777 MLK Blvd., Macon, Georgia—Decorative fences

GROWTH STRATEGY

The overall growth strategy of the company is to obtain as many contracts as it can. The owners plan to bid on government contracts in Georgia, including local, state, and federal. In addition to government contracts, the owners will also bid on commercial jobs, including fencing for cemeteries, rail yards, etc. The company will also become affiliated with commercial construction and landscaping companies in the area. Fortress Fence Company plans to achieve strong financial growth during the first two years of operation by obtaining a reputation for quality work.

Percent Profits Three- Year Projection

The following charts show how the owners think their time will be spent.

Year 1

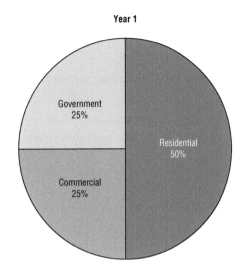

Year 2

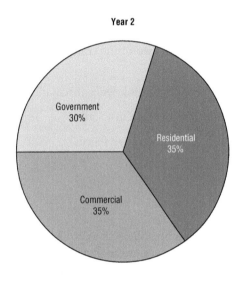

Year 3

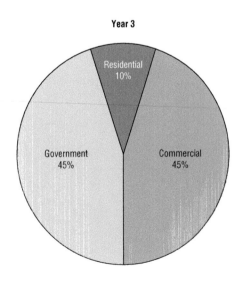

Sales and Marketing

According to the Small Business Development Center, referrals serve as the main advertising method for fence installation for residential customers. However, bidding on contracts will be the method for obtaining commercial and government projects. The company will also become affiliated with a major construction company in Warner Robbins, Georgia.

The owners of Fortress Fence Company have identified key advertising avenues and tactics for gaining residential customers.

Advertising

- Running ads in area newspapers.

- Placing an ad in the yellow pages.

- Placing ads on Internet sites i.e. Greg's List, Mandy's List.

- Social media

In addition to conventional advertising, the company will rely on quality work, great customer service, and fair prices to generate customers through referrals.

FINANCIAL ANALYSIS

Start-up costs

Start-up costs will consist mainly of tools and inventory. The owners will rent a warehouse/office space in Macon. At first, they will keep inventory for what they think they will need for the month. This will keep their start-up costs as low as possible until money starts flowing into the business. The owners both have trucks and will convert those to business use.

Estimated start-up costs

Chain link inventory	$20,000
Farm fence inventory	$ 5,000
Vinyl fence inventory	$10,000
Wood panels inventory	$15,000
Metal fence inventory	$25,000
Supplies/tools	$ 3,000
Fence accessories	$ 2,500
Business license	$ 250
Website design	$ 1,000
Initial advertising	$ 1,500
Total	**$83,250**

Estimated Monthly Income

In the beginning, the owners expect to install at least two fences per week. The average cost for installing a chain link fence is $14 per linear foot, and the average size fence is 200 linear feet. So the owners expect to make at least $20,000 per month. Factors, including a change in price of materials, the property's terrain, and total linear footage will determine the total cost of each project.

Prices for residential services

[Per linear foot]

Chain link	$14
Wooden privacy 6 ft.	$17
Metal (aluminum)	$40
Vinyl	$30
Wrought iron	$50
Picket	$30
Farm	$20

Estimated Monthly Expenses

Payroll will be the largest monthly expense. This will be based on hours worked.

Estimated monthly expenses

Office/warehouse space	$ 1,000
Inventory	$ 5,000
Bank loan	$ 1,200
Electricity	$ 100
Water	$ 50
Phone/Internet	$ 100
Advertising	$ 150
Insurance	$ 400
Wages for owners (est.)	$ 8,000
Wages for technicians (est.)	$ 3,200
Total	**$19,200**

Profit/Loss

The owners take a conservative approach and estimate $3,200 in profit each month for the first six months. Profits are expected to increase as project bids are won. As word of the business spreads, Fortress Fence Company estimates that income will double in months 7 to 12 and it will hire four additional employees, making the monthly expenses increase from $19,200 to $25,600.

Estimated profits months 1–6

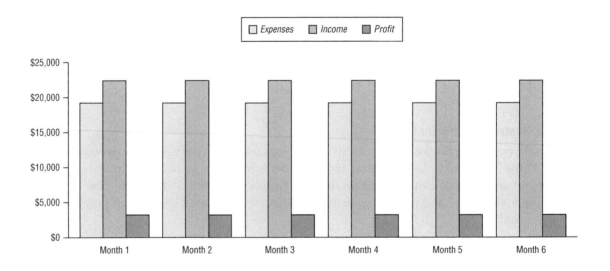

Estimated profits months 7–12

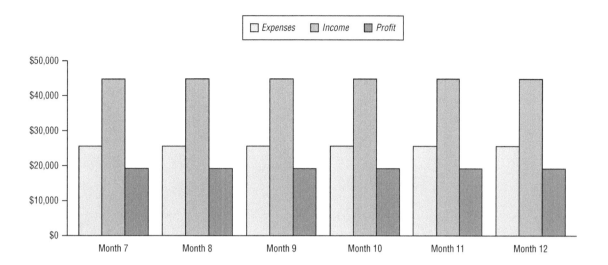

Financing

The owners would like to take out a business line of credit for the amount needed to cover the start-up costs and the three months' operating expenses. This loan would be in the amount of $125,850.

Repayment Plan

The owners will pay a $1,200 loan payment each month. At the end of each year, the owners will apply 10% of the annual profit to the loan. The owners plan to repay the line of credit in five and one half years.

Repayment plan

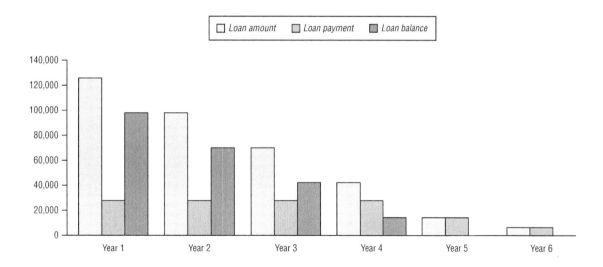

Interior Design Company

Make It Your Own Space Inc.

141 Normandy
Las Vegas, NV 89101

Gerald Rekve

Business plan for a group of professional interior designers planning on providing services to the residential and the commercial sectors.

This business plan appeared in a previous volume of Business Plans Handbook. It has been updated for this volume.

EXECUTIVE SUMMARY

The design business enjoys strong demand as people continue to buy or move into new homes, and remodel old ones. According to *Houzz*, nearly half of Americans plan to redecorate or remodel in the next five years, compared with 15-30 percent in the previous five years. Consumer confidence is picking up, and people are interested in improving their home for aesthetic purposes as well as resale value.

The interior design business is a go–out–of–your–house kind of home business. While doing the business aspects inside the home, most of the sales will be done at the client's home or office as you evaluate the space, match color swatches to existing furniture and measure windows for draperies, etc. With the vast amount of cable channels now available/the increased amount of the television network viewing time, there are at least 50 new TV Shows which focus on one form of interior design themes. There have been countless books and magazines published for the sector.

Both of the owners of this new design business have been trained and have worked in this sector for a number of years. These skills will play a big role in the success of the business.

The growth of this industry sector overall pairs well with the fact the city we are setting the shop up in is growing and is projected to grow for at least the next 18 years. With little competition from qualified designers in this booming market, we are confident we will get a strong market share in the first year.

BUSINESS STRATEGY

The American Society of Interior Designers defines an interior designer as someone "professionally trained to create a functional and quality interior environment. Qualified through education, experience and examination, a professional designer can identify, research and creatively resolve issues and lead to a healthy, safe and comfortable physical environment."

The keywords here are "professionally trained and qualified." Regulations dictate that only those who have met or exceeded a certain level of accredited education and, in some states, passed the qualifying exam administered by the National Council for Interior Design Qualification, can use the title of Interior Designer. In 18 states, they must be licensed before they can be called an Interior Designer. We will either hire designers who are accredited or, after a period of mentoring, offer to assist the designer by paying a portion of the costs for the education. This will allow us to offer our clients the best services.

Based on market stats, designers held about 58,900 jobs in 2014. Four out of 10 were self–employed. With this small percentage being self–employed, we are confident our ability to hire qualified staff will be easy in our market. In fact, there is a design school in our region that graduates about 40 students every six months.

Designers work in a number of different industries, depending on their design specialty. Most industrial designers, for example, work for engineering or architectural consulting firms or for large corporations. We will offer our services to these sectors, allowing these companies the freedom of not having to hire a full-time designer.

ORGANIZATION

Management Summary

Lisa Kurtis—CEO
Lisa has a degree in designing and Business Administration from University of California at Berkeley. Lisa had worked after graduating in 2006 with a small furniture–manufacturing firm for about 5 years. Then she started working for one of the largest homebuilders in California. After working in home building, making a lot of contacts, Lisa started her own design business. With her training, Lisa will hire the key staff persons to fill the required roles.

Tracy Trane—CIO
Tracy also graduated from University of California at Berkeley in 2007 with honors in Finance. Tracy worked with Lisa at the homebuilders and saw the opportunity to start her own business. While the risks of starting their own business were scary, they were comforted with the fact that both had husbands who were making enough money to keep the family supported.

Financial Analysis
Both owners had used several methods to finance this business.

Lisa Kurtis
1. Used the money she had accumulated over 5 years of saving (Approximately $15,000)

2. Has a newer family van, which will be used as a company van. Logos and decals will be added to the van

3. Already has computers and office equipment, which will be used for the business

4. Applied with the Women's Entrepreneur Foundation for a loan for her share in the operating capital of the business

Tracy Trane
1. Tracy will invest $20,000

2. Has a newer van which also will be listed as company property and have all logos

3. Will supply the required software to run the business, both accounting and design

4. Will co–apply with the Women's Entrepreneur Foundation for the operating line of credit

SERVICES

The design business is multi–faceted. We will provide work as a product–driven designer or as a design consultant.

The product–driven designer is a hands–on designer who combines the task of conceptualizing the look of the given space with marketing a wide variety of products. This is the common track of start–up designers. The designer often markets various products and even offers free design advice if the client buys all of the products from him or her. Buyers of their products are often allotted a certain number of hours of free design advice; if more time is needed, the per-hour fee is charged. A product–driven designer also charges a per-hour rate to customers who seek their advice but buy products from another company. A hefty percentage of the designer's income is generated from product sales.

Our staff has worked in the business for a long time with an established reputation and a long list of references; we can focus on offering design–consulting services instead. We will not sell or market any product, but instead offer advice about the design of a room or an office. We will be selling our design expertise, not any product.

MARKET ANALYSIS

There are two types of markets for interior design: residential and commercial. Residential interior design focuses on the planning and/or specifying of interior materials and products used in private residences. In terms of scope and contract amount, residential jobs are often smaller, but offer a higher profit margin particularly if you are marketing the products to be used in designing the rooms.

Commercial jobs, on the other hand, are often much bigger in scope but the bidding that often accompanies the contract can push down your profit margin. Commercial design covers a wide variety of specialties, such as entertainment (e.g. movies, theater, videos, theme parks, clubs, dramatic and musical theater); facilities management (e.g. office moves or expansions); government/institutional (e.g. government offices, embassies, museums), health care (e.g. hospitals, nursing homes, long-term care facilities); retail or store planning (e.g. boutiques, department stores, malls, food retailing centers); hospitality/restaurant (e.g. country clubs, hotels, cruise ships); and offices.

Based on city and regional statistics last year there was over 10,600 permits purchased for new commercial and home construction, as well renovations. Based on this number and the available designers in the field, we are confident that we will gain a strong market share. All construction firms we talked with told us that they bring in designers from other cities to help with projects. If we offered quality work and competitive prices, they would give us work.

Competition

Right at this moment in the market, we have a few competitors. Based on their offerings and training, we believe we will win more profitable jobs due to these lack of skills on their part.

1. **PaperPlus Wallpaper & Design**—This firm has a staff of 7, of which 4 are installers, 2 are retail sales staff and one is the accountant. The owner basically does it all. They offer design consultations, however these are very limited as the focus is always on the products they sell, not what products are new or available in the market.

2. **Las Vegas Design Team**—This company has a staff of 5, all of which are in sales and are designers. While this company does a lot of business, they only have a designer who is educated and has been certified as a professional designer. We believe once we open up shop, this firm will try to hire

qualified staff. In the short-term this will be beneficial to us; over time, though, clients will see the quality of work. We believe this firm will only be able to get contracts that are low-bidder-win types where quality is not an issue and the potential for profit may be limited.

3. **Brady and Sons Interiors**—This firm has a staff of 16, however none are designers and they just give their best opinions. They tend not to go after our clients, but they will take a sale if it walks in the door. Their fee for designers is half our fee. Our goal will be to co–contract with this company and offer our consultations to this firm under contract. That way they will still make money for the referral and we will offer their clients top dollar services.

4. **Home–based Designers**—There are five listed in the phone book. We called each one and after lengthy communications, three had indicated that they would be happy to contract to us for work; this way they could reduce their costs and be able to work on larger projects that required more staff. All three of these designers are certified.

Start–Up

Our interior design business requires basic office supplies and equipment such as computers, telephones, and scanner. In addition to the standard word processing and spreadsheet software, we will invest in AutoCAD software to present more professional looking design solutions to our clients with three–dimensional realism. AutoCAD software will cost from $1,000 to $2,500 depending on the specific applications we purchase.

We also need to buy books of samples, which are the lifeblood of a design business. Manufacturers of wallpapers, paint and carpets produce samples costing about $250 each representing various products in all sorts of design and colors. We will try negotiating with sales representatives, as they can give some of these sample books for free, particularly if they see the potential that you can sell their product.

When buying samples, we will be very careful of companies that will require us to purchase pre–selected samples on a monthly basis—even if we don't need it. The assumption is that you run a showroom to keep all the unused samples. Wallpaper and large fabric companies are particularly notorious for this practice.

Monthly Operating Expenses

For the first six months, both partners will not take a salary out of the company. After this period, they will each split a 35% share of the net profits each month.

1. Office Rental—$900 monthly

2. Telephone—$75 monthly

3. Office Equipment—$5,000 (for book value only; owner invested)

4. Software—$2,500 (for book value only; owner invested)

5. Postage—$50

6. Special Tools—$2,600 (for book value only; owner invested)

7. Advertising—$1,500

8. Company Van—Gas, Repair and Maintain—$500 monthly

Company Van—Both owners transferred ownership of their vans to the business. Both are free and clear of any debt and are valued at $12,000 and $16,000 according to the *Kelly Blue Book*.

We will develop strategic alliances with local builders, realtors and home improvement firms. This will allow us to have a several lines of revenue into our company.

Here is a breakdown of the revenue sources we will have.

1. Retail Clients—walk–in or phone quotes

2. Realtor—for their clients' homes

3. Home improvement companies

4. Commercial builders of office and home complexes

5. Home builders associations

6. Furniture stores

7. Paint and wall paper stores

8. Flower shops

9. Architects and developers

10. We will also develop a weekly advice column in the local newspaper and try to set up a talk–type show on the local cable 10 channels. This channel is free to use as long as the information provided is key to the public's interest.

Pricing Structure

Fee structures vary widely, depending on the designer, complexity of the project, geographical location and a host of other factors. Some of the ways interior designer's charges for their services include:

*   Fixed fee (or flat fee)—The designer identifies a specific sum to cover costs, exclusive of reimbursement for expenses. One total fee applies to the complete range of services, from conceptual development through layouts, specifications and final installation.

*   Hourly fee—Some designers charge based on the actual time spent on a project or specific service, with fees ranging from $75 to $200 per hour, based on the required detail and other professionals who may need to be consulted.

*   Percentage fee—Compensation is computed as a percentage of construction/project costs.

*   Cost plus—A designer purchases materials, furnishings and services (e.g., carpentry, drapery workrooms, picture framing, etc.) at cost and sells to the client at the designer's cost plus a specified percentage agreed to by the client. The service charge is often put at 20–30 percent.

*   Retail—Others charge their clients the retail price of furnishings, furniture and all other goods they get wholesale, keeping the difference as designer's fee and services. Retail establishments offering design services commonly use this method. With this method, clients get the designers services at a price no greater than he or she would have paid for the products at retail.

*   Per square foot—Often used for large commercial properties, the charge is based on the area of the project.

Our staff designers require a retainer fee before the start of a design project. A retainer is an amount of money paid by the client to the designer and applied to the balance due at the termination of the project.

Income Potential

What is unique about the interior design business is that you never do the same job twice. It will be hard to place a specific price on individual projects. What you will earn from a job that requires redecoration of an entire room from the carpet, wallpaper to upholstery will be different from a job that requires you to put up drapes to ten windows.

According to Industry statistics, on the Design Business, an interior designer earns an average of $883 per job. If you are working at four jobs per month, you can expect monthly sales of $3,532. Interior designers can thus expect to earn about $42,384; the median wage of interior designers in 2014 was

$48,840. For exceptional designers with a solid track record on our staff, this will be their base pay. The owners' percentage will be 1.5 times this base pay, or $73,260 per year.

Our goal is to have 5 designers on staff; this will make our first year gross profit of $390,720 and gross revenue of $781,440.

The goal over time will be to increase the number of clients per designer per month. This will result in increased revenues. This will happen once we get better known for our services.

Training, Other Qualifications, and Advancement

The reason we put this in our business plan, is to always be reminded of the fact that our staff and our training will be the key to our success in the designers business. We will continue to follow the guide we listed below, as well make amendments to it as we require.

Creativity is crucial in all design occupations. People in this field must have a strong sense of the aesthetic—an eye for color and detail, a sense of balance and proportion, and an appreciation for beauty. Sketching ability is helpful for most designers, but it is especially important for fashion designers. A good portfolio—a collection of examples of a person's best work—is often the deciding factor in getting a job. Except for floral design, formal preparation in design is necessary.

Educational requirements for entry–level positions vary. Some design occupations, notably industrial design, require a bachelor's degree. Interior designers normally need a college education, in part because few clients—especially commercial clients—are willing to entrust responsibility for designing living and working space to a designer with no formal credentials.

Interior design is the only design field subject to government regulation. According to the American Society for Interior Designers, 21 States and the District of Columbia require interior designers to be licensed. Because licensing is not mandatory in all states, an interior designer's professional standing is important. Membership in a professional association usually requires the completion of 3 or 4 years of postsecondary education in design, at least 2 years of practical experience in the field, and passage of the National Council for Interior Design qualification examination. We will meet these standards at the high point.

Set, lighting, and costume designers typically have college degrees in their particular area of design. A Master of Fine Arts (MFA) degree from an accredited university program further establishes one's design credentials. Membership in the United Scenic Artists, Local 829, is a nationally recognized standard of achievement for scenic designers.

In contrast to the other design occupations, a high school diploma ordinarily suffices for floral design jobs. Most floral designers learn their skills on the job. When employers hire trainees, they generally look for high school graduates who have a flair for color and a desire to learn. Completion of formal training, however, is an asset for floral designers, particularly for advancement to the chief floral designer level. Vocational and technical schools offer programs in floral design, usually lasting less than a year, while 2– and 4–year programs in floriculture, horticulture, floral design, or ornamental horticulture are offered by community and junior colleges, and colleges and universities.

Formal training for some design professions is also available in 2– and 3–year professional schools that award certificates or associate degrees in design. Graduates of 2–year programs normally qualify as assistants to designers. The Bachelor of Fine Arts degree is granted at 4–year colleges and universities. The curriculum in these schools includes art and art history, principles of design, designing and sketching, and specialized studies for each of the individual design disciplines, such as garment construction, textiles, mechanical and architectural drawing, computerized design, sculpture, architec- ture, and basic engineering. A liberal arts education, with courses in merchandising, business admin- istration, marketing, and psychology, along with training in art, also is a good background for most design fields. Additionally, persons with training or experience in architecture qualify for some design occupations, particularly interior design.

Computer–aided design (CAD) increasingly is used in all areas of design, except floral design, so many employers expect new designers to be familiar with the use of the computer as a design tool. For example, industrial designers extensively use computers in the aerospace, automotive, and electronics industries. Interior designers use computers to create numerous versions of interior space designs—making it possible for a client to see and choose among several designs; images can be inserted, edited, and replaced easily and without added cost. In furniture design, a chair's basic shape and structure may be duplicated and updated, by applying new upholstery styles and fabrics with the use of computers.

The National Association of Schools of Art and Design currently accredits about 200 postsecondary institutions with programs in art and design; most of these schools award a degree in art. Some award degrees in industrial, interior, textile, graphic, or fashion design. Many schools do not allow formal entry into a bachelor's degree program, until a student has finished a year of basic art and design courses successfully. Applicants may be required to submit sketches and other examples of their artistic ability.

The Foundation for Interior Design Education Research also accredits interior design programs and schools. Currently, there are more than 120 accredited programs in the United States and Canada, located in schools of art, architecture, and home economics.

Individuals in the design field must be creative, imaginative, persistent, and able to communicate their ideas in writing, visually, or verbally. Because tastes in style and fashion can change quickly, designers need to be well read, open to new ideas and influences, and quick to react to changing trends. Problem–solving skills and the ability to work independently and under pressure are important traits. People in this field need self–discipline to start projects on their own, to budget their time, and to meet deadlines and production schedules. Good business sense and sales ability also are important, especially for those who freelance or run their own business.

Beginning designers usually receive on–the–job training, and normally need 1 to 3 years of training before they advance to higher–level positions. Experienced designers in large firms may advance to chief designer, design department head, or other supervisory positions. Some designers become teachers in design schools and colleges and universities. Some experienced designers open their own firms.

Growth Strategy

Despite projected faster–than–average employment growth, designers in most fields—with the exception of floral and furniture design—are expected to face keen competition for available positions. We will use this to make sure we hire the most qualified staff.

Overall, the employment of designers is expected to grow slower than the average for all occupations through the year 2020. In addition to employment growth, many job openings will result from the need to replace designers who leave the field. Increased demand for industrial designers will stem from the continued emphasis on product quality and safety; the demand for new products that are easy and comfortable to use; the development of high–technology products in medicine, transportation, and other fields; and growing global competition among businesses. Rising demand for professional design of private homes, offices, restaurants and other retail establishments, and institutions that care for the rapidly growing elderly population should spur employment growth of interior designers. Demand for fashion, textile, and furniture designers should remain strong, because many consumers are concerned with fashion and style.

Earnings for average staff

Median annual earnings for designers in all specialties except interior design were $37,960 in 2013. The middle 50 percent earned between $23,946 and $57,122. The lowest 10 percent earned less than $17,914 and the highest 10 percent earned over $88,803. Median annual earnings in the industries employing the largest numbers of designers, except interior designers, in 2012 were as follows:

1. Engineering and architectural services—$53,690

2. Apparel, piece goods, and notions—$49,920

3. Mailing, reproduction, and stenographic services—$46,800

4. Retail stores, not elsewhere classified—$21,450

Median annual earnings for interior designers were $41,288 in 2013. The middle 50 percent earned between $30,654 and $55,341. The lowest 10 percent earned less than $23,868 and the highest 10 percent earned over $85,553. Median annual earnings in the industries employing the largest numbers of interior designers in 2012 were as follows:

1. Engineering and architectural services—$42,900

2. Furniture and home furnishings stores—$36,140

3. Miscellaneous business services—$34,840

Median annual earnings of merchandise displayers and window dressers were $23,634 in 2013. The lowest 10 percent earned less than $16,484; the highest 10 percent, over $37,583.

According to the Industrial Designers Society of America, the average base salary for an industrial designer with 1 to 2 years of experience was about $40,300 in 2013. Staff designers with 5 years of experience earned $50,700 whereas senior designers with 8 years of experience earned $66,300. Industrial designers in managerial or executive positions earned substantially more—up to $650,000 annually; however, $97,500 to $130,000 was more representative.

Design Specialties

Designers often specialize in one or more specific types of interior design.

- **Residential**—Residential interior design focuses on the design, professional design team coordination, planning, budgeting, specifying/purchasing and furnishings installation of private homes, including the specialty areas of the kitchen, bath, home theater, home office, and custom product design. Interior projects include new construction, renovation, historic renovation and model homes, with expertise in universal and sustainable design. A residential designer is often involved in interior detailing of background elements like ceiling designs, specialty trim and case work including interior doors and door hardware, both architectural and decorative lighting, coordination of audio–visual and communication technology, organizational and storage needs, interior finish schedules of walls, ceilings and floors, in addition to selections of appliances, plumbing, and flooring materials. Residential designers also provide specification and purchasing services to procure materials, furniture, accessories and art.

- **Information Technology**—Today's information technology environment has a profound effect upon the interior design profession. Consulting in areas outside our traditional training, we must now assist our clients with decisions on home wiring and cable needs, switching and security systems, computer hardware placement and space requirements for accompanying equipment, home theater electronics, and more. While we will offer advice, our Information Tech staff will have final say on the placements because while we are trained to envision the design of the total space, we understand how each individual issue affects another and the key importance of advanced planning. The majority of American homes are now wired with computers in multiple rooms. Designers must consider and advise their clients on linking computer systems, installing appropriate circuits and using multiple phone, cable and wireless options. Design issues once confined to the office now affect the home as well as the "home office" becomes a more standard feature in today's household. Functional equipment placement, wire management and a host of other technological and ergonomic challenges are now a regular part of a residential designer's work. Thin screen technology is being married with larger, multiple–speaker audio and theater–quality video systems that require specialized skills for proper installation and acoustics. Systems are being installed in just about any place, including on the ceiling, and many clients are requesting special "home theater rooms." Today's information technology advancements will soon allow our computers to link to our video systems, creating new challenges and opportunities in the design of home spaces. Already privacy and parental supervision issues arising from the information technology boom are affecting the function of every floor plan in the home. Our designers are trained to interview clients, to help them explore in depth their needs and tutor them as to possible future requirements that will improve their lifestyle. We are the natural link to help educate our clients about the future direction of information technology in the home. We must continually reeducate ourselves so we have the knowledge and sources to solve our clients' problems. However, we must also know our limitations and refer clients to appropriate sources to adequately address their needs.

- **Our Designers Service Sectors**—We will hire designers with these skill–sets, so we can offer our clients services in all these areas.

- **Commercial**—ASID divides commercial design into the following sub–specialties: 1) Entertainment—Entertainment design brings together the use of interiors, lighting, sound and other technologies for movies, television, videos, dramatic and musical theater, clubs, concerts, theme parks and industrial projects. 2) Facilities Management—A facilities manager develops schedules for building upkeep and maintenance, addressing safety and health issues and lighting and acoustics needs. A facilities manager also plans and coordinates office moves or expansions, and serves as project manager during construction or renovation. 3) Government/Institutional—A government designer is familiar with the very specific needs and requirements associated with working with government agencies, such as military bases, federal buildings or government offices. An institutional designer focuses on projects such as childcare, educational, religious, correctional and recreational facilities, fire and police stations, courts, embassies, libraries, auditoriums, museums and transportation terminals. 4) Health Care—Health care designers create environments for hospitals; clinics; examination rooms; surgical suites; mobile units; hospice care homes; nursing, assisted living or long term care facilities; or any other health care environment. 5) Hospitality/ Restaurant—Hospitality design focuses on environments that entertain or host the public, including nightclubs, restaurants, theaters, hotels, city and country clubs, golf facilities, cruise ships and conference facilities. 6) Office—Office design focuses on the public and private areas utilized by corporate and professional service firms. 7) Retail/Store Planning—Retail design and store planning concentrate on retail venues, including boutiques, department stores, outlets, showrooms, food retailing centers and shopping malls.

Approaches—The following are not design specialties but rather approaches to design that cut across design specialties.

- **Sustainable Design**—Also referred to as "green" design or "eco–design," sustainable design is concerned with the environmental/ecological, economic, ethical and social aspects and impacts of design.

- **Universal Design**—An extension of "barrier–free" design, universal design employs products and solutions originally developed for individuals with disabilities to increase ease of use, access, safety and comfort for all users.

Interior Painting Service

Eyecatching Interiors LLC

1510 Battery Way
Charleston, SC 29417

Eric Patrick McMahon

The mission of Eyecatching Interiors is to offer high quality interior commercial and residential painting services. The company will accomplish this by using the highest quality materials and apply them in the most professional manner. Every customer will be dealt with in a personal and friendly manner and every project will be viewed as a personal reflection of the company.

This business plan appeared in a previous volume of Business Plans Handbook. It has been updated for this volume.

EXECUTIVE SUMMARY

Eyecatching Interiors' Objectives

Eyecatching Interiors is an interior painting contractor with combined experience of over thirty years in the industry. The company is located at 1510 Battery Way in Charleston, South Carolina. The company emphasizes the highest quality of work for all of its jobs, regardless of size. The foundation of the company is Brett Taylor. Originally trained as a union painter, Brett brings experience and knowledge to every job. The company had previously been a sole proprietorship, with Brett Taylor being the only employee. Currently the company has contracts with nine builders with several others interested. One man cannot meet the demand, thus the company must grow to add the additional customers. The company intends to add an additional employee, Joe Taylor, who will be on site and paint four days a week and do office work one day a week. His addition will allow the company to meet its growing demand as well as lighten the workload for Brett Taylor. The purpose of this plan is to guide the company through this expansion and evolution. It will be a guide for the company as it adds an employee and modernizes its operations. The company currently has no intention to become a huge painting contractor and wishes to stay at two employees for the foreseeable future.

The main objective of the company is to become a family owned and operated business. Joe Taylor will join as a minority owner and become the director of operations. He has a degree in entrepreneurship from College of Charleston along with six years of experience in the industry. He often worked part time and in the summers for the company. Brett and Joe's background makes them the perfect team to expand the company. It is very important to keep the family atmosphere in the company so as to make every customer feel like a member of the family.

The company currently does mainly new residential home painting and does work for nine builders. Karl Brown Construction is becoming the company's largest customer, with over one hundred homes planned in one sub–division. The company started out building three to four homes a year and has grown to twenty homes a year, and has plans for continued growth. Eyecatching Interiors must grow with this client to meets its growing demand. The company hopes to continue to grow its residential new construction segment and add a few new contractors to its customer list. The company also plans to expand its commercial segment with small specialized projects. Eyecatching Interiors is a quality driven company, thus it is not in the interest of the company to perform jobs that do not require a quality finish.

Eyecatching Interiors has been successful for fifteen years and has developed a fine reputation. The company will count on reputation and customer referrals to reach its goals.

The objectives for Eyecatching Interiors over the next three years are:

- Transition into a family owned and operated business

- Continue to profitably offer the highest quality interior finishes and service

- Modernize and update business practices

Mission

The mission of Eyecatching Interiors is to offer high quality interior commercial and residential painting services. The company will accomplish this by using the highest quality materials and apply them in the most professional manner. Every customer will be dealt with in a personal and friendly manner and every project will be viewed as a personal reflection of the company.

Keys to Success

Keys to success for the company will include:

1. Maintaining a reputation of high quality and professional service

2. Professional appearance of all employees

3. Not sacrificing quality for profit

COMPANY SUMMARY

Eyecatching Interiors is a limited liability company based in Charleston, South Carolina that provides commercial and residential interior painting. The company has been in existence for twenty five years and is based on over thirty years' experience by its founder, Brett Taylor. The company will be a family owned and operated business consisting of Brett Taylor and Joe Taylor. Joe Taylor will function as the director of operations for the company, dealing with the business end of the company. Joe will also offer his service in the field three to four days a week depending on the needs of the company. Brett Taylor will be the primary painter and estimator; he will be concerned with bidding on new jobs as well as managing existing projects. Currently the company is about 85% residential and 15% commercial. The majority of the work is residential new construction, mainly focused in the Charleston County area. This area is experiencing rapid growth, especially in new construction. Eyecatching Interiors has formed strong relationships with several builders in the area and looks to strengthen these existing relationships as well as develop new relationships. The company also has well established relationships with several interior designers; this work is usually high-end and very time consuming. Currently the company is owned and operated by Brett Taylor; he is also the sole employee. The company lacks formal bookkeeping and invoicing practices and lacks modernization. The work is currently performed with a pencil and an adding machine. For the company to continue to be successful, it is important for it to modernize.

Company Ownership

Eyecatching Interiors is a limited liability company with two partners: Joe Taylor and Brett Taylor. Joe Taylor will become president of the company and will primarily function as head of operations. He will work in the business side about two days a week and paint the remainder of the week. Brett Taylor will be the head foreman and function as site supervisor and estimator. The company will be owned as follows:

- 70% owned by Brett Taylor

- 30% owned by Joe Taylor

Company History

Eyecatching Interiors was founded as a sole proprietorship by Brett Taylor and has been in business for 15 years. The company's founder has 30 years' experience in the painting industry and was trained as a union painter. He had worked at a union shop for 15 years when he decided to start his own company. Currently, Eyecatching Interiors has a broad customer base that includes: residential builders, private homeowners, interior designers, and real estate management companies. The majority of revenues come from residential new construction primarily in the Charleston County area. Eyecatching Interiors currently does work for 4 builders in the area and has been approached by additional builders. The company also has a mix of residential clients that act as fillers when work slows down. Many of these customers are willing to wait for our service. If construction on a new home slows, we can call a client in waiting and complete the job. This helps offset some of the seasonal slow-downs that affect the new construction industry. The company averages about one major commercial project a year and a handful of smaller office repaints.

Some of Eyecatching Interiors' previous projects include:

- Several custom homes in St. Albans

- Club house at Deer Creek Golf Course

- Kohler City Plaza, a 20,000 square foot commercial space comprised of a restaurant, hardware store, and office space

- Glaze Creek sewer treatment facility in Barnhart, Missouri

- 10,000 square foot home in Town and Country

- 3-story medical office building in Creve Coeur, Missouri

Eyecatching Interiors' clients include:
Residential Builders:

- A Grade Construction

- Eric Loberg Contracting

- Eagle Eye Construction

- Karl Brown Construction

- Pinnacle Homes

- Smith Construction

- Sturdy Custom Homes

- True Homes

Interior Designers:

- Painters R Us

- Unique Design

Real Estate Managers/Developers:

- Bill Quinn

- Hayden Smith

- Steve Holcomb

Services

Eyecatching Interiors provides complete interior painting for the residential and commercial markets. The emphasized service for the company is woodwork. Eyecatching Interiors prides itself in the finest quality woodwork and takes pride in all of its projects. The company uses the highest quality products from Benjamin Moore Paints and insists on using oil enamel for all woodwork. This method of finishing is all but lost with the advent of latex paint and the spray gun, but it is what sets Eyecatching Interiors apart from its competitors. All enamel woodwork is first prepped, which involves spackling, caulking, and sanding. A first coat of enamel is then brushed on followed by a light sanding. After the additional sanding a final coat is applied. (For higher end work this may involve an additional one to two coats.) This method of finishing woodwork is labor intensive and leads to higher costs but the overall product is well worth the added cost to our clients.

Eyecatching Interiors also provides finishes for walls and can apply these coatings by either rolling or spraying. On new spec homes in large subdivisions the preferred method of application is spraying, primarily because of its low cost to the builder. Again, quality plays a role as a PVA drywall primer is sprayed on all surfaces first. After allowing time for the primer to dry, a finish coat is sprayed on. This can be accomplished in less than 8 hours for a house of about 2,500 square feet. The company can accomplish this task with one spray man and one apprentice. Due to the experience of its painters, the company can spray a house without backrolling, which is when you go over the sprayed surface with a roller to get rid of any runs. This is a common practice among less experienced, less skilled painters. Eyecatching Interiors has the skills and experience to spray a surface without having runs or heavy spots. Experience, skill, and quality are all characteristics of the service the company provides to all its customers.

MARKET ANALYSIS

Eyecatching Interiors will focus on two broad categories in the industry; the commercial market and the residential market. The commercial market will not be a major emphasis but it is an area with planned growth for the company. The emphasis in this sector will primarily be high-end offices and commercial spaces. The company cannot compete in the cookie cutter office market. The company would hurt its brand image by doing this kind of work. Eyecatching Interiors could definitely make a name for itself in the restaurant industry. Fine restaurants place an emphasis on interior finishes, since they create the overall atmosphere. Restaurants also provide highly visible displays of the company's work. Eyecatching Interiors has previous experience in the restaurant industry, with such projects as Hilfinger's, The Shrimp House, and Joseph's. The company can exploit these past accomplishments to gain new work in the market. Eyecatching Interiors also plans on expanding into the commercial office loft market, which is a market that is experiencing tremendous growth. The company is currently forming a relationship with an emerging real estate developer, Office Spaces LLC, which specializes in these kinds of projects in the Charleston region. Eyecatching Interiors is currently in preliminary discussions on a renovation of a 46,000 square foot building on Morris in Charleston. This project would entail twelve to fifteen residential lofts and possibly three to four restaurants and potential retail space. Office Spaces LLC already has thirty five buildings planned for redevelopment in the next five years. This relationship could prove to be very valuable as redevelopment of the city continues to grow in popularity.

Another area of emphasis is the residential new construction market, which has been the company's main emphasis for the past fifteen years. Eyecatching Interiors currently has contracts with six builders for all of their projects. This segment is attractive because a relationship is developed between the sub–contractor and the builder; the relationship is such that you are guaranteed all of that builders work. The only way you will lose the work is if you make a huge mistake or do not take care of the builder. This means, barring a major mistake, you have a steady stream of work guaranteed. This is advantageous to the company because it doesn't have to spend a lot of time and effort seeking out new work. Currently the company focuses on the Charleston County area for new construction. The company does all the work for six builders in this region and has another builder interested in acquiring its services. One of the builders, A Grade Construction, has recently broken ground on a development of one hundred homes in the Mt. Pleasant area. Each home equals about $5,850 in revenue for the company. Eyecatching Interiors has also reached an agreement with Pinnacle Homes for twenty eight homes in the Summerville, South Carolina area.

Reasons new home construction market should be pursued:

- The 45–64 age bracket is expected to have the greatest population gains in the U.S from 2013–2020, with an expected increase of 29%

- This age bracket is likely to be at its peak earnings and looking to move into bigger, more luxurious homes

- Strong relationships with existing builders

- Twenty years' experience in the new home construction market

Reasons Charleston County should be an emphasized region:

- The company has developed a name for itself in the region with around 200 homes completed

- Charleston County has experienced rapid growth in population

- 14.9% increase in population from 2000–2010

- Number three in population growth in the state from 2000–2010 and has recently moved to number two

- A rise in income means more new homes and bigger new homes

- Lots are priced considerably less than lots found in western counties

- Absence of union builders means lower construction costs

- Continued urban sprawl

Eyecatching Interiors will also focus on "active adult housing" and retirement complexes. This is a market that could provide substantial dividends for the company as the country's population grows older. The 65+ age bracket is expected to increase 29% between the 2013 and 2020, which means an increased need for "active adult housing." Eyecatching Interiors needs to work with the builders it already does work for to begin to exploit the rising demand for older adult housing. This would be a fairly easy transition for Eyecatching Interiors because the building methods are very similar. The company is already entering the market, with a new ten unit retirement condominium complex on the horizon.

The company will also emphasize adding more interior designers as clients. Currently the company does work for two designers, including Unique Design. Interior designers provide a source of work that is frequently very detailed and high–end, something that Eyecatching Interiors excels at. Interior designers also provide a steady source of work, like builders. These projects are usually such that bring pride to the company and could be added to the portfolio of work. Interior designers could also provide the high-end commercial work that Eyecatching Interiors desires.

Eyecatching Interiors also does work for property management firms. Currently the company does work for two major property managers and usually does about five or six projects a year for these clients. This is a great segment because it offers work when new construction may slow down. In the winter when most new construction slows, the company can jump over and complete projects for the property management firms. These projects are usually small enough to be fillers between jobs; this segment is essential to maintaining incoming cash flow.

Market Segmentation

Eyecatching Interiors will focus on three market segments:

1. Residential Builders—This segment is comprised of home builders and represents the main focus of the company. This segment provides a steady stream of work for the company and currently accounts for about sixty percent of total revenue. This segment is crucial because of the intense loyalty of the builder to the sub–contractor. Most of the builders the company currently does work for have been working with the company for at least ten years. After ten years of working together a bond is formed, a bond that is so strong that it becomes nearly impossible to break. The key to maintaining the bond is taking care of the customer; we provide a one-year warranty for all new homes free of charge and do not charge for additional touch ups. Offering small services free of charge goes a long way in keeping the builder happy and committed to the company. A high-quality paint job really helps sell a house and it is why many builders turn to Eyecatching Interiors. Currently the company is not large enough to handle the growing number of builders interested in acquiring our services. The demand is definitely there; the company needs to expand to meet the heightened demand. The current trend in the new home segment, especially custom homes, is enameled woodwork and dark colors. This trend requires better quality finishes and better quality applications. This growing trend is very advantageous to Eyecatching Interiors because of the high quality finishes it provides.

2. Commercial—The commercial segment the company is pursuing is high-end commercial space, such as restaurants and office lofts. Due to the type of service Eyecatching Interiors provides, the costs are too high for the typical cookie cutter office space. Eyecatching Interiors needs to attach its name to projects that will bring prestige to the overall brand image of the company. These clients will frequently require detailed paint schemes with many techniques required. Often faux finishes will be requested, and Eyecatching Interiors is fully capable of providing these services. Eyecatching Interiors uses Painters R Us for all of its decorative finish work; including faux finishing and specialized murals. Painters R Us is hired as a sub–contractor, which allows the customer to deal with one company: Eyecatching Interiors. These clients will also request wallpaper, which again Eyecatching Interiors can provide. The company has a paper hanger that does all of work as a sub–contractor. Commercial projects are desired because they are large projects that can add to the overall portfolio of the company.

3. Other—This segment is composed of several smaller market segments Eyecatching Interiors will pursue. A major aspect of this segment is interior designers. Interior designers often request tailored service and often require very intricate and time–consuming finishes. Again Eyecatching Interiors' alliance with Painters R Us and a quality paper hanger allows the company to apply nearly any interior finish. Interior designers provide a steady stream of work for the company but also require a lot of time, as many projects are quite drawn out. This is why Eyecatching Interiors wants to limit the number of designers to about four or five. Another aspect of this segment is real estate management firms. These are companies and individuals that the company has longstanding relations with. This segment requires repaints of properties that range from apartment complexes to doctors' offices. This segment is great for providing a steady stream of work, especially when the building season slows. The company does not wish to pursue this segment too dramatically as it doesn't fit with the overall scheme of the company. The company does wish to maintain existing

clients because of the longstanding relationships and to keep the steady stream of work. The final aspect of this segment is miscellaneous jobs; these are often jobs the company picks up off referrals. These jobs are usually small but provide good filler work for when things are slow.

Target Market Segment Strategy

Eyecatching Interiors recognizes that its quality and skills capabilities position it in a higher-end customer segment. Each segment was chosen because of its relationship to quality and skill required. The new home construction segment was chosen because it is increasingly requiring higher quality painting. A quality paint job is often what distinguishes one new home from another, especially in a time when new homes are increasingly looking alike. Builders are often willing to pay more for a paint job if they know it will help sell the home faster. Custom home builders also want a quality finish because it makes their work look better and it pleases the discerning homeowner. A quality paint job accentuates the woodwork and often makes or breaks the trim carpenter's work. Trim carpenters want the assurance of a skilled painter following them because the painter can hide errors and emphasize the trim. The high-end commercial segment again needs quality above cost. If a restaurant requires detailed finishes, they will be willing to pay more for it to look right. The finish is often what sets the mood for any restaurant. Interior designers often require the most detailed and exotic finishes and thus look for the best painting companies, with little concern for cost. Their clients are usually very affluent and thus capable and willing to pay more for a unique finish. Each segment is meant to mirror image the high-quality service Eyecatching Interiors provides.

Competition

Eyecatching Interiors falls in the painting and paper hanging industry: NAICS 23832. The painting and paper hanging industry is very diverse and fragmented. In 2016 there were 242,374 industry establishments in the United States that employed 401,150 people. The industry produced $48 billion in income in 2015. Most of the contractors in the industry are small independent contractors; these small contractors usually have between one and ten employees and account for 47% of all painters and paperhangers. Most of Eyecatching Interiors' competitors are small to mid–size, with the average number of employees being around five. In the residential new construction segment, there are several competitors trying to gain access to the lucrative builder. The strategy employed by most competitors is low cost provider. These companies claim to provide high-quality service but don't charge enough to actually provide the quality service. Eyecatching Interiors cannot and will not become the low cost painter and thus distinguishes itself from the numerous low cost painting companies. Many of these shops do not employ higher-trained painters but rather laborers who happen to paint. They pay their employees ten dollars an hour and give about an ten dollar an hour quality job. These contractors spray anything and everything and emphasize speed over quality. Eyecatching Interiors is a quality painting company and thus has its own niche which distinguishes itself from the multitude of painting companies.

In this industry, the service and professionalism in which the service is provided is also a distinguishing factor. Eyecatching Interiors prides itself in being a company that emphasizes personal relations. The company goes out of its way to provide the best service possible for every client. Every employee is issued 5 white t–shirts with the company name, which they are required to wear every day. Employees are expected to wear clean whites and are required to wear boots. All shirts are to be tucked in and a belt is to be worn. This professional appearance presents a positive image of the company; very few painting companies have such strict rules on uniform. In fact many do not have a uniform, which makes the company look bad and the trade itself bad. Eyecatching Interiors considers its employees to be crafts-men, not merely painters.

Competition in the painting industry is very intense, especially among the small to mid–size contractors. Companies are competing for a multitude of work and must look for innovative ways to distinguish themselves. The main tactic used by companies is lowering their cost. Price wars are quite common in the painting industry, especially when contractors are fighting to gain access to a builder or subdivision. Most of the work is acquired by word of mouth; nothing can replace having a satisfied customer tell a friend. This is especially true with painting contractors who specialize in residential repaints. You may do a house for a family in a sub–division and they will tell all their friends in that sub–division, suddenly you have ten homes in one sub–division. A key is building a good relationship and reputation with your paint supplier; frequently people will turn to those who supply the paint for the best painter. In new construction, aligning with builders with good reputations serve to bolster your reputation and may lead to additional work. Contractors often post yard signs in front of new projects as a form of advertisement. If you provide quality service, the customers will find you.

Competition and Buying Patterns by Segment

- Residential New Construction—This segment has a definite barrier to entry that makes obtaining new contracts very difficult. In this segment builders create strong relationships with their sub-contractors and often stick with one contractor for each trade. What this means is that in order to gain additional work you have to get the builder to break the relationship. This is not easy because a friendship has been formed and it is a very big hassle to switch contractors. The plus side to this barrier is that once you get in, you have that barrier protecting you. As long as you provide quality finishes and service you keep the barrier protecting you. The competitors in this market include: Colonial Painting and Exterior Painting and Drywall, as well as numerous other small contractors who employ two to four people. These competitors all claim to provide quality service, thus just saying you provide quality is not enough. Painting is very visible, thus you have to prove that you provide quality. There are, however, customers who do not recognize quality and look at the bottom line. These are customers Eyecatching Interiors has no desire to pursue—first because we will probably be too costly and second our work will not be appreciated. Therefore the company wishes to pursue clients who appreciate quality and understand that quality comes at a price. There are painting contractors who provide quality work at a price comparable to Eyecatching Interiors. One way Eyecatching Interiors distinguishes itself from comparable competitors is the added service it offers. There are no additional charges for touch up and change orders will often be performed without a surcharge. This may seem to cut in on profits but in the long run it creates a greater relationship with the builder. It's the little things you do free of charge that really set you apart from competitors. Two major competitors, Ernest Painting and Perfection Painting, charge $150 per change order. These additional costs can add up quickly, especially on larger projects. Builders appreciate the break and become even more loyal to you when you show that you are looking out for them.

- Commercial—The commercial segment has a loyalty that is similar, but not as strong as the residential new construction. In the commercial repaint segment you often get jobs by word of mouth. People will often ask friends and colleagues who does their painting; this is how we get a majority of the work. Once you get the job you are most likely going to be repainting the office again in three to five years, especially if you do a good job. The competition in this segment is however very competitive and many jobs are won through bidding. An edge that Eyecatching Interiors has is the thirty plus years of experience of Brett Taylor. He has done almost everything and understands what is involved in a particular job. The commercial new construction/renovation is a segment the company is beginning to pursue. This is a highly competitive segment, where every job is bid on. There is rarely an instance where you are guaranteed the work. The competitors range from smaller painting contractors with three or more employees to large union shops with twenty or more employees. The union shops often charge more than a nonunion shop, but on many projects a nonunion contractor will not be permitted to bid. This is the reason Eyecatching Interiors plans on pursuing smaller-scale projects with contractors who do not use one hundred percent union subs.

- Other—This segment is composed primarily of two smaller segments: interior designers and property managers. The interior designer segment is a great source of work, especially work that can add prestige to the company. This segment is marked by a barrier to entry, much the same as the residential new construction segment. Interior designers tend to stick with a single painting contractor because they know and trust your work. In addition, the contractor has a better understanding of the style and look the designer is after because they have worked together before. It is very rare that an interior designer will bounce between several painting contractors. The competitors in this segment tend to be much smaller, usually with no more than three employees. They also tend be older painters who have been around for a long time and understand the business. This is a real specialty niche with very few actual competitors. It is really difficult to target interior designers because they frequently already have a painter. This is the reason why Eyecatching Interiors does not wish to actively pursue the interior designer segment, but rather maintain the existing relationships and possibly pick up additional clients along the way. The other segment is the property manager segment. This is a small segment for Eyecatching Interiors and is composed mostly of longtime clients, many of whom are also builders/developers. In the segment as a whole the competition is brutal, as price is the main factor for most clients. Contractors such as Schaffer Painting and Berkner Painting are some of the bigger nonunion contractors that pursue this segment. Eyecatching Interiors does not plan on pursuing this segment primarily because it is so price driven. There are very few property managers who care about quality when it comes to apartment and office complexes. The clients the company already has in this segment have been clients for over ten years and continue to use us because of the existing relationship. It is in the interest to maintain these relationships because as previously stated many of these clients are also builders. If you take care of them, they will take care of you.

GROWTH STRATEGY

The strategy of Eyecatching Interiors is quite simple—to continue to provide the highest quality finishes to its clients. The company wishes to maintain its course while adding a few additional contractors; one being Subdivision Development LLC. A strategy for sudden and rapid growth would jeopardize the quality and service that has been a trademark of the company for so many years. In fact, the small size of the company gives a more personal feel to all projects, as the clients deal directly with the owners of the company. In order to add the additional contractors, Joe Taylor will have to work three to four days a week and spend the remaining time doing paperwork and setting up new work. This will free time up for Brett Taylor and allow him to do what he does best–paint. Currently Brett is overworked, often working seven days a week to keep up with the demand. The additional help of Joe will reduce his workload and lead to better efficiency overall. The company is currently in the dark ages; everything is done on paper and there is no computerized invoicing system in place. Joe intends on improving the operating efficiency of the company by having a more automated invoicing system, most likely QuickBooks Online that will track sales and expenses of the company. Brett looked at books as a sidebar to painting and thus did not spend a great deal of time and effort getting them done. The plan is to modernize the bookkeeping system so that it is not such a big task and to where it benefits the entire company. Joe's education will allow him to do the bookwork in a more efficient and timely manner than Brett.

Competition

The company has a competitive edge over its competition in the quality of work provided. Eyecatching Interiors emphasizes quality on all jobs, regardless of size and the company will do whatever it takes to do the job right. The site supervisor, Brett Taylor, provides a competitive advantage because of his thirty plus years of experience. He has seen everything in his career and is thus able to overcome most obstacles. The sheer professionalism of Eyecatching Interiors keeps its customers happy and it is a true trademark of the company's work.

Marketing & Sales

The marketing strategy is focused around generating more new home contracts and adding new commercial contracts. The emphasis of Eyecatching Interiors has and will continue to be residential new construction. Currently the company has no existing marketing plan; in fact the company is not even listed in the phone book. The reason being is that the company doesn't want to do work for people it doesn't know. The company has grown simply because of reputation and word of mouth. The plan then is to continue to rely on reputation and word of mouth to continue to grow, but with some added marketing efforts. The company will for the first time have a listed number; a simple listing will be posted in the local Yellow Pages. The company will also place signs in front of its projects, proclaiming: "Another Quality Job By Eyecatching Interiors." The company plans on having Benjamin Moore Paints pay for a portion of the sign to have their name on it; this will help defer some of the costs of the advertisement. The company also plans on advertising its name in local home and designer magazines, in order to attract the higher-end clientele.

The company will generate sales through existing contacts and through its reputation. A solid customer base already exists; there is already too much work lined up for one man. The company has projects lined up into 2017. Currently the company is forced to put clients off and sometimes turn them down. Brett Taylor averages over fifty hours a week working. The addition of Joe will add relief to Brett and allow the company to take care of all of its clients.

The average new home runs between $5,850 and $6,500 and is between 2,500 to 3,000 square feet. The large custom homes and commercial projects are all bid by Brett Taylor. He estimates the total time and material required and usually adds between twenty and thirty percent to that. For the very large and detailed custom homes the sales procedure is to quote a ball park price, but to charge time and material. These jobs are frequently very difficult to safely bid because of the complicated finishes and frequent changes made by the homeowners. In the end the customer comes out ahead because in order to bid the project safely you would really have to pad the price.

MANAGEMENT SUMMARY

Joe Taylor will become the director of operations. He has six years experience in the painting industry and a degree in Entrepreneurship from the College of Charleston. His business education and underlying knowledge and understanding of the industry will allow him to effectively manage the operations of the company. His tasks will include recruiting new work, handling payroll and insurance, and the general operations of the business. He will also work about four days a week in the field painting with Brett Taylor.

Brett Taylor, the other principal, will be the primary painter and estimator. His thirty years experience in the industry will allow him to efficiently manage jobs and troubleshoot any issues that should arise during a job. He will also become the estimator for the company; again his experience affords him the capability to effectively bid jobs.

The company also has an accountant, Greg Lombardo, who keeps track of the company's financials; the company will be linked to his office via QuickBooks Online. This will allow for optimal cash flow management for the company as it can easily monitor cash in–flows and out–flows.

Personnel Plan

The personnel plan assumes paying Brett Taylor $40 an hour and paying Joe Taylor $30 an hour. Brett Taylor is currently making $40 an hour, so his wage will remain the same. He could easily find a job in a large paint shop making about the same wage if you included the benefits package. A talented and experienced painter is worth every bit of $40 an hour. Joe Taylor earned $20 an hour during the summer as an apprentice and has become a very good painter. He has run entire jobs on his own and has shown that he understands the business. He also has the business skills and knowledge to handle the company's day to day operations.

FINANCIAL ANALYSIS

Eyecatching Interiors is currently a small independent painting contractor. The goal of the company is to add Joe as an additional painter and as the director of operations. His addition will allow for the company's sales to increase dramatically from 2017 to the end of 2018. This growth will continue through 2019 as the company benefits from the added efficiency of having Joe with the company. He will be billed at $60 an hour but only costs the company $30 an hour, therefore he alone brings in an additional $30 an hour of profit. After the year FY 2019 the company will experience minor growth– 3% from FY 2019 to FY 2020 and 2% growth from FY 2020 to FY 2021. The company will be quite content at this level of sales and does not wish to grow any larger. Eyecatching Interiors wants to maintain its quality and fears that too much growth can lead to a decline in quality. There comes a point where a company becomes so big that it cannot effectively monitor the quality of services. The company does not want to borrow to fund future expansion. Joe has $30,000 which he intends on keeping as reserve for any unforeseen events. This keeps the company from going to the bank for a credit line. The overall office expenses will increase in the beginning due to the addition of a computer and software. This investment will pay off in the long run as it will cut the time to do paperwork in half, if not more. The truck expenses category includes Brett's van and Joe's 4–Runner which are both paid off; this line item also includes gas and miscellaneous repairs. The company will now have to pay workman's compensation as it adds Joe as a full–time employee. This was not needed before because Brett was the only employee. The rate is based off a quote per $130 of total payroll. The insurance line item includes insurance for both vehicles and contractor's general liability insurance. The company intends on paying dividends as shown in the Pro Forma Cash Flow Statement.

The dividends will be divided according to ownership; 70% to Brett Taylor and 30% to Joe Taylor. Please look to the Appendix for Past Performance and Pro Forma Financial Statements.

Past performance

	FY2014	FY2015	FY2016
Sales	169,241	172,595	57,669
Materials	47,387	48,326	16,147
Labor	78,000	79,560	24,960
Payroll taxes	10,920	11,138	3,494
COGS	136,307	139,025	44,602
Gross profit	32,933	33,570	13,067
Expenses			
Truck expense	11,847	12,082	4,037
Insurance	1,157	1,170	1,216
Legal/professional services	677	690	231
Office expense	1,015	1,036	346
Meals/entertainment	338	345	115
Depreciation	3,385	3,452	1,153
Other	5,923	6,041	2,018
Total expenses	**24,343**	**24,815**	**9,116**
Net income before taxes	**8,590**	**8,754**	**3,951**
Taxes	2,577	2,626	1,185
Net income	**6,013**	**6,128**	**2,766**

Assumptions:

• 2016 is calculated from the January 1 to the end of April.
• Labor is the wages earned and payroll taxes are based on a 14% rate.
• The insurance category is for both vehicle insurance and contractor's liability insurance.
• The tax is based on a 30% rate.

Pro forma profit and loss

	FY2016	FY2017	FY2018	FY2019
Sales	160,618	293,800	302,614	308,666
Materials	40,154	73,450	75,654	77,167
Labor	57,408	119,600	121,394	122,244
Taxes	8,037	16,744	16,995	17,114
COGS	97,562	193,050	197,048	199,410
Gross profit	63,055	100,750	105,567	109,256
Expenses				
Truck expense	10,790	17,628	18,157	18,520
Insurance	1,820	1,924	1,950	2,028
Workman's comp	5,275	12,895	13,088	13,154
Legal/professional services	642	1,175	1,210	1,235
Office expense	16,062	17,628	18,157	18,520
Meals/entertainment	642	1,175	1,210	1,235
Payroll	10,400	10,400	10,400	10,400
Depreciation	3,212	5,876	6,052	6,173
Other	5,622	10,283	10,591	10,803
Total expenses	**54,466**	**78,984**	**80,816**	**82,067**
Net income before taxes	**8,589**	**21,766**	**24,750**	**27,188**
Taxes	2,577	6,530	7,425	8,157
Net income	**6,012**	**15,236**	**17,325**	**19,032**

Assumptions:

• 2016 is calculated from June 1, when the strategy is implemented, to December 31.
• Truck expense includes gas and repairs.
• Insurance is comprised of auto insurance and liability for the business.
• The payroll row is based off 8 hours a week spent on bookwork.
• Workman's Comp is a rate based on total wages.
• Payroll taxes are 14% and taxes are 30%.
• Materials are estimated at 25% of total sales, this is based off previous percentages for the company.

Pro forma balance sheet

Assets	FY2016	FY2017	FY2018	FY2019
Current assets				
Accounts receivable	3,250	3,900	2,600	3,250
Cash	23,453	5,460	6,500	6,500
Inventory	260	455	260	260
Other current assets	3,900	4,160	4,550	4,550
Total current assets	**30,863**	**13,975**	**13,910**	**14,560**
Long-term assets				
Long-term assets	26,000	26,650	26,650	26,650
Accumulated depreciation	3,212	5,876	6,053	6,187
Total long-term assets	**22,788**	**20,774**	**20,597**	**20,463**
Total assets	**53,651**	**34,749**	**34,507**	**35,023**
Liabilities and capital				
Current liabilities				
Accounts payable	1,105	1,170	1,170	1,235
Other current liabilities	780	1,300	1,040	1,105
Total current liabilities	**1,885**	**2,470**	**2,210**	**2,340**
Long-term liabilities				
Total liabilities	**1,885**	**2,470**	**2,210**	**2,340**
Paid-in capital	6,500	2,600	0	0
Retained earnings	39,254	14,443	14,972	13,651
Earnings	6,013	15,236	17,325	19,032
Total capital	**51,766**	**32,279**	**32,297**	**32,683**
Total capital and liabilities	**53,651**	**34,749**	**34,507**	**35,023**

Pro forma annual cash flow

	FY2016	FY2017	FY2018	FY2019
Cash received				
Cash from operations				
Cash sales	160,618	293,800	302,614	308,665.5
Cash from receivables	2,600	3,250	3,900	3,250
Subtotal from operations	**163,218**	**297,050**	**306,514**	**311,916**
Additional cash received				
Subtotal cash received	**163,218**	**297,050**	**306,514**	**311,916**
Expenditures				
Expenditures from operations				
Cash spending	72,800	149,500	153,400	156,000
Payment of accounts payable	64,897	123,500	124,800	127,400
Subtotal spent on operations	**137,697**	**273,000**	**278,200**	**283,400**
Purchase other current assets	0	260	390	0
Purchase long-term assets	0	650	0	0
Dividends	0	6,500	13,000	13,000
Subtotal cash spent	**137,697**	**280,410**	**291,590**	**296,400**
Net cash flow	25,520	16,640	14,924	15,516
Cash balance	**29,420**	**46,060**	**60,984**	**76,500**

Projected cash flow—FY2016

	June	July	Aug	Sept	Oct	Nov	Dec
Cash received							
Cash from operations							
Cash sales	22,945	23,660	23,790	23,595	22,360	22,168	22,100
Cash from receivables	2,600	0	0	0	0	0	0
Subtotal from operations	**25,545**	**23,660**	**23,790**	**23,595**	**22,360**	**22,168**	**22,100**
Additional cash received	0	0	0	0	0	0	0
Subtotal cash received	**25,545**	**23,660**	**23,790**	**23,595**	**22,360**	**22,168**	**22,100**
Expenditures							
Expenditures from operations							
Cash spending	10,400	10,400	10,400	10,400	10,400	10,400	10,400
Payment of accounts payable	9,178	9,464	9,516	9,438	8,944	8,867	8,840
Subtotal spent on operations	**19,578**	**19,864**	**19,916**	**19,838**	**19,344**	**19,267**	**19,240**
Subtotal cash spent	**19,578**	**19,864**	**19,916**	**19,838**	**19,344**	**19,267**	**19,240**
Net cash flow	5,967	3,796	3,874	3,757	3,016	2,900	2,860
Cash balance	**9,217**	**13,013**	**16,887**	**20,644**	**23,660**	**26,560**	**29,420**

Microbrewery

Hangtown Brew Co., Inc.

1002 Placerville Road
Placerville, CA 95667

Claire Moore

Hangtown Brew Co., Inc. (HBC) will be a microbrewery located in Placerville, California. On family-owned land zoned for agriculture.

EXECUTIVE SUMMARY

In an industry dominated by giant mass producers there exists a flourishing market for microbreweries. A microbrewery produces a limited amount of beer, typically less than 15,000 U.S. barrels per year with most of its product sold off-site. Microbreweries sell to the public by one or more of the following methods: the traditional three-tier system (brewer to wholesaler to retailer to consumer); the two-tier system (brewer acting as wholesaler to retailer to consumer); and, directly to the consumer through carry-outs and/or on-site tap-room or restaurant sales.

Hangtown Brew Co., Inc. (HBC) will be a microbrewery located in Placerville, California. On family-owned land zoned for agriculture. This business plan covers the startup phase of the business and a brief outline for future growth.

BBL stands for "barrels." A barrel of beer is 31 gallons and the standard size for a keg is a half barrel. HBC plans to start production at 3,000 barrels to be expanded to 7,500 by the end of year five. HBC creates its beer with a 30-barrel system operating at two brews a week. We will be expanding our reach with the help of a distribution company that is established in the craft beer market.

Initially the HBC will produce 75 percent ales and 25 percent lagers. The beer will be sold in kegs through a local distributor for resale to the Northern California beer market. Our facilities will include a taproom where customers can sample and purchase 12-ounce bottles of product.

We also offer refills in 32-ounce and 64-ounce growlers. A growler is an amber-colored glass jug that can be refilled in our taproom. HBC growlers bear our logo and sell for $6 unfilled.

We will offer six beers on tap with plans to expand to 16 by the end of year five.

Long-term goals include expanding capacity to 7,500 barrels (BBL) per year and adding a canning line.

Microbreweries have a competitive advantage in regards to their unique craft beverages that appeal to local consumers. Microbreweries increase their market share by increasing the awareness of their consumers, sustainable brewing and environmental stewardship, and by innovating their brands and product lines.

Therefore, our marketing strategy will be grounded in building our brand and establishing HBC as the premier, locally produced brewed beverages.

Owner investment and investment from interested parties, an Angel investor and generous leasing terms have given HBC a significant cash infusion with which to begin production.

Sales projections are based on research conducted with the help of a student from California Polytechnic Institute, San Luis Obispo. The student used figures obtained from a working microbrewery in the Monterey area of California. Projections place HBC gross sales revenues in excess of $1 million by the end of year three.

OBJECTIVES

HBC's objectives for the first five years of operations include the following:

- Establish and maintain the highest quality by utilizing quality ingredients and maintaining a motivated staff.
- Create profitable relationships with local beer distributors.
- Establish profitability and use the funds for expansion.
- Expand our line of beers with new unique recipes.
- Add a canning line.

COMPANY SUMMARY

Owners Jim Johnson, Larry Reinhardt and Karen Trainer formulated the idea that would become HBC in 2014. They then focused all of their energy on creating the business plan and raising funds for startup. After almost two years of research, writing and polishing the business plan was finalized in late 2015. Although the plan changed many times it is expected that it will continue to change as HBC moves forward.

During this pre-startup phase HBC also accomplished the following:

- Created the business name and incorporated in California
- Conducted market research
- Established a business bank account
- Began development of marketing strategy and materials
- Began working with a web site developer
- Researched equipment
- Worked with a brewery supplier to map out the brewpub design/layout
- Worked with an architect on plans to renovate the location
- Began site buildout
- A business license was obtained
- A building permit was purchased from the county Building Services Department
- Application for the beer manufacturers license was begun with the Department of Alcoholic Beverage Control (ABC); the license was finalized in November 2015

A beer manufacturer's license authorizes the sale of beer, and permits consumer consumption of beer on the manufactures' premises. The beer manufacturers license permits beer tasting and minors are allowed on the premises as long as the proprietor operates under specific conditions (Section 23357.3), regulated by the California State Board of Equalization. Only a certain number of licenses are given out in each county; fortunately permits can be acquired via pre-existing permit holders, for a fixed annual fee.

Our company name is rooted in the history of Placerville, formerly Hangtown and Old Dry Diggins; it has its roots in mining and was once known for its notorious reputation for vigilante justice carried out by hangings.

The history of Placerville represents several important points in California history, from gold mining, to the Pony Express, to railroad history. Today Placerville features many historical buildings and markers, including the Fountain-Tallman Soda Works (now the Fountain & Tallman Museum), the John Pearson Soda Works, the Combellack-Blair House, Confidence Hall, Hangman's Tree, the Church of Our Savior, the Placerville Bell, and the Hangtown Gold Bug Park & Mine.

As of the 2010 Census, Placerville's population was 10,389 people. Main Street and Downtown are popular tourist destinations, and nearby Apple Hill, known for its wineries and orchards, is east of here. Placerville is located on Highway 50, approximately 44 miles east of Sacramento and 62 miles west of South Lake Tahoe. (SierraNevadaGeotourism.com).

By late-2015 HBC had its brewing license and its first brewmaster on board and began the search for a distributor. Production began in the fall of 2015. In January of 2016 HBC signed a distribution agreement with DBI Beverage, Sacramento.

As one of the ten DBI Beverage warehouses in California, Sacramento supplies on and off-premise retail accounts in the six California counties (whether whole or in part) of El Dorado, Nevada, Placer, Sacramento, Sierra and Yolo.

After nearly two years of hard work HBC opened its doors in February 2016. Our brewmaster has produced three batches already and continues to fine tune his recipes.

COMPANY OWNERSHIP

Hangtown Brew Co., Inc. is a California corporation owned by Jim Johnson, Larry Reinhardt and Karen Trainer. Other owners of company stock include the 12 investors who have helped HBC become a reality.

COMPANY LOCATION

HBC is located on 20 acres of farmland near the heart of Placerville, California. The taproom opens to a cozy picnic and patio area with a view of the Sierra foothills.

The brewery grows 11 acres of blackberries, raspberries and blueberries to use in some of its beers as well as its hard cider, which is available in the spring and summer.

The land and buildings are owned by Jim Johnson, Sr. HBC, Inc. is leasing the land and buildings from Mr. Johnson for $2,500 per month.

The location has the following advantages:

- It is easily accessible from major freeways

- Has plentiful space for parking

- Within minutes of downtown Placerville

- Proximity to wineries, Apple Hill and other tourist destinations

- With 20 acres, there is plenty of room to expand

- The existing warehouse has 20-foot-high ceilings

- Favorable lease terms

The facilities will include the following room parameters:

- Retail/taproom

- Supplies area

- Product inventory storage

- Ingredient storage

- Brewhouse and fermentation areas

- Walk-in cooler

- Shipping/receiving area

- Packaging area

- Staff room

- Office

- Restrooms (ADA accessible)

Buildout of the 10,000 sf space included bringing the premises up to code for electrical, plumbing (including restrooms), handicap access and floor modification in the brewing area to a 1/8"—1/4" pitch for draining of waste water.

STARTUP SUMMARY

HBC has incurred the following costs in its startup phase.

Buildout costs	$475,000
Brewhouse equipment	$390,575
Other	$ 55,500
Legal/accounting	$ 1,750
Licenses	$ 3,200
Deposits	$ 1,200
Consulting	$ 1,500
Marketing	$ 2,200
Web site	$ 1,300
Office equipment	$ 950
Total costs	**$934,175**
Other startup costs	
Supplies inventory	$ 7,500
POS	$ 5,000
Security	$ 6,000
Signage	$ 25,000
Furnishings/décor	$ 12,000
Total other	**$ 55,500**

Detail of brewhouse equipment purchased are listed below.

Equipment (stainless, electric)

30 barrel pub brewing system complete, used	$225,000
5 x 30 bbl fermenters	$ 48,000
1 x 30 bbl bright tank	$ 16,500
Steam boiler & equipment	$ 10,000
Barrels	$ 13,000
Kegging equipment	$ 12,375
Lab Equipment	$ 3,000
Grain storage bins	$ 12,000
Kegs	$ 7,000
Bottling line: used 12 head filler, crowner, labeler, sparger	$ 40,000
Piping, hosing, etc.	$ 3,700
Total	**$390,575**

The brewhouse was supplied Prospero Equipment Corp. in Windsor, California. It is a 30-barrel complete turnkey system.

INITIAL FINANCING

During our pre-startup phase all three owners engaged in fundraising efforts that realized $700,000 in startup funding.

The financial investments came from the following sources:

- Owners

- Friends/Relatives

- Key "Angel" investors

- Kickstarter campaign

Investments from friends, relatives and Angels lead to more investments from people who they knew. In all HBC received equity funding from a total of 15 people (including the founders) in varying amounts.

The Kickstarter campaign ran for three months in late 2015 garnered nearly $30,000 in funding from 208 backers. The funds have been used to help complete the taproom opened in February 2016.

The signature HBC tee and hat were sent as their reward and for those who can make it to our taproom, a free pint awaits them. Each contributor was also sent a printable coupon that can presented in the taproom for their free brew.

The Kickstarter campaign was such a success that we plan to initiate another campaign in year two in order to raise funds to help acquire a canning line. Since we expect to have an even larger following by then it is possible that we will be able to raise twice as much in that campaign.

PRODUCTS

Currently HBC has four product lines:

- Ales

- Lagers

- Cider

- Accessories

Ales: Comprising 75 percent of our product line including Hangtown Blond, Pony Express Red Amber and Prospector Scotch.

Lagers: Because of brewmaster Larry Reinhardt's roots in German brewery practices HBC is currently focusing on German-style kolsch lagers. Germany's answer to the British pale ale, kolsch is the palest of the German beers getting its characteristic slightly fruity flavor from its own special ale yeast with which the brew is cool-fermented and then aged and mellowed near freezing point.

HBC plans to offer two beers year-round: Hangtown Blond and Goldpan Kolsch. Our other recipes will be offered seasonally with the menu changing every three months. Our menu now includes six different beers and we have plans to expand to 16 beers by year five.

Cider: Because of our location near Apple Hill we decided a logical choice was to produce hard cider as well. This decision was confirmed by projected trends in the brewing industry in a January 2016 article at Fortune.com.

Accessories: We also produce and sell hats, tees and accessories with our logo. Future plans include the addition of glassware, 6-bottle tote and can cozy all monogrammed with the HBC logo.

The brewery and taproom are open from 11 a.m. to 6 p.m. Saturday through Thursday and Fridays until 7 p.m. Two Fridays a month, the taproom stays open until 9 p.m. and food trucks are stationed to serve customers while they listen to live music in the courtyard.

BEER SALES

HBC will also sell and refill growlers in the taproom. Both 32 and 64-ounce sizes will be accommodated. While we prefer to refill growlers that bear our logo, California law allows breweries to refill third party brand growler as long as the label is covered. The cost of refilling a 64-ounce growler will range from $12 to $20 depending on the beer. We will have stickers available with our logo if the customer with a third-party growler wants it.

Our 12-head bottling machine allows us to fill and sell 12-ounce bottles. It can fill up to 4,000 bottles per hour. For our first three years of operation we plan to use a mobile canning service, Can Van, to can our product. In year two we will begin our campaign to raise funds to acquire our own canning line. The expected price will be at least $120,000.

In the taproom customers can purchase pints for $5 and five 3-ounce tastes for $7.50.

PRODUCTION

In our first three years of operation HBC will produce 3,000 barrels per year: 75 percent (2,250 bbl) Ales and 25 percent (750 bbl) Lager.

Production will take place 50 weeks/year as follows:

- Ales—25 cycles/fermenter/year (50 brewing weeks / 2-week fermentation)
- Lagers—12.5 cycles/fermenter/year (50 brewing weeks / 4-week fermentation)

Our current system is a 30-barrel 4-vessel system with 5 x 30 bbl fermenters and 1 x 30 bbl bright tank. The brewhouse turns crushed grain, water, and hops into wort. From there the wort temperature drops, it is moved to fermenters, and yeast is added to turn the wort to beer. For a 4-vessel brewhouse you have one vessel for each step, mash tun, lauter tun, boil kettle, and whirlpool. The incredible advantage of the 4-vessel system comes in the ability to perform multiples steps at the same time.

In order to allow for future expansion to 7,500 barrels by year five HBC will need to add more fermenters. If it maintains its ratio of 75/25 ales to lagers then it must add 375 bbl of capacity. We would prefer to add four-60 bbl fermenters because this would also allow more production per brew. Production would increase from two to five days per week.

DISTRIBUTION STRATEGY

In addition to self-distribution HBC has completed an agreement with a distributor DBI Beverage, Sacramento who will ensure that our products are available at bars, pubs and restaurants in Northern California.

Our web site will include an interactive map where consumers can find out where they can buy our beers as well as hours and events at our taproom.

MARKET ANALYSIS SUMMARY

According to the Brewers Association, there were just under 2,400 microbreweries in the U.S. at the end of 2015. The rate of growth from 2014 to 2015 was 21.6 percent.

In 2013, 2014 and 2015 hundreds of microbreweries came online while the number of annual closings ranged between 30 and 40 each year. The year 2014 was the high point with 635 microbrewery startups.

This business climate is due to the legalization of brew pubs in 1978. Current legislation provides excise tax breaks and marketing advantages to microbreweries which helps them stay competitive as evidenced by the success of Sierra Nevada Brewing Co. and The Boston Beer Co.

One reason microbreweries continue to succeed is because of their regulatory environment. Large brewers (brewers that sell over 60,000 barrels yearly) must pay $18 per barrel in excise tax, while small breweries only pay $7 per barrel (First Research 2011).

One factor in the success of a microbrewery is its ability to produce a variety of beers. Mass producers, in their quest to gain market share, tend to focus their efforts on generalized product offerings. They cannot efficiently distribute a large variety of beers.

This characteristic of their strategy allows microbreweries to fill the gap by targeting consumers who are looking for new malt beverages and unique tastes. The explosion in the number of microbreweries is a reflection of the change in consumer preferences and a shift in demand for premium craft beer.

The lifestyle index for alcoholic beverages is highest for microbrews, which suggests that more people drink craft beer than any other alcoholic beverage. The county population is 184,000 and it is estimated that 28,681 of those people drink microbrew beer.

MARKET SEGMENTATION

Hangtown Brew Co. (HBC) will be a microbrewery located in Placerville, California. On family-owned land zoned for agriculture. Agricultural zoned land receives subsidized water, which is useful because it takes 75 liters of water to make a single 250 ml glass of beer (First Research 2011).

HBC will neighbor two vineyards and a brewery, a mile away from the American River. The American River attracts thousands of tourists because that is where gold was discovered in California and the river perpetuates one of the largest whitewater rafting industries in California. HBC will experience immediate exposure to agritourism, and tourists will enjoy our 20 acres of beautiful foothill terrain, a view of the American River valley, and premium craft beer.

A new casino opened locally, and will attract even more tourism to the area. Approximately 16,880,272 people in the U.S. drink craft beer and visit gambling casinos according to research from Standard Rate & Data Service.

There are two market segments for our product:

- Local residents in and around Placerville

- Tourists visiting the area: wineries, Apple Hill, casinos, Lake Tahoe, etc.

Placerville is located in El Dorado county in the Sierra foothills of Northern California. It can be reached by way of two major highways: Highway 50 and Highway 49.

It is part of two of California's twelve State tourism regions, Gold Country and High Sierra, actively marketed by the California Travel and Tourism Commission and its private sector partners through the Visit California program and VisitCalifornia.com.

According to a May 2014 report prepared by Dean Runyan Associates for the Tourism Commission and the Governor's Office of Business Development (GO-Biz), total direct travel spending in California was $109.6 billion in 2013 (preliminary).

A 2014 study, "Bay to Tahoe Basin Recreation and Tourism Travel Impact Study" examined the relationship of major Northern California urban areas and the "rural areas" of El Dorado, Placer, Amador, and Nevada counties and the bi-state Lake Tahoe Basin as defined by tourism travel. The study found that a large portion of visitors to the study area come from Sacramento, San Jose and the Bay Area by way of Highway 50. Overall survey respondents indicated that they travel to the area more during non-winter months.

Data obtained from the user surveys was extrapolated over the entire populations of the three metro areas (using 2010 Census data) to calculate that over 4 million visitors make close to 8 million trips annually to the area.

While respondents indicated a high awareness of sightseeing and recreational activities, they were not as aware of the agritourism, wineries and restaurants to be had. Two activities that respondents rated as top reasons they do or might stop on the way to their destination(s) in the area were: restaurants or a unique culinary experience (53 percent) and shopping (52 percent).

El Dorado County has a population of 184,000 people and approximately 50,900 wage and salary jobs. The per capita income is $59,340 and the average salary per worker is $52,929. Employment across Northern California increased by 3.4 percent in 2014, whereas employment in the Sacramento Valley (consisting of Sacramento, Yolo, Placer, El Dorado, Yuba and Sutter counties) increased by 2.7 percent. In El Dorado County, 1,400 wage and salary jobs were gained, representing a growth rate of 2.8 percent. The unemployment rate improved substantially, falling from 8.5 percent in 2013 to 7.0 percent in 2014.

The most recent economic survey of El Dorado County also forecast the following:

- Total employment is expected to increase by 2.8 percent in 2015. From 2015 to 2020, the growth rate is forecasted to average 1.7 percent per year

- Over the 2015-2020 period, population growth is expected to average 0.6 percent per year.

- Real per capita income is expected to rise by 5.9 percent in 2015. Between 2015 and 2020, real per capita income will increase by 1.9 percent per year.

The typical craft beer consumer is a Caucasian male between the ages of 21 to 55 years who makes $50,000 or more a year. HBC Company expects over 50% of sales to come from individuals fitting this profile.

MARKETING PLAN

The marketing plan will be focused on creating a brand identity that the public will associate with a fun and quality craft beer. As our product line includes both darker ales and lighter fare, we will not only target the typical male beer enthusiast but also female customers who generally prefer a subtler flavor.

Our marketing efforts will include the following strategies:

- *Print advertising:* including marketing materials aimed at the tourist visitors to the area.

- *Web site:* Information on our company, our beers, staff and farm including tours and tastings.

- *Promotional items:* hats and tees bearing our logo and address will take our brand into far flung regions along with our satisfied customers.

HBC has completed the design of a signature trademark to be used in our marketing materials and on labels for our products. The services of an attorney were obtained to carry out a trademark search and registering of the valid trademark for HBC.

SALES STRATEGY

Beer distribution is a separate industry within the beer industry. The main roles of beer distributors are to purchase the beer from the brewers, market the beer to the retailers, store the beer before it is sold to the retailers, and then sell the beer to the retailers. Retailers include outlets such as restaurants, liquor stores, hotels, bars, taverns, pubs, supermarkets, and convenience stores. Typically, distributors work on a 25% gross margin for microbrewed beers. The advantage of having a distributor is that distributors reduce brewers' capital requirements and assume the responsibility of retailer non-payment for products.

TACTICAL OBJECTIVES

HBC has identified the following tactical objectives for future activities that can be tied to specific marketing strategies, tracked and managed.

- Establish strong relationships with local beer distributors in selected sales areas.

- Establish and maintain 50 percent minimum gross profit margin.

- Achieve a profitable return on investment within three years.

- To develop a cash flow that is capable of paying all salaries and grow the business by the end of year three.

COMPETITIVE EDGE

The craft beer market has experienced explosive growth that is predicted to continue into the future. Because craft beers tend to be marketed to a select geographic area it is possible to build a loyal following based on familiarity.

HBC has competitive advantage because of several factors:

- Experienced, award-winning staff

- Commitment to purity and quality on a consistent basis

- Commitment to the Sierra foothills community

- Innovative recipes from our brewmaster

Moreover, HBC has secured a distributor and has plans to cultivate other distribution channels. Our distributor, DBI, Sacramento was chosen for its dedication to craft beer demonstrated by the following:

- A craft manager who is beer passionate

- Education of their sales staff on the craft segment

- Marketing plans with specific and measurable goals

MANAGEMENT SUMMARY

The HBC team is led by its owners and follows the philosophy of producing the highest quality product.

Jim Johnson—General Manager/President: responsible for operations and marketing. Jim has been a member of the Sacramento beer industry since 1993 when he was Bar Manager for one of the original craft beer bars in the region. Jim is a graduate of the American Brewer's Guild who built his skills at the Sacramento Brewing Company and Beermann's Beerwerks. During his career Jim has performed every task from working the brew dock to brewing signature microbrews. In total, Jim has more than 80 medals and awards from sanctioned commercial brewing competitions.

Larry Reinhardt—Brewmaster and Vice President: Larry became a certified brewmaster in his home town of Munich, Germany at the prestigious Doemens Academy. Disappointed with the decline in brewery culture in Germany, Larry immigrated to the U.S. in 2000. Larry brings with him a wealth of experience and skill in the art of craft brewing.

Karen Trainer—Brewery Manager and Secretary/Treasurer: Karen has an extensive background in the culinary industry where she was manager for several Sacramento restaurants. After becoming a fan of home brewing Karen turned her attention toward the brewery industry and now serves as the HBC general manager.

PERSONNEL PLAN

In addition to owners Jim Johnson and Larry Reinhardt, HBC has assembled a phenomenal brewing staff who bring with them decade's worth of knowledge and skill.

Craig Watson—brewmaster and production supervisor: was head of a major craft brewery in Santa Cruz for 2 years where he was responsible for a combined 130,000 bbls of production.

Don Freeman was head brewer at a Sacramento brewery and a graduate of the Siebel Institute's Concise Course in Brewing Technology, is a certified Beer Judge Certification Program (BJCP) judge and Cicerone.

Future hires include:

- Door person—part time

- Beer server—part time

- Assistant taproom manager

- Assistant production supervisor

MILESTONES

Task	Delivery date
Begin business plan	Jan-14
Begin equipment search	Feb-14
Location found, lease negotiated	May-14
Completed brewery design plans	Oct-14
Finalized logo design and registration of trademark	Dec-14
Began brewery buildout	Jan-15
Corporation formed, IRS EIN obtained	Jan-15
Search for brewmaster	Jun-15
Order equipment	Jul-15
Began work on web site	Oct-15
Beer manufacturer license application	Nov-15
Beer manufacturer license obtained	Nov-15
Brewery testing/optimization	Nov-15
Business plan completion	Dec-15
Distributor secured	Jan-16
Taproom opens	Feb-16

FINANCIAL PLAN

Pro forma profit and loss

	Year 1	Year 2	Year 3
Sales	**$725,000**	**$925,000**	**$1,200,000**
Cost of goods sold:			
Material, supplies	$170,000	$235,000	$ 337,000
Labor	$100,000	$136,000	$ 136,000
Packaging/bottling/canning	$ 35,000	$ 50,000	$ 70,000
Total direct costs	**$305,000**	**$421,000**	**$ 543,000**
Gross profit	**$420,000**	**$504,000**	**$ 657,000**
Gross profit %	58%	54%	55%
Expenses			
Depreciation	$ 91,453	$ 91,453	$ 91,453
Payroll	$150,000	$180,000	$ 195,000
Payroll taxes	$ 25,000	$ 31,600	$ 33,100
Employee benefits	$ 12,500	$ 15,800	$ 16,550
Sales & marketing	$ 25,000	$ 26,000	$ 27,000
Sales commission	$ 21,750	$ 27,750	$ 36,000
Utilities/phone	$ 15,000	$ 16,000	$ 16,000
Insurance	$ 3,200	$ 3,200	$ 3,200
Fees/licenses	$ 875	$ 975	$ 975
Office expense	$ 1,400	$ 1,400	$ 1,400
Repairs/maintenance	$ 6,500	$ 7,500	$ 8,000
Legal/accounting	$ 2,500	$ 2,500	$ 2,500
Property tax	$ 850	$ 850	$ 850
Professional dues/subscription	$ 785	$ 785	$ 785
Rent	$ 30,000	$ 30,000	$ 30,000
Other	$ 1,200	$ 2,500	$ 4,500
Total operating expenses	**$388,013**	**$438,313**	**$ 467,313**
Earnings before interest and taxes	$ 31,988	$ 65,688	$ 189,688
Interest expense			
Net earnings	$ 31,988	$ 65,688	$ 189,688
Income tax	$ 4,798	$ 11,422	$ 57,228
Net profit	**$ 27,190**	**$ 54,266**	**$ 132,460**
Net profit/sales	**4%**	**6%**	**11%**
Monthly break even revenue	$ 69,457		
Percent variable cost	42%		
Estimated monthly fixed costs	$ 29,220		

Projected balance sheet

Assets	Year 1	Year 2	Year 3
Current assets			
Cash in bank	$ 12,100	$ 32,835	$235,767
Account receivable	$ 2,800	$ 4,500	$ 15,000
Inventory	$ 18,500	$ 15,000	$ 28,000
Other current assets			
Total current assets	**$ 33,400**	**$ 52,335**	**$278,767**
Fixed assets			
Improvements	$475,000	$475,000	$475,000
Equipment	$439,525	$439,525	$439,525
Less: depreciation	($ 91,453)	($182,905)	($274,358)
Total assets	**$856,473**	**$783,955**	**$918,935**
Liabilities			
Current liabilities			
Accounts payable	$129,283	$ 2,500	$ 5,020
Current maturities loan			
Total current liabilities	**$129,283**	**$ 2,500**	**$ 5,020**
Long term liabilities loan			
Total liabilities	**$129,283**	**$ 2,500**	**$ 5,020**
Paid-in capital	$700,000	$700,000	$700,000
Net profit	**$ 27,190**	**$ 54,266**	**$132,460**
Retained earnings		$ 27,190	$ 81,455
Total capital	**$ 27,190**	**$ 81,455**	**$213,915**
Total liabilities & capital	**$856,473**	**$783,955**	**$918,935**

Professional Photographer

Finns Fine Photography

35090 23 Mile Road
New Baltimore, MI 48047

Zuzu Enterprises

Finns Fine Photography will re-tool its established business to take advantage of the changing nature of photography. Efficiencies due to the switch to digital photography as well as the clients' preferences for location shots will allow Finns to downsize the studio size and lease the remaining square footage for added income to the business.

EXECUTIVE SUMMARY

Finns Fine Photography will re-tool its established business to take advantage of the changing nature of photography. Efficiencies due to the switch to digital photography as well as the clients' preferences for location shots will allow Finns to downsize the studio size and lease the remaining square footage for added income to the business.

INDUSTRY ANALYSIS

Professional photography is a $10 billion industry in the United States. Photographers held about 124,900 jobs in 2014, with approximately 3 in 5 photographers being self-employed. Employment of photographers is projected to grow 3 percent from 2014 to 2024, slower than the average for all occupations. Overall growth will be limited because of the decreasing cost of digital cameras and the increasing number of amateur photographers and hobbyists. However, employment of self-employed photographers is projected to grow 9 percent from 2014 to 2024. Demand for portrait photographers will continue as people continue to want new portraits.

The Photography industry has experienced several changes as digital cameras and postproduction technologies have increasingly affected operators. While photographers are benefiting from the changes by increasing their efficiency and availability, consumers are now able to take professional-quality images without the need of a specialist. Nevertheless, revenue is expected to improve slightly in the next five years as operators focus on niche markets, such as events, sports, and church directory photography, to sustain demand. Industry revenue will continue to increase despite a constantly shifting technological landscape.

MARKET ANALYSIS

The City of New Baltimore is located in the northeast corner of Macomb County bordering beautiful Anchor Bay located on the coastline of Lake St. Clair. The City is approximately 30 minutes northeast of downtown Detroit, Michigan. New Baltimore is 4.6 square miles with a population of 12,084 as of April of 2010. It is the fastest growing community in Macomb County and is projected to be so for the next 10 years.

New Baltimore is close to Chesterfield, Ira Township, Casco, Lenox, China, East China, Marine City, and St. Clair, bordering both Macomb County and St. Clair County.

The town sits on the waterfront along Lake St. Clair's Anchor Bay, and offers a public park, beach, and downtown shopping district.Throughout its history, New Baltimore has been linked to the regional economy by virtue of the city's access to the waterfront and the region's transportation network. It enjoys easy access from both I-94 and M-29.

The population of New Baltimore in 2014 was 12,269, with 100% being urban. Since 2000, the population has grown 65.7%. The median resident age is 40.7 years, with 94% of the population being white. 51% of the population is female with 49% male.

The estimated median household income in 2013 was $78,377 compared to $60,699 in 2000. By contrast, the estimated median household income in 2013 across the state of Michigan was $48,273.

The estimated median house or condo value in 2013 was $160,340, much higher than the state median value of $117,500.

As of March, 2016 the cost of living index in New Baltimore was 87.8, which is less than the U.S. average of 100.

Target Markets

Finns Fine Photography focuses on several market segments, including:

- Wedding photography

- Senior photography

- Sports photography, including baseball, softball, karate, middle school and high school sports teams, and dance

- Family/baby portraits

- Theater portraits

Within a 30-mile radius of Finns Fine Photography, there are:

- 4 dance studios

- 6 Little league organizations

- 3 baseball travel teams

- 4 softball organizations, including various levels of travel softball

- 3 AYSO soccer organizations

- 5 high schools

- 12 middle schools

- 1 gymnastics school

- 3 martial arts studios

- 1 youth theater

Finns already has established relationships with many of these organizations and is regularly hired as their professional photographer.

PERSONNEL

Anyone can use their cell phone to take a picture and many people fancy themselves "photographers," but there are many qualities necessary to be a successful photographer who can consistently take quality shots. These qualities include:

- *Artistic ability.* Photographers capture their subjects in images, and they must be able to evaluate the artistic quality of a photograph. Photographers need a "good eye"—the ability to use colors, shadows, shades, light, and distance to compose good photographs.

- *Business skills.* Photographers must be able to plan marketing strategies, reach out to prospective clients, and anticipate seasonal employment.

- *Computer skills.* Most photographers do their own postproduction work and must be familiar with photo-editing software. They also use computers to maintain a digital portfolio.

- *Customer-service skills.* Photographers must be able to understand the needs of their clients and propose solutions to any problems that arise.

- *Detail oriented.* Photographers who do their own postproduction work must be careful not to overlook details and must be thorough when editing photographs. In addition, photographers accumulate many photographs and must maintain them in an orderly fashion.

- *Interpersonal skills.* Photographers often photograph people. They must communicate effectively to achieve a certain composition in a photograph.

Photographer

Finn Shuster has been in the photography business for 25 years. Over this time, he has established himself as a reliable photographer with a great eye who is willing to do anything to please his customer and perfect his craft. This combination of integrity and artistry has served him well and he has many long-term commitments from local organizations.

Other

Mary Shuster, Finn's wife, oversees and manages the day-to-day office activities including scheduling appointments, billing, and product delivery. She has an attention to business detail that her more artistic husband does not.

SERVICES

Today, most photographers use digital cameras instead of the traditional film cameras. Digital cameras capture images electronically, so the photographer can edit the image on a computer. Images can be stored on portable memory devices, such as compact disks, memory cards, and flash drives. Once the raw image has been transferred to a computer, photographers can use processing software to crop or modify the image and enhance it through color correction and other specialized effects. Photographers who edit their own pictures use computers, high-quality printers, and editing software.

Photographers use their technical expertise, creativity, and composition skills to produce and preserve images that tell a story or record an event. They:

- Select the site and props used in the photographs

- Analyze and plan the composition of photographs

- Use various photographic techniques and lighting equipment

- Capture subjects in commercial-quality photographs

- Enhance the subject's appearance with natural or artificial light

- Use photo-enhancing software to make changes, corrections, and alter the look of the photograph to serve the client's desires

- Maintain a digital portfolio to demonstrate their work

Finns Fine Photography is no exception. From site selection to composition, to lighting and enhancing, Finn Shuster is able to produce unique, quality photographs that prove to customers again and again the importance of hiring an experienced photographer.

PRODUCTS

In addition to prints and digital copies of the completed photographs, Finns Fine Photography offers a full line of photo products as well as framing services. Photo products include:

- Banners

- Blankets

- Buttons

- Canvas prints

- Ceramic mugs and travel mugs

- Graduation announcements

- Holiday cards

- Keychains

- Magazine covers

- Magnets

- Mouse pads

- Photo books

- Photo cases

- Photo collages

- Statuettes

- Throw pillows

- Tote bags

- Trading cards

- Wall decals

- Water bottles

- Wedding invitations

OPERATIONS

Operations are changing for Finns Fine Photography. Digital photography is changing the nature of the business and allowing for more freedom and flexibility. Less physical space is needed for development and storage of negatives, as more reliance is placed on computers and the cloud.

The switch to digital photography is not the only change. The needs and wants of clients are shifting as well. It is rare that customers want to come in to the studio for posed shots involving intricate backdrops and props. Instead, clients are interested in outdoor or location shoots that use the natural world instead of formal furniture arrangements and the like. Clients may wish to have professional photos taken in their own home, school, park, or studio rather than the more formal and unnatural setting of a studio shot. With this change in tastes and preferences, there is much less need for props and thus, the room to store them as well.

What all of this means to Finns is a need for more a streamlined, compact space. Our 3,129 square foot facility is more than we require and is being under-utilized. We plan to purge outdated and unused furniture and props, selling them whenever possible to obtain as much value as we can. 25 years' worth of negatives will be digitized and stored electronically, then disposed of. We anticipate the newly revised business to need approximately 1,000 square feet, which will include a meeting place to sit with potential clients, go over available plans and options, etc.; a small studio to accommodate posed baby and family photos with limited backdrops and props; and an office with computer and storage equipment where image storage and manipulation occurs.

The remaining 2,000 square feet will be leased to another business for an additional revenue stream.

Equipment

Due to the service nature of the industry, capital intensity is low; for every dollar spent on wages, the industry spends about $0.11 on equipment. Capital investment for the industry is in the form of printing equipment, high-end cameras and computer technology.

Cameras, lighting and other equipment is already owned and used by Finns Fine Photography. A computer is also owned and used for order processing and billing, as well as another dedicated to software for photo touch-ups and manipulation.

An additional computer will be purchased to aid in the storage of the digital images. Offsite data backup will also be added to ensure the safety of our stock and trade.

Hours of Operation

Finns Fine Photography has flexible hours to accommodate both current and potential clients as well as to visit the sites where we will work.

Demand for certain types of photographers may fluctuate with the season. For example, the demand for wedding photographers typically increases in the spring and summer. Below is a generalized yearly schedule of the most common types of portraits:

- January—family portraits
- February—family portraits
- March—Dance, martial arts, youth theater, middle/high school sports
- April—Dance, martial arts
- May—Dance, softball, baseball, soccer, martial arts, gymnastics, weddings
- June—softball, baseball, soccer, gymnastics, weddings
- July—softball, baseball, soccer, weddings

- August—senior pictures, weddings
- September—senior pictures, middle/high school sports
- October—senior pictures
- November—senior pictures, family portraits, middle/high school sports
- December—family portraits, youth theater, middle/high school sports

Location

Finns Fine Photography is located in a freestanding building at 35090 23 Mile Road in New Baltimore, a major thoroughfare. The lot is approximately one acre, located in a high-traffic and visibility area near a Kroger shopping complex. The property is zoned as retail space.

Built in 1982, the property was completely renovated in 2011. With 3,129 square feet, built on a concrete foundation, the building is on one floor. The average size of the retail space is augmented by the above-average sized lot relative to other retail spaces in the area.

The approximate value of the building itself is $135,000. The Shusters' own the building outright after ownership was transferred via a quit claim deed in 2003 from Finn's father. Yearly taxes are approximately $7,000.

LEGAL

The legal firm of Harley and Guster has been retained to help with lease negotiations and contract preparation for the newly available space.

FINANCIAL

With three parties having already expressed interest in the property, it is anticipated that the 2,000 square feet will leased at a rate of $16 per square foot per year, or $32,000. This averages $2,667 per month in additional income for Finns Fine Photography.

Property Management Company

Premiere Property Management

34542 Main St.
Mount Carmel, IL 62863

Zuzu Enterprises

Premiere Property Management has a dedicated leadership and staff who have a common goal—to serve our customers quickly and professionally. Our unique approach to business ensures that you are not just a number or an association name when you call; you are a customer with a name.

EXECUTIVE SUMMARY

Premiere Property Management has a dedicated leadership and staff who have a common goal—to serve our customers quickly and professionally. Our unique approach to business ensures that you are not just a number or an association name when you call; you are a customer with a name. We promise to make every effort to get to know you and serve each customer's unique needs.

Some people may question the need for a management company to handle the day-to-day activities of the Condo or Homeowners' Association. A management company can be essential to the successful operation of these organizations, taking care of such business affairs as arranging meetings, developing and implementing the budget, performing full-service accounting, overseeing vendors to the community, and enforcing the rules and regulations in a uniform and fair fashion.

While the association board may be able to do it themselves in an effort to be fiscally responsible, you must remember that board members are usually volunteers with their own lives, jobs, and other responsibilities. Their interests and abilities may vary, and may not be up to the task of managing finances or other affairs for the group. A professional property management company alleviates this responsibility and assumes much of the liability as well. Choosing the *right* management company allows you to enjoy your home and maintain the property values of your Association.

MISSION STATEMENT

Our mission is to exceed our condominium, subdivision, and commercial property and investment property customer's expectations by providing the highest level of customer service, professionalism, and industry expertise. We will achieve these goals primarily by providing courteous service, complete availability to all customers, frequent site inspections, and attention to all details great and small.

VISION

To be a recognized leader in the field of Association Management in Southeast Illinois.

CORE VALUES

Our Core Values include:

- Passion for Our Clients
- Integrity & Ethics
- Communication
- Teamwork
- Experience
- Modernization
- Pro-Active Management
- Excellence
- Efficiency
- Socially & Environmentally Conscious

Passion for Our Clients: We are passionately committed to our Associations, their Board of Directors and Owners. We enjoy sharing our ideas and improving the Associations we partner with. We are dedicated to client satisfaction.

Integrity & Ethics: We are committed to the highest standards of ethical and professional behavior and endeavor to instill proper conduct in all our employees and independent contractors. We act ethically and legally as we work to meet and exceed our contractual commitments to Associations. We take responsibility for our behavior and our performance.

Communication: We believe communication is the central component to effective management. Through communication we can truly understand and meet the needs of our Associations to create long-term, win-win partnerships.

Teamwork: We operate as a coordinated body of collective wisdom and embrace the thoughts and ideas of our Associations' representatives. Everyday our employees and independent contractors strive to discover and implement cohesive solutions to Association challenges.

Experience: The management team has a combined experience of 35 years in the property management industry. During that time, we have developed solid relationships with many professional service providers. These professional relationships provide Premiere Property Management with confidence when securing bids for our Associations. The pre-screened contractors have proven that they are reputable and will provide quality service at a competitive price. Also, we have experienced all different types of scenarios and worked closely with different associations, companies, and personality types. Our experience is invaluable and immensely helpful to our clients.

Modernization: We value, encourage and empower our employees and independent contractors to modernize their efforts to increase efficiency and accuracy. We support them in challenging conventional wisdom and practices in the property management field. We develop plans to use technology to exceed our customer's expectations.

Pro-Active Management: We are pro-active every day in our actions with our Boards, owners and independent contractors. We support quality assurance and personal discipline in all our endeavors. We seek to pro-actively identify and rectify issues before they become problems. We regularly visit complexes to seek out ways to improve and maintain architectural integrity. We implement preventative maintenance procedures to circumvent costly repairs. We keep abreast of the evolving property management industry and support the changes necessary to keep our Associations current with procedures and technology.

Excellence: We meet or exceed all professional and contractual expectations and obligations to our Associations. We strive to deliver reliable and exceptional service and focus on achieving excellence. Our employees and independent contractors are dedicated, loyal and honorable.

Efficiency: We operate a streamlined organization that prides itself on solving issues in a lean, economical manner, while maintaining the highest of standards. We deliver a great value for a great price.

Socially & Environmentally Conscious: We believe in respecting, preserving, and promoting the neighborhoods we work in. We operate in an environmentally sensitive manner. We are active and involved members of the community and our industry.

INDUSTRY ANALYSIS

Property Management is a $75 billion dollar industry in the United States with approximately 231,000 companies employing nearly 775,000 people. Operating conditions for the Property Management industry are expected to remain positive over the next five years with the industry expected to grow at an annual rate of 4.6%. The value of residential construction is expected to expand rapidly due to improved consumer confidence and low interest rates, causing an increase in the housing stock including condominiums, site condos, and other residential subdivisions. As a result, the U.S. homeownership rate is projected to increase, and more consumers will require property management services.

MARKET ANALYSIS

Property Types
Premiere Property Management will primarily focus their attention on the following markets:

- Condominiums

- Residential Subdivision Associations

Property owners of condominiums and houses in residential subdivisions tend to have more specific needs and requirements from the broader property management industry. Those who own their own property tend to take more pride in their homes and are willing to follow rules set forth to increase their property values and investment.

Service Area
Serving Southeast Illinois, including Clay, Cumberland, Crawford, Edwards, Jasper, Lawrence, Richland, Wabash, Wayne, and White Counties.

SERVICES

Operational Management
- Site Management

- Being a Board Advisor/Partner

- Conscientious Association Administration

Premiere Property Management has vast experience in representing Associations of all sizes. In every assignment, our goal is to assist the Association in maintaining its physical property, enhancing lifestyles and protecting each owner's investment. Successful management of Associations is a full-time specialization, calling for training, experience, and an understanding of the laws affecting Associations.

Premiere Property Management's Operational Management program offers comprehensive Association operational assistance and can be divided into Site Management, Board Advisor/Partner, and Administrative Management.

Premiere Property Management offers the following site management services:

- Regular on-site inspections of grounds, structure, and common area conditions as well as looking for violations of restrictions.

- Organize and establish a liaison for repair work on common areas as directed by the Board of Directors.

- Continuous recommendations for long-term maintenance needs.

- Prepare bids, negotiate contracts, retain, schedule, and oversee common area maintenance, major maintenance needs, and other required services. Collaborate with independent contractors when necessary.

- Recruit, hire and train all Association personnel (if applicable) as directed by the Board of Directors.

- Prepare preventative maintenance schedules and assist in insurance claim processing.

Premiere Property Management offers the following services for your Board of Directors:

- Offer advice and direction to the Association regarding their governing process and responsibilities.

- Assist Board of Directors in administering and enforcing the Association's master deed, bylaws, and rules and regulations.

- Inform the Association concerning significant and relevant legislation, insurance, financial practices, court decisions, or tax rulings pertaining to Associations which come to the Manager's attention.

- Attend certain meetings to discuss any events, review contractor bids, contracts and performance and be prepared to answer any questions or offer advice as needed.

- Preparation of special reports and assistance with Association newsletter, as requested by Board.

- Interface with specialists retained by Association for specific tasks.

- Provide assistance with conducting annual meetings and elections.

- Ensure compliance and advise Board regarding Federal, State, and Local Association rules and regulations.

From systematic record-keeping to resale certification, Premiere Property Management understands the demands of successful administration. We ensure that our client's records are maintained and regularly updated to increase operational efficiency and chronological integrity. We have a detailed filing system for paper documents that allows for quick access to necessary items when applicable. In addition, our computer software allows for even quicker retrieval of our extensive online archives. We are proud to offer our clients access to some of their financial and compliance-related data via our computer software online in real-time.

In addition to this, Premiere Property Management offers the following administrative services:

- Maintain custody and ensure all Association records are current and available for Board and owner review.

- Maintain master mailing list, owner list and individual files for each owner in the Association.

- Coordinate and attend the Association's Annual Meeting and other meetings where voting takes place. This includes preparation of meeting notices, agendas, nomination forms, proxies, and administering proper ballot and election procedures.

- Premiere Property Management provides basic information about the Association as requested by a seller, prospective buyer, or agent for items such as a condominium questionnaire or status/paid dues letter mandated by law or the Association documents. Costs for preparation of these items will be borne by those parties requesting such services.

- Prepare general correspondence dealing with routine operational matters between the Association and owners, contractors, agents, government officials, or other entities.

- Prepare and mail appropriate notices and letters to current and new owners.

- Our staff is also prepared to compile notes from Board members and assemble newsletters accordingly.

Maintenance Services

- Maintenance Management

- Preventative Maintenance

- Property Inspections

- Emergency Services Program

Financial Management

- Collection of Dues

- Bookkeeping

- Financial Reporting

- Budgeting

- Investments

Independent Contractor Management

Premiere Property Management can hire high quality and value-oriented maintenance providers as Associations require. Premiere Property Management will always work diligently to minimize costs, which includes obtaining competitive bids for routine maintenance items like landscaping and snow removal as well as expensive capital maintenance projects. After we've collected the bids, we will make a recommendation based on the cost and reputation of the contractor. Of course, the final decision will be made by the Board of Directors.

Premiere Property Management offers the following contractor management services:

- Prepare bids, negotiate contracts, retain, schedule, and oversee common area maintenance, major maintenance needs, and other required services. Collaborate with independent contractors when necessary.

- Write specifications for maintenance contracts and prepare and distribute bid specifications on routine services for Board review and approval.

- Develop a competitive bidding process for projects and services where the cost will exceed the approved spending limitation as set forth in the Management Agreement.

- Guide and assist the Association on the selection of contractors, materials and equipment and facilitate the Board's final decision.

- Maintain extensive "approved" independent contractor database of contractors with proven track records. Monitor their workmanship and performance for possible removal from the "approved" list.

- Allow "approved" independent contractors access to their work that has been assigned or is outstanding via online website.

- All independent contractors are required to sign the Premiere Property Management "Work Right" Ethical Contract to ensure a clear understanding of behavior and decision making while working for our clients.

- Periodically inspect Association for performance and supervision of contractors and ensure that completed work conforms to Association standards and meets contract requirements.

- Obtain certificates of insurance from contractors providing services to the Association and confirm all contractors have appropriate insurance coverage.

Insurance Administration and Risk Management

Premiere Property Management is skilled in risk management, the process of making and carrying out decisions that will minimize the unfavorable effects of accidental losses at a community Association. We have extensive contacts within the insurance industry to help the Board of Directors secure appropriate coverage at a reasonable rate. In addition, Premiere Property Management is experienced in one of the most important, but least exercised skills in Insurance Administration, determining when not to submit a claim under the master insurance policy. Premiere Property Management can assist the Board of Directors in securing the appropriate coverage for property and liability insurance.

Following is a list of insurance administration services provided by Premiere Property Management:

- Counsel and advise the Board concerning generally accepted industry standards.

- Assist the Board of Directors in developing an insurance program that offers the appropriate coverage and defines the different types of insurance and endorsements a community Association needs: Property and Liability, Umbrella, Directors and Officers (Covering the actions of a Board as a whole), Workers Compensation, Building Ordinance, Boiler and Machinery (if applicable) and Flood (if applicable).

- Assist, secure and monitor annual insurance policies.

- Ensure that insurance coverage is at least the minimum coverage set forth in the Declaration of Covenants.

- Assist the Association and its qualified insurance agent in placing the required insurance by providing required information.

- Receive and report to the insurance agent any known incident which may result in an insurance claim for which the Association may have responsibility.

- Report to the Association any accidents, fires, or other claims related to the management, maintenance, and operation of the Association's property.

- Coordinate and administer insurance claims on behalf of the Association.

- Prepare the necessary information to assist the insurance carrier in the event of a workers compensation audit.

- Provide annual review of coverage, costs and obtain competitive bids.

- Analyze the Association's exposure to possible loss.

- Explore alternative risk management techniques and determine if appropriate.

- Implement the risk management techniques decided upon by the Board and monitor the results.

Compliance
- Ensuring Architectural Integrity
- Covenant Enforcement

Communication and Meetings

We believe that providing the proper management to an Association centers around communication. The systems and personnel of Premiere Property Management are geared towards increasing communication between the owners, the Board, and the property management company.

One of the most effective ways to help increase support of Board decisions is through communication. If the owners are informed of the issues facing their Association and understand why the Board makes the decisions that it does, then they are more likely to support and comply with those Association decisions. In addition, effective communication also allows owners to voice their comments, requests, concerns and ideas so that the Board can make its decisions based on the best interests of the entire membership. Premiere Property Management plays a key role in building a sense of community and positively affecting owners' perceptions of their Association through consistent communications and management.

The Premiere Property Management Association Communication & Meetings services include:

- Board Communication & Meetings
- Owner Communication & Meetings

Website Services

We are proud to offer custom Association websites with secure on-line access to private Association information. Owners have the convenience of securely viewing their personal account information real-time. In addition, Board Members can view financials and approve invoices on-line.

OPERATIONS

Equipment

General Business Technology
- Each employee is equipped with the latest computer, software, and communications equipment in order to perform their daily activities at the highest level.
- Digital cameras, scanners and advanced copiers assist our staff in their daily work.
- Our email and website structure provides effective interaction with our Associations and independent contractors.
- Owners can report Association violations, architectural requests or maintenance needs online through our website.

Financial-Related Technology
- We allow for the utilization of automatic payment processing interaction with banks to receive owner's payments.
- Our software combines the owner's database with financial transactions providing seamless data to clients.
- Owners can pay dues online with one-time electronic checks, credit card or opt to automatically have their bank account drafted monthly for reliable payment of dues.
- We provide website services which allow for each Association to have their own website and links to important information.

Hours of Operation

Premiere Property Management is accessible to Boards, owners and contractors 24-hours a day through our real-time, secure online access to financial, maintenance, and compliance information.

To speak directly with an employee, our office hours include:

Monday—Thursday, 9 a.m.—4:30 p.m.

Friday, 9 a.m.—4 p.m.

Closed for lunch from noon to 1 p.m. daily

We are available by phone, fax, email, and postal mail in addition to our secure website.

Payment Processing

Association dues payments are accepted in a number of ways:

- Mail a check or money order
- Automatically deducted from a checking or savings account
- Online e-check or credit card payments
- Pay directly at the management office by walking the payment in or utilizing the drop box

MEMBERSHIPS

Premiere Property Management id a proud member of both UCOI and CAI. These organizations are crucial to our success with continued education opportunities and other valuable experiences. Each organization is detailed below.

United Condominium Owners of Illinois

UCOI was organized by individuals who had leadership roles in their own community associations and whose express desire was to improve the operation of community associations and, in particular, condominium associations, through education, communication, and political assertiveness as it relates to issues affecting condominium associations. UCOI's board is comprised solely of individuals who reside in condominium associations and the focus of the attention is to improve the operation and development of condominium association's internet casino in concert with other service oriented organizations and/or entities which serve condominium associations. We continue to strive to improve the services provided to our member associations while maintaining the unique attributes of our composition and direction. We are the oldest organization in the State of Illinois representing the interests of condominium associations and importantly our Board of Directors is not comprised of nor controlled by representatives of profit oriented organizations or entities. We have grown dramatically in recent years and are encouraged that the leadership role which we have earned here in Illinois on behalf of condominium associations will continue to allow us to serve our members even more effectively going into the 22nd Century.

UCOI GOALS

- Develop and maintain programs which represent the best interests of all condominium owners through educational forums and publications.
- Encourage and enhance the condominium lifestyle as a more carefree, economical and independent home ownership.
- Inform and educate members to administer their associations with knowledge, good judgment and even-handedness for the well-being of all.

- Represents members setting forth the interests of condominium associations through the legislative process. UCOI is the only organization that is designed solely to represent the interests of condominium and community associations in Illinois.

- Inform members of potential legislation relating to issues affecting home ownership, particularly condominium ownership.

- Join and participate in national organizations with goals common to UCOI and condominium ownerships and lifestyle.

Community Associations Institute

Founded in 1973, CAI and its U.S. and international chapters provide information, education and resources to the homeowner leaders and professionals who govern and manage homeowners associations, condominium communities and cooperatives. CAI's 33,000-plus members include community association board members, other homeowner leaders, community managers, association management firms and other professionals who support common-interest communities. CAI serves associations by:

- Advancing excellence through seminars, workshops, conferences and education programs

- Publishing the largest collection of resources available on community association management and governance

- Advocating on behalf of community associations and their residents before legislatures, regulatory bodies and the courts

- Conducting research and serving as an international clearinghouse for information, innovations and best practices

CAI believes community associations should strive to exceed the expectations of their residents. Our mission is to inspire professionalism, effective leadership and responsible citizenship, ideals that are reflected in communities that are preferred places to call home.

CAI also offers a directory of credentialed service professionals and downloadable resources for Community Operations and Management, including those on the following topics:

- Bidding and Contracting
- Board Meetings & Decision Making
- Community Leadership
- Community Operations
- Financial Management
- Human Resources Management
- Insurance & Risk Management
- Maintenance
- Rule Development & Enforcement

Real Estate Drone Business

Remington Aerial Imagery Inc.

2965 Williams St.
Westchester, TX 89758

Paul Greenland

Remington Aerial Imagery Inc. is a newly established provider of aerial photography and videography services for residential and commercial realtors, property owners, and property managers.

EXECUTIVE SUMMARY

Remington Aerial Imagery Inc. is a newly established provider of aerial photography and videography services for residential and commercial realtors, property owners, and property managers. The business uses an aerial drone (quad copter) to take stunning still photography and video images of properties, improving their salability to prospective buyers, and their features to prospective tenants, investors, and/or customers.

The business is being established by Jim Remington, an experienced photographer/videographer at Westchester Hospital. After using drones on a recreational basis, Hayes developed an interest in combining his knowledge of drone operation with his existing professional skills in traditional photography and videography. After receiving a Section 333 waiver from the Federal Aviation Administration and liability insurance, Remington is now able to establish a lucrative full-time business that requires minimal startup capital and overhead.

INDUSTRY ANALYSIS

Popularly known as "drones," unmanned aerial vehicles (UAVs), unmanned aircraft systems (UAS), or remotely-piloted aircraft (RPA), these devices are typically quad copters that feature an autopilot and corresponding software, along with physical components such as GPS modules, pressure sensors, gyros, accelerometers, magnetometers, and cameras. Their use has increased significantly in a wide range of industries and industry segments, including real estate, property management, agriculture, cinematography, surveying, mapping, energy (oil and gas), insurance (claims processing), weddings, conservation, and powerline/utility management. By capturing video footage and still images, and utilizing specialized accessories, drones can be used for a variety of applications. These include inspection, analysis, data collection, evaluation, observation, and monitoring/surveillance.

Federal Aviation Administration

The main government agency overseeing the use of drones in the United States is the Federal Aviation Administration (FAA), whose mission is "to provide the safest, most efficient aerospace system in the world." According to the FAA, the introduction of unmanned aircraft systems has presented the agency with a variety of challenges. Therefore, FAA has taken "an incremental approach to safe UAS integration." The latest information from FAA regarding the commercial and recreational use of drones, including details regarding registration, regulations and policies, publications, and temporary flight restrictions, is available at: https://www.faa.gov/uas.

Additionally, several industry organizations have emerged to serve the drone market. These include the Association for Unmanned Vehicle Systems International (AUVSI) and the Academy of Model Aeronautics (AMA).

Association for Unmanned Vehicle Systems International

AUVSI bills itself as "the world's largest nonprofit organization devoted exclusively to advancing the unmanned systems and robotics community." The organization's base of approximately 7,500 members includes individuals from the academic sector, as well as both government and industry. It provides members with industry data, a magazine, daily news updates, and more. Additional details are available at: http://www.auvsi.org.

Academy of Model Aeronautics

Based in Muncie, Indiana, the Academy of Model Aeronautics "is a world-class association of modelers organized for the purpose of promotion, development, education, advancement, and safeguarding of modeling activities. The Academy provides leadership, organization, competition, communication, protection, representation, recognition, education, and scientific/technical development to modelers." Although the organization is geared toward the recreational segment, including model airplane clubs, it includes approximately 175,000 members and is open to anyone interested in the subject of model aviation. More information is available at: http://www.modelaircraft.org.

National Association of Realtors

With approximately 1 million members, the National Association of Realtors (NAR) is the largest trade association representing individuals within the commercial and residential real estate industries, including salespeople, brokers, appraisers, and property managers. NAR offers 54 state and territory associations and 1,300 local associations and boards. The NAR has useful information regarding the use of drones on its Web site, including articles, videos, and legal/regulatory updates. More information is available at: http://www.realtor.org/law-and-ethics/drones-frequently-asked-questions.

Industry Safety

In conjunction with the FAA, the AUVSI and the AMA have developed an educational campaign called "Know Before You Fly" to promote safe and responsible drone use. The campaign includes useful information, which is available at: http://knowbeforeyoufly.org.

MARKET ANALYSIS

According to data from the market research and consulting company Radiant Insights Inc., the drone market was estimated at $6.8 billion in 2016 and was expected to reach $36.9 billion by 2022. The firm's report, "Drone Market Shares, Strategies, and Forecasts, Worldwide, 2016 to 2022," provides detailed information regarding several market segments, including photography and videography.

Following the Great Recession, the national real estate market was improving by the end of 2015. According to data from the NAR, the real estate market was growing throughout most of the country, with the median home price of existing single-family homes increasing in 81 percent of measured markets. The NAR provides quarterly updates of home prices, both nationally and on a regional basis.

Target Markets

Remington Aerial Imagery will provide aerial photography and videography services for:

*   Residential and commercial realtors

*   Property owners

*   Property managers

Local Property Market Overview

The Westchester, Texas, market was home to a population of 880,500 people in 2015, with an average household income of $82,182. At that time, the market had 364,903 housing units, about 97 percent of which were occupied. Following housing growth of 18.7 percent between 2000 and 2010, the market was projected to grow 20.4 percent between 2010 and 2020. Between 2015 and 2020, growth of 7.1 percent was anticipated. In 2015 the market was home to 65 real estate agencies, which collectively represented some 15,500 real estate agents. Beyond realtors, individual private home sellers were a smaller, yet significant, target market for Remington Aerial Imagery.

Commercial real estate, in particular, is a lucrative niche for drone businesses. Owners, managers, and sellers of non-residential, investment-grade properties such as retail establishments, industrial facilities, warehouses, distribution centers, medical centers, office buildings, and hotels seek videography and photography for various reasons, including content for property listings, Web sites, social media, television production, corporate videos, brochures, and more. In a market comparison of the nation's top 10 commercial real estate markets conducted by Ballard & Associates, Westchester ranked fifth nationally.

Competition

Because there is a low barrier to entry, competition can be stiff for providers of traditional/general drone photography and videography services. The Westchester market already is served by several reputable providers. However, with a sizable population and one of the nation's strongest real estate markets, there is ample opportunity for growth.

Drone operators serving the real estate market not only face strong competition from other reputable providers, they also must compete with opportunistic providers whose main objective is making fast money. For a minimal investment, it is possible for individuals with little or no technical and professional skills to purchase a drone and begin marketing services to prospective customers. By providing poor service, or operating without the appropriate FAA exemption and liability insurance coverage, these types of providers tarnish the reputation of all drone operations, including legitimate, skilled operators.

For this reason, Jim Remington will emphasize his local community roots (including service with several local charitable organizations) when promoting his business to prospective customers. Additionally, he will become a member of the Westchester Chamber of Commerce and the Trenton County Realtors Association, which will reinforce his position as a legitimate provider of quality aerial photography and videography services.

SERVICES

Remington Aerial Imagery will provide aerial photography and videography services for residential and commercial realtors, property owners, and property managers. The company will begin all projects with an initial consultation (on-site and/or via phone), during which Jim Remington will discuss the scope of services to be provided for a given customer. This information will be used to provide a detailed time and cost estimate based on the scope of photography/videography services to be provided.

Once the customer has signed off on the estimate, Jim Remington will make arrangements to provide aerial photography/videography services. Typically, Remington will provide a series of high-quality still images, as well as a video fly-around of the property, with close-ups of key areas identified by the customer. Remington will use his video editing skills to provide a polished video clip highlighting a property's best features.

Remington Aerial Imagery typically will charge $200 to shoot one hour of video footage, edited down to the equivalent of a one-minute clip (e.g., four 15-second clips, two 30-second clips, one 60-second clip, etc.). The business will charge $100 for one hour of still photography and 25 edited images. The client will be provided with all "raw" footage and images, as well as the edited images. Clients in need of more extensive videography and photography services will be provided the option of additional service hours at 20 percent off the first-hour rate.

Customers will have access to their data for inspection/download for a period of 30 days, after which they will be provided with a fee-based option for long-term storage. Jim Remington has secured cloud-based storage space through a third-party, which he can mark up, providing him with a reasonable profit (and a source of passive income).

OPERATIONS

Location
Remington Aerial Imagery will operate as a home-based business, thereby minimizing overhead expenses.

Transportation
Jim Remington will use his personal vehicle for business use, and reimburse himself for mileage from the corporation.

Business Structure
Remington Aerial Imagery is organized as an S corporation in the state of Texas. This business structure will allow the owner to receive half of his revenue in the form of salary, while taking the rest as quarterly profits that are not subject to Social Security and Medicare taxes. Additionally, the corporation provides the owner with a certain level of liability protection.

Equipment
The equipment used by Remington Aerial Imagery is simple to operate. The company's drone is a high-end quad copter equipped with high-resolution still and video (1080p) cameras. Remington invested approximately $2,000 in his equipment, which he will insure against damage. Additionally, Remington will maintain an inventory of spare parts, extra batteries, and other accessories to ensure smooth/efficient operations.

Legal
Remington Aerial Imagery has received a grant of exemption in accordance with Section 333 and a civil Certificate of Waiver or Authorization from the Federal Aviation Administration, allowing the business to use its drone commercially. More information regarding this required commercial certification is available at: http://www.faa.gov/uas/civil_operations. In addition, Remington has obtained an appropriate level of liability insurance for the business in partnership with his insurance agent.

PERSONNEL

Remington Aerial Imagery is being established by Jim Remington, an experienced photographer/videographer. After using drones on a recreational basis, Remington developed an interest in combining his knowledge of drone operation with his existing professional skills in traditional photography and videography. Remington honed his skills with drones by starting out with inexpensive models, mastering the basics, and gradually purchasing more expensive drones. Additionally, he took advantage of a short advanced training course offered by a local model aviation club.

Independent Contractors

Beginning in the second year of operation, Remington Aerial Imagery will develop and maintain a pool of freelance drone operators, in order to efficiently meet client demand during peak times and provide coverage when Jim Remington is not available. Jim has established stringent criteria to ensure that his contractors meet minimum quality, reliability, and skill standards.

Professional & Advisory Support

Remington Aerial Imagery has retained the services of Bryson & Associates, a local accounting firm, to assist with bookkeeping and tax preparation. The company also has established a business checking account with Westchester Credit Union, which offers low fees compared to leading national banks. The business also will use a hosted version of a popular accounting software application to simplify bookkeeping and financial management.

GROWTH STRATEGY

Jim Remington has established the following annual goals for his new business:

Year One: Focus on building awareness of Remington Aerial Imagery in the Westchester market. Bill an average of 950 service hours. Generate net profit of $600 on revenue of $129,400.

Year Two: Continue to increase visibility of Remington Aerial Imagery in the local market. Increase annual service hours to 1,650. Generate net profit of $56,900 on revenue of $178,100.

Year Three: Maintain awareness of the business in the local market. Increase Remington Aerial Imagery's annual service hours to 2,063. Generate net profit of $53,950 on revenue of $239,800.

The following table shows a detailed breakdown of Remington Aerial Imagery's projected average annual service hours for the first three years of operations:

Average annual service hours	2016	2017	2018
Realtors-videography	150	250	313
Realtors-photography	250	350	438
Individual home sellers-videography	50	150	188
Individual home sellers-photography	100	200	250
Property management firms-videography	100	200	250
Property management firms-photography	150	250	313
Building owners-videography	50	100	125
Building owners-photography	100	150	188
Total	950	1,650	2,063

MARKETING & SALES

To develop an effective marketing plan for Remington Aerial Imagery, Jim Remington had conversations with realtors, property owners, building managers, and other industry players to determine the most effective tactics for promoting the business. Based in part on these conversations, the following tactics were identified:

1. A high-quality, color brochure describing the benefits of aerial photography and videography. Jim Remington will include testimonials from customers, in order to convince prospects to use his business' services.

2. Membership in the Westchester Chamber of Commerce, providing an opportunity to build relationships and gain exposure among area business leaders, property owners, and decision-makers.

3. Real estate agency meetings: Jim Remington will visit at least one of the city's largest real estate agencies every week. He will attempt to schedule a brief (15-minutes or less) presentation during one of the agency's regular sales meetings, providing him with the opportunity to showcase his abilities in front of large groups (35-50 realtors) of prospects. Remington specifically will pursue realtors selling upper-end, "executive" homes, who are more likely to see aerial photography/videography as a worthwhile investment. Office managers at real estate agencies are ideal contacts for getting on meeting agendas. Remington has included a video testimonial from a successful area realtor in his presentation.

4. A multi-faceted social media marketing strategy including Facebook, Twitter, LinkedIn, and Instagram, providing multiple ways to connect with the business' target markets.

5. Quarterly postcard mailings to Westchester's top-producing real estate agents (obtained from the Trenton County Realtors Association) and property management firms (obtained from a business directory at the Westchester Public Library). Jim Remington will use a local mail shop to prepare and send the mailings, saving valuable time.

6. A public relations strategy that involves guest columns and/or news stories in both free and subscription-based newspapers distributed throughout the Westchester market.

7. A Web site with complete details about Remington Aerial Imagery, including profiles of the owner, details of the services provided, and sample video and imagery.

8. Exhibition and networking at area home shows.

9. Professional stationery (business cards, envelopes, letterhead, etc.) featuring the Remington Aerial Imagery name.

FINANCIAL ANALYSIS

Following are projected annual revenue and expenses for Remington Aerial Imagery's first three years of operations:

	2016	2017	2018
Revenue			
Realtors-videography	$ 30,000	$ 50,000	$ 62,500
Realtors-photography	$ 25,000	$ 35,000	$ 43,750
Individual home sellers-videography	$ 10,000	$ 30,000	$ 37,500
Individual home sellers-photography	$ 10,000	$ 20,000	$ 25,000
Property management firms-videography	$ 20,000	$ 40,000	$ 50,000
Property management firms-photography	$ 15,000	$ 25,000	$ 31,250
Building owners-videography	$ 10,000	$ 20,000	$ 25,000
Building owners-photography	$ 10,000	$ 15,000	$ 18,750
Total	**$130,000**	**$235,000**	**$293,750**
Expenses			
Salary	$ 65,000	$100,000	$125,000
Payroll tax	$ 9,750	$ 15,000	$ 18,750
Independent contractor labor	$ 25,000	$ 33,000	$ 65,000
Equipment	$ 5,000	$ 5,000	$ 5,000
Mileage	$ 2,000	$ 2,250	$ 2,500
Data storage	$ 2,500	$ 3,000	$ 3,500
Office supplies	$ 600	$ 600	$ 600
Telecommunications	$ 1,100	$ 1,100	$ 1,100
Legal & regulatory	$ 1,000	$ 500	$ 500
Accounting	$ 950	$ 1,050	$ 1,150
Postage	$ 500	$ 600	$ 700
Internet	$ 1,000	$ 1,000	$ 1,000
Marketing	$ 15,000	$ 15,000	$ 15,000
Total expenses	**$129,400**	**$178,100**	**$239,800**
Net profit	**$ 600**	**$ 56,900**	**$ 53,950**

Senior Safety Specialist

Fall Prevention Specialists Inc.

6825 Monroe Ave. W.
Forrester Hills, NC 27000

Paul Greenland

Fall Prevention Specialists Inc. is a senior safety specialist business with an important mission: helping senior citizens avoid preventable injuries.

EXECUTIVE SUMMARY

Fall Prevention Specialists Inc. is a senior safety specialist business with an important mission: helping senior citizens avoid preventable injuries. The business is being established by Jessica Martin, a Certified Occupational Therapy Assistant. Martin will operate the business in partnership with her husband, Tim, a local firefighter. Jessica will continue to work in her professional field on a part-time basis, allowing her to satisfy her entrepreneurial spirit and build a promising part-time business with strong growth potential into a full-time operation.

INDUSTRY ANALYSIS

Fall Prevention Specialists is part of the so-called "aging in place" industry, which plays a key role in helping people remain safely in their homes for as long as possible. According to figures from the National Association of Home Builders, aging in place-related home modifications total roughly $25 billion per year, a small but growing segment of the home improvement industry's overall revenues ($214 billion). As the population ages, many older adults face the reality that they have not saved enough to transition to assisted living facilities, making the need for safety-related devices and home improvements more pressing than ever.

The need for innovative new solutions is evident by initiatives such as "Re-defining Home: Home Today, Home Tomorrow," a design challenge sponsored by the AARP, AARP Foundation, Home Matters and Wells Fargo Housing Foundation that inspires architects to "address the future housing needs for millions of Americans." Beyond home designers, the initiative has grown to include startup companies that help lower-income individuals remain safely at home, through the "2016 Aging in Place $50k Challenge." Additionally, in 2015 AARP and J.P. Morgan Asset Management established a new "Innovation Fund," with the goal of investing in early-to-late-stage companies that were developing solutions to improve the lives of older adults in three categories: Aging at Home, Convenience and Access to Healthcare, and Preventative Health.

MARKET ANALYSIS

National & State Outlook

According to *The State of Aging and Health in America 2013,* a report developed by the Centers for Disease Control and Prevention (CDC), U.S. Department of Health and Human Services, the population of older adults in the United States is experiencing unprecedented growth. Key drivers for this growth include the aging baby boomer population, as well as longer life spans in general.

Based on data from the U.S. Census Bureau, the number of individuals over the age of 65 totaled 40.2 million in 2010 (13% of the population). This figure is projected to reach 54.8 million (16.1%) by 2020 and 72.1 million (19.3%) by 2030. In North Carolina, specifically, adults over age 65 accounted for 12.4 percent of the population in 2010. Consistent with national trends, this figure is projected to increase, reaching 13.7 percent by 2015, 15.1 percent by 2020, 16.6 percent by 2025, and 17.8 percent by 2030.

The CDC reports that one in three adults over the age of 65 falls every year, resulting in approximately 2 million trips to the emergency room. Falls can have a variety of consequences, ranging from scrapes and bruises to hip fractures and serious brain injuries. In fact, fall-related injuries and broken hips result in about 700,000 hospitalizations per year. The CDC reports that fall-related injuries are expensive for everyone, resulting in direct medical costs of approximately $34 billion in 2013 alone. Fall-related hospital stays cost an average of $35,000, with approximately 78 percent of those costs covered by Medicare.

Local Outlook

The population of Forrester Hills, North Carolina, included 73,717 people (29,284 households) in 2015. Individuals over the age of 65 accounted for 11.8 percent of the population. By 2020 the population is projected to reach 74,937, at which time individuals over 65 will account for 13.7 percent of the population. In particular, individuals in the 65-74 age range will experience a 25.1 percent population increase.

According to data from a leading consumer research firm, in 2015 households in Forrester Hills spent an average of $3,739 on healthcare expenditures. Although health insurance represented the majority of this figure, medical-related supplies and equipment totaled about $400 per household. By 2020 this figure was expected to reach approximately $500 per household.

Beyond Forrester Hills, significant senior populations also exist in several nearby communities, including Bentonville, Liberty Cove, Island Lake, and Barkleyville, offering opportunities for growth beyond the business' initial primary market.

SERVICES

Fall Prevention Specialists has one important mission: helping senior citizens avoid preventable injuries. To accomplish this, Jessica and Tim Martin have committed to learning as much as possible about products that seniors can use to make their living environments as safe as possible. They have devoted a considerable amount of time to performing online research, reading product reviews, and talking to senior citizens and sales representatives to learn about both traditional and emerging fall prevention solutions. The owners will combine their professional knowledge (occupational therapy and fire safety) with this solutions-focused research to (1) assess a client's living environment, (2) develop a safety plan with specific product recommendations, and (3) manage contractors capable of performing installations/modifications.

To make their services as affordable and flexible as possible, the Martins will offer each component individually:

Home Safety Assessment ($50)

Using a home safety assessment tool developed by a leading university, the owners will conduct a thorough, room-by-room assessment of their customer's living space. This will involve identifying potential environmental hazards and safety risks, such as insufficient lighting, cracked or uneven pavement, and broken or missing railings. In addition, other factors affecting the customer's risk level will be considered, including illness or disease, vision impairment, limitations from a recent surgical procedure (e.g., a hip or knee replacement, etc.), and poor physical health.

Once a thorough assessment has been completed, the owners will then develop a comprehensive report outlining all identified safety issues. These will be used to develop a "risk score," which will provide the customer with an objective safety ranking of their living space.

Home Safety Plan ($100)

Following the aforementioned Home Safety Assessment, Fall Prevention Specialists will provide customers with the option of purchasing a custom home safety plan that includes specific recommendations for improvement. Whenever possible, a variety of potential solutions (e.g., from different vendors, and at different price points) will be provided to address each safety risk that was identified. Examples of potential solutions include, but are not limited to:

- Automatic Stove Control Devices
- Bath Mats
- Bed Rails
- Bedside Canes
- Cable Covers (to avoid tripping)
- Carpet Trims
- Clutter Removal
- Contrast Flooring (between transition areas)
- Cordless Telephones with Answering Machine Access
- Door Mounted Mail Catchers (for mail slots)
- Fall Detection Systems
- Fall Mats
- Furniture Risers
- Ice Tips (for canes)
- Indoor Grab Bars
- Indoor Motion Sensor Lights
- Lighted Remote Controls with Large Buttons
- Loose Wires (stapling/securing)
- Motion Sensing LED Lights (for hallways/stairs)
- Motion Sensing Security Lamps
- Nonslip Socks/Safe Shoes
- Nonslip Steps/Stair Treads
- Outdoor Grab Bars

- Railing Installation/Repair

- Raised Toilet Seats

- Rubber Threshold Ramps

- Rug Pads

- Security Gates (for pets/grandchildren)

- Standing Canes

- Stepladders with Trays/Rubber Steps

- Walk-In Bathtubs

- Wireless Doorbells

Some safety concerns can be addressed inexpensively, without the need for home modifications. For example, customers may be advised to get rid of loose throw rugs, use no-stick tape in their bathtub or shower, install a higher toilet seat, rearrange furniture, use a grabbing tool to avoid the need for stepladders, remove extension cords, lower their hot water heater's temperature setting, or wear non-slip shoes in the house.

Contractor Management ($50/hour)

In many cases, the Home Safety Assessment and Home Safety Plan will be all that is required by the customer. Many customers likely will have friends or family members who can assist them with purchasing and installing the required solutions. In other cases, customers already will have established relationships with home repair specialists or contractors that they will prefer to use. However, some of Fall Prevention Specialists' customers will desire assistance in identifying and managing contractors to perform product installations and/or home modifications. In this case, the Martins will provide contractor management services at a rate of $50 per hour. This will entail (1) identifying a contractor from a list of quality, pre-screened companies, (2) meeting with the contractor to define the project scope, (3) ordering specialized equipment, (4) arranging a mutually convenient date and time for the work to be performed, and (5) ensuring that the contractor performs quality work that meets the customer's expectations. Customers are required to pay the contractor directly for all work that is performed.

Payment

Fall Prevention Specialists will require that customers pre-pay for all services using a check or credit card. For contractor management services, customers typically will be required to pay for a two-hour minimum ($100), with the balance due upon completion of the project. The Martins estimate that, on average, most contractor management projects will require four hours of work.

OPERATIONS

Facility & Location

Fall Prevention Specialists will operate as a home-based business. The Martins have dedicated a small room in their house that will be used exclusively for businesses purposes. Consultations with prospective customers, as well as the provision of services, will occur in customers' homes. Customers can communicate with the Martins by dialing their business phone number, which has been programmed to ring on their mobile phones.

Hours of Operation

Fall Prevention Specialists will provide services on a flexible schedule, including evening and weekend hours, to accommodate the owners' work schedules and the needs of their customers.

LEGAL

Fall Prevention Specialists will maintain appropriate liability and automotive insurance policies (available upon request).

PERSONNEL

A native of Appleton, Wisconsin, Jessica Martin is the president of Fall Prevention Specialists. After graduating with an Associate's degree from Statesville University, which offered a program accredited by the Accreditation Council for Occupational Therapy Education, in 2004, Jessica completed fieldwork and successfully passed the National Board for Certification in Occupational Therapy exam. She then began working as a Certified Occupational Therapy Assistant at Central Appleton Hospital. In that role, Jessica works with patients in a variety of age ranges, including senior citizens, to help them recover from orthopedic surgeries, strokes, and other health conditions. Jessica will continue to work in this rapidly-growing field, while establishing a part-time business with full-time potential.

Tim Martin is vice president and treasurer of Fall Prevention Specialists. Tim began his career as a paramedic before becoming a firefighter. With 15 years on the force, he currently holds the rank of lieutenant and has an excellent reputation in the local community.

Although a fall prevention business can be established and operated by anyone, the Martins will have an advantage in the business because of the knowledge and credibility associated with their existing professional occupations.

Professional & Advisory Support

Fall Prevention Specialists has established a business banking account with Appleton Community Bank, including a merchant account for accepting credit card payments. Tax advisement is provided by Daniels & Grayson PC. In addition, legal services are provided by the Law offices of Walsh & Myers LP.

GROWTH STRATEGY

Year One: Establish Fall Prevention Specialists in the local community as a part-time business. Focus on developing a reputation for reliability, trustworthiness, and excellent customer service, realizing that word-of-mouth referrals will be essential to growing the business. Become a member of the Better Business Bureau and the local Chamber of Commerce. Generate net profit of $14,150 on revenue of $75,000.

Year Two: Continue to build Fall Prevention Specialists' reputation locally and achieve focused growth. Generate net profit of $38,900 on revenue of $145,000.

Year Three: Transition Fall Prevention Specialists from a part-time operation to a full-time operation. Generate net profit of $69,400 on revenue of $215,000.

By category, Fall Prevention Specialists' owners anticipate that business volume will break down as follows:

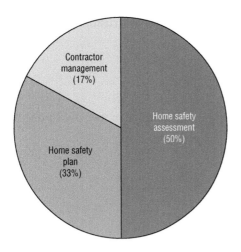

Weekly	2016	2017	2018
Home safety assessment ($50)	6	10	14
Home safety plan ($100)	4	8	12
Contractor management ($50/hour)	2	4	6

Annual	2016	2017	2018
Home safety assessment ($50)	300	500	700
Home safety plan ($100)	200	400	600
Contractor management ($50/hour)	100	200	300

Weekly	2016	2017	2018
Home safety assessment ($50)	$300	$ 500	$ 700
Home safety plan ($100)	$400	$ 800	$1,200
Contractor management ($50/hour)	$800	$1,600	$2,400

Annual	2016	2017	2018
Home safety assessment ($50)	$15,000	$ 25,000	$ 35,000
Home safety plan ($100)	$20,000	$ 40,000	$ 60,000
Contractor management ($50/hour)	$40,000	$ 80,000	$120,000
	$75,000	$145,000	$215,000

Fall Prevention Specialists' owners also have projected overall annual revenue and expenses for the first three years of operations:

	2016	2017	2018
Gross revenue	**$75,000**	**$145,000**	**$215,000**
Expenses			
Salaries	$35,000	$ 70,000	$100,000
Payroll taxes	$ 5,250	$ 10,500	$ 15,000
Marketing	$15,000	$ 20,000	$ 25,000
Business insurance	$ 1,200	$ 1,200	$ 1,200
Mobile telecommunications	$ 1,350	$ 1,350	$ 1,350
Software	$ 2,500	$ 2,500	$ 2,500
Office supplies	$ 550	$ 550	$ 550
Equipment	$ 1,500	$ 750	$ 750
Misc.	$ 500	$ 500	$ 500
	$62,850	$107,350	$146,850
Total expenses	**$60,850**	**$106,100**	**$145,600**
Net profit	**$14,150**	**$ 38,900**	**$ 69,400**

Specialty Coffee Roaster

High Sierra Coffee, Inc.

2187 Pinenut Way
Carson Valley, NV 89701

Claire Moore

High Sierra Coffee, Inc. (HSC) is specialty coffee micro-roaster. We seek to source our coffee primarily from small growers guaranteeing as much as possible, the responsible functioning of the supply chain in maintaining a healthy and prosperous balance of social, environmental, and economic capital.

EXECUTIVE SUMMARY

According to a consumer survey conducted in 2015 by the National Coffee Association of America (NCAA), 48 percent of U.S. coffee cups are perceived by the consumer to be specialty. The retail value of the U.S. coffee market is estimated to be $48 billion dollars with specialty comprising approximately 55 percent value share. Thirty-one percent of consumers aged 18+ drank specialty coffee yesterday, and 35 percent of 18 to 24 year olds said that they drink specialty coffee on a daily basis.

A 2014 study of drinking trends by the Specialty Coffee Association of America (SCAA) found that consumers desire more and better tasting coffee. The market share of specialty cups is now 51 percent, passing non-specialty for the first time. Trends indicate that there has been sustained growth for specialty coffee over the past five years. The increase in daily specialty coffee consumption is currently being driven by espresso-based beverages.

Because coffee passes through so many hands from cultivation to cup, the standard for defining specialty coffee has proven challenging. Ric Rhinehart, Executive Director of the Specialty Coffee Association of America, attempted to distill a working definition in an article for SCAA, "What is Specialty Coffee?"

"From the green stage to the final beverage there are other standards either currently in place or in the process of being developed. For example, the SCAA Brewing Standard for preparation of drip coffee defines the proper ratios of water to coffee, the proper extraction, brewing temperature and holding temperature and time," Rhinehart explained. "In the final analysis specialty coffee will be defined by the quality of the product, whether green bean, roasted bean or prepared beverage and by the quality of life that coffee can deliver to all of those involved in its cultivation, preparation and degustation."

High Sierra Coffee, Inc. (HSC) is specialty coffee micro-roaster. We seek to source our coffee primarily from small growers guaranteeing, as much as possible, the responsible functioning of the supply chain in maintaining a healthy and prosperous balance of social, environmental, and economic capital.

TARGET MARKET SEGMENTS

HSC provides its customers with specialty coffee that has been roasted on our premises according to our special roasting system. Our customers fall into three distinct groups: wholesale customers including hotels, motels, bed/breakfast, casinos, resorts and food establishments that serve our coffee; retailers including establishments that sell our packaged coffees; and customers at our web site.

HSC coffee is sold to the public in one pound bags either whole bean or ground. Many varieties are available in decaf. The average price per bag of coffee is $13.80. Coffee subscriptions are available as well.

MANAGEMENT

HSC is led by roaster Joel Stein and production manager Mindy Weist. They have assembled a team of experienced and dedicated professionals who help make HSC a premier coffee roaster.

OBJECTIVES

We know that customers demand a quality experience when drinking their daily brew. Our farmers expect to be treated fairly and to be paid according to their product. Likewise, our employees expect to be persons and not just personnel and to share in the success that they help to create.

Therefore, our objectives include:

- To always ensure that our product is fresh as evidenced by the "roast on date" that we include on every package of coffee and by shipping orders on the same day.

- To maintain the highest commitment to sustainability in our roastery, with our retail partners and with our customers.

- To source as much coffee direct from small growers as much as possible.

KEYS TO SUCCESS

High Sierra Coffee has identified three factors that will ensure the success of our venture. These keys to success include:

- Our unique combination of technical expertise in roasting along with our creativity in roasting and blending flavors.

- Our roasting technique which includes accurate and consistent batch weight portioning, a proper balance of convective and radiant heat for optimum chemical conversion and flavor development.

- Our marketing plan that will help us to systematize the development of sales venues for our products.

MISSION

Our mission at HSC is to provide the world's finest coffees and roast them with care to bring out the full flavors and aromatics that great coffee can have. Our success is grounded in strong and lasting relationships with the coffee farmers who grow our beans and with our customers who can always expect to receive the best coffee experience.

COMPANY SUMMARY

Owners Joel Stein and Mindy Wiest joined forces to form High Sierra Coffee in 2015 in Truckee, California. After years of building their careers, both had moved to the Sierra foothills in search of a better quality of life and the opportunity to pursue their dream of business ownership.

Operations began in Truckee, California but the company soon moved to a larger and more affordable space in Carson Valley, Nevada. The move has proven to be financially successful, allowing us to expand our efforts while maintaining a workable debt ratio.

Carson Valley offers many amenities to businesses in order to help them relocate to Nevada. The state's business-friendly attitude and low taxes, along with affordable property costs and transportation infrastructure make it an ideal choice for HSC.

Carson Valley combines a rural feel, with ranches along many of the main roadways and open space all around. Traffic is rarely congested, yet with the major North-South artery of Hwy 395 slowing down to 25 mph and serving as the Main Street, it connects easily with Carson City and Reno as well Hwy 50 and Interstate 80 for travel to the East and West.

Our roastery is located in a bustling industrial park that is near to residential and shopping centers. We made use of our large picture window in the front of our space to install a sign with our logo and contact information. A menu of our products is also a key feature in the window. We invite the public to stop by and purchase coffee and we plan to hold tours, brewing classes and tastings several time a year.

COMPANY OWNERSHIP

When HSC moved to Nevada the owners, Joel Stein and Mindy Wiest, changed the ownership structure from a partnership to a Nevada corporation.

Joel and Mindy each contributed $50,000 during the startup phase. Other investors have contributed $75,000 in additional investments.

HSC has no need for additional investment at this time and currently carries no long-term debt. In year two HSC will purchase and deploy a custom hybrid coffee truck complete with solar power system and equipment for making coffee, tea, espresso and smoothie drinks. Total cost is estimated at $45,000, part of which will be funded with a five-year auto loan personally secured by Joel and Mindy.

STARTUP SUMMARY

In 2015 HSC acquired the following equipment in order to begin operations:

Startup equipment

Computer	$ 850
Printer/copier/scanner/fax	$ 200
Software: MS Office, QuickBooks	$ 400
Furniture	$ 1,500
12 kilo Trabattoni roaster	$29,500
Used probat UW201 roller grinder	$28,000
Actionpac programmable vibratory bagger	$ 7,000
Huller/sheller	$ 1,000
Bulk storage	$ 3,000
Brewers	$14,000
Freezer	$ 750
Scale	$ 375
Total equipment	**$86,575**

Other startup costs

Supplies inventory	$ 1,500
Security	$ 2,000
Signage	$ 6,000
Brochures, cards, stationery	$ 225
Graphic design	$ 2,000
Web site development	$ 2,975
Legal/accounting	$ 2,500
Total other	**$17,200**

PRODUCTS

HSC will offer a seasonal selection of single-origin coffees, limited-release offerings and year-round selections that are, we feel, the best expression of coffee's diverse traditions and origins. In our continual search for quality coffee from around the world, we engage in quality development at every state of the coffee chain as well such as brewing experimentation, initiatives at origin, and improving the information available to our customers on our packaging and online. Wherever possible, the beans are organic, and in some cases, they are better than that—they grow wild.

We offer both whole bean and ground product sold in either 16-ounce whole bean bags for resale and home use or 5-pound bags for market coffee bars and bulk coffee containers. Cafes and restaurants may purchase both 16-ounce retail bags and 5-pound bulk bags, organic tea, filters, coffee sleeves, and specialty chocolate and sugars.

At our home location we offer 16-ounce retail bags, organic tea, equipment purchasing assistance, coffee brewing and cupping training.

Our roast levels fall into the following categories:

* Full-city Roast

* Medium Roast

* Dark Roast

* Coffee subscriptions

* Flavored Coffee: French vanilla or Hazelnut

* Decaffeinated

Coffee of the Month: Each month we will offer a blend of our choosing based on new arrival coffees, varietal rotation and unique flavors that come our way. These are sold at a discount to our customers.

Our decaffeinated products are either mountain water processed or chemically decaffeinated coffees which offer the fullest flavor of our decaf coffee offerings.

Along with traditional roasts such as French, Italian and Vienna, we have developed our own varietal and signature blends. Some of our signature blends include the following:

- *High Sierra House Blend:* our signature house blend has a moderate acidity and rich full body with spicy aroma and the rich flavor of sweet spice.

- *Shades of Tahoe Blend:* a multi-roast blend of premium coffees with a rich, nutty flavor followed with a smooth sweet finish.

- *Mountain Meadows Blend:* a blend of two beans from the high peaks of Guatemala that create a sweet, rich cup with a hint of caramel, vanilla and milk chocolate.

- *Colombia Alta Bourbon:* a medium roast, sweet cup with soft notes of chocolate and traditional spice.

- *Certified Organic/ Fair Trade Guatemala Cafe Amarillo:* A hint of maple sugar and chocolate melt into fragrances of strawberry, apricot, and dark honey.

Customers can choose from a variety of grind types including:

- Whole bean
- Drip
- French press
- Pour over cone
- Espresso home
- Percolator
- Espresso commercial
- Turkish

Prices for coffee will range from $13 to $18 for a one-pound bag. We welcome wholesale inquiries and seek to create a customized specialty coffee program for our wholesale customers. Wholesale prices for a 5-pound bag of coffee will vary from $34 to $325 per bag depending on flavor and country of origin.

HSC will also offer several teas from black, green, oolong, decaf and herbal.

Tea products will include the following:

- Assam
- Ceylon
- China gunpowder
- Darjeeling
- China floral ti kuan yin
- Earl Grey
- English Breakfast
- Various herbals

OTHER PRODUCTS

Customers can purchase a number of gift items from our web site.

- Aeorpress Brew Kit
- Chemex Brew Kit

- Crema Pro Home Barista Kit

- French Press Kit

- Gourmet Coffee Gift Boxes

We also sell equipment, grinders, tools and parts from our site. Available products range from hi-end espresso machines for over $2,000 to frothing thermometers. We have established an account with drop shipping company, Doba, for fulfillment of any orders other than for coffee.

After the buyer orders and pays us we log into our Doba account and order the product at wholesale cost. Our profit is the difference between what we pay and what we sell the item for. Doba will ship the product directly to our customer.

SUBSCRIPTIONS

Consumers can sign up for subscriptions and receive a 16-ounce bag of coffee on a monthly basis. Prices include shipping and handling. Customers realize a savings of anywhere from 10 to 25 percent off the regular prices and can choose from whole bean or ground. We will choose the specific coffee blend based on new arrival coffees, varietal rotation and unique flavors that come our way.

Subscriptions are as follows:

- Six-month subscription $80

- Twelve-month subscription $150

In 2017 our wholesale subscription service will include an option to receive keg service. We will make regular deliveries of cold-brew coffee in kegs. Customers can lease a kegerator from us which will be used to house and cool a keg of cold-brewed coffee to be served on tap. This idea has met with a lot of enthusiasm by many of our customers, especially the casinos.

The year 2017 will also see the roll-out of our coffee truck where we will serve hot and cold-brewed coffee, tea and smoothies along with baked goods and sandwiches that we purchase from a local bakery. The coffee truck will be deployed at community events and can be hired as part of catering services.

MARKET SEGMENTATION

Coffee is one of the most widely consumed beverages both worldwide and in the U.S. The coffee market is segmented into growers, roasters and retailers. As of 2012, Brazil lead the world in coffee production with about 3 million metric tons of coffee. According to the International Coffee Organization, there has been an estimated increase of 1.4 percent in global coffee production in 2015/16 compared to 2014/15. The average annual growth rate in global coffee consumption since 2011 is 2.5 percent.

In 2013 roast and ground coffee took the largest market share with 36 percent of retail sales. Leaders in at-home coffee sales are Folgers and Maxwell. The past several years have seen the rise in popularity of coffee chains selling coffee to go. The leaders in this segment are Starbucks and Dunkin Brands, Inc. with a combined market share of almost 50 percent in 2011.

According to Statista.com, American consumers spend an average of $21.32 per week on coffee. When choosing where to buy, taste is the deciding factor in where they will purchase their coffee. Statistics compiled in a January 2016 survey indicate that 70 percent of coffee cups were consumed at home, 13 percent at work. Again, roasted coffee was the most common type of coffee consumed at home in the

U.S. People in the U.S. consumed 20.1 million bags of roasted coffee, 1.3 million bags of soluble coffee and 0.15 million bags of coffee pods in 2009.

More current data indicates that there is a growing popularity with home brewing machines like Keurig that make a single cup. Twenty-seven percent of survey respondents owned one of these machines in 2015.

Our products appeal to a wide and varied demographic. Although the per capita consumption of coffee is about half of what it was at its peak in 1946, Americans are spending more money than ever on coffee, coffee-making products and other coffee-related items. Data from Statistica.com indicates that U.S. coffee and snack shops grossed just over $31 billion dollars in 2015 as part of a trend of steady growth.

HSC will sell it products to the following market groups:

- *Wholesale:* Businesses that serve coffee to the public can take advantage of our wholesale bulk pricing. This market includes: hotels, resorts, coffee shops, caterers and cafes.

- *Wholesale:* Grocery stores and other sellers of food products are also prime candidates for our products.

- *Retail:* Many of our wholesale customers not only brew and sell our coffee, they choose to sell our one pound bags of product.

- *Retail:* Sales to consumer through our web site, home location and coffee truck: HSC sells one pound bags of coffee to retail consumers. We also offer a coffee subscription program that features discounted pricing and automatic shipment of a specially chosen flavor each month.

Many of our wholesale customers also act as retailers for our coffees and teas. Some of our wholesale customers who also sell our product retail include:

- Alpina Café in South Lake Tahoe, CA

- Freel Perk Coffee Shop in Meyers, CA

- Karen's Bakery and Café in Folsom, CA

- Placerville Natural Foods Coop in Placerville, CA

- Great Basin Community Food Co-op in Reno, NV

TRENDS IN COFFEE

Our research on what is trending in coffee consumption has revealed the following:

- Cold brew

- Cold brew cocktails

- Draft coffee

- Signature sweetened drinks

- Use of the cherry skin to make coffee flour for baking

- Focus on specialty coffee beverages

- Focus on Espresso-based beverages

- Focus on different water sources used in brew

- Coffee/tea combinations brewed together

- Adding chicory to brew, especially cold brew

- Changing role of barista from server to mixologist

- Increased focus on the technology of coffee beverage production
- Renewed interest in new varieties due to threat of coffee-leaf rust disease

Based on this information we are developing new blends such as a coffee/tea combination and a coffee/chicory blend. We also plan on offering cold-brew services on tap by subscription and on our coffee truck.

While coffee is more popular in the U.S. and Europe, tea also has its followers. In 2014 the major tea producing countries of China, India, Kenya, Sri Lanka and Indonesia produced about 5 million metrics tons. Per capita consumption of tea in the U.S. was 8.9 gallons in 2012, up from 7.89 gallons in 2000.

According to a December 2013 article by Drew Silver at PewResearch.org, "Although more green coffee is produced globally than tea – 8.5 million metric tons versus 4.7 million metric tons of tea in 2011, according to the Food and Agriculture Organization– it takes only about two grams of tea to make a cup, compared with 10 grams of coffee. As a result, as British geographer David Grigg wrote, worldwide 'three cups of tea are drunk for every one of coffee.'"

Experts expect that the demand for tea will continue to grow as consumers become more aware of the health benefits of tea and the emergence of new flavors sparks interest.

HSC will continue to market quality teas and experiment with new flavors and drink combinations.

MARKETING STRATEGY

Wholesale venues include restaurants, cafes, bakeries and resorts that will brew and serve our coffee to their guests. Many of these customers will also want to sell our packaged coffees to their guests as will grocery stores.

Part of our marketing strategy with wholesale customers includes providing them with marketing materials and signage to help them sell our coffee. For example, we provide a full-color poster each month to help them in their promotional efforts. We also work with our wholesale customers on how to display our product, even providing bins if necessary.

Another strategy that is part of our commitment to contributing to the success of our wholesale customers is to offer classes in brewing and tasting on their premises. These have been particularly successful at bakeries, grocery stores and food co-ops. Once consumers discover how to bring out the flavors in their brew they are motivated to purchase them on a regular basis. We also encourage our wholesale customers to allow their employees to attend our classes so that they know more about the coffees and therefore become better ambassadors for sales.

HSC research has also revealed that we have a competitive advantage with our proximity to Reno and its gambling establishments. Through Don Sheldon's contacts HSC has developed several lucrative contracts with casinos to provide regular coffee service. Roasted coffee will be delivered daily, Monday through Friday, within 48 hours of being roasted.

In 2017 we will be adding cold brew keg service to our wholesale customers. By using a subscription model, we will deliver freshly ground and ready to brew coffee along with cold brew kegs that are installed in the clients' location inside a kegerator to keep it cold.

Workers and customers of the client can self-serve the cold brew in the same way that beer would be served. The taps are emblazoned with the HSC name and logo.

Our field testing of this program has been met with great enthusiasm by customers and potential customers. We feel that it will significantly boost our sales by expanding our brand.

Our web site is the hub of our retail sales strategy for the present. We have taken great care in designing an engaging and user-friendly site. Visitors can read our blog and learn about flavors and blends, our roasting process, even about our travels to visit the farmers who grow our beans.

All interactions at the web site are designed with the user in mind and with the aim of building product recognition and brand loyalty. Customers can buy products and join our subscription program at the site.

In 2017 HSC will ramp up sales to the public with the addition of our custom coffee truck. We are working with a local automobile renovation specialty company to modify a Chevy express cutaway truck as a hybrid solar/gas vehicle for serving coffee drinks, tea, smoothies and baked goods.

The truck will have a full wrap showing our logo, web site address and contact information. The HSC truck will appear at public events from Carson Valley to Reno to Truckee and will be available for hire at special events.

MANAGEMENT TEAM

Joel Stein is a California native born in Truckee. What began as a part-time job during college turned into a drive to be the best coffee technician in the U.S. His quest took him around the world where he visited nearly every coffee-producing country on earth. Now, his personal relationships with the coffee producers allows him to have an influential hand in the beans that will become his final product.

His travels took him eventually to the Ivy League Barista Academy (ILBA) in San Diego, California where he completed his training in cupping, roasting, grinding, sensory cup tasting, green coffee, tea sommelier and coffee cart business management. Joel is the master roaster and tea blender for High Sierra Coffee.

Mindy Wiest is a graduate of the business program at California State University, San Francisco. In her career Mindy has worked for major marketing firms in San Francisco. She took her business training to the next level at Boot Coffee campus in San Rafael, California. The coursework taken qualified Mindy to earn her accreditation by the Specialty Coffee Association of America (SCAA). Mindy is HSC's roaster and production manager.

Don Sheldon is HSC's wholesale delivery and marketing director. Don is a graduate of the business program at University of Nevada, Reno. Don has worked in every facet of marketing from copywriting to managing ad campaigns. Don has extensive experience in the casino industry and his many contacts have made it possible for HSC to secure several significant accounts to supply coffee to casinos and resorts in the Reno/Tahoe areas.

MILESTONES

In order to ensure that HSC meets its goals and objectives, the following milestones have been identified.

Task	End date
Begin business plan	3/1/2015
Finalized logo design and registration of trademark	4/1/2015
Order equipment	4/1/2015
Began work on web site	7/1/2015
Open roastery	7/1/2015
Secure first major account	9/1/2015
Business plan completion	12/1/2015
Location found, Carson valley, lease negotiated	1/15/2016
Corporation formed, IRS EIN obtained	1/15/2016
Begin operation of coffee truck	1/15/2017
Begin keg service	2/15/2017
Profitability	12/31/2017

PERSONNEL PLAN

HSC anticipated the following personnel requirements.

Personnel plan	Year 1	Year 2	Year 3
Joel	$18,000	$ 24,000	$ 32,000
Mindy	$18,000	$ 24,000	$ 32,000
Don	$18,000	$ 24,000	$ 32,000
Assistant roaster/shipper	$12,000	$ 12,000	$ 22,000
Coffee truck operator		$ 10,000	$ 20,000
Secretary/bookkeeper	$12,000	$ 15,000	$ 20,000
Total people	**5**	**6**	**6**
Total payroll	**$78,000**	**$109,000**	**$158,000**

FINANCIAL PLAN

Pro forma profit and loss

	Year 1	Year 2	Year 3
Sales	**$132,000**	**$325,000**	**$475,000**
Cost of goods sold:			
Material, supplies, packaging	$ 46,200	$113,750	$166,250
Gross profit	**$ 85,800**	**$211,250**	**$308,750**
Gross profit %	**65%**	**65%**	**65%**
Expenses			
Depreciation	$ 9,458	$ 13,958	$ 13,958
Payroll	$ 78,000	$109,000	$158,000
Payroll taxes	$ 7,800	$ 10,900	$ 15,800
Employee benefits	$ 3,900	$ 5,450	$ 7,900
Sales & marketing	$ 7,500	$ 6,000	$ 6,000
Utilities/phone	$ 6,500	$ 7,500	$ 7,500
Insurance	$ 3,200	$ 3,200	$ 3,200
Fees/licenses	$ 875	$ 975	$ 975
Office expense	$ 1,400	$ 1,400	$ 1,400
Repairs/maintenance	$ 2,700	$ 2,400	$ 2,500
Legal/accounting	$ 1,800	$ 1,800	$ 1,800
Professional dues/subscription	$ 785	$ 785	$ 785
Rent	$ 15,000	$ 15,000	$ 15,000
Automobile	$ 5,000	$ 5,500	$ 6,600
Lease: delivery van	$ 4,800	$ 4,800	$ 4,800
Other	$ 1,200	$ 2,500	$ 2,500
Total operating expenses	**$149,918**	**$191,168**	**$248,718**
Earnings before interest and taxes	($ 64,118)	$ 20,083	$ 60,033
Interest expense		$ 767	$ 606
Net earnings	($ 64,118)	$ 19,316	$ 59,427
Income tax	$ —	$ 3,012	$ 10,008
Net profit	**($ 64,118)**	**$ 16,304**	**$ 49,419**
Net profit/sales	**−49%**	**5%**	**10%**
Monthly break even revenue	$ 19,741		
Percent variable cost	35%		
Estimated monthly fixed costs	$ 12,832		

Projected balance sheet

Assets	Year 1	Year 2	Year 3
Current assets			
Cash in bank	$ 22,215	$ 31,359	$ 88,102
Account receivable	$ 250	$ 1,200	$ 1,200
Inventory	$ 4,500	$ 5,000	$ 6,000
Other current assets			
Total current assets	**$ 26,965**	**$ 37,559**	**$ 95,302**
Fixed assets			
Equipment	$ 94,575	$ 94,575	$ 94,575
Coffee truck		$ 45,000	$ 45,000
Less: depreciation	($ 9,458)	($ 23,415)	($ 37,373)
Total assets	**$112,083**	**$153,719**	**$197,505**
Liabilities & capital			
Current liabilities			
Accounts payable	$ 1,200	$ 2,200	$ 2,400
Current maturities loan			
Total current liabilities	**$ 1,200**	**$ 2,200**	**$ 2,400**
Long term liabilities			
Truck loan		24,333	18,500
Total liabilities	**$ 1,200**	**$ 26,533**	**$ 20,900**
Paid-in capital	$175,000	$175,000	$175,000
Net profit	**($ 64,118)**	**$ 16,304**	**$ 49,419**
Retained earnings		($ 64,118)	($ 47,814)
Total capital	**($ 64,118)**	**($ 47,814)**	**$ 1,605**
Total liabilities & capital	**$112,083**	**$153,719**	**$197,505**

Tow Truck Operator

Rescue Wrecker Service, LLC

876 Sycamore Road
Ashburn, GA 31714

Fran Fletcher

Rescue Wrecker Service, LLC is located in Ashburn, Georgia and is owned and operated by Rocky Smith. Mr. Smith has ten years of experience in the business.

BUSINESS SUMMARY

Rescue Wrecker Service, LLC is located in Ashburn, Georgia and is owned and operated by Rocky Smith. Mr. Smith has ten years of experience in the business. After working for another company, Mr. Smith decided it was time to go out on his own.

According to the Bureau of Labor Statistics, the job outlook for tow truck operators is expected to increase by 5% over the next decade. Thousands of automobiles a day travel this major north-south corridor between Michigan and Florida. Interstate 75 runs through the heart of Ashburn and will provide the majority of customers for the business. Rescue Wrecker Service is located in a prime location for helping motorists in need of towing or roadside assistance.

Rescue Wrecker Service will offer the following services to residential and business clients:

Towing services
- Tractor trailers
- Automobiles
- Motorcycles

Roadside Assistance
- Mobile tire changing
- Towing service
- Fuel delivery
- Oil delivery
- Jump starts
- Battery services
- Lockout assistance

There are several businesses in the area offering similar services, but none more dedicated to success and to providing excellent customer service as Mr. Smith.

The overall growth strategy of Rescue Wrecker Service is to become a preferred service provider through the American Travelers Association and major insurance companies. The owner recognizes the importance of advertising and customer referrals. The company will make every effort to provide excellent customer service and to provide roadside assistance services as quickly as possible.

The owner anticipates modest profits from the beginning. During the first year of operation, he expects a steady increase in income and profits as his advertising methods become established and as he starts receiving referrals from satisfied customers. If projections are correct, Mr. Smith will need to hire additional workers and buy additional equipment during the second year.

Start-up costs will include purchasing a tow truck and a service truck that are used but in excellent working condition. The owner is currently seeking financing in the amount of $188,400 to cover start-up expenses. Payments will be made monthly and 20 percent of the annual profits will be paid on the loan at the end of each year. If profits are as anticipated, the loan will be repaid within four years.

COMPANY DESCRIPTION

Location

Rescue Wrecker Service is located at 876 Sycamore Road, Ashburn, GA. Mr. Smith is renting office space that includes a fenced-in lot. This fenced-in lot can hold a total of twenty-five vehicles that have been towed. This location is easily accessible from the Interstate.

Hours of Operation

Rescue Wrecker Service will operate as follows:

24 Hours a Day, 365 Days a Year

Personnel

Rocky Smith (owner)

Mr. Smith has been driving a tow truck for ten years. He will perform all accounting duties and will manage daily operations. If needed, he will drive one of the trucks or advise his drivers when difficult towing situations arise.

Employees

Two experienced, full-time drivers will be hired.

Services

All services are offered 24 hours a day, 365 days a year.

Towing services

- Tractor trailers

- Automobiles

- Motorcycles

Roadside Assistance

- Mobile tire changing

- Towing service

- Fuel delivery

- Oil delivery

- Jump starts

- Battery services
- Lockout assistance

MARKET ANALYSIS

Industry Overview

According to the Bureau of Labor Statistics, the job outlook for tow truck operators is expected to increase by 5% over the next decade. Thousands of automobiles travel this major north-south corridor between Michigan and Florida each day. Interstate 75 runs through the heart of Ashburn and will provide the majority of customers for the business. Rescue Wrecker Service is located in a prime location for helping these motorists that are in need of towing or roadside assistance.

Target Market

Customers seeking towing services and roadside assistance within a 30-mile radius of Ashburn, Georgia are the target market for Rescue Wrecker Service. This includes travelers as well as the residents of Ashburn.

Competition

Rescue Wrecker Service competes with five other towing services within a 60-mile radius. They are:

1. Allied Towing, Cordele, Georgia
2. Arabi Towing, Arabi, Georgia
3. Benson's Wrecker Service, Tifton, Georgia
4. Chula Towing, Chula, Georgia
5. Tommy's Wrecker Service, Sycamore, Georgia

Rescue Wrecker Service plans to set itself apart from the competition by becoming an American Travelers Association preferred service provider. As a preferred service provider, customers can feel confident that Rescue Wrecker Service meets the highest standards of service and professionalism.

GROWTH STRATEGY

The overall growth strategy of Rescue Wrecker Service is to become a preferred service provider through the American Travelers Association and major insurance companies. The owner recognizes the importance of advertising and customer referrals. The company will make every effort to provide excellent customer service and to provide roadside assistance services as quickly as possible.

The owner expects the business to perform well in the first year of operation and anticipates hiring additional drivers and buying additional equipment later in the first year of operation.

Sales and Marketing

The company has identified key sales and marketing tactics to support the company's growth strategy.

Marketing that will target travelers includes:

- Meeting the requirements of the American Travelers Association and three major insurance companies to become a preferred service provider
- Working with GPS service providers to ensure that business information is correct

- Renting two billboards on the Interstate along both the north and southbound lanes
- Signing up with the Georgia State Patrol, Sheriff's Office, and Police Department to participate in the rotation of towing services

Advertising targeting local customers will include:

- Advertising in area newspapers
- Sponsoring the local high school's booster club fundraiser

FINANCIAL ANALYSIS

Start-up Costs

The owner will need to purchase a tow truck and a service truck to start the business and meet the American Travelers Association standards.

Estimated start-up costs

Tow truck	$100,000
Service truck	$ 82,000
Business license	$ 100
Initial advertising	$ 500
Insurance	$ 4,000
Legal fees	$ 1,800
Total	**$188,400**

Estimated Monthly Expenses

Monthly expenses are expected to remain constant each month.

Monthly expenses

Loan payment	$ 3,000
Rent	$ 500
Phone/Internet	$ 100
Advertising (including billboard rental)	$ 200
Insurance	$ 200
Wages owner	$ 4,000
Wages employees	$12,000
Service products (oil, batteries, etc.)	$ 450
Total	**$20,450**

Estimated Monthly Income

The number of jobs will determine monthly income. Services will be offered 24 hours a day, 365 days a year. The two drivers will rotate working during the day and being on call at night.

Prices for Services

Service	Price
Towing service	$200
Battery quick charge	$75
Battery replacement	$75 plus battery cost
Fuel delivery	$75
Oil delivery	$75
Tire change	$125
Lock out	$125

Profit/Loss

According to estimated expenses and income data, modest profits are expected from the beginning and are expected to steadily increase as referrals grow and advertising measures become established.

Demand for services should remain constant all year, with a slight increase during the summer months and December, when there is an increase in travel. Conservative estimates indicate that ten people will call for roadside assistance each day, for a monthly income of $30,000. Roadside assistance is expected to increase to fifteen customers a day in December and from June to September.

Profits will be used to purchase additional equipment and hire employees as needed.

Monthly profit/loss

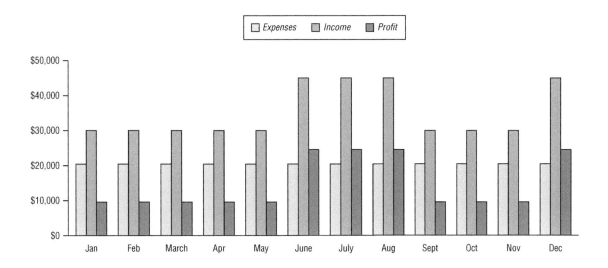

Yearly profit/loss

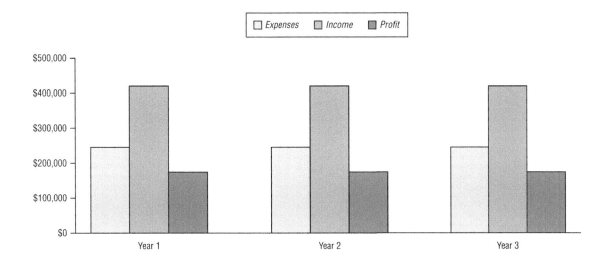

Financing

Rescue Wrecker Service is currently seeking financing in the amount of $188,400. This would cover start-up costs, including a tow truck and service truck. The business will pay $3,000 per month toward the loan and will also pay 20% of the annual profit toward the loan at the end of each year. The Repayment Plan chart shows that the loan will be completely paid within four years.

Repayment plan

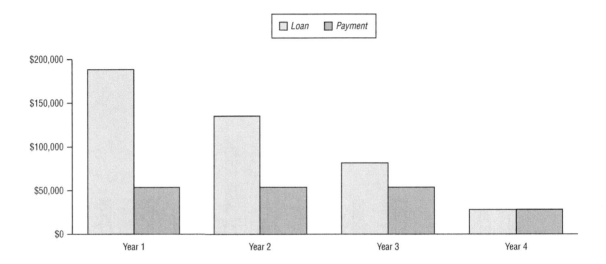

Virtual Assistant

ExecAssist, LLC

4545 Fruitvale Road
Lincoln, CA 95648

Claire Moore

ExecAssist, LLC is a start up virtual assistant business providing online executive business support services and project management to companies. We specialize in project managing web development and design projects, operations management and design direction. The company is a limited liability company with Linda Hardy as the sole owner.

EXECUTIVE SUMMARY

ExecAssist, LLC is a start up virtual assistant business providing online executive business support services and project management to companies. We specialize in project managing web development and design projects, operations management and design direction. The company is a limited liability company with Linda Hardy as the sole owner.

THE MARKET FOR SERVICES

A virtual assistant (VA) is an independent contractor who works from a remote location to provide services to one or more clients.

Situations where a businesses that can benefit from hiring a VA include:

- A small or startup company that can't afford a full-time employee
- Those with a need for a specialized skill
- When the employee need not be on site
- A business owner who travels a lot and needs a virtual employee
- When it's clear what tasks need to be done but staffing is lacking
- When systems and training are in place to manage a VA

Typical tasks that can be delegated to a VA include:

- Bookkeeping
- Online research
- Data entry

149

- Project management

- Creating reports and presentations

- Correspondence: includes notes, cards, emails

- Travel coordination: research, booking, creating itineraries

- Scheduling: managing calendars, scheduling appointments, responding to invitations, event planning

- Executive assistance

- Online marketing

- Social media: research, write/edit blog posts, update social media feeds such as Twitter

MARKET SEGMENTS

We have identified two key market segments upon which we will focus. We will focus on businesses that are conducting web design and development as part of their marketing efforts and generate at least $150,000 in revenues each year.

It is our belief, based on our research, that businesses of this size are more likely to seek subcontractors to handle certain administrative tasks on a regular basis. Moreover, they are more likely to have developed to the point where they need to scale the business to the next level. They will also be more likely to have the budget allocated to pay for the services.

Clients in this category demand a virtual assistant (VA) who has expertise and is proactive and who goes the extra mile. Because of our extensive experience in business we are confident that we can meet and exceed these expectations.

We will also focus on small agencies that have their own clients and web/development/design projects for those clients. These companies are at the point where they are expanding from "organized chaos" to the need for a solid, actual business process is usually where the owners see the need for a project manager to join the team.

SERVICES

Services provided by ExecAssist will include the following:

- Business and project management: oversee, maintain and provide progress updates for a project or program.

- Help in choosing and setting up project management software, internal team communication development, auditing processes, setting up and maintaining business development systems, developing and managing support and maintenance plans.

- Marketing and writing: creation of deliverables such as press releases, blog posts and reports.

Our pricing plans are customized according to our clients' needs. Pricing options include: hourly, bundle, project based and monthly retainer. Generally speaking, our hourly rate will range from $35 to as high as $125 depending on the project.

COMPETITIVE EDGE

Our competitive edge is based on Linda Hardy's vast work experience and her contacts in the industry. Over the past 20 years Linda has worked her way up from secretary to marketing professional to project manager.

Over the years she has both worked on or managed web development and marketing campaigns for some of the most prestigious companies in the U.S.

Most VA companies offer general administrative services. Our advantage is the years of expertise that Linda has acquired in managing projects and servicing CEO-level executives. Because of her background she can quickly grasp and take on the challenges presented to her.

Linda's approach for ExecAssist is meeting with the client and conducting a Needs Assessment that is designed to proactively create a plan of action.

Often a company will engage a VA service for a task such as marketing without having a clear idea of a strategy. Linda's approach helps the client to focus on goals, objectives and strategies for achieving desired results within a stated time frame and budget.

Because of her track record of working in project management, Linda's expertise is valued by development/design agencies. In her capacity as an independent project manager she has already received several inquiries from small agencies that are in need of help in completing projects.

With Linda on board these agencies will be able to take on projects that would have been beyond their scope.

MANAGEMENT TEAM

Linda Hardy earned her MBA in Marketing and Finance from University of California, Berkeley. Her professional experience includes administrative, business, sales and marketing, management and support for marketing and web development teams.

Her experience has given her the ability to lead, view projects in the long-range, and stay focused. Linda has gained the praise of her past and current employers and clients due to her keen attention to detail and organizational skills plus her ability to quickly grasp and assess situations and formulate a results-driven action plan.

After working for web design and marketing agencies for over 20 years Linda felt that it was time to fulfill her dream of forming her own company. Apparently she was not the only one who saw freelancing in her future.

Suddenly she was finding that prospective clients were approaching her for help. Even her employer offered to send business her way once she had her company in place. It seemed that the time was right and years of putting away funds for just such a venture were about to pay off.

KEYS TO SUCCESS

- The ability to provide executive-level support.
- An experienced project manager who can act proactively to get things done.
- Expert record-keeping and billing on projects.
- Access to a team of virtual experts to help in completing tasks.

MISSION

ExecAssist, LLC helps growing firms to achieve their business goals from project management to email management, from writing support to administration. Our services support and prices are tailored to our clients' unique needs.

OBJECTIVES

- Generate five contracts in 2016.

- Increase revenue steadily from 2016 to 2018.

- To generate annual gross revenues of $60,000 by year three.

COMPANY SUMMARY

ExecAssist, LLC has been structured as a single member California limited liability company with Linda Hardy as the sole member.

COMPANY OWNERSHIP

Linda Hardy is the sole member and owner of the company. She will personally invest all startup funding.

ExecAssist will operate from Linda Hardy's home where she has a bedroom dedicated to housing the equipment, supplies and records of the company.

STARTUP SUMMARY

We have invested in the following equipment and software.

Start-up expenses

Licenses	$ 150
Legal/accounting	$1,500
Supplies	$ 125
Advertising	$ 550
Software	$ 575
Web site development	$ 600
Total start-up expenses	**$3,500**

Item	Estimated cost if purchased
Computer/printer/copier/scanner/fax	$1,700
Telephone/cell phone	$ 875
Tablet computer	$ 650
Storage/filing/shelving	$ 135
Adding machine	$ 40
Paper shredder	$ 75
Clock	$ 20
Desk/table/chair	$ 460
Desk lamp: full spectrum	$ 45
Total	**$4,000**

SERVICES

ExecAssist will provide executive level services to its clients. We will specialize in providing the following services:

- Business management
- Shopping cart and payment methods integrations assistance
- Autoresponder/newsletter assistance
- Affiliate program management
- Social media management
- Web analytics integrations
- Project management: oversee, maintain and provide progress updates for a project or program
- Plan collaboration, clearly defining project objectives
- Writing technical and functional specifications
- Establishing realistic project milestones and monitoring deadlines
- Budget management
- Progress reports
- Team member management/correspondence

Our services begin with a free 30-minute consultation where we can get acquainted. Once we know more about your concerns and business goals we move on to the next phase where we contract for a 30-day trial where we perform a needs assessment. Then we can then create a proposal for achieving the client's goals and objectives.

We expect that many of our clients will be small agencies that have their own clients and web/development/design projects for those clients. Our major functions with those clients will include:

- Managing projects to completion
- Assisting company owners to create, solidify and/or fix their internal project processes

TOOLS USED

We are skilled in using the following tools in providing client services:

- Microsoft's Team Foundation Server
- BaseCamp
- ClientSpot
- Smartsheet
- Highrise
- 1Shopping Cart
- PayPal
- Aweber
- Constant Contact

- iContact
- MailChimp
- Microsoft Excel
- Outlook
- Gmail
- Google Calendar
- Google Docs
- Survey Monkey
- Microsoft PowerPoint
- Microsoft Word
- Hootsuite Social Media Platform
- Drop Box
- Twhirl
- Social Oomph
- Dasheroo-Social Media Dashboard
- JIRA for task definition and tracking

We will employ the following tools to help us manage our business.

- *Google Apps for work:* calendar, online storage and video meetings managed virtually and shared as needed
- *Dropbox:* online storage of documents that can be accessed from anywhere
- *Boomerang:* a Gmail app to schedule and track emails
- *Bluehost:* WordPress web site hosting
- *WordPress.org:* web software to create site and blog
- *StudioPress:* WordPress themes to use on web site
- *AWebber:* autoresponder and email marketing service
- *QuickBooks Online:* bookkeeping in the cloud with added services such as credit card processing and online invoicing, billing and payments processing
- *AnyDesk:* allows remote connection in order to demonstrate tasks and offer presentations
- *HubStaff:* track the time to complete VA tasks
- *SEM Rush Search Engine Optimization Tool:* find valuable keywords, track competitive sites, analyze web sites

MARKET ANALYSIS

Based on our research and our past work experience we have identified the core market that we will specialize in serving. This market is comprised of firms that are experiencing growing pains and so are aware that they need expert assistance. There is no question that if they are to grow that they must invest in the people and services that will take them to the next level.

As a VA we can help our clients to be more flexible and efficient with their projects without compromising quality, timing or budget.

TARGET MARKET

Our ideal client possesses the following characteristics:

- They are in the process of expanding staff (including subcontractors)

- They are starting to take on larger projects and more projects per year

- They are moving toward restructuring the services that they offer

- They are struggling to find a process or system to fit their project needs

This target market is in transition. The company founders find that they can no longer wear all the hats and need assistance with work, process and management.

Our ideal client is a firm that is seeking a contract of between four and six months although longer contracts are welcome.

The key services that we have found of importance to this category of client include:

- The ability to manage projects from start to finish (or from wherever we enter the picture).

- Help in creating and implementing their internal project processes.

- Help in choosing and setting up project management software, internal team communication development, auditing processes, setting up and maintaining business development systems, developing and managing support and maintenance plans.

MARKETING STRATEGY

Project management is basically the art of making sure that things get done. This is often not the first thought of a company that is in the throes of growing pains. Consequently we find that our initial consultation is critical in securing a services contract that will benefit both the client and our firm.

We offer a free 30-minute consultation with the client as a way to get acquainted with them. This is appealing because the client feels that they are getting free advice. The purpose of the consultation is for us to gather the information so that we can move on to the next phase of client development.

We believe that it is important to quickly move to the next step in the process where the prospect will be expected to pay for an assessment of their needs and a written proposal for services. This "skin in the game" approach is important because it communicates to the prospect that there is value to be gained from working with us.

We will sign up a prospective client for an initial 30-day engagement at a significantly reduced fee. At the end of the month we will present an in-depth, researched and collaborative proposal.

If clients are willing to pay for a 30-day engagement, are involved and available during this time, and are truly excited about the future opportunities that signals this could be a long-lasting, collaborative relationship. If they drop out at this point then they aren't the kind of client we want because they don't recognize the value of what we can provide. The idea of paying for a proposal can be a surprise to some clients—and it's just not a good fit for others, depending on what services they are in need of.

The trial retainer helps clients gain confidence that this is the right path forward, and it builds trust in the chosen partner agency from the beginning.

Once we have gone through a needs assessment with the client we write up a proposal that details what we can do for them and what the benefits of those services will be in terms of both growth in revenues and cost savings.

In the end, the goals for the client are identified and based in reality. It's not about making an educated guess or repeating what the client thinks the brand should want to achieve.

WEB PLAN AND WEB MARKETING

Because we serve clients regardless of their location, our web site and online tools are critical to our success.

Our site will include a description of our company and our services, a short biography of Linda Hardy and a contact form that allows a prospect to ask us for more information.

A key strategy that will be employed on our company web site is a blog that will be updated on a regular basis with articles on topics of interest to our target customers. The goals associated with the blog include:

- Establish our expertise

- Develop a relationship of trust

- Inform about the benefits of project management services

- Inform about our suite of services

- Describe case studies of how we have been successful in helping our clients

- Include testimonials from satisfied clients

It is our objective to educate the client on the benefit of coordinating their needs into a project that entails coordination of resource requirements and promised timelines.

The arguments for the benefits of project management services tend to be a recurring theme when dealing with prospective clients. It should help to flatten out the learning curve if prospects read about the benefits and the consequent return on investment through articles on our blog.

Because of her experience in marketing Linda Hardy will be able to handle many of the tasks involved in initially creating the web site and attracting traffic. Linda is an expert in creating sites with WordPress and is familiar with third-party tools that add functionality to the site.

We will be contracting with an independent firm to carry on the regular maintenance, hosting, storage and upgrading of our site.

PERSONNEL PLAN

Another benefit of having worked for years in design and marketing is the catalog of contacts of other freelancers. Linda can call upon the help of proven writers, programmers, designers, artists and others to complete any work that must be subcontracted out.

She will also engage the services of a virtual assistant to help her with her own billing, correspondence and bookkeeping for the company.

MILESTONES

ExecAssist plans to achieve the following milestones.

Milestone	Start	End
Business plan	December 2015	February 2016
Web design	November 2015	February 2016
Brochures & cards	January 2016	January 2016
Logo design	December 2015	December 2015
Hire a virtual office assistant	January 2016	January 2016

FINANCIAL PLAN

Pro forma profit and loss

	Year 1	Year 2	Year 3
Sales	$25,000	$40,000	$60,000
Direct cost of sales: subcontractors	$ 6,250	$14,000	$21,000
Gross margin	**$18,750**	**$26,000**	**$39,000**
Gross margin %	**75%**	**65%**	**65%**
Expenses			
Advertising	$ 1,250	$ 1,500	$ 1,800
Virtual office assistant	$ 6,000	$ 6,000	$ 6,000
Depreciation	$ 400	$ 400	$ 400
Phone/Internet	$ 640	$ 960	$ 960
Insurance: errors omissions/life/disability	$ 350	$ 350	$ 400
Web site fees	$ 250	$ 250	$ 250
Web site maintenance	$ 400	$ 400	$ 400
Software/app subscriptions	$ 2,400	$ 2,500	$ 2,600
Professional dues/memberships	$ 750	$ 750	$ 750
Books/subscriptions	$ 200	$ 250	$ 300
Office supplies	$ 200	$ 250	$ 300
Auto	$ 2,000	$ 2,200	$ 2,400
Travel	$ 575	$ 600	$ 850
Other expenses	$ 400	$ 600	$ 800
Total operating expenses	**$15,815**	**$17,010**	**$18,210**
Net profit	**$ 2,935**	**$ 8,990**	**$20,790**
Net profit/sales	**12%**	**22%**	**35%**

Pro forma balance sheet

Assets	Year 1	Year 2	Year 3
Current assets			
Cash	$3,335	$ 9,390	$21,190
Other current assets	$ 0	$ 0	$ 0
Total current assets	**$3,335**	**$ 9,390**	**$21,190**
Long-term assets			
Long-term assets	$4,000	$ 4,000	$ 4,000
Accumulated depreciation	($ 400)	($ 400)	($ 400)
Total long-term assets	**$3,600**	**$ 3,600**	**$ 3,600**
Total assets	**$6,935**	**$12,990**	**$24,790**
Liabilities and capital			
Current liabilities			
Accounts payable	$ 0	$ 0	$ 0
Other current liabilities	$ 0	$ 0	$ 0
Subtotal current liabilities	**$ 0**	**$ 0**	**$ 0**
Long-term liabilities	$ 0	$ 0	$ 0
Total liabilities	**$ 0**	**$ 0**	**$ 0**
Paid in capital	$4,000	$ 4,000	$ 4,000
Earnings	$2,935	$ 8,990	$20,790
Total capital	**$6,935**	**$12,990**	**$24,790**
Total liabilities and capital	**$6,935**	**$12,990**	**$24,790**

Writing & Editing Business

Ellen Smith Communications Inc.

1904 Mason St., Apt. 2
Piedmont, IL 60014

Paul Greenland

Ellen Smith Communications Inc. is a writing and editing business specializing in corporate and business communications.

EXECUTIVE SUMMARY

Ellen Smith Communications Inc. is a Piedmont, Illinois-based writing and editing business specializing in corporate and business communications. The business is being established by Ellen Smith, a highly skilled copywriter and editor who has decided to work independently following nearly 25 years in corporate marketing and public relations.

Before establishing Ellen Smith Communications, Ellen was the marketing and PR manager for Piedmont Health System, where she helped to lead marketing and media relations for a major acute care hospital, regional medical center, free-standing outpatient cancer center, home healthcare agency, 16 primary care and multi-specialty clinics, 2,000 employees and more than 380 active and courtesy staff physicians from 70 specialties. In that role she served as the senior writer and editor for all corporate communications, with responsibility for researching, writing, editing, and disseminating news releases, feature stories, story pitches, blog and social media posts, speeches, talking points, and other communications.

Additionally, Ellen has maintained a successful freelance business for 15 years. In that role, she has developed extensive experience writing marketing-related articles for trade magazines, as well as white papers and case studies for marketing agencies and organizations. Her existing freelance business will form the nucleus of Ellen Smith Communications. In this plan, she has developed a thoughtful growth strategy that focuses on scaling up work with her existing customers, as well as new business development that capitalizes on her specialized healthcare industry experience.

Ellen is a member of several professional organizations, including the Independent Writers of Chicago, the Editorial Freelancers Association, and the Public Relations Society of America. She holds an undergraduate degree from North Park University and an editing certificate from the University of Chicago.

INDUSTRY ANALYSIS

According to the 2016-17 edition of the *Occupational Outlook Handbook*, published by the Bureau of Labor Statistics, U.S. Department of Labor, in 2014 there were approximately 136,500 writers and authors working in the United States, about 66 percent of whom were self-employed. The greatest opportunities for independent writers typically exist near major cities where there are large concentrations of customers. However, high-speed Internet and wireless communications have significantly changed this, allowing writers to work remotely from almost anywhere. Self-employed writers enjoy the benefit of independence and flexibility. However, those who are successful are adept at managing their business well, dealing with irregular and cyclical work, and setting aside time to market themselves on a consistent basis.

Professional Resources

Several professional organizations help writers to improve their craft, network with fellow writers and editors, and find new clients. In addition, individuals like Ellen Smith also may belong to trade organizations that are specific to their particular industry. Ellen Smith is a member of the following organizations:

American Society of Journalists and Authors

Headquartered in New York, the American Society of Journalists and Authors (ASJA) is perhaps the oldest professional organization for independent nonfiction writers, with roots dating back to 1948. The ASJA counts more than 1,000 freelance writers among its membership base, all of whom have met specific professional and experience-related criteria. Members benefit from local chapters, seminars and workshops, and an exclusive referral service. More information is available at: www.asja.org.

Editorial Freelancers Association

Also based in New York, but offering regional chapters throughout the world, is the Editorial Freelancers Association (EFA). Established in 1970, the EFA provides members with benefits such as job listings, a newsletter, a membership directory, as well as networking and educational opportunities. More information is available at: http://www.the-efa.org.

Society for Healthcare Strategy & Market Development

Because of her specialized experience, Ellen Smith is a member of the Society for Healthcare Strategy & Market Development (SHSMD). Part of the American Hospital Association, SHSMD bills itself as "the largest and most prominent voice and resource for healthcare strategists, planners, marketers, and communications and public relations professionals nationwide." The organization's approximately 4,000 members include professionals at hospitals and healthcare systems, consulting firms, and advertising/public relations agencies. Members benefit from online discussion forums, job postings, newsletters, and an annual conference with engaging speakers. More information is available at: www.shsmd.org.

MARKET ANALYSIS

For writers specializing in corporate communications, prospects typically fall into one of three categories:

1. *Business-to-consumer (B2C):* Businesses that market products and services to the consumer market. In the online retail category alone, the B2C segment was worth approximately $350 billion in 2015, according to data from the firm Forrester Research.

2. *Business-to-business (B2B):* Businesses that market products and services to other businesses. Compared to the B2C sector, Forrester Research valued the B2B market at $780 billion, illustrating the significant investments companies make in this area.

3. *Internal Communications:* Content that organizations target toward their employees and/or members, including newsletters, intranet sites, etc. Organizations make significant investments in this area to ensure high levels of engagement with their constituents.

Ellen Smith Communications will perform work in all three of these categories. Rather than concentrating on large organizations that are likely to have robust in-house marketing/communications staff and existing agency relationships, Ellen will target her services toward smaller and mid-sized companies with sales of $25 million-$100 million. Many companies in this category have money earmarked for marketing and advertising, but are pressed for time, short-staffed, or inexperienced handling things independently.

Another key target market will be third parties such as advertising agencies and marketing/public relations firms. Although third parties typically pay writers less (because they marked the writers' services up when billing their own clients), they often handle all communications with the ultimate end-user and may offer the benefit of a more steady stream of work.

Because writers and editors with highly specialized skills in a particular field or industry are often in greater demand than generalists, Ellen Smith will leverage her healthcare industry experience when seeking new customers. These will include hospitals, healthcare systems, physician practices, manufacturers of medical devices and products, and more.

Using a tool available at her local public library, Ellen has developed a custom report to identify prospects in a 60-mile radius from her home, dividing prospects into 15, 30, and 60-mile bands. The entire market area includes 10,000, 20,000, and 140,000 business establishments, respectively. Using North American Industry Classification System (NAICS) codes (used by the federal government to classify businesses based on their activities) and annual sales figures, Ellen refined the list to include establishments that were likely to be excellent prospects for business, including:

Primary Market (by NAICS)

- 339112—Surgical and Medical Instrument Manufacturing
- 339113—Surgical Appliance and Supplies Manufacturing
- 541810—Advertising Agencies
- 541820—Public Relations Agencies
- 621111—Offices of Physicians (except Mental Health Specialists)
- 621340—Offices of Physical, Occupational and Speech Therapists, and Audiologists
- 621391—Offices of Podiatrists
- 621399—Offices of All Other Miscellaneous Health Practitioners
- 621493—Freestanding Ambulatory Surgical and Emergency Centers
- 621498—All Other Outpatient Care Centers
- 621512—Diagnostic Imaging Centers
- 621610—Home Health Care Services
- 622110—General Medical and Surgical Hospitals
- 622310—Specialty (except Psychiatric and Substance Abuse) Hospitals

Secondary Market (by NAICS)

- 339114—Dental Equipment and Supplies Manufacturing
- 339115—Ophthalmic Goods Manufacturing
- 621112—Offices of Physicians, Mental Health Specialists
- 621210—Offices of Dentists
- 621310—Offices of Chiropractors

- 621320—Offices of Optometrists
- 621330—Offices of Mental Health Practitioners (except Physicians)
- 621491—HMO Medical Centers
- 621492—Kidney Dialysis Centers
- 621511—Medical Laboratories
- 621910—Ambulance Services
- 621991—Blood and Organ Banks
- 621999—All Other Miscellaneous Ambulatory Health Care Services
- 622210—Psychiatric and Substance Abuse Hospitals
- 623110—Nursing Care Facilities (Skilled Nursing Facilities)
- 623210—Residential Intellectual and Developmental Disability Facilities
- 623311—Continuing Care Retirement Communities
- 623312—Assisted Living Facilities for the Elderly
- 624120—Services for the Elderly and Persons with Disabilities

Ellen will use the tactics outlined in the Marketing & Sales section of this plan to grow her business, beginning with prospects in her primary market. Eventually, she will expand her marketing efforts to prospects in the secondary market.

SERVICES

Estimates

Ellen Smith will begin all projects by meeting with clients (by phone or in person) to gain as much information as possible about their specific project, and what their specific goals, objectives, and expectations are. Additionally, she will identify the specific sources that will be used to produce the content her client needs. This may include existing corporate materials; trade/industry associations; or interviews with customers, employees, and subject matter experts. She will then use this information to provide the client with a detailed, written time and cost estimate that includes details regarding timelines/ deliverables, rounds of included revisions, the number of interviews to be conducted, research hours, delivery format, etc. If the client is agreeable to the estimate, Ellen will require them to sign off on it.

Payment

In most cases, Ellen Smith will request that new clients provide half of the agreed-upon fee in advance, with the remainder due upon successful completion. For longer-term projects (e.g., annual reports, corporate histories, etc.), Ellen will request one-third of her fee in advance, another one-third midway through the project, and the final one-third due upon successful completion.

Process

With any marketing communications project, Ellen Smith will obtain as much information as possible from her client prior to the start of work. By asking lots of questions, she will be in the best position to meet their expectations the very first time. As part of this process, she will gain a firm understanding of:

1. The company/product/service being featured.
2. What differentiates the company/product/service in the marketplace (e.g., the unique selling proposition). This step also may include gathering information regarding the competitive landscape.

3. Who the target audience is and what their needs, goals, desires, and concerns are. This critical step will help Ellen make a strong connection with her client's customers. Whenever possible, she will focus on communicating the benefits of her customer's product or service to the target market, as opposed to leading with information about specific features.

Once Ellen has obtained all of the necessary information to complete the project, she will proceed with research, interviews, and writing. Ultimately, she will provide her customer with a draft for their review and approval.

Fees

Ellen typically charges $100 per hour for general corporate copywriting services. Following are average charges for projects, along with typical ranges:

- Annual Reports: $9,000 ($1,500-$16,500)

- Blog Posts: $750 ($500-$2,500)

- Brochures: $3,500 ($500-$10,500)

- Business Plans $4,500 ($1,500-$12,500)

- Company Histories: $45,000 ($5,000-$150,000)

- Company Profiles: $1,500 ($750-$2,500)

- Newsletters: $3,000 ($1,500-$6,500)

- Press Releases: $900 ($750-$1,500)

- Direct Mail: $3,500 ($1,000-$7,500)

- Advertorials: $850 ($500-$2,000)

- Advertising: $4,500 ($500-$9,500)

- White Papers: $8,000 ($5,000-$12,500)

- Case Studies: $750 ($500-$1,500)

In addition to copywriting, Ellen also is an experienced editor who can help shape, polish and rewrite copy. She typically charges $70 per hour for copyediting services.

Specialties

In particular, Ellen has substantial experience with two types of corporate copywriting (white papers and case studies). For the past 15 years, Ellen literally has completed hundreds of projects in these categories on a freelance basis for several marketing firms:

1. *White Papers.* A combination of corporate literature and magazine content, white papers are useful tools for educating business prospects on a variety of topics. They are a key tool for generating leads for companies, and ultimately bringing in new revenue. Beyond their dominance in the technology field, white papers are now used in a wide range of industries, including healthcare. Writing successful white papers can result in repeat business for writers, which is significant, considering that the fee for writing a 10-page white paper can range between $5,000 and $10,000 or more.

2. *Case Studies.* Case studies are another extremely useful tool that companies can use to showcase their products or services in action. Case studies, which can be distributed in multiple ways (e.g., at trade shows, on sales calls, online, to trade magazines, as pitches to magazine editors, etc.), are success stories that demonstrate how a company provided a solution to a customer's challenge or problem.

OPERATIONS

One key advantage of a freelance writing business is low overhead. Ellen spent considerable time researching a variety of options that will allow her to operate her business in a high-impact, efficient manner, at the lowest possible cost.

Location

Ellen Smith will maintain dedicated home office space for her business. In addition to a desktop computer, she has purchased a multi-function printer with scanning, faxing, and copying capabilities.

Business Structure

Ellen Smith Communications is organized as an S corporation in the state of Illinois. This business structure will allow the owner to receive half of her revenue in the form of salary, while taking the rest as quarterly profits that are not subject to Social Security and Medicare taxes. Additionally, the corporation provides the owner with a certain level of liability protection.

Telecommunications

Ellen has secured broadband Internet and telephone service from her local cable provider. Additionally, she obtained an inexpensive toll-free number through the service, Grasshopper, which she can configure to ring anywhere (e.g., her cell phone, desk phone, etc.). For a small fee, she had her telephone greeting recorded by a professional voice artist, helping her to maintain a professional image for the business.

Accounting

In addition to working with a local accountant, who will handle payroll and tax preparation, Ellen purchased a subscription to the online accounting software, FreshBooks, which offers tools for project tracking, invoicing, billing, expense tracking, and more.

Liability Insurance

Ellen Smith has obtained an affordable liability policy for her business in partnership with a local insurance broker.

PERSONNEL

Ellen Smith is a highly skilled copywriter and editor who has decided to work independently following nearly 25 years in corporate marketing and public relations. Before establishing Ellen Smith Communications, Ellen was the marketing and PR manager for Piedmont Health System, where she helped to lead marketing and media relations for a major acute care hospital, regional medical center, freestanding outpatient cancer center, home healthcare agency, 16 primary care and multi-specialty clinics, 2,000 employees and more than 380 active and courtesy staff physicians from 70 specialties. In that role she served as the senior writer and editor for all corporate communications, with responsibility for researching, writing, editing, and disseminating news releases, feature stories, story pitches, blog and social media posts, speeches, talking points, and other communications.

Additionally, Ellen has maintained a successful freelance business for 15 years. In that role, she has developed extensive experience writing marketing-related articles for trade magazines, as well as white papers and case studies for marketing agencies and organizations.

Ellen is a member of several professional organizations, including the Independent Writers of Chicago, the Editorial Freelancers Association, and the Public Relations Society of America. She holds an undergraduate degree from North Park University, and an editing certificate from the University of Chicago.

Professional & Advisory Support

Ellen Smith Communications has retained the services of McPherson & Ruth, a local accounting firm, to assist with bookkeeping and tax preparation. The company also has established a business checking account with Piedmont Credit Union, which offers low fees compared to leading national banks. Andrew Johnson, a local business attorney, assisted with the business' incorporation, as well as standard business agreements that Ellen Smith can customize for use with her clients.

GROWTH STRATEGY

Ellen Smith's existing base of freelance customers will form the foundation of her new writing and editing business. Currently, she relies upon a handful of key clients for the majority of her business, which generates revenue of approximately $30,000 per year. In particular, two advertising agencies account for 75 percent of her freelancing income, followed by trade magazines (15%), and several local (non-healthcare) organizations (10%).

The growth strategy for Ellen Smith Communications will focus on the following main themes:

• Maximizing business with existing clients.

• New business growth, especially with companies in the primary market.

• Diversification to minimize financial risk.

Ellen has established the following growth targets for the first three years of operations:

Year One: Generate annual revenue of $60,000, or an average of $5,000 per month/$1,250 per week. Diversify customer base so that organizations account for 20 percent of business, followed by advertising/marketing agencies (65%), and trade magazines (15%).

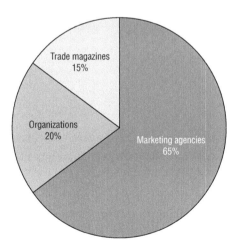

Year Two: Generate annual revenue of $80,000, or an average of $6,666 per month/$1,666 per week. Diversify customer base so that organizations account for 35 percent of business, followed by advertising/marketing agencies (55%), and trade magazines (10%).

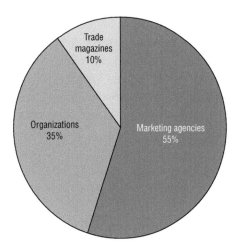

Year Three: Generate annual revenue of $100,000, or an average of $8,333 per month/$2,083 per week. Diversify customer base so that organizations account for 55 percent of business, followed by advertising/marketing agencies (35%), and trade magazines (10%).

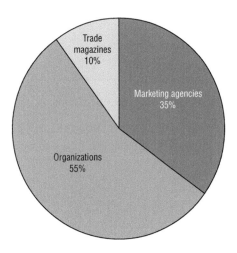

MARKETING & SALES

In speaking with other writers, Ellen has discovered that the key to marketing success for her communications business is staying visible with prospects on a consistent basis through a variety of different channels. To accomplish this, she will rely upon the following marketing tactics:

1. *Direct Mailings.* Ellen has obtained names at no cost from a business database at her local library, based on the criteria specified in the Market Analysis section of this plan. She has exported the data into a spreadsheet, which she can use to send out a steady stream of mailings to prospects.

2. *Cold Calling.* In addition to sending mailings to the aforementioned list of prospects, Ellen will maximize her response rate by making follow-up phone calls.

3. *Local Networking.* Ellen will read local business publications (including the Piedmont Chamber of Commerce's newsletter) to identify when new marketing/PR directors have been hired at local companies. This will provide her with an opportunity to send them a congratulatory letter/e-mail, and offer up her business as a potential resource.

4. *Professional Networking.* Ellen will attend conferences and regional meetings hosted by the professional organizations listed in the Industry Analysis section of this plan. Additionally, she will participate in online discussions held on message boards.

5. *Online Job Boards.* On a regular basis, Ellen will monitor online job postings on subscription-based sites such as Flexjobs.com, as well as membership-only job boards provided by the professional organizations to which she belongs.

6. *Providing Exceptional Service.* Ellen takes great pride in the fact that she has never missed a deadline. She follows through on promises to all of her customers, showing up for meetings on-time and delivering projects as-promised. This is a key differential that sets her apart from competitors.

7. *Web Site.* Ellen has developed a simple Web site that includes a portfolio of clips, testimonials from satisfied customers, a brief bio, and contact information.

8. *Stationary.* To look professional, Ellen worked with a local graphic designer to develop her own letterhead, envelopes, thank-you cards, and business cards.

9. *Social Media.* Ellen will maintain a presence on LinkedIn to identify and connect with prospects.

10. *Chamber of Commerce.* A membership in the local Chamber of Commerce will provide Ellen with an opportunity to network with local business owners and decision makers.

FINANCIAL ANALYSIS

Following are projected annual revenue and expenses for Ellen Smith Communications' first three years of operations:

	2016	2017	2018
Revenue	**$60,000**	**$80,000**	**$100,000**
Expenses			
Salary	$30,000	$40,000	$ 50,000
Payroll tax	$ 4,500	$ 6,000	$ 7,500
Books & subscriptions	$ 250	$ 250	$ 250
Equipment	$ 500	$ 500	$ 500
Memberships	$ 500	$ 500	$ 500
Office supplies	$ 450	$ 500	$ 550
Telecommunications (VoIP)	$ 300	$ 300	$ 300
Telecommunications (mobile)	$ 510	$ 510	$ 510
Telecommunications (toll-free)	$ 280	$ 300	$ 320
Legal & regulatory	$ 125	$ 125	$ 125
Accounting	$ 1,100	$ 1,100	$ 1,100
Postage	$ 500	$ 600	$ 700
Internet	$ 1,000	$ 1,000	$ 1,000
Marketing	$ 2,000	$ 2,000	$ 2,000
Total expenses	**$42,015**	**$53,685**	**$ 65,355**
Net profit	**$17,985**	**$26,315**	**$ 34,645**

BUSINESS PLAN TEMPLATE

USING THIS TEMPLATE

A business plan carefully spells out a company's projected course of action over a period of time, usually the first two to three years after the start-up. In addition, banks, lenders, and other investors examine the information and financial documentation before deciding whether or not to finance a new business venture. Therefore, a business plan is an essential tool in obtaining financing and should describe the business itself in detail as well as all important factors influencing the company, including the market, industry, competition, operations and management policies, problem solving strategies, financial resources and needs, and other vital information. The plan enables the business owner to anticipate costs, plan for difficulties, and take advantage of opportunities, as well as design and implement strategies that keep the company running as smoothly as possible.

This template has been provided as a model to help you construct your own business plan. Please keep in mind that there is no single acceptable format for a business plan, and that this template is in no way comprehensive, but serves as an example.

The business plans provided in this section are fictional and have been used by small business agencies as models for clients to use in compiling their own business plans.

GENERIC BUSINESS PLAN

Main headings included below are topics that should be covered in a comprehensive business plan. They include:

Business Summary

Purpose
Provides a brief overview of your business, succinctly highlighting the main ideas of your plan.

Includes

- Topic Headings and Subheadings
- Page Number References

Table of Contents

Purpose
Organized in an Outline Format, the Table of Contents illustrates the selection and arrangement of information contained in your plan.

Includes

- Name and Type of Business
- Description of Product/Service
- Business History and Development
- Location
- Market

- Competition
- Management
- Financial Information
- Business Strengths and Weaknesses
- Business Growth

Business History and Industry Outlook

Purpose

Examines the conception and subsequent development of your business within an industry specific context.

Includes

- Start-up Information
- Owner/Key Personnel Experience
- Location
- Development Problems and Solutions
- Investment/Funding Information
- Future Plans and Goals

- Market Trends and Statistics
- Major Competitors
- Product/Service Advantages
- National, Regional, and Local Economic Impact

Product/Service

Purpose

Introduces, defines, and details the product and/or service that inspired the information of your business.

Includes

- Unique Features
- Niche Served
- Market Comparison
- Stage of Product/Service Development

- Production
- Facilities, Equipment, and Labor
- Financial Requirements
- Product/Service Life Cycle
- Future Growth

Market Examination

Purpose

Assessment of product/service applications in relation to consumer buying cycles.

Includes

- Target Market
- Consumer Buying Habits
- Product/Service Applications
- Consumer Reactions
- Market Factors and Trends

- Penetration of the Market
- Market Share
- Research and Studies
- Cost
- Sales Volume and Goals

Competition

Purpose

Analysis of Competitors in the Marketplace.

Includes

- Competitor Information
- Product/Service Comparison
- Market Niche

- Product/Service Strengths and Weaknesses
- Future Product/Service Development

Marketing

Purpose

Identifies promotion and sales strategies for your product/service.

Includes

- Product/Service Sales Appeal
- Special and Unique Features
- Identification of Customers
- Sales and Marketing Staff
- Sales Cycles
- Type of Advertising/ Promotion
- Pricing
- Competition
- Customer Services

Operations

Purpose

Traces product/service development from production/inception to the market environment.

Includes

- Cost Effective Production Methods
- Facility
- Location
- Equipment
- Labor
- Future Expansion

Administration and Management

Purpose

Offers a statement of your management philosophy with an in-depth focus on processes and procedures.

Includes

- Management Philosophy
- Structure of Organization
- Reporting System
- Methods of Communication
- Employee Skills and Training
- Employee Needs and Compensation
- Work Environment
- Management Policies and Procedures
- Roles and Responsibilities

Key Personnel

Purpose

Describes the unique backgrounds of principle employees involved in business.

Includes

- Owner(s)/Employee Education and Experience
- Positions and Roles
- Benefits and Salary
- Duties and Responsibilities
- Objectives and Goals

Potential Problems and Solutions

Purpose

Discussion of problem solving strategies that change issues into opportunities.

Includes

- Risks
- Litigation
- Future Competition
- Economic Impact
- Problem Solving Skills

Financial Information

Purpose

Secures needed funding and assistance through worksheets and projections detailing financial plans, methods of repayment, and future growth opportunities.

Includes

- Financial Statements
- Bank Loans
- Methods of Repayment
- Tax Returns
- Start-up Costs
- Projected Income (3 years)
- Projected Cash Flow (3 Years)
- Projected Balance Statements (3 years)

Appendices

Purpose

Supporting documents used to enhance your business proposal.

Includes

- Photographs of product, equipment, facilities, etc.
- Copyright/Trademark Documents
- Legal Agreements
- Marketing Materials
- Research and or Studies
- Operation Schedules
- Organizational Charts
- Job Descriptions
- Resumes
- Additional Financial Documentation

Fictional Food Distributor

Commercial Foods, Inc.

3003 Avondale Ave.
Knoxville, TN 37920

This plan demonstrates how a partnership can have a positive impact on a new business. It demonstrates how two individuals can carve a niche in the specialty foods market by offering gourmet foods to upscale restaurants and fine hotels. This plan is fictional and has not been used to gain funding from a bank or other lending institution.

STATEMENT OF PURPOSE

Commercial Foods, Inc. seeks a loan of $75,000 to establish a new business. This sum, together with $5,000 equity investment by the principals, will be used as follows:

- Merchandise inventory $25,000
- Office fixture/equipment $12,000
- Warehouse equipment $14,000
- One delivery truck $10,000
- Working capital $39,000
- Total $100,000

DESCRIPTION OF THE BUSINESS

Commercial Foods, Inc. will be a distributor of specialty food service products to hotels and upscale restaurants in the geographical area of a 50 mile radius of Knoxville. Richard Roberts will direct the sales effort and John Williams will manage the warehouse operation and the office. One delivery truck will be used initially with a second truck added in the third year. We expect to begin operation of the business within 30 days after securing the requested financing.

MANAGEMENT

A. Richard Roberts is a native of Memphis, Tennessee. He is a graduate of Memphis State University with a Bachelor's degree from the School of Business. After graduation, he worked for a major manufacturer of specialty food service products as a detail sales person for five years, and, for the past three years, he has served as a product sales manager for this firm.

B. John Williams is a native of Nashville, Tennessee. He holds a B.S. Degree in Food Technology from the University of Tennessee. His career includes five years as a product development chemist in gourmet food products and five years as operations manager for a food service distributor.

Both men are healthy and energetic. Their backgrounds complement each other, which will ensure the success of Commercial Foods, Inc. They will set policies together and personnel decisions will be made jointly. Initial salaries for the owners will be $1,000 per month for the first few years. The spouses of both principals are successful in the business world and earn enough to support the families.

They have engaged the services of Foster Jones, CPA, and William Hale, Attorney, to assist them in an advisory capacity.

PERSONNEL

The firm will employ one delivery truck driver at a wage of $8.00 per hour. One office worker will be employed at $7.50 per hour. One part-time employee will be used in the office at $5.00 per hour. The driver will load and unload his own trucks. Mr. Williams will assist in the warehouse operation as needed to assist one stock person at $7.00 per hour. An additional delivery truck and driver will be added the third year.

LOCATION

The firm will lease a 20,000 square foot building at 3003 Avondale Ave., in Knoxville, which contains warehouse and office areas equipped with two-door truck docks. The annual rental is $9,000. The building was previously used as a food service warehouse and very little modification to the building will be required.

PRODUCTS AND SERVICES

The firm will offer specialty food service products such as soup bases, dessert mixes, sauce bases, pastry mixes, spices, and flavors, normally used by upscale restaurants and nice hotels. We are going after a niche in the market with high quality gourmet products. There is much less competition in this market than in standard run of the mill food service products. Through their work experiences, the principals have contacts with supply sources and with local chefs.

THE MARKET

We know from our market survey that there are over 200 hotels and upscale restaurants in the area we plan to serve. Customers will be attracted by a direct sales approach. We will offer samples of our products and product application data on use of our products in the finished prepared foods. We will cultivate the chefs in these establishments. The technical background of John Williams will be especially useful here.

COMPETITION

We find that we will be only distributor in the area offering a full line of gourmet food service products. Other foodservice distributors offer only a few such items in conjunction with their standard product line. Our survey shows that many of the chefs are ordering products from Atlanta and Memphis because of a lack of adequate local supply.

SUMMARY

Commercial Foods, Inc. will be established as a foodservice distributor of specialty food in Knoxville. The principals, with excellent experience in the industry, are seeking a $75,000 loan to establish the business. The principals are investing $25,000 as equity capital.

The business will be set up as an S Corporation with each principal owning 50% of the common stock in the corporation.

Fictional Hardware Store

Oshkosh Hardware, Inc.

123 Main St.
Oshkosh, WI 54901

The following plan outlines how a small hardware store can survive competition from large discount chains by offering products and providing expert advice in the use of any product it sells. This plan is fictional and has not been used to gain funding from a bank or other lending institution.

EXECUTIVE SUMMARY

Oshkosh Hardware, Inc. is a new corporation that is going to establish a retail hardware store in a strip mall in Oshkosh, Wisconsin. The store will sell hardware of all kinds, quality tools, paint, and housewares. The business will make revenue and a profit by servicing its customers not only with needed hardware but also with expert advice in the use of any product it sells.

Oshkosh Hardware, Inc. will be operated by its sole shareholder, James Smith. The company will have a total of four employees. It will sell its products in the local market. Customers will buy our products because we will provide free advice on the use of all of our products and will also furnish a full refund warranty.

Oshkosh Hardware, Inc. will sell its products in the Oshkosh store staffed by three sales representatives. No additional employees will be needed to achieve its short and long range goals. The primary short range goal is to open the store by October 1, 1994. In order to achieve this goal a lease must be signed by July 1, 1994 and the complete inventory ordered by August 1, 1994.

Mr. James Smith will invest $30,000 in the business. In addition, the company will have to borrow $150,000 during the first year to cover the investment in inventory, accounts receivable, and furniture and equipment. The company will be profitable after six months of operation and should be able to start repayment of the loan in the second year.

THE BUSINESS

The business will sell hardware of all kinds, quality tools, paint, and housewares. We will purchase our products from three large wholesale buying groups.

In general our customers are homeowners who do their own repair and maintenance, hobbyists, and housewives. Our business is unique in that we will have a complete line of all hardware items and will be able to get special orders by overnight delivery. The business makes revenue and profits by servicing our customers not only with needed hardware but also with expert advice in the use of any product we sell. Our major costs for bringing our products to market are cost of merchandise of 36%, salaries of $45,000, and occupancy costs of $60,000.

Oshkosh Hardware, Inc.'s retail outlet will be located at 1524 Frontage Road, which is in a newly developed retail center of Oshkosh. Our location helps facilitate accessibility from all parts of town and reduces our delivery costs. The store will occupy 7500 square feet of space. The major equipment involved in our business is counters and shelving, a computer, a paint mixing machine, and a truck.

THE MARKET

Oshkosh Hardware, Inc. will operate in the local market. There are 15,000 potential customers in this market area. We have three competitors who control approximately 98% of the market at present. We feel we can capture 25% of the market within the next four years. Our major reason for believing this is that our staff is technically competent to advise our customers in the correct use of all products we sell.

After a careful market analysis, we have determined that approximately 60% of our customers are men and 40% are women. The percentage of customers that fall into the following age categories are:

Under 16: 0%
17-21: 5%
22-30: 30%
31-40: 30%
41-50: 20%
51-60: 10%
61-70: 5%
Over 70: 0%

The reasons our customers prefer our products is our complete knowledge of their use and our full refund warranty.

We get our information about what products our customers want by talking to existing customers. There seems to be an increasing demand for our product. The demand for our product is increasing in size based on the change in population characteristics.

SALES

At Oshkosh Hardware, Inc. we will employ three sales people and will not need any additional personnel to achieve our sales goals. These salespeople will need several years experience in home repair and power tool usage. We expect to attract 30% of our customers from newspaper ads, 5% of our customers from local directories, 5% of our customers from the yellow pages, 10% of our customers from family and friends, and 50% of our customers from current customers. The most cost effect source will be current customers. In general our industry is growing.

MANAGEMENT

We would evaluate the quality of our management staff as being excellent. Our manager is experienced and very motivated to achieve the various sales and quality assurance objectives we have set. We will use a management information system that produces key inventory, quality assurance, and sales data on a weekly basis. All data is compared to previously established goals for that week, and deviations are the primary focus of the management staff.

GOALS IMPLEMENTATION

The short term goals of our business are:

1. Open the store by October 1, 1994
2. Reach our breakeven point in two months
3. Have sales of $100,000 in the first six months

In order to achieve our first short term goal we must:

1. Sign the lease by July 1, 1994
2. Order a complete inventory by August 1, 1994

In order to achieve our second short term goal we must:

1. Advertise extensively in Sept. and Oct.
2. Keep expenses to a minimum

In order to achieve our third short term goal we must:

1. Promote power tool sales for the Christmas season
2. Keep good customer traffic in Jan. and Feb.

The long term goals for our business are:

1. Obtain sales volume of $600,000 in three years
2. Become the largest hardware dealer in the city
3. Open a second store in Fond du Lac

The most important thing we must do in order to achieve the long term goals for our business is to develop a highly profitable business with excellent cash flow.

FINANCE

Oshkosh Hardware, Inc. Faces some potential threats or risks to our business. They are discount house competition. We believe we can avoid or compensate for this by providing quality products complimented by quality advice on the use of every product we sell. The financial projections we have prepared are located at the end of this document.

JOB DESCRIPTION-GENERAL MANAGER

The General Manager of the business of the corporation will be the president of the corporation. He will be responsible for the complete operation of the retail hardware store which is owned by the corporation. A detailed description of his duties and responsibilities is as follows.

Sales

Train and supervise the three sales people. Develop programs to motivate and compensate these employees. Coordinate advertising and sales promotion effects to achieve sales totals as outlined in budget. Oversee purchasing function and inventory control procedures to insure adequate merchandise at all times at a reasonable cost.

Finance

Prepare monthly and annual budgets. Secure adequate line of credit from local banks. Supervise office personnel to insure timely preparation of records, statements, all government reports, control of receivables and payables, and monthly financial statements.

Administration

Perform duties as required in the areas of personnel, building leasing and maintenance, licenses and permits, and public relations.

Organizations, Agencies, & Consultants

A listing of Associations and Consultants of interest to entrepreneurs, followed by the Small Business Administration Regional Offices, Small Business Development Centers, Service Corps of Retired Executives offices, and Venture Capital and Finance Companies.

Associations

This section contains a listing of associations and other agencies of interest to the small business owner. Entries are listed alphabetically by organization name.

American Business Women's Association
9100 Ward Pkwy.
PO Box 8728
Kansas City, MO 64114-0728
(800)228-0007
E-mail: abwa@abwa.org
Website: http://www.abwa.org
Jeanne Banks, National President

American Franchisee Association
53 W Jackson Blvd., Ste. 1157
Chicago, IL 60604
(312)431-0545
E-mail: info@franchisee.org
Website: http://www.franchisee.org
Susan P. Kezios, President

American Independent Business Alliance
222 S Black Ave.
Bozeman, MT 59715
(406)582-1255
E-mail: info@amiba.net
Website: http://www.amiba.net
Jennifer Rockne, Director

American Small Businesses Association
206 E College St., Ste. 201
Grapevine, TX 76051
800-942-2722
E-mail: info@asbaonline.org
Website: http://www.asbaonline.org/

American Women's Economic Development Corporation
216 East 45th St., 10th Floor
New York, NY 10017

(917)368-6100
Fax: (212)986-7114
E-mail: info@awed.org
Website: http://www.awed.org
Roseanne Antonucci, Exec. Dir.

Association for Enterprise Opportunity
1601 N Kent St., Ste. 1101
Arlington, VA 22209
(703)841-7760
Fax: (703)841-7748
E-mail: aeo@assoceo.org
Website: http://www.microenterprise
works.org
Bill Edwards, Exec.Dir.

Association of Small Business Development Centers
c/o Don Wilson
8990 Burke Lake Rd.
Burke, VA 22015
(703)764-9850
Fax: (703)764-1234
E-mail: info@asbdc-us.org
Website: http://www.asbdc-us.org
Don Wilson, Pres./CEO

BEST Employers Association
2505 McCabe Way
Irvine, CA 92614
(949)253-4080
800-433-0088
Fax: (714)553-0883
E-mail: info@bestlife.com
Website: http://www.bestlife.com
Donald R. Lawrenz, CEO

Center for Family Business
PO Box 24219
Cleveland, OH 44124
(440)460-5409
E-mail: grummi@aol.com
Dr. Leon A. Danco, Chm.

Coalition for Government Procurement
1990 M St. NW, Ste. 400
Washington, DC 20036
(202)331-0975
E-mail: info@thecgp.org
Website: http://www.coalgovpro.org
Paul Caggiano, Pres.

Employers of America
PO Box 1874
Mason City, IA 50402-1874
(641)424-3187
800-728-3187
Fax: (641)424-1673
E-mail: employer@employerhelp.org
Website: http://www.employerhelp.org
Jim Collison, Pres.

Family Firm Institute
200 Lincoln St., Ste. 201
Boston, MA 02111
(617)482-3045
Fax: (617)482-3049
E-mail: ffi@ffi.org
Website: http://www.ffi.org
Judy L. Green, Ph.D., Exec.Dir.

Independent Visually Impaired Enterprisers
500 S 3rd St., Apt. H
Burbank, CA 91502
(818)238-9321
E-mail: abazyn@bazyncommunications
.com
Website: http://www.acb.org/affiliates
Adris Bazyn, Pres.

International Association for Business Organizations
3 Woodthorn Ct., Ste. 12
Owings Mills, MD 21117
(410)581-1373
E-mail: nahbb@msn.com
Rudolph Lewis, Exec. Officer

181

International Council for Small Business
The George Washington University
School of Business and Public
Management
2115 G St. NW, Ste. 403
Washington, DC 20052
(202)994-0704
Fax: (202)994-4930
E-mail: icsb@gwu.edu
Website: http://www.icsb.org
Susan G. Duffy. Admin.

International Small Business Consortium
3309 Windjammer St.
Norman, OK 73072
E-mail: sb@isbc.com
Website: http://www.isbc.com

Kauffman Center for Entrepreneurial Leadership
4801 Rockhill Rd.
Kansas City, MO 64110-2046
(816)932-1000
E-mail: info@kauffman.org
Website: http://www.entreworld.org

National Alliance for Fair Competition
3 Bethesda Metro Center, Ste. 1100
Bethesda, MD 20814
(410)235-7116
Fax: (410)235-7116
E-mail: ampesq@aol.com
Tony Ponticelli, Exec.Dir.

National Association for the Self-Employed
PO Box 612067
DFW Airport
Dallas, TX 75261-2067
(800)232-6273
E-mail: mpetron@nase.org
Website: http://www.nase.org
Robert Hughes, Pres.

National Association of Business Leaders
4132 Shoreline Dr., Ste. J & H
Earth City, MO 63045
Fax: (314)298-9110
E-mail: nabl@nabl.com
Website: http://www.nabl.com/
Gene Blumenthal, Contact

National Association of Private Enterprise
PO Box 15550
Long Beach, CA 90815
888-224-0953
Fax: (714)844-4942

Website: http://www.napeonline.net
Laura Squiers, Exec.Dir.

National Association of Small Business Investment Companies
666 11th St. NW, Ste. 750
Washington, DC 20001
(202)628-5055
Fax: (202)628-5080
E-mail: nasbic@nasbic.org
Website: http://www.nasbic.org
Lee W. Mercer, Pres.

National Business Association
PO Box 700728
5151 Beltline Rd., Ste. 1150
Dallas, TX 75370
(972)458-0900
800-456-0440
Fax: (972)960-9149
E-mail: info@nationalbusiness.org
Website: http://www.nationalbusiness
.org
Raj Nisankarao, Pres.

National Business Owners Association
PO Box 111
Stuart, VA 24171
(276)251-7500
(866)251-7505
Fax: (276)251-2217
E-mail: membershipservices@nboa.org
Website: http://www.rvmdb.com.nboa
Paul LaBarr, Pres.

National Center for Fair Competition
PO Box 220
Annandale, VA 22003
(703)280-4622
Fax: (703)280-0942
E-mail: kentonp1@aol.com
Kenton Pattie, Pres.

National Family Business Council
1640 W. Kennedy Rd.
Lake Forest, IL 60045
(847)295-1040
Fax: (847)295-1898
E-mail: lmsnfbc@email.msn.com
Jogn E. Messervey, Pres.

National Federation of Independent Business
53 Century Blvd., Ste. 250
Nashville, TN 37214
(615)872-5800
800-NFIBNOW
Fax: (615)872-5353
Website: http://www.nfib.org
Jack Faris, Pres. and CEO

National Small Business Association
1156 15th St. NW, Ste. 1100
Washington, DC 20005
(202)293-8830
800-345-6728
Fax: (202)872-8543
E-mail: press@nsba.biz
Website: http://www.nsba.biz
Rob Yunich, Dir. of Communications

PUSH Commercial Division
930 E 50th St.
Chicago, IL 60615-2702
(773)373-3366
Fax: (773)373-3571
E-mail: info@rainbowpush.org
Website: http://www.rainbowpush.org
Rev. Willie T. Barrow, Co-Chm.

Research Institute for Small and Emerging Business
722 12th St. NW
Washington, DC 20005
(202)628-8382
Fax: (202)628-8392
E-mail: info@riseb.org
Website: http://www.riseb.org
Allan Neece, Jr., Chm.

Sales Professionals USA
PO Box 149
Arvada, CO 80001
(303)534-4937
888-736-7767
E-mail: salespro@salesprofessionals-
usa.com
Website: http://www.salesprofessionals-
usa.com
Sharon Herbert, Natl. Pres.

Score Association - Service Corps of Retired Executives
409 3rd St. SW, 6th Fl.
Washington, DC 20024
(202)205-6762
800-634-0245
Fax: (202)205-7636
E-mail: media@score.org
Website: http://www.score.org
W. Kenneth Yancey, Jr., CEO

Small Business and Entrepreneurship Council
1920 L St. NW, Ste. 200
Washington, DC 20036
(202)785-0238
Fax: (202)822-8118
E-mail: membership@sbec.org
Website: http://www.sbecouncil.org
Karen Kerrigan, Pres./CEO

Small Business in Telecommunications
1331 H St. NW, Ste. 500
Washington, DC 20005
(202)347-4511
Fax: (202)347-8607
E-mail: sbt@sbthome.org
Website: http://www.sbthome.org
Lonnie Danchik, Chm.

Small Business Legislative Council
1010 Massachusetts Ave. NW, Ste. 540
Washington, DC 20005
(202)639-8500
Fax: (202)296-5333
E-mail: email@sblc.org
Website: http://www.sblc.org
John Satagaj, Pres.

Small Business Service Bureau
554 Main St.
PO Box 15014
Worcester, MA 01615-0014
(508)756-3513
800-343-0939
Fax: (508)770-0528
E-mail: membership@sbsb.com
Website: http://www.sbsb.com
Francis R. Carroll, Pres.

Small Publishers Association of North America
1618 W Colorado Ave.
Colorado Springs, CO 80904
(719)475-1726
Fax: (719)471-2182
E-mail: span@spannet.org
Website: http://www.spannet.org
Scott Flora, Exec. Dir.

SOHO America
PO Box 941
Hurst, TX 76053-0941
800-495-SOHO
E-mail: soho@1sas.com
Website: http://www.soho.org

Structured Employment Economic Development Corporation
915 Broadway, 17th Fl.
New York, NY 10010
(212)473-0255
Fax: (212)473-0357
E-mail: info@seedco.org
Website: http://www.seedco.org
William Grinker, CEO

Support Services Alliance
107 Prospect St.
Schoharie, NY 12157
800-836-4772
E-mail: info@ssamembers.com

Website: http://www.ssainfo.com
Steve COle, Pres.

United States Association for Small Business and Entrepreneurship
975 University Ave., No. 3260
Madison, WI 53706
(608)262-9982
Fax: (608)263-0818
E-mail: jgillman@wisc.edu
Website: http://www.ususbe.org
Joan Gillman, Exec. Dir.

Consultants

This section contains a listing of consultants specializing in small business development. It is arranged alphabetically by country, then by state or province, then by city, then by firm name.

Canada

Alberta

Tenato
1229A 9th Ave. SE
Calgary, AB, Canada T2G 0S9
(403)242-1127
Fax: (403)261-5693
E-mail: jdrew@tenato.com
Website: http://www.tenato.com

Varsity Consulting Group
School of Business
University of Alberta
Edmonton, AB, Canada T6G 2R6
(780)492-2994
Fax: (780)492-5400

British Columbia

Andrew R. De Boda Consulting
1523 Milford Ave.
Coquitlam, BC, Canada V3J 2V9
(604)936-4527
Fax: (604)936-4527
E-mail: deboda@intergate.bc.ca

Reality Marketing Associates
3049 Sienna Ct.
Coquitlam, BC, Canada V3E 3N7
(604)944-8603
Fax: (604)944-4708
E-mail: info@realityassociates.com
Website: http://www.realityassociates.com

Pinpoint Tactics Business Consulting
5525 West Blvd., Ste. 330
Vancouver, BC, Canada V6M 3W6
(604)263-4698

E-mail: info@pinpointtactics.com
Website: http://www.pinpointtactics.com

Ketch Consulting Inc.
6890 Winnifred Pl.
Victoria, BC, Canada V8M 1N1
(250)661-1208
E-mail: info@ketch.ca
Website: http://www.ketch.ca

Mahigan Consulting Services
334 Skawshen Rd.
West Vancouver, BC, Canada V7P 3T1
(604)210-3833
Fax: (778)285-2736
E-mail: info@mahiganconsulting.com
Website: http://www.mahiganconsulting.com

Nova Scotia

The Marketing Clinic
1384 Bedford Hwy.
Bedford, NS, Canada B4A 1E2
(902)835-4122
Fax: (902)832-9389
E-mail: office@themarketingclinic.ca
Website: http://www.themarketingclinic.ca

Ontario

The Cynton Co.
17 Massey St.
Brampton, ON, Canada L6S 2V6
(905)792-7769
Fax: (905)792-8116
E-mail: cynton@home.com
Website: http://www.cynton.com

CRO Engineering Ltd.
1895 William Hodgins Ln.
Carp, ON, Canada K0A 1L0
(613)839-1108
Fax: (613)839-1406
E-mail: J.Grefford@ieee.ca

Business Plan World
PO Box 1322, Sta. B
Mississauga, ON, Canada L4Y 4B6
(709)643-8544
E-mail: theboss@businessplanworld.com
Website: http://www.businessplanworld.com

JPL Consulting
236 Millard Ave.
Newmarket, ON, Canada L3Y 1Z2
(416)606-9124
E-mail: sales@jplbiz.ca
Website: http://www.jplbiz.ca

Black Eagle Consulting 2000 Inc.
451 Barclay Cres.
Oakville, ON, Canada L6J 6H8
(905)842-3010
Fax: (905)842-9586
E-mail: info@blackeagle.ca
Website: http://www.blackeagle.ca

Care Concepts & Communications
21 Spruce Hill Rd.
Toronto, ON, Canada M4E 3G2
(416)420-8840
E-mail: info@cccbizconsultants.com
Website: http://www.cccbizconsultants
.com

FHG International Inc.
14 Glengrove Ave. W
Toronto, ON, Canada M4R 1N4
(416)402-8000
E-mail: info@fhgi.com
Website: http://www.fhgi.com

Harrison Pricing Strategy Group Inc.
1235 Bay St., Ste. 400
Toronto, ON, Canada M5R 3K4
(416)218-1103
Fax: (416) 827-8595

Ken Wyman & Associates Inc.
64 Lamb Ave.
Toronto, ON, Canada V
(416)362-2926
Fax: (416)362-3039
E-mail: kenwyman@compuserve.com

Quebec

PGP Consulting
17 Linton
Dollard-des-Ormeaux, QC, Canada H9B
1P2
(514)796-7613
Fax: (866)750-0947
E-mail: pierre@pgpconsulting.com
Website: http://www.pgpconsulting.com

Komand Consulting
1250 Rene Levesque Blvd.,W
22nd Fl., Ste. 2200
Montreal, QC, Canada H3B 4W8
(514)934-9281
Fax: (514)934-0770
E-mail: info@komand.ca
Website: http://www.komand.ca

Saskatchewan

Banda Marketing Group
410 - 22nd St. E, Ste. 810
Saskatoon, SK, Canada S7K 5T6
(306) 343-6100

Fax: (306) 652-1340
E-mail: admin@bandagroup.com
Website: http://www.bandagroup.com

Oracle Planning
106 28th St. W
Saskatoon, SK, Canada, S7L 0K2
(306) 717-5001
Fax: (650)618-2742

United states

Alabama

Business Planning Inc.
2090 Columbiana Rd., Ste. 2950
Vestavia Hills, AL 35216
(205)824-8969
Fax: (205)824-8939
E-mail: kmiller@businessplanninginc.com
Website: http://www. business
planninginc.com

Tradebank of Eastern Alabama
400 S St. E
Talladega, AL 35160
(256)761-9051
Fax: (256)761-9227

Alaska

Alaska Business Development Center
840 K St., Ste. 202
Anchorage, AK 99501
(907)562-0335
Free: 800-478-3474
Fax: (907)562-6988
E-mail: info@abdc.org
Website: http://www.abdc.org

Arizona

Carefree Direct Marketing Corp.
8001 E Serene St.
PO Box 3737
Carefree, AZ 85377-3737
(480)488-4227
Fax: (480)488-2841

Management 2000
39342 S Winding Trl.
Oro Valley, AZ 85737
(520)818-9988
Fax: (520)818-3277
E-mail: m2000@mgmt2000.com
Website: http://www.mgmt2000.com

CMAS
5125 N 16th St.
Phoenix, AZ 85016

(602)395-1001
Fax: (602)604-8180

Moneysoft Inc.
1 E Camelback Rd. #550
Phoenix, AZ 85012
Free: 800-966-7797
E-mail: mbray@moneysoft.com
Website: http://www.moneysoft.com

Harvey C. Skoog
7151 E Addis Ave.
Prescott Valley, AZ 86314
(928)772-1448

The De Angelis Group Inc.
9815 E Bell Rd., Ste. 120
Scottsdale, AZ 85260
(480)609-4868
Fax: (480)452-0401
E-mail: info@thedeangelisgroup.com
Website: http://www.thedeangelisgroup.com

Incendo Marketing L.L.C.
7687 E Thunderhawk Rd., Ste. 100
Scottsdale, AZ 85255
(480)513-4208
Fax: (509)561-9011

Sauerbrun Technology Group Ltd.
7979 E Princess Dr., Ste. 5
Scottsdale, AZ 85255-5878
(602)502-4950
Fax: (602)502-4292
E-mail: info@sauerbrun.com
Website: http://www.sauerbrun.com

Van Cleve Associates
6932 E 2nd St.
Tucson, AZ 85710
(520)296-2587
Fax: (520)296-3358

Variantia
6161 N Canon del Pajaro
Tucson, AZ 85750
(520)577-7680

Louws Management Corp.
PO Box 130
Vail, AZ 85641
(520)664-1881
Fax: (928)222-0086
E-mail: info@louwstraining.com
Website: http://www.louwsmanagement
.com

California

Thomas E. Church & Associates Inc.
PO Box 2439
Aptos, CA 95001
(831) 662-7950

Fax:(831) 684-0173
E-mail: thomase2@trueyellow.net
Website: http://www.thomas_church
.ypgs.net

AB Manley Partners Worldwide L.L.C.
1428 S Marengo Ave.
Alhambra, CA 91803-3096
(626) 457-8841

Lindquist Consultants-Venture Planning
225 Arlington Ave.
Berkeley, CA 94707
(510)524-6685
Fax: (510)527-6604

One Page Business Plan Co.
1798 Fifth St.
Berkeley, CA 94710
(510)705-8400
Fax: (510)705-8403
E-mail: info@onepagebusinessplan.com
Website: http://www.onepagebusiness
plan.com

WordCraft Creative Services
2687 Shasta Rd.
Berkeley, CA 94708
(510) 848-5177
Fax:(510) 868-1006
E-mail: info@wordcraftcreative.com
Website: http://www.wordcraft
creative.com

Growth Partners
1566 La Pradera Dr., Ste. 5
Campbell, CA 95008
(408) 871-7925
Fax: (408) 871-7924
E-mail: mark@growth-partners.com
Website: http://www.growth-partners
.com

The Success Resource
25773 Flanders Pl.
Carmel, CA 93923
(831) 236-0732

W and J PARTNERSHIP
PO Box 2499
18876 Edwin Markham Dr.
Castro Valley, CA 94546
(510)583-7751
Fax: (510)583-7645
E-mail: wamorgan@wjpartnership.com
Website: http://www.wjpartnership.com

JB Associates
21118 Gardena Dr.
Cupertino, CA 95014
(408)257-0214

Fax: (408)257-0216
E-mail: semarang@sirius.com

House Agricultural Consultants
1105 Kennedy Pl., Ste. 1
Davis, CA 95616
(916)753-3361
Fax: (916)753-0464
E-mail: infoag@houseag.com
Website: http://www.houseag.com/

3C Systems Co.
16161 Ventura Blvd., Ste. 815
Encino, CA 91436
(818)907-1302
Fax: (818)907-1357
E-mail: mark@3CSysCo.com
Website: http://www.3CSysCo.com

Technical Management Consultants
3624 Westfall Dr.
Encino, CA 91436-4154
(818)784-0626
Fax: (818)501-5575
E-mail: tmcrs@aol.com

Rainwater-Gish & Associates
317 3rd St., Ste. 3
Eureka, CA 95501
(707)443-0030
Fax: (707)443-5683

MedMarket Diligence L.L.C.
51 Fairfield
Foothill Ranch, CA 92610-1856
(949) 859-3401
Fax: (949) 837-4558
E-mail: info@mediligence.com
Website: http://www.mediligence.com

Global Tradelinks
451 Pebble Beach Pl.
Fullerton, CA 92835
(714)441-2280
Fax: (714)441-2281
E-mail: info@globaltradelinks.com
Website: http://www.globaltradelinks.com

Larson Associates
1440 Harbor Blvd., Ste. 800
Fullerton, CA 92835
(714)529-4121
Fax: (714)572-3606
E-mail: ray@consultlarson.com
Website: http://www.consultlarson.com

Strategic Business Group
800 Cienaga Dr.
Fullerton, CA 92835-1248
(714)449-1040
Fax: (714)525-1631

Burnes Consulting
20537 Wolf Creek Rd.
Grass Valley, CA 95949
(530)346-8188
Free: 800-949-9021
Fax: (530)346-7704
E-mail: kent@burnesconsulting.com
Website: http://www.burnesconsulting
.com

International Health Resources
PO Box 2738
Grass Valley, CA 95945
Website: http://www.futureofhealthcare
.com

Pioneer Business Consultants
9042 Garfield Ave., Ste. 211
Huntington Beach, CA 92646
(714)964-7600

Fluor Daniel Inc.
3353 Michelson Dr.
Irvine, CA 92612-0650
(949)975-2000
Fax: (949)975-5271
E-mail: sales.consulting@fluordaniel.com
Website: http://www.fluor.com

MCS Associates
18881 Von Karman, Ste. 1175
Irvine, CA 92612
(949)263-8700
Fax: (949)263-0770
E-mail: info@mcsassociates.com
Website: http://www.mcsassociates.com

Savvy Communications
9730 Soda Bay Rd., Ste. 5035
Kelseyville, CA 95451-9576
(707) 277-8078
Fax:(707) 277-8079

Sky Blue Consulting Inc.
4165 Executive Dr.
Lafayette, CA 94549
(925) 283-8272

Comprehensive Business Services
3201 Lucas Cir.
Lafayette, CA 94549
(925)283-8272
Fax: (925)283-8272

The Ribble Group
27601 Forbes Rd., Ste. 52
Laguna Niguel, CA 92677
(714)582-1085
Fax: (714)582-6420
E-mail: ribble@deltanet.com

Norris Bernstein, CMC
9309 Marina Pacifica Dr. N
Long Beach, CA 90803

(562)493-5458
Fax: (562)493-5459
E-mail: norris@ctecomputer.com
Website: http://foodconsultants.com/
bernstein/

Horizon Consulting Services
1315 Garthwick Dr.
Los Altos, CA 94024
(415)967-0906
Fax: (650)967-0906

Blue Garnet Associates L.L.C.
8055 W Manchester Ave., Ste. 430
Los Angeles, CA 90293
(310) 439-1930
Fax: (310) 388-1657
E-mail: hello@bluegarnet.net
Website: http://www.bluegarnet.net

CAST Management Consultants Inc.
700 S Flower St., Ste. 1900
Los Angeles, CA 90017
(213) 614-8066
Fax: (213) 614-0760
E-mail: info@castconsultants.com
Website: http://www.castconsultants.com

Rubenstein/Justman Management Consultants
11620 Wilshire Blvd., Ste. 750
Los Angeles, CA 90025
(310)445-5300
Fax: (310)496-1450
E-mail: info@rjmc.net
Website: http://www.rjmc.net

F.J. Schroeder & Associates
1926 Westholme Ave.
Los Angeles, CA 90025
(310)470-2655
Fax: (310)470-6378
E-mail: fjsacons@aol.com
Website: http://www.mcninet.com/
GlobalLook/Fjschroe.html

Western Management Associates
5777 W Century Blvd., Ste. 1220
Los Angeles, CA 90045
(310)645-1091
Free: (888)788-6534
Fax: (310)645-1092
E-mail: gene@cfoforrent.com
Website: http://www.cfoforrent.com

Inspiration Quest Inc.
PO Box 90
Mendocino, CA 95460
(415) 235-6002
E-mail: info@inspirationquest.com
Website: http://www.inspirationquest
.com

Heron Advisory Group
9 Heron Dr.
Mill Valley, CA 94941
(415) 380-8611
Fax: (415) 381-9044
E-mail: janetmca@pacbell.net
Website: http://www.hagroup.biz

Emacula Consulting Group
131 Draeger Dr., Ste. A
Moraga, CA 94556
(925) 388-6083
Fax: (267) 589-3151
E-mail: drochlin@emacula.com
Website: http://www.emacula.com

BizplanSource
1048 Irvine Ave., Ste. 621
Newport Beach, CA 92660
Free: 888-253-0974
Fax: 800-859-8254
E-mail: info@bizplansource.com
Website: http://www.bizplansource.com
Adam Greengrass, President

The Market Connection
20051 SW Birch St., Ste 310
Newport Beach, CA 92660
(949)851-6313
Fax: (949)833-0283

Intelequest Corp.
722 Gailen Ave.
Palo Alto, CA 94303
(415)968-3443
Fax: (415)493-6954
E-mail: frits@iqix.com

Beblie, Brandt & Jacobs Inc.
19 Brista del Lago
Rancho Santa Margarita, CA 92618
(949)589-5120
Fax: (949)203-6225
E-mail: darcy@bbjinc.com

California Business Incubation Network
225 Broadway, Ste. 2250
San Diego, CA 92101
(619)237-0559
Fax: (619)237-0521

The Drake Group
824 Santa Clara Pl.
San Diego, CA 92109-7224
(858) 488-3911
Fax: (810) 454-4593
E-mail: cdrake@drakegroup.com
Website: http://www.drakegroup.com

G.R. Gordetsky Consultants Inc.
11414 Windy Summit Pl.
San Diego, CA 92127

(858)487-4939
E-mail: gordet@pacbell.net

Noorany Marketing Resources
3830 Valley Centre Dr., Ste. 705
San Diego, CA 92130
(858) 792-9559
Fax: (858) 259-2320
E-mail: heidi@noorany.com
Website: http://www.noorany.com

Freeman, Sullivan & Co.
1101 Montgomery St., 15th Fl.
San Francisco, CA 94104
Website: http://www.fscgroup.com

PKF Consulting Corp.
50 California St., 19th Fl.
San Francisco, CA 94111
(415)788-3102
Fax: (415)433-7844
E-mail: callahan@pkfc.com
Website: http://www.pkfc.com

Welling & Woodard Inc.
1067 Broadway
San Francisco, CA 94133
(415)776-4500
Fax: (415)776-5067

Highland Associates
16174 Highland Dr.
San Jose, CA 95127
(408)272-7008
Fax: (408)272-4040

Leckrone Law Corp.
4010 Moorpark Ave., Ste. 215
San Jose, CA 95117-1843
(408) 243-9898
Fax: (408) 296-6637

ORDIS Inc.
6815 Trinidad Dr.
San Jose, CA 95120-2056
(408)268-3321
Free: 800-446-7347
Fax: (408)268-3582
E-mail: ordis@ordis.com
Website: http://www.ordis.com

Bay Area Tax Consultants and Bayhill Financial Consultants
1840 Gateway Dr.
San Mateo, CA 94404
(650)378-1373
Fax: (650)585-5444
E-mail: admin@baytax.com
Website: http://www.baytax.com/

Helfert Associates
111 St. Matthews, Ste. 307
San Mateo, CA 94401

(650)377-0540
Fax: (650)377-0472

Mykytyn Consulting Group Inc.
185 N Redwood Dr., Ste. 200
San Rafael, CA 94903
(415)491-1770
Fax: (415)491-1251
E-mail: info@mcgi.com

Omega Management Systems Inc.
3 Mount Darwin Ct.
San Rafael, CA 94903-1109
(415)499-1300
Fax: (415)492-9490
E-mail: information@omegamgt.com

Manex Consulting
2010 Crow Canyon Pl., Ste. 320
San Ramon, CA 94583
(925) 807-5100
Website: http://
www.manexconsulting.com

Brincko Associates Inc.
530 Wilshire Blvd., Ste. 201
Santa Monica, CA 90401
(310)553-4523
Fax: (310)553-6782

hE Myth
131B Stony Cir., Ste. 2000
Santa Rosa, CA 95401
(541)552-4600
Free: 800-300-3531
E-mail: info@emyth.com
Website: http://www.emyth.com

Figueroa Farms L.L.C.
PO Box 206
Santa Ynez, CA 93460
(805) 686-4890
Fax: (805) 686-2887
E-mail: info@figueroafarms.com
Website: http://www.FigueroaFarms.com

Reilly, Connors & Ray
1743 Canyon Rd.
Spring Valley, CA 91977
(619)698-4808
Fax: (619)460-3892
E-mail: davidray@adnc.com

RJR Associates
1639 Lewiston Dr.
Sunnyvale, CA 94087
(408)737-7720
E-mail: bobroy@rjrassoc.com
Website: http://www.rjrassoc.com

Schwafel Associates
333 Cobalt Way, Ste. 107
Sunnyvale, CA 94085

(408)720-0649
Fax: (408)720-1796
E-mail: schwafel@ricochet.net
Website: http://www.patca.org

The International Coverting Institute
5200 Badger Rd
Terrebonne, CA 97760
(503) 548-1447
Fax: (503) 548-1618

GlobalReady
1521 Kirk Ave.
Thousand Oaks, CA 91360
(805) 427-4131
E-mail: info@globalready.com
Website: http://www.globalready.com

Staubs Business Services
23320 S Vermont Ave.
Torrance, CA 90502-2940
(310)830-9128
Fax: (310)830-9128
E-mail: Harry_L_Staubs@Lamg.com

Enterprise Management Corp.
17461 Irvine Blvd., Ste. M
Tustin, CA 92780
(714) 505-1925
Fax: (714) 505-9691
E-mail: cfotogo@companycfo.com
Website: http://www.companycfo.com

Out of Your Mind . . . and Into the Marketplace
13381 White Sands Dr.
Tustin, CA 92780-4565
(714)544-0248
Free: 800-419-1513
Fax: (714)730-1414
Website: http://www.business-plan.com

Ingman Company Inc.
7949 Woodley Ave., Ste. 120
Van Nuys, CA 91406-1232
(805)650-9353
Fax: (805)984-2979

Innovative Technology Associates
3639 E Harbor Blvd., Ste. 203E
Ventura, CA 93001
(805)650-9353

Grid Technology Associates
20404 Tufts Cir.
Walnut, CA 91789
(909)444-0922
Fax: (909)444-0922

Bell Springs Publishing
PO Box 1240
Willits, CA 95490
(707)459-6372

E-mail: bellsprings@sabernet
Website: http://www.bellsprings.com

Hutchinson Consulting and Appraisal
23245 Sylvan St., Ste. 103
Woodland Hills, CA 91367
(818)888-8175
Free: 800-977-7548
Fax: (818)888-8220
E-mail: r.f.hutchinson-cpa@worldnet
.att.net

Colorado

Sam Boyer & Associates
4255 S Buckley Rd., No. 136
Aurora, CO 80013
(303)766-1557
Free: 800-785-0485
Fax: (303)766-8740
E-mail: samboyer@samboyer.com
Website: http://www.samboyer.com/

Associated Enterprises Ltd.
183 Pauls Ln.
Bailey, CO 80421

Comer & Associates LLC
5255 Holmes Pl.
Boulder, CO 80303
(303) 786-7986
Fax: (303)895-2347
E-mail: jerry@comerassociates.com
Website: http://www.comerassociates
.com

Ameriwest Business Consultants Inc.
3725 E. Wade Ln.
Colorado Springs, CO 80917
(719)380-7096
Fax: (719)380-7096
E-mail: email@abchelp.com
Website: http://www.abchelp.com

GVNW Consulting Inc.
2270 La Montana Way
Colorado Springs, CO 80936
(719)594-5800
Fax: (719)594-5803
Website: http://www.gvnw.com

M-Squared Inc.
755 San Gabriel Pl.
Colorado Springs, CO 80906
(719)576-2554
Fax: (719)576-2554

Foxhall Consulting Services
2532 Dahlia St.
Denver, CO 80207
(303)355-7995
Fax: (303)377-0716

E-mail: michael@foxhallconsulting.com
Website: http://www.foxhallconsulting
.com

KLA Associates
2352 Humboldt St.
Denver, CO 80205-5332
(303)830-8042

Wilson Hughes Consulting LLC
2100 Humboldt St., Ste. 302
Denver, CO 80205
Website: http://www.wilsonhughes
consultingllc.com

Co-Active Communications Corp.
400 Inverness Pkwy., Ste. 200
Englewood, CO 80112-6415
(303)771-6181
Fax: (303)771-0080

Thornton Financial FNIC
1024 Centre Ave., Bldg. E
Fort Collins, CO 80526-1849
(970)221-2089
Fax: (970)484-5206

Extelligent Inc.
8400 E Crescent Pky., Ste. 600
Greenwood Village, CO 80111
(720)201-5672
E-mail: info@extelligent.com
Website: http://www.extelligent.com

Western Capital Holdings Inc.
10050 E Applwood Dr.
Parker, CO 80138
(303)841-1022
Fax: (303)770-1945

Connecticut

Christiansen Consulting
56 Scarborough St.
Hartford, CT 06105
(860)586-8265
Fax: (860)233-3420
Website: http://www.Christiansen
Consulting.com

Follow-up News
185 Pine St., Ste. 818
Manchester, CT 06040
(860)647-7542
Free: 800-708-0696
Fax: (860)646-6544
E-mail: Followupnews@aol.com

Musevue360
555 Millbrook Rd.
Middletown, CT 06457
(860)463-7722
Fax: (860)346-3013

E-mail: jennifer.eifrig@musevue360.com
Website: http://www.musevue360.com

Alltis Corp.
747 Farmington Ave., Ste. 6
New Britain, CT 06053
(860)224-1300
Fax: (860)224-1700
E-mail: info@alltis.com
Website: http://www.alltis.com

Kalba International Inc.
116 McKinley Ave.
New Haven, CT 06515
(203)397-2199
Fax: (781)240-2657
E-mail: kalba@comcast.net
Website: http://www.kalbainternational
.com

Lovins & Associates Consulting
357 Whitney Ave.
New Haven, CT 06511
(203)787-3367
Fax: (203)624-7599
E-mail: Alovinsphd@aol.com
Website: http://www.lovinsgroup.com

JC Ventures Inc.
4 Arnold St.
Old Greenwich, CT 06870-1203
(203)698-1990
Free: 800-698-1997
Fax: (203)698-2638

Charles L. Hornung Associates
52 Ned's Mountain Rd.
Ridgefield, CT 06877
(203)431-0297

Greenwich Associates
6 High Ridge Park
Stamford, CT 06905
(203)629-1200
Fax: (203)629-1229
E-mail: lisa@greenwich.com
Website: http://www.greenwich.com

Management Practice Inc.
216 W Hill Rd.
Stamford, CT 06902
(203)973-0535
Fax: (203)978-9034
E-mail: mpayne@mpiweb.com
Website: http://www.mpiweb.com

RealBusinessPlans.com
156 Westport Rd.
Wilton, CT 06897
(914)837-2886

E-mail: ct@realbusinessplans.com
Website: http://www.RealBusinessPlans
.com

Wellspring Consulting LLC
198 Amity Rd., 2nd Fl.
Woodbridge, CT 06525
(203)387-7192
Fax: (203)387-1345
E-mail: info@wellspringconsulting.net
Website: http://www.wellspring
consulting.net

Delaware

Focus Marketing
61-7 Habor Dr.
Claymont, DE 19703
(302)793-3064

Daedalus Ventures Ltd.
PO Box 1474
Hockessin, DE 19707
(302)239-6758
Fax: (302)239-9991
E-mail: daedalus@mail.del.net

The Formula Group
PO Box 866
Hockessin, DE 19707
(302)456-0952
Fax: (302)456-1354
E-mail: formula@netaxs.com

Selden Enterprises Inc.
2502 Silverside Rd., Ste. 1
Wilmington, DE 19810-3740
(302)529-7113
Fax: (302)529-7442
E-mail: selden2@bellatlantic.net
Website: http://
www.seldenenterprises.com

District of Columbia

The Breen Consulting Group LLC
1101 Pennsylvania Ave, NW, 7th Fl.
Washington, DC 20004
(877)881-4688
E-mail: sales@joebreen.com
Website: http://www.joebreen.com

Catalysr IpF
1514Upshur St. NW
Washington, DC 20011
(202)230-2662
E-mail: contact@catalystipf.com
Website: http://www.catalystipf.com

Smith, Dawson & Andrews Inc.
1150 Connecticut Ave., Ste. 1025
Washington, DC 20036
(202)835-0740

Fax: (202)775-8526
E-mail: webmaster@sda-inc.com
Website: http://www.sda-inc.com

1000 Cranes LLC
1425 K St. NW, Ste. 350
Washington, DC 20005
(202)587-2737
E-mail: info@1000cranes.com
Website: http://www.1000cranes.com

Florida

BackBone, Inc.
20404 Hacienda Court
Boca Raton, FL 33498
(561)470-0965
Fax: 516-908-4038
E-mail: BPlans@backboneinc.com
Website: http://www.backboneinc.com

Dr. Eric H Shaw and Associates
500 South Ocean Blvd., Ste. 2105
Boca Raton, FL 33432
(561)338-5151
E-mail: ericshaw@bellsouth.net
Website: http://www.ericshaw.com

E.N. Rysso & Associates
180 Bermuda Petrel Ct.
Daytona Beach, FL 32119
(386)760-3028
E-mail: erysso@aol.com

Eric Sands Consulting Services
6750 N. Andrews Ave., Ste. 200
Fort Lauderdale, FL 33309
(954)721-4767
Fax: (954)720-2815
E-mail: easands@aol.com
Website: http://
www.ericsandsconsultig.com

F.A. McGee Inc.
800 Claughton Island Dr., Ste. 401
Miami, FL 33131
(305)377-9123

Strategic Business Planning Co.
12000 Biscayne Blvd., Ste. 203
Miami, FL 33181
(954)704-9100
E-mail: info@bizplan.com
Website: http://www.bizplan.com

Professional Planning Associates, Inc.
1440 NE 35th St.
Oakland Park, FL 33334
(954)829-2523
Fax:(954)537-7945
E-mail: Mgoldstein@proplana.com
Website: http://proplana.com
Michael Goldstein, President

Hunter G. Jackson Jr.
3409 Canoga Dr.
Orlando, FL 32861-8272
(407)245-7682
E-mail: hunterjackson@juno.com

F. Newton Parks
210 El Brillo Way
Palm Beach, FL 33480
(561)833-1727
Fax: (561)833-4541

Hughes Consulting Services LLC
522 Alternate 19
Palm Harbor, FL 34683
(727)631-2536
Fax: (727)474-9818
Website: http://consultinghughes.com

Avery Business Development Services
2506 St. Michel Ct.
Ponte Vedra Beach, FL 32082
(904)280-8840
Fax: (904)285-6033

Dufresne Consulting Group Inc.
10014 N Dale Mabry, Ste. 101
Tampa, FL 33618-4426
(813)264-4775
Fax: (813)264-9300
Website: http://www.dcgconsult.com

Tunstall Consulting LLC
13153 N. Dale Mabry Hwy., Ste. 200
Tampa, FL 33618
(813)968-4461
Fax: (813)961-2315
Website: http://www.tunstallconsulting
.com

The Business Planning Institute, LLC.
580 Village Blvd., Ste. 150
West Palm Beach, FL 33409
(561)236-5533
Fax: (561)689-5546
Website: http://www.bpiplans.com

Georgia

Fountainhead Consulting Group, Inc.
3970 Old Milton Pkwy, Ste. 210
Atlanta, GA 30005
(770)642-4220
Website: http://www.fountainhead
consultinggroup.com/

CHScottEnterprises
227 Sandy Springs P., NE, Ste. 720702
Atlanta, GA 30358
(770)356-4808
E-mail: info@chscottenterprises.com
Website: http://www.chscottenterprises
.com

US Business Plan Inc.
1200 Barrett Pky., Ste. 4-400
Kennesaw, GA 30144
(770)794-8000
Website: http://www.usbusinessplan.com

Business Ventures Corp.
1650 Oakbrook Dr., Ste. 405
Norcross, GA 30093
(770)729-8000
Fax: (770)729-8028

Tom C. Davis CPA LLC
1808-A Plum St.
Valdosta, GA 31601
(229)247-9801
Fax:(229) 244-7704
E-mail: mail@tcdcpa.com
Website: http://www.tcdcpa.com/

Illinois

TWD and Associates
431 S Patton
Arlington Heights, IL 60005
(847)398-6410
Fax: (847)255-5095
E-mail: tdoo@aol.com

Management Planning Associates Inc.
2275 Half Day Rd., Ste. 350
Bannockburn, IL 60015-1277
(847)945-2421
Fax: (847)945-2425

Phil Faris Associates
86 Old Mill Ct.
Barrington, IL 60010
(847)382-4888
Fax: (847)382-4890
E-mail: pfaris@meginsnet.net

Seven Continents Technology
787 Stonebridge
Buffalo Grove, IL 60089
(708)577-9653
Fax: (708)870-1220

Grubb & Blue Inc.
2404 Windsor Pl.
Champaign, IL 61820
(217)366-0052
Fax: (217)356-0117

ACE Accounting Service Inc.
3128 N Bernard St.
Chicago, IL 60618
(773)463-7854
Fax: (773)463-7854

AON Consulting Worldwide
200 E Randolph St., 10th Fl.
Chicago, IL 60601

(312)381-4800
Free: 800-438-6487
Fax: (312)381-0240
Website: http://www.aon.com

FMS Consultants
5801 N Sheridan Rd., Ste. 3D
Chicago, IL 60660
(773)561-7362
Fax: (773)561-6274

Grant Thornton
800 1 Prudential Plz.
130 E Randolph St.
Chicago, IL 60601
(312)856-0001
Fax: (312)861-1340
E-mail: gtinfo@gt.com
Website: http://www.grantthornton.com

Kingsbury International Ltd.
5341 N Glenwood Ave.
Chicago, IL 60640
(773)271-3030
Fax: (773)728-7080
E-mail: jetlag@mcs.com
Website: http://www.kingbiz.com

MacDougall & Blake Inc.
1414 N Wells St., Ste. 311
Chicago, IL 60610-1306
(312)587-3330
Fax: (312)587-3699
E-mail: jblake@compuserve.com

James C. Osburn Ltd.
6445 N. Western Ave., Ste. 304
Chicago, IL 60645
(773)262-4428
Fax: (773)262-6755
E-mail: osburnltd@aol.com

Tarifero & Tazewell Inc.
211 S Clark
Chicago, IL 60690
(312)665-9714
Fax: (312)665-9716

Human Energy Design Systems
620 Roosevelt Dr.
Edwardsville, IL 62025
(618)692-0258
Fax: (618)692-0819

China Business Consultants Group
931 Dakota Cir.
Naperville, IL 60563
(630)778-7992
Fax: (630)778-7915
E-mail: cbcq@aol.com

Center for Workforce Effectiveness
500 Skokie Blvd., Ste. 222
Northbrook, IL 60062
(847)559-7777

Fax: (847)559-8778
E-mail: office@cwelink.com
Website: http://www.cwelink.com

Smith Associates
1320 White Mountain Dr.
Northbrook, IL 60062
(847)480-7200
Fax: (847)480-9828

Francorp Inc.
20200 Governors Dr.
Olympia Fields, IL 60461
(708)481-2900
Free: 800-372-6244
Fax: (708)481-5885
E-mail: francorp@aol.com
Website: http://www.francorpinc.com

Camber Business Strategy Consultants
1010 S Plum Tree Ct
Palatine, IL 60078-0986
(847)202-0101
Fax: (847)705-7510
E-mail: camber@ameritech.net

Partec Enterprise Group
5202 Keith Dr.
Richton Park, IL 60471
(708)503-4047
Fax: (708)503-9468

Rockford Consulting Group Ltd.
Century Plz., Ste. 206
7210 E State St.
Rockford, IL 61108
(815)229-2900
Free: 800-667-7495
Fax: (815)229-2612
E-mail: rligus@RockfordConsulting.com
Website: http://www.Rockford
Consulting.com

RSM McGladrey Inc.
1699 E Woodfield Rd., Ste. 300
Schaumburg, IL 60173-4969
(847)413-6900
Fax: (847)517-7067
Website: http://www.rsmmcgladrey.com

A.D. Star Consulting
320 Euclid
Winnetka, IL 60093
(847)446-7827
Fax: (847)446-7827
E-mail: startwo@worldnet.att.net

Indiana

Bingham Economic Development Advisors
8900 Keystone Xing
Indianapolis, IN 46240
(317)968-5576

Ketchum Consulting Group
7575 Copperfield Way
Indianapolis, IN 46256
(317)845-5411
Fax: (317)842-9941

Cox and Company
3930 Mezzanine Dr. Ste A
Lafayette, IN, 47905
(765)449-4495
Fax: (765)449-1218
E-mail: stan@coxpa.com

Iowa

McCord Consulting Group Inc.
3425 Sycamore Ct. NE
Cedar Rapids, IA 52402
(319)378-0077
Fax: (319)378-1577
E-mail: sam@mccordgroup.com

Management Solutions L.L.C.
3815 Lincoln Pl. Dr.
Des Moines, IA 50312
(515)277-6408
Fax: (515)277-3506

Kansas

Aspire Business Development
10955 Lowell Ave., Ste. 400
Overland Park, KS 66210
(913)660-9400
Free: (888)548-1504
Website: http://www.aspirekc.com

Maine

Pan Atlantic SMS Group Inc.
6 City Ctr., Ste. 200
Portland, ME 04101
(207)871-8622
Fax: (207)772-4842
E-mail: pmurphy@panatlanticsmsgroup
.com
Website: http://www.panatlanticsms
group.com

Maryland

Clemons & Associates Inc.
5024-R Campbell Blvd.
Baltimore, MD 21236
(410)931-8100
Fax: (410)931-8111
E-mail: info@clemonsmgmt.com
Website: http://www.clemonsmgmt.com

Employee Benefits Group Inc.
4405 E West Hwy., Ste. 202
Bethesda, MD 20814
(301) 718-4637

Fax: (301) 907-0176
E-mail: info@ebg.com
Website: http://www.ebg.com

Burdeshaw Associates Ltd.
4701 Sangamore Rd.
Bethesda, MD 20816-2508
(301)229-5800
Fax: (301)229-5045
E-mail: jstacy@burdeshaw.com
Website: http://www.burdeshaw.com

Michael E. Cohen
5225 Pooks Hill Rd., Ste. 1119 S
Bethesda, MD 20814
(301)530-5738
Fax: (301)530-2988
E-mail: mecohen@crosslink.net

World Development Group Inc.
5800 Madaket Rd., Ste. 100
Bethesda, MD 20816
(301) 320-0971
Fax: (301) 320-0978
E-mail: wdg@worlddg.com
Website: http://www.worlddg.com

Creative Edge Consulting
6047 Wild Ginger Ct.
Columbia, MD 21044
(443) 545-5863
Website: http://
www.creativeedgeconsulting.org

Paul Yelder Consulting
9581 Standon Pl.
Columbia, MD 21045
(410) 740-8417
E-mail: consulting@yelder.com
Website: http://www.yelder.com

Hammer Marketing Resources
19118 Silver Maple Ct.
Hagerstown, MD 21742
(301) 733-8891
Fax: (305) 675-3277

Strategies
8 Park Center Ct., Ste. 200
Owings Mills, MD 21117
(410)363-6669
Fax: (410)363-1231
E-mail: info@strategiescorp.net
Website: http://www.strategiescorp.net

Managance Consulting and Coaching
1708 Chester Mill Rd.
Silver Spring, MD 20906
(301) 260-9503
E-mail: info@managance.com
Website: http://www.managance.com

Andrew Sussman & Associates
13731 Kretsinger
Smithsburg, MD 21783
(301)824-2943
Fax: (301)824-2943

Massachusetts

Geibel Marketing and Public Relations
PO Box 611
Belmont, MA 02478-0005
(617)484-8285
Fax: (617)489-3567
E-mail: jgeibel@geibelpr.com
Website: http://www.geibelpr.com

Bain & Co.
131 Dartmouth St.
Boston, MA 02116
(617)572-2000
Fax: (617)572-2427
E-mail: corporate.inquiries@bain.com
Website: http://www.bain.com

Fairmont Consulting Group
470 Atlantic Ave., 4th Fl.
Boston, MA 02210
(617)217-2401
Fax: (617)939-0262
E-mail: info@fairmontcg.com
Website: http://www.fairmontcg.com

Information & Research Associates
PO Box 3121
Framingham, MA 01701
(508)788-0784

Walden Consultants Ltd.
252 Pond St.
Hopkinton, MA 01748
(508)435-4882
Fax: (508)435-3971
Website: http://www.waldenconsultants
.com

Consulting Resources Corp.
6 Northbrook Park
Lexington, MA 02420
(781)863-1222
Fax: (781)863-1441
E-mail: res@consultingresources.net
Website: http://www.consultingre
sources.net

Mehr & Co.
31 Woodcliffe Rd.
Lexington, MA 02421
(781)372-1055

Real Resources
27 Indian Hill Rd.
Medfield, MA 02052
(508)359-6780

VMB Associates Inc.
115 Ashland St.
Melrose, MA 02176
(781)665-0623
Fax: (425)732-7142
E-mail: vmbinc@aol.com

The Company Doctor
14 Pudding Stone Ln.
Mendon, MA 01756
(508)478-1747
Fax: (508)478-0520

Data and Strategies Group Inc.
190 N Main St.
Natick, MA 01760
(508)653-9990
Fax: (508)653-7799
E-mail: dsginc@dsggroup.com
Website: http://www.dsggroup.com

The Enterprise Group
73 Parker Rd.
Needham, MA 02494
(617)444-6631
Fax: (617)433-9991
E-mail: lsacco@world.std.com
Website: http://www.enterprise-group.com

PSMJ Resources Inc.
10 Midland Ave.
Newton, MA 02458
(617)965-0055
Free: 800-537-7765
Fax: (617)965-5152
E-mail: psmj@tiac.net
Website: http://www.psmj.com

Non Profit Capital Management
41 Main St.
Sterling, MA 01564
(781)933-6726
Fax: (781)933-6734

Michigan

BBC Entrepreneurial Training & Consulting LLC
803 N Main St.
Ann Arbor, MI 48104
(734)930-9741
Fax: (734)930-6629
E-mail: info@bioconsultants.com
Website: http://www.bioconsultants.com

Center for Simplified Strategic Planning Inc.
2219 Packard Rd., Ste. 13
Ann Arbor, MI 48104
(734)995-3465
E-mail: tidd@cssp.com
Website: http://www.cssp.com

Walter Frederick Consulting
1719 South Blvd.
Ann Arbor, MI 48104
(313)662-4336
Fax: (313)769-7505

Aimattech Consulting LLC
568 Woodway Ct., Ste. 1
Bloomfield Hills, MI 48302
(248) 540-3758
Fax: (248) 540-3011
E-mail: dpwconsult@aol.com
Website: http://www.aimattech.com

QualSAT International Inc.
30777 NW Highway., Ste. 101
Farmington Hills, MI 48334
866-899-0020
Fax: (248)932-3801
E-mail: info@qualsat.com
Website: http://www.qualsat.com

Fox Enterprises
6220 W Freeland Rd.
Freeland, MI 48623
(989)695-9170
Fax: (989)695-9174

T. L. Cramer Associates LLC
1788 Broadstone Rd.
Grosse Pointe Woods, MI 48236
(313)332-0182
E-mail: info@tlcramerassociates.com
Website: http://www.tlcramerassociates
.com

G.G.W. and Associates
1213 Hampton
Jackson, MI 49203
(517)782-2255
Fax: (517)782-2255

BHM Associates Inc.
2817 Canterbury Dr.
Midland, MI 48642
(989) 631-7109
E-mail: smiller@bhmassociates.net
Website: http://www.bhmassociates.net

MarketingHelp Inc.
6647 Riverwoods Ct. NE
Rockford, MI 49341
(616) 866-1198
Website: http://www.mktghelp.com

Rehmann, Robson PC
5800 Gratiot
Saginaw, MI 48605
(989)799-9580
Fax: (989)799-0227
E-mail: info@rehmann.com
Website: http://www.rehmann.com

Private Ventures Inc.
16000 W 9 Mile Rd., Ste. 504
Southfield, MI 48075
(248)569-1977
Free: 800-448-7614
Fax: (248)569-1838
E-mail: pventuresi@aol.com

JGK Associates
14464 Kerner Dr.
Sterling Heights, MI 48313
(810)247-9055
Fax: (248)822-4977
E-mail: kozlowski@home.com

Cool & Associates Inc.
921 Village Green Ln., Ste. 1068
Waterford, MI 48328
(248)683-1130
E-mail: jcool@cool-associates.com
Website: http://www.cool-associates.com

Griffioen Consulting Group Inc.
6689 Orchard Lake Rd., Ste. 295
West Bloomfield, MI 48322
(888)262-5850
Fax: (248)855-4084
Website: http://www.griffioenconsulting.com

Minnesota

Health Fitness Corp.
31700 W 82nd St., Ste. 200
Minneapolis, MN 55431
(952)831-6830
E-mail: info@hfit.com
Website: http://www.hfit.com

Consatech Inc.
PO Box 1047
Burnsville, MN 55337
(612)953-1088
Fax: (612)435-2966

Kaes Analytics Inc.
14960 Ironwood Ct.
Eden Prairie, MN 55346
(952)942-2912

DRI Consulting
2 Otter Ln.
Saint Paul, MN 55127
(651)415-1400
Fax: (651)415-9968
E-mail: dric@dric.com
Website: http://www.dric.com

Markin Consulting
12072 87th Pl. N
Maple Grove, MN 55369
(763)493-3568
Fax: (763)322-5013
E-mail: markin@markinconsulting.com

Website: http://www.markinconsulting
.com

Minnesota Cooperation Office for Small Business & Job Creation Inc.
5001 W 80th St., Ste. 825
Minneapolis, MN 55437
(612)830-1230
Fax: (612)830-1232
E-mail: mncoop@msn.com
Website: http://www.mnco.org

Power Systems Research
1365 Corporate Center Curve, 2nd Fl.
St. Paul, MN 55121
(612)905-8400
Free: (888)625-8612
Fax: (612)454-0760
E-mail: Barb@Powersys.com
Website: http://www.powersys.com

Missouri

Business Planning and Development Corp.
4030 Charlotte St.
Kansas City, MO 64110
(816)753-0495
E-mail: humph@bpdev.demon.co.uk
Website: http://www.bpdev.demon.co.uk

CFO Service
10336 Donoho
St. Louis, MO 63131
(314)750-2940
E-mail: jskae@cfoservice.com
Website: http://www.cfoservice.com

Nebraska

International Management Consulting Group Inc.
1309 Harlan Dr., Ste. 205
Bellevue, NE 68005
(402)291-4545
Free: 800-665-IMCG
Fax: (402)291-4343
E-mail: imcg@neonramp.com
Website: http://www.mgtconsulting.com

Heartland Management Consulting Group
1904 Barrington Pky.
Papillion, NE 68046
(402)952-5339
Fax: (402)339-1319

Nevada

The DuBois Group
865 Tahoe Blvd., Ste. 108
Incline Village, NV 89451

(775)832-0550
Free: 800-375-2935
Fax: (775)832-0556
E-mail: DuBoisGrp@aol.com

New Hampshire

Wolff Consultants
10 Buck Rd.
Hanover, NH 03755
(603)643-6015

BPT Consulting Associates Ltd.
12 Parmenter Rd., Ste. B-6
Londonderry, NH 03053
(603)437-8484
Free: (888)278-0030
Fax: (603)434-5388
E-mail: bptcons@tiac.net
Website: http://www.bptconsulting.com

New Jersey

Delta Planning Inc.
138 Hillcrest Dr.
Denville, NJ 07834
(913)625-1742
Free: 800-672-0762
Fax: (973)625-3531
E-mail: DeltaP@worldnet.att.net
Website: http://deltaplanning.com

Kumar Associates Inc.
1004 Cumbermeade Rd.
Fort Lee, NJ 07024
(201)224-9480
Fax: (201)585-2343
E-mail: mail@kumarassociates.com
Website: http://kumarassociates.com

John Hall & Company Inc.
14 Houston Rd.
Little Falls, NJ 07424
(973)680-4449
Fax: (973)680-4581
E-mail: jhcompany@aol.com

Market Focus
12 Maryland Rd.
Maplewood, NJ 07040
(973)378-2470
Fax: (973)378-2470
E-mail: mcss66@marketfocus.com

Distinctive Marketing Inc.
516 Bloomfield Ave., Ste. 7
Montclair, NJ 07042
(973)746-9114
Fax: (973)783-5555
Website: http://www.distinctivemktg
.com

Vanguard Communications Corp.
45 S Park Pl., Ste. 210
Morristown, NJ 07960
(973)605-8000
Fax: (973)605-8329
Website: http://www.vanguard.net/

Bedminster Group Inc.
16 Arrowhead Dr.
Neshanic Station, NJ 08853
 (908)347-0006
Fax: (908)369-4767
E-mail: info@bedminstergroup.com
Website: http://www.bedminstergroup
.com

ConMar International Ltd.
1405 Rte. 18, Ste. 200
Old Bridge, NJ 08857
(732)607-6415
Fax: (732)607-6480
Website: http://www.conmar-intl.com

PA Consulting Group
600 Alexander Pk., Ste. 209A
Princeton, NJ 08540
(609)806-0800
Fax: (609)936-8811
E-mail: info@paconsulting.com
Website: http://www.pa-consulting.com

Aurora Marketing Management Inc.
66 Witherspoon St., Ste. 600
Princeton, NJ 08542
(908)904-1125
Fax: (908)359-1108
E-mail: aurora2@voicenet.com
Website: http://www.auroramarketing
.net

Schkeeper Inc.
130-6 Bodman Pl.
Red Bank, NJ 07701
(732)219-1965
Fax: (732)530-3703
Website: http://www.schkeeper.com

Henry Branch Associates
2502 Harmon Cove Twr.
Secaucus, NJ 07094
(201)866-2008
Fax: (201)601-0101
E-mail: hbranch161@home.com

Robert Gibbons & Company Inc.
46 Knoll Rd.
Tenafly, NJ 07670-1050
(201)871-3933
Fax: (201)871-2173

PMC Management Consultants Inc.
6 Thistle Ln.
Three Bridges, NJ 08887-0332

(908)788-1014
Free: 800-PMC-0250
Fax: (908)806-7287
E-mail: inguiry@pmc-management.com
Website: http://www.pmc-management
.com

R.W. Bankart & Associates
20 Valley Ave., Ste. D-2
Westwood, NJ 07675-3607
(201)664-7672

New Mexico

Vondle & Associates Inc.
4926 Calle de Tierra, NE
Albuquerque, NM 87111
(505)292-8961
Fax: (505)296-2790
E-mail: vondle@aol.com

InfoNewMexico
2207 Black Hills Rd., NE
Rio Rancho, NM 87124
(505)891-2462
Fax: (505)896-8971

New York

Powers Research and Training Institute
PO Box 78
Bayville, NY 11709
(516)628-2250
Fax: (516)628-2252
E-mail: powercocch@compuserve.com
Website: http://www.nancypowers.com

Consortium House
296 Wittenberg Rd.
Bearsville, NY 12409
(845)679-8867
Fax: (845)679-9248
E-mail: eugenegs@aol.com
Website: http://www.chpub.com

Progressive Finance Corp.
3549 Tiemann Ave.
Bronx, NY 10469
(718)405-9029
Free: 800-225-8381
Fax: (718)405-1170

Wave Hill Associates Inc.
2621 Palisade Ave., Ste. 15-C
Bronx, NY 10463
(718)549-7368
Fax: (718)601-9670
E-mail: pepper@compuserve.com

Management Insight
96 Arlington Rd.
Buffalo, NY 14221
(716)631-3319

Fax: (716)631-0203
E-mail: michalski@foodserviceinsight.com
Website: http://www.foodserviceinsight
.com

**Samani International Enterprises,
Marions Panyaught Consultancy**
2028 Parsons
Flushing, NY 11357-3436
(917)287-8087
Fax: 800-873-8939
E-mail: vjp2@biostrategist.com
Website: http://www.biostrategist.com

Marketing Resources Group
71-58 Austin St.
Forest Hills, NY 11375
(718)261-8882

**Mangabay Business Plans &
Development**

Subsidiary of Innis Asset Allocation
125-10 Queens Blvd., Ste. 2202
Kew Gardens, NY 11415
(905)527-1947
Fax: 509-472-1935
E-mail: mangabay@mangabay.com
Website: http://www.mangabay.com
Lee Toh, Managing Partner

ComputerEase Co.
1301 Monmouth Ave.
Lakewood, NY 08701
(212)406-9464
Fax: (914)277-5317
E-mail: crawfordc@juno.com

Boice Dunham Group
30 W 13th St.
New York, NY 10011
(212)924-2200
Fax: (212)924-1108

Elizabeth Capen
27 E 95th St.
New York, NY 10128
(212)427-7654
Fax: (212)876-3190

Haver Analytics
60 E 42nd St., Ste. 2424
New York, NY 10017
(212)986-9300
Fax: (212)986-5857
E-mail: data@haver.com
Website: http://www.haver.com

The Jordan, Edmiston Group Inc.
150 E 52nd Ave., 18th Fl.
New York, NY 10022
(212)754-0710
Fax: (212)754-0337

KPMG International
345 Park Ave.
New York, NY 10154-0102
(212)758-9700
Fax: (212)758-9819
Website: http://www.kpmg.com

Mahoney Cohen Consulting Corp.
111 W 40th St., 12th Fl.
New York, NY 10018
(212)490-8000
Fax: (212)790-5913

Management Practice Inc.
342 Madison Ave.
New York, NY 10173-1230
(212)867-7948
Fax: (212)972-5188
Website: http://www.mpiweb.com

Moseley Associates Inc.
342 Madison Ave., Ste. 1414
New York, NY 10016
(212)213-6673
Fax: (212)687-1520

Practice Development Counsel
60 Sutton Pl. S
New York, NY 10022
(212)593-1549
Fax: (212)980-7940
E-mail: pwhaserot@pdcounsel.com
Website: http://www.pdcounsel.com

Unique Value International Inc.
575 Madison Ave., 10th Fl.
New York, NY 10022-1304
(212)605-0590
Fax: (212)605-0589

The Van Tulleken Co.
126 E 56th St.
New York, NY 10022
(212)355-1390
Fax: (212)755-3061
E-mail: newyork@vantulleken.com

Vencon Management Inc.
301 W 53rd St.
New York, NY 10019
(212)581-8787
Fax: (212)397-4126
Website: http://www.venconinc.com

Werner International Inc.
55 E 52nd, 29th Fl.
New York, NY 10055
(212)909-1260
Fax: (212)909-1273
E-mail: richard.downing@rgh.com
Website: http://www.wernertex.com

Zimmerman Business Consulting Inc.
44 E 92nd St., Ste. 5-B
New York, NY 10128
(212)860-3107
Fax: (212)860-7730
E-mail: ljzzbci@aol.com
Website: http://www.zbcinc.com

Overton Financial
7 Allen Rd.
Peekskill, NY 10566
(914)737-4649
Fax: (914)737-4696

Stromberg Consulting
2500 Westchester Ave.
Purchase, NY 10577
(914)251-1515
Fax: (914)251-1562
E-mail: strategy@stromberg_
consulting.com
Website: http://www.stromberg_
consulting.com

**Innovation Management
Consulting Inc.**
209 Dewitt Rd.
Syracuse, NY 13214-2006
(315)425-5144
Fax: (315)445-8989
E-mail: missonneb@axess.net

M. Clifford Agress
891 Fulton St.
Valley Stream, NY 11580
(516)825-8955
Fax: (516)825-8955

Destiny Kinal Marketing Consultancy
105 Chemung St.
Waverly, NY 14892
(607)565-8317
Fax: (607)565-4083

Valutis Consulting Inc.
5350 Main St., Ste. 7
Williamsville, NY 14221-5338
(716)634-2553
Fax: (716)634-2554
E-mail: valutis@localnet.com
Website: http://www.valutisconsulting
.com

North Carolina

Best Practices L.L.C.
6320 Quadrangle Dr., Ste. 200
Chapel Hill, NC 27514
(919)403-0251
Fax: (919)403-0144
E-mail: best@best:in/class
Website: http://www.best-in-class.com

Norelli & Co.
1340 Harding Pl.
Charlotte, NC 28204
(704)376-5484
Fax: (704)376-5485
E-mail: consult@norelli.com
Website: http://www.norelli.com

North Dakota

Center for Innovation
Ina Mae Rude Entrepreneur Ctr.
4200 James Ray Dr.
Grand Forks, ND 58203
(701)777-3132
Fax: (701)777-2339
E-mail: info@innovators.net
Website: http://www.innovators.net

Ohio

Transportation Technology Services
208 Harmon Rd.
Aurora, OH 44202
(330)562-3596

Empro Systems Inc.
4777 Red Bank Expy., Ste. 1
Cincinnati, OH 45227-1542
(513)271-2042
Fax: (513)271-2042

Alliance Management International Ltd.
1440 Windrow Ln.
Cleveland, OH 44147-3200
(440)838-1922
Fax: (440)838-0979
E-mail: bgruss@amiltd.com
Website: http://www.amiltd.com

Bozell Kamstra Public Relations
1301 E 9th St., Ste. 3400
Cleveland, OH 44114
(216)623-1511
Fax: (216)623-1501
E-mail: jfeniger@cleveland.bozellkamstra
.com
Website: http://www.bozellkamstra.com

Cory Dillon Associates
111 Schreyer Pl. E
Columbus, OH 43214
(614)262-8211
Fax: (614)262-3806

Holcomb Gallagher Adams
300 Marconi, Ste. 303
Columbus, OH 43215
(614)221-3343
Fax: (614)221-3367
E-mail: riadams@acme.freenet.oh.us

Young & Associates
PO Box 711
Kent, OH 44240
(330)678-0524
Free: 800-525-9775
Fax: (330)678-6219
E-mail: online@younginc.com
Website: http://www.younginc.com

Robert A. Westman & Associates
8981 Inversary Dr. SE
Warren, OH 44484-2551
(330)856-4149
Fax: (330)856-2564

Oklahoma

Innovative Partners L.L.C.
4900 Richmond Sq., Ste. 100
Oklahoma City, OK 73118
(405)840-0033
Fax: (405)843-8359
E-mail: ipartners@juno.com

Oregon

INTERCON - The International Converting Institute
5200 Badger Rd.
Crooked River Ranch, OR 97760
(541)548-1447
Fax: (541)548-1618
E-mail: johnbowler@crookedriverranch
.com

Talbott ARM
HC 60, Box 5620
Lakeview, OR 97630
(541)635-8587
Fax: (503)947-3482

Management Technology Associates Ltd.
2768 SW Sherwood Dr, Ste. 105
Portland, OR 97201-2251
(503)224-5220
Fax: (503)224-5334
E-mail: lcuster@mta-ltd.com
Website: http://www.mgmt-tech.com

Pennsylvania

Healthscope Inc.
400 Lancaster Ave.
Devon, PA 19333
(610)687-6199
Fax: (610)687-6376
E-mail: health@voicenet.com
Website: http://www.healthscope.net/

Elayne Howard & Associates Inc.
3501 Masons Mill Rd., Ste. 501
Huntingdon Valley, PA 19006-3509
(215)657-9550

GRA Inc.
115 West Ave., Ste. 201
Jenkintown, PA 19046
(215)884-7500
Fax: (215)884-1385
E-mail: gramail@gra-inc.com
Website: http://www.gra-inc.com

Mifflin County Industrial Development Corp.
Mifflin County Industrial Plz.
6395 SR 103 N
Bldg. 50
Lewistown, PA 17044
(717)242-0393
Fax: (717)242-1842
E-mail: mcide@acsworld.net

Autech Products
1289 Revere Rd.
Morrisville, PA 19067
(215)493-3759
Fax: (215)493-9791
E-mail: autech4@yahoo.com

Advantage Associates
434 Avon Dr.
Pittsburgh, PA 15228
(412)343-1558
Fax: (412)362-1684
E-mail: ecocba1@aol.com

Regis J. Sheehan & Associates
Pittsburgh, PA 15220
(412)279-1207

James W. Davidson Company Inc.
23 Forest View Rd.
Wallingford, PA 19086
(610)566-1462

Puerto Rico

Diego Chevere & Co.
Metro Parque 7, Ste. 204
Metro Office
Caparra Heights, PR 00920
(787)774-9595
Fax: (787)774-9566
E-mail: dcco@coqui.net

Manuel L. Porrata and Associates
898 Munoz Rivera Ave., Ste. 201
San Juan, PR 00927
(787)765-2140
Fax: (787)754-3285
E-mail: m_porrata@manuelporrata.com
Website: http://manualporrata.com

South Carolina

Aquafood Business Associates
PO Box 13267
Charleston, SC 29422

(843)795-9506
Fax: (843)795-9477
E-mail: rraba@aol.com

Profit Associates Inc.
PO Box 38026
Charleston, SC 29414
(803)763-5718
Fax: (803)763-5719
E-mail: bobrog@awod.com
Website: http://www.awod.com/gallery/
business/proasc

Strategic Innovations International
12 Executive Ct.
Lake Wylie, SC 29710
(803)831-1225
Fax: (803)831-1177
E-mail: stratinnov@aol.com
Website: http://www.strategicinnovations
.com

Minus Stage
Box 4436
Rock Hill, SC 29731
(803)328-0705
Fax: (803)329-9948

Tennessee

Daniel Petchers & Associates
8820 Fernwood CV
Germantown, TN 38138
(901)755-9896

Business Choices
1114 Forest Harbor, Ste. 300
Hendersonville, TN 37075-9646
(615)822-8692
Free: 800-737-8382
Fax: (615)822-8692
E-mail: bz-ch@juno.com

RCFA Healthcare Management Services L.L.C.
9648 Kingston Pke., Ste. 8
Knoxville, TN 37922
(865)531-0176
Free: 800-635-4040
Fax: (865)531-0722
E-mail: info@rcfa.com
Website: http://www.rcfa.com

Growth Consultants of America
3917 Trimble Rd.
Nashville, TN 37215
(615)383-0550
Fax: (615)269-8940
E-mail: 70244.451@compuserve.com

Texas

Integrated Cost Management Systems Inc.
6001 W I-20, Ste. 209
Arlington, TX 76094-0206
(817)475-2945
E-mail: abm@icms.net
Website: http://www.icms.net

Business Resource Software Inc.
1779 Wells Branch Pky.
Austin, TX 78728
Free: 800-423-1228
Fax: (512)251-4401
E-mail: info@brs-inc.com
Website: http://www.brs-inc.com

Erisa Adminstrative Services Inc.
12325 Hymeadow Dr., Bldg. 4
Austin, TX 78750-1847
(512)250-9020
Fax: (512)250-9487
Website: http://www.cserisa.com

R. Miller Hicks & Co.
1011 W 11th St.
Austin, TX 78703
(512)477-7000
Fax: (512)477-9697
E-mail: millerhicks@rmhicks.com
Website: http://www.rmhicks.com

Pragmatic Tactics Inc.
3303 Westchester Ave.
College Station, TX 77845
(409)696-5294
Free: 800-570-5294
Fax: (409)696-4994
E-mail: ptactics@aol.com
Website: http://www.ptatics.com

Zaetric Business Solutions LLC
27350 Blueberry Hill, Ste. 14
Conroe, TX 77385
(713)621-4885
Fax: (713)824-1654
E-mail: inquiries@zaetric.com
Website: http://www.zaetric.com

Perot Systems
12404 Park Central Dr.
Dallas, TX 75251
(972)340-5000
Free: 800-688-4333
Fax: (972)455-4100
E-mail: corp.comm@ps.net
Website: http://www.perotsystems.com

ReGENERATION Partners
3811 Turtle Creek Blvd., Ste. 300
Dallas, TX 75219

(214)559-3999
Free: 800-406-1112
E-mail: info@regeneration-partner.com
Website: http://www.regeneration-
partners.com

High Technology Associates
5739 Longmont Ln.
Houston, TX 77057
(713)963-9300
Fax: (713)963-8341
E-mail: baker@hta-usa.com
Website: http://www.high-technology-
associates.com

SynerImages LLC
1 Riverway, Ste. 1700
Houston, TX 77056
(713)840-6442
Fax: (713)963-8341
Website: http://www.synerimages.com

PROTEC
4607 Linden Pl.
Pearland, TX 77584
(281)997-9872
Fax: (281)997-9895
E-mail: p.oman@ix.netcom.com

Bastian Public Relations
614 San Dizier
San Antonio, TX 78232
(210)404-1839
E-mail: lisa@bastianpr.com
Website: http://www.bastianpr.com
Lisa Bastian CBC

Business Strategy Development Consultants
PO Box 690365
San Antonio, TX 78269
(210)696-8000
Free: 800-927-BSDC
Fax: (210)696-8000

Utah

Vector Resources
7651 S Main St., Ste. 106
Midvale, UT 84047-7158
(801) 352-8500
Fax: (801) 352-8506
E-mail: info@vectorresources.com
Website: http://www.vectorresources
.com

StreetMaker Inc.
524 West 440 South
Orem, UT 84058-6115
(801)607-2246
Fax: (800)561-4928
E-mail: contact@streetmaker.com
Website: http://www.streetmaker.com

Biomedical Management Resources
PO Box 521125
Salt Lake City, UT 84152-1125
(801)272-4668
Fax: (801)277-3290
E-mail: SeniorManagement@Biomedical
Management.com
Website: http://
www.biomedicalmanagement.com

Marriott Consulting Inc.
6945 S Knudsen Ridge Cir.
Salt Lake City, UT 84121
(801)944-5000
Fax: (801)947-9022
E-mail: info@marriottconsulting.com
Website: http://www.marriott
consulting.com

Virginia

Crown Consulting Inc.
1400 Key Blvd., Ste. 1100
Arlington, VA 22209
(703)650-0663
Fax: (703)243-1280
E-mail: info@crownci.com
Website: http://www.crownci.com

Dare Mighty Things
901 N Glebe Rd., Ste. 1005
Arlington, VA 22203
(703)752-4331
Fax: (703)752-4332
E-mail: info@daremightythings.com
Website: http://www.daremightythings
.com

Elliott B. Jaffa
2530-B S Walter Reed Dr.
Arlington, VA 22206
(703)931-0040

Koach Enterprises - USA
5529 N 18th St.
Arlington, VA 22205
(703)241-8361
Fax: (703)241-8623

AMX International Inc.
9016 Triple Ridge Rd.
Fairfax Station, VA 22039-3003
(703)864-7046
Fax: (703)690-9994
E-mail: info@amxi.com
Website: http://www.amxi.com

Joel Greenstein & Associates
6212 Nethercombe Ct.
McLean, VA 22101
(703) 893-1888

John C. Randall and Associates Inc.
10197 Georgetown Rd.
Mechanicsville, VA 23116
(804)746-4450

Charles Scott Pugh (Investor)
4101 Pittaway Dr.
Richmond, VA 23235-1022
(804)560-0979
Fax: (804)560-4670

Robert Martens & Co.
2226 Floyd Ave.
Richmond, VA 23220
(804) 342-8850
Fax: (804)342-8860
E-mail: rm@robertmartens.com
Website: http://www.robertmartens.com

William W. Garry Inc.
PO Box 61662
Virginia Beach, VA 23466
(757) 467-7874
E-mail: drbillgarry@freeyellow.com

Regis J. Sheehan & Associates
500 Belmont Bay Dr.
Woodbridge, VA 22191-5445
(703)491-7377

Washington

Burlington Consultants
10900 NE 8th St., Ste. 900
Bellevue, WA 98004
(425)688-3060
Fax: (425)454-4383
E-mail: partners@burlington
consultants.com
Website: http://www.burlington
consultants.com

Perry L. Smith Consulting
800 Bellevue Way NE, Ste. 400
Bellevue, WA 98004-4208
(425)462-2072
Fax: (425)462-5638

St. Charles Consulting Group
1420 NW Gilman Blvd.
Issaquah, WA 98027
(425)557-8708
Fax: (425)557-8731
E-mail: info@stcharlesconsulting.com
Website: http://www.stcharlesconsulting
.com

**Independent Automotive Training
Services**
PO Box 334
Kirkland, WA 98083
(425)822-5715
E-mail: ltunney@autosvccon.com
Website: http://www.autosvccon.com

Kahle Associate Inc.
6203 204th Dr. NE
Redmond, WA 98053
(425)836-8763
Fax: (425)868-3770
E-mail: randykahle@kahleassociates.com
Website: http://www.kahleassociates.com

Dan Collin
3419 Wallingord Ave N, No. 2
Seattle, WA 98103
(206)634-9469
E-mail: dc@dancollin.com
Website: http://members.home.net/
dcollin/

ECG Management Consultants Inc.
1111 3rd Ave., Ste. 2700
Seattle, WA 98101-3201
(206)689-2200
Fax: (206)689-2209
E-mail: ecg@ecgmc.com
Website: http://www.ecgmc.com

**Northwest Trade Adjustment
Assistance Center**
900 4th Ave., Ste. 2430
Seattle, WA 98164-1001
(206)622-2730
Free: 800-667-8087
Fax: (206)622-1105
E-mail: matchingfunds@nwtaac.org
Website: http://www.taacenters.org

Business Planning Consultants
S 3510 Ridgeview Dr.
Spokane, WA 99206
(509)928-0332
Fax: (509)921-0842
E-mail: bpci@nextdim.com

West Virginia

**Stanley & Associates Inc./
BusinessandMarketingPlans.com**
1687 Robert C. Byrd Dr.
Beckley, WV 25801
(304)252-0324
Free: 888-752-6720
Fax: (304)252-0470
E-mail: cclay@charterinternet.com
Website: http://
www.BusinessandMarketingPlans.com
Christopher Clay

Wisconsin

White & Associates Inc.
5349 Somerset Ln. S
Greenfield, WI 53221
(414)281-7373
Fax: (414)281-7006
E-mail: wnaconsult@aol.com

Small business administration regional offices

This section contains a listing of Small Business Administration offices arranged numerically by region. Service areas are provided. Contact the appropriate office for a referral to the nearest field office, or visit the Small Business Administration online at www.sba.gov.

Region 1

U.S. Small Business Administration
Region I Office
10 Causeway St., Ste. 812
Boston, MA 02222-1093
Phone: (617)565-8415
Fax: (617)565-8420
Serves Connecticut, Maine, Massachusetts, New Hampshire, Rhode Island, and Vermont.

Region 2

U.S. Small Business Administration
Region II Office
26 Federal Plaza, Ste. 3108
New York, NY 10278
Phone: (212)264-1450
Fax: (212)264-0038
Serves New Jersey, New York, Puerto Rico, and the Virgin Islands.

Region 3

U.S. Small Business Administration
Region III Office
1150 First Avenue Suite 1001
King of Prussia, PA 19406
(610)382-3092
Serves Delaware, the District of Columbia, Maryland, Pennsylvania, Virginia, and West Virginia.

Region 4

U.S. Small Business Administration
Region IV Office
233 Peachtree St. NE
Harris Tower 1800
Atlanta, GA 30303
Phone: (404)331-4999
Fax: (404)331-2354
Serves Alabama, Florida, Georgia, Kentucky, Mississippi, North Carolina, South Carolina, and Tennessee.

Region 5

U.S. Small Business Administration
Region V Office
500 W. Madison St.
Citicorp Center, Ste. 1150
Chicago, IL 60661
Phone: (312)353-0357
Fax: (312)353-3426
Serves Illinois, Indiana, Michigan, Minnesota, Ohio, and Wisconsin.

Region 6

U.S. Small Business Administration
Region VI Office
4300 Amon Carter Blvd., Ste. 108
Fort Worth, TX 76155
Phone: (817)684-5581
Fax: (817)684-5588
Serves Arkansas, Louisiana, New Mexico, Oklahoma, and Texas.

Region 7

U.S. Small Business Administration
Region VII Office
1000 Walnut Suite 530
Kansas City, MO 64106
Phone: (816)426-4840
Fax: (816)426-4848
Serves Iowa, Kansas, Missouri, and Nebraska.

Region 8

U.S. Small Business Administration
Region VIII Office
721 19th St., Ste. 400
Denver, CO 80202
Phone: (303)844-0500
Fax: (303)844-0506
Serves Colorado, Montana, North Dakota, South Dakota, Utah, and Wyoming.

Region 9

U.S. Small Business Administration
Region IX Office
330 N Brand Blvd., Ste. 1200
Glendale, CA 91203
Phone: (818)552-3437
Fax: (818)552-0344
Serves American Samoa, Arizona, California, Guam, Hawaii, Nevada, and the Trust Territory of the Pacific Islands.

Region 10

U.S. Small Business Administration
Region X Office
2401 Fourth Ave., Ste. 400
Seattle, WA 98121
Phone: (206)553-5676
Fax: (206)553-4155
Serves Alaska, Idaho, Oregon, and Washington.

Small business development centers

This section contains a listing of all Small Business Development Centers, organized alphabetically by state/U.S. territory, then by city, then by agency name.

Alabama

Alabama SBDC

UNIVERSITY OF ALABAMA
2800 Milan Court Suite 124
Birmingham, AL 35211-6908
Phone: 205-943-6750
Fax: 205-943-6752
E-Mail: wcampbell@provost.uab.edu
Website: http://www.asbdc.org
Mr. William Campbell Jr, State Director

Alaska

Alaska SBDC

UNIVERSITY OF ALASKA - ANCHORAGE
430 West Seventh Avenue, Suite 110
Anchorage, AK 99501
Phone: 907-274 -7232
Fax: 907-272-0565
E-Mail: Isaac.Vanderburg@aksbdc.org
Website: http://www.aksbdc.org
Isaac Vanderburg, State Director

American Samoa

American Samoa SBDC

AMERICAN SAMOA COMMUNITY COLLEGE
P.O. Box 2609
Pago Pago, American Samoa 96799
Phone: 011-684-699-4830
Fax: 011-684-699-6132
E-Mail: hthweatt.sbdc@hotmail.com
Website: www.as-sbdc.org
Mr. Herbert Thweatt, Director

Arizona

Arizona SBDC

MARICOPA COUNTY COMMUNITY COLLEGE
2411 West 14th Street, Suite 114
Tempe, AZ 85281
Phone: 480-731-8720
Fax: 480-731-8729

E-Mail: janice.washington@domail
.maricopa.edu
Website: http://www.azsbdc.net
Janice Washington, State Director

Arkansas

Arkansas SBDC

UNIVERSITY OF ARKANSAS

2801 South University Avenue
Little Rock, AR 72204
Phone: 501-683-7700
Fax: 501-683-7720
E-Mail: jmroderick@ualr.edu
Website: http://asbtdc.org
Ms. Janet M. Roderick, State Director

California

California - Northern California Regional SBDC

Northern California SBDC

HUMBOLDT STATE UNIVERSITY

1 Harpst Street 2006A, 209 Siemens Hall
Arcata, CA, 95521
Phone: 707-826-3920
Fax: 707-826-3912
E-Mail: Kristin.Johnson@humboldt.edu
Website: https://www.norcalsbdc.org
Kristin Johnson, Regional Director

California - Northern California SBDC

CALIFORNIA STATE UNIVERSITY - CHICO

35 Main St., Rm 203rr
Chico, CA 95929-0765
Phone: 530-898-5443
Fax: 530-898-4734
E-Mail: dripke@csuchico.edu
Website: https://www.necsbdc.org
Mr. Dan Ripke, Interim Regional Director

California - San Diego and Imperial SBDC

SOUTHWESTERN COMMUNITY COLLEGE

880 National City Boulevard, Suite 103
National City, CA 91950
Phone: 619-216-6721
Fax: 619-216-6692
E-Mail: awilson@swccd.edu
Website: http://www.SBDCRegional
Network.org
Aleta Wilson, Regional Director

California - UC Merced SBDC

UC Merced Lead Center

UNIVERSITY OF CALIFORNIA - MERCED

550 East Shaw, Suite 105A
Fresno, CA 93710
Phone: 559-241-6590
Fax: 559-241-7422
E-Mail: dhowerton@ucmerced.edu
Website: http://sbdc.ucmerced.edu
Diane Howerton, State Director

California - Orange County/Inland Empire SBDC

Tri-County Lead SBDC

CALIFORNIA STATE UNIVERSITY - FULLERTON

800 North State College Boulevard,
SGMH 5313
Fullerton, CA 92834
Phone: 714-278-5168
Fax: 714-278-7101
E-Mail: kmpayne@fullerton.edu
Website: http://www.leadsbdc.org
Katrina Payne Smith, Lead Center Director

California - Los Angeles Region SBDC

LONG BEACH CITY COLLEGE

4900 E. Conant Street, Building 2
Long Beach, CA 90808
Phone: 562-938-5006
Fax: 562-938-5030
E-Mail: jtorres@lbcc.edu
Website: http://www.smallbizla.org
Jesse Torres, Lead Center Director

Colorado

Colorado SBDC

COLORADO SBDC

1625 Broadway, Suite 2700
Denver, CO 80202
Phone: 303-892-3864
Fax: 303-892-3848
E-Mail: Kelly.Manning@state.co.us
Website: http://
www.www.coloradosbdc.org
Ms. Kelly Manning, State Director

Connecticut

Connecticut SBDC

UNIVERSITY OF CONNECTICUT

2100 Hillside Road, Unit 1044
Storrs, CT 06269
Phone: 855-428-7232

E-Mail: ecarter@uconn.edu
Website: www.ctsbdc.com
Emily Carter, State Director

Delaware

Delaware SBDC

DELAWARE TECHNOLOGY PARK

1 Innovation Way, Suite 301
Newark, DE 19711
Phone: 302-831-4283
Fax: 302-831-1423
E-Mail: jmbowman@udel.edu
Website: http://www.delawaresbdc.org
Mike Bowman, State Director

District of Columbia

District of Columbia SBDC

HOWARD UNIVERSITY

2600 6th Street, NW Room 128
Washington, DC 20059
Phone: 202-806-1550
Fax: 202-806-1777
E-Mail: darrell.brown@howard.edu
Website: http://www.dcsbdc.com/
Darrell Brown, Executive Director

Florida

Florida SBDC

UNIVERSITY OF WEST FLORIDA

11000 University Parkway, Building 38
Pensacola, FL 32514
Phone: 850-473-7800
Fax: 850-473-7813
E-Mail: mmyhre@uwf.edu
Website: http://www.floridasbdc.com
Michael Myhre, State Director

Georgia

Georgia SBDC

UNIVERSITY OF GEORGIA

1180 East Broad Street
Athens, GA 30602
Phone: 706-542-6762
Fax: 706-542-7935
E-mail: aadams@georgiasbdc.org
Website: http://www.georgiasbdc.org
Mr. Allan Adams, State Director

Guam

Guam Small Business Development Center

UNIVERSITY OF GUAM

Pacific Islands SBDC
P.O. Box 5014 - U.O.G. Station

Mangilao, GU 96923
Phone: 671-735-2590
Fax: 671-734-2002
E-mail: casey@pacificsbdc.com
Website: http://www.uog.edu/sbdc
Mr. Casey Jeszenka, Director

Hawaii

Hawaii SBDC

UNIVERSITY OF HAWAII - HILO
200 W. Kawili Street, Suite 107
Hilo, HI 96720
Phone: 808-974-7515
Fax: 808-974-7683
E-Mail: cathy.wiltse@hisbdc.org
Website: http://www.hisbdc.org
Cathy Wiltse, State Director

Idaho

Idaho SBDC

BOISE STATE UNIVERSITY
1910 University Drive
Boise, ID 83725
Phone: 208-426-3838
Fax: 208-426-3877
E-mail: ksewell@boisestate.edu
Website: http://www.idahosbdc.org
Katie Sewell, State Director

Illinois

Illinois SBDC

DEPARTMENT OF COMMERCE AND ECONOMIC OPPORTUNITY
500 E. Monroe
Springfield, IL 62701
Phone: 217-524-5700
Fax: 217-524-0171
E-mail: mark.petrilli@illinois.gov
Website: http://www.ilsbdc.biz
Mr. Mark Petrilli, State Director

Indiana

Indiana SBDC

INDIANA ECONOMIC DEVELOPMENT CORPORATION
One North Capitol, Suite 700
Indianapolis, IN 46204
Phone: 317-232-8805
Fax: 317-232-8872
E-mail: JSchpok@iedc.in.gov
Website: http://www.isbdc.org
Jacob Schpok, State Director

Iowa

Iowa SBDC

IOWA STATE UNIVERSITY
2321 North Loop Drive, Suite 202
Ames, IA 50010
Phone: 515-294-2030
Fax: 515-294-6522
E-mail: lshimkat@iastate.edu
Website: http://www.iowasbdc.org
Lisa Shimkat, State Director

Kansas

Kansas SBDC

FORT HAYS STATE UNIVERSITY
214 SW Sixth Street, Suite 301
Topeka, KS 66603
Phone: 785-296-6514
Fax: 785-291-3261
E-mail: panichello@ksbdc.net
Website: http://www.fhsu.edu/ksbdc
Greg Panichello, State Director

Kentucky

Kentucky SBDC

UNIVERSITY OF KENTUCKY
One Quality Street
Lexington, KY 40507
Phone: 859-257-7668
Fax: 859-323-1907
E-mail: lrnaug0@uky.edu
Website: http://www.ksbdc.org
Becky Naugle, State Director

Louisiana

Louisiana SBDC

UNIVERSITY OF LOUISIANA - MONROE

College of Business Administration
700 University Avenue
Monroe, LA 71209
Phone: 318-342-5507
Fax: 318-342-5510
E-mail: rkessler@lsbdc.org
Website: http://www.lsbdc.org
Rande Kessler, State Director

Maine

Maine SBDC

UNIVERSITY OF SOUTHERN MAINE
96 Falmouth Street P.O. Box 9300
Portland, ME 04104
Phone: 207-780-4420
Fax: 207-780-4810

E-mail: mark.delisle@maine.edu
Website: http://www.mainesbdc.org
Mark Delisle, State Director

Maryland

Maryland SBDC

UNIVERSITY OF MARYLAND
7100 Baltimore Avenue, Suite 401
College Park, MD 20742
Phone: 301-403-8300
Fax: 301-403-8303
E-mail: rsprow@mdsbdc.umd.edu
Website: http://www.mdsbdc.umd.edu
Renee Sprow, State Director

Massachusetts

Massachusetts SBDC

UNIVERSITY OF MASSACHUSETTS
23 Tillson Farm Road
Amherst, MA 01003
Phone: 413-545-6301
Fax: 413-545-1273
E-mail: gparkin@msbdc.umass.edu
Website: http://www.www.msbdc.org
Georgianna Parkin, State Director

Michigan

Michigan SBTDC

GRAND VALLEY STATE UNIVERSITY
510 West Fulton Avenue
Grand Rapids, MI 49504
Phone: 616-331-7480
Fax: 616-331-7485
E-mail: boesen@gvsu.edu
Website: http://www.misbtdc.org
Nancy Boese, State Director

Minnesota

Minnesota SBDC

MINNESOTA SMALL BUSINESS DEVELOPMENT CENTER
1st National Bank Building
332 Minnesota Street, Suite E200
St. Paul, MN 55101-1349
Phone: 651-259-7420
Fax: 651-296-5287
E-mail: Bruce.Strong@state.mn.us
Website: http://www.mnsbdc.com
Bruce H. Strong, State Director

Mississippi

Mississippi SBDC

UNIVERSITY OF MISSISSIPPI
122 Jeanette Phillips Drive
P.O. Box 1848

University, MS 38677
Phone: 662-915-5001
Fax: 662-915-5650
E-mail: wgurley@olemiss.edu
Website: http://www.mssbdc.org
Doug Gurley, Jr., State Director

Missouri

Missouri SBDC

UNIVERSITY OF MISSOURI
410 South 6th Street, ?200 Engineering North
Columbia, MO 65211
Phone: 573-882-9206
Fax: 573-884-4297
E-mail: bouchardc@missouri.edu
Website: http://www.missouribusiness.net
Chris Bouchard, State Director

Montana

Montana SBDC

DEPARTMENT OF COMMERCE
301 S. Park Avenue, Room 114
Helena, MT 59601
Phone: 406-841-2746
Fax: 406-841-2728
E-mail: adesch@mt.gov
Website: http://www.sbdc.mt.gov
Ms. Ann Desch, State Director

Nebraska

Nebraska SBDC

UNIVERSITY OF NEBRASKA - OMAHA
200 Mammel Hall, 67th & Pine Streets
Omaha, NE 68182
Phone: 402-554-2521
Fax: 402-554-3473
E-mail: rbernier@unomaha.edu
Website: http://nbdc.unomaha.edu
Robert Bernier, State Director

Nevada

Nevada SBDC

UNIVERSITY OF NEVADA - RENO
Reno College of Business, Room 411
Reno, NV 89557-0100
Phone: 775-784-1717
Fax: 775-784-4337
E-mail: males@unr.edu
Website: http://www.nsbdc.org
Sam Males, State Director

New Hampshire

New Hampshire SBDC

UNIVERSITY OF NEW HAMPSHIRE
10 Garrison Avenue
Durham, NH 03824-3593
Phone: 603-862-2200
Fax: 603-862-4876
E-mail: Mary.Collins@unh.edu
Website: http://www.nhsbdc.org
Mary Collins, State Director

New Jersey

New Jersey SBDC

RUTGERS UNIVERSITY
1 Washington Park, 3rd Floor
Newark, NJ 07102
Phone: 973-353-1927
Fax: 973-353-1110
E-mail: bhopper@njsbdc.com
Website: http://www.njsbdc.com
Brenda Hopper, State Director

New Mexico

New Mexico SBDC

SANTA FE COMMUNITY COLLEGE
6401 Richards Avenue
Santa Fe, NM 87508
Phone: 505-428-1362
Fax: 505-428-1469
E-mail: russell.wyrick@sfcc.edu
Website: http://www.nmsbdc.org
Russell Wyrick, State Director

New York

New York SBDC

STATE UNIVERSITY OF NEW YORK
22 Corporate Woods, 3rd Floor
Albany, NY 12246
Phone: 518-443-5398
Fax: 518-443-5275
E-mail: j.king@nyssbdc.org
Website: http://www.nyssbdc.org
Jim King, State Director

North Carolina

North Carolina SBDTC

UNIVERSITY OF NORTH CAROLINA
5 West Hargett Street, Suite 600
Raleigh, NC 27601
Phone: 919-715-7272
Fax: 919-715-7777
E-mail: sdaugherty@sbtdc.org
Website: http://www.sbtdc.org
Scott Daugherty, State Director

North Dakota

North Dakota SBDC

UNIVERSITY OF NORTH DAKOTA
1200 Memorial Highway, PO Box 5509
Bismarck, ND 58506
Phone: 701-328-5375
Fax: 701-250-4304
E-mail: dkmartin@ndsbdc.org
Website: http://www.ndsbdc.org
David Martin, State Director

Ohio

Ohio SBDC

OHIO DEPARTMENT OF DEVELOPMENT
77 South High Street, 28th Floor
Columbus, OH 43216
Phone: 614-466-2711
Fax: 614-466-1789
E-mail: ezra.escudero@development.ohio.gov
Website: http://www.ohiosbdc.org
Ezra Escudero, State Director

Oklahoma

Oklahoma SBDC

SOUTHEAST OKLAHOMA STATE UNIVERSITY
1405 N. 4th Avenue, PMB 2584
Durant, OK 74701
Phone: 580-745-2955
Fax: 580-745-7471
E-mail: wcarter@se.edu
Website: http://www.osbdc.org
Grady Pennington, State Director

Oregon

Oregon SBDC

LANE COMMUNITY COLLEGE
1445 Willamette Street, Suite 5
Eugene, OR 97401
Phone: 541-463-5250
Fax: 541-345-6006
E-mail: gregorym@lanecc.edu
Website: http://www.bizcenter.org
Mark Gregory, State Director

Pennsylvania

Pennsylvania SBDC

UNIVERSITY OF PENNSYLVANIA

The Wharton School
3819-33 Chestnut Street, Suite 325
Philadelphia, PA 19104

Phone: 215-898-1219
Fax: 215-573-2135
E-mail: cconroy@wharton.upenn.edu
Website: http://pasbdc.org
Christian Conroy, State Director

Puerto Rico

Puerto Rico SBDC

INTER-AMERICAN UNIVERSITY OF PUERTO RICO
416 Ponce de Leon Avenue, Union Plaza,
Tenth Floor
Hato Rey, PR 00918
Phone: 787-763-6811
Fax: 787-763-6875
E-mail: cmarti@prsbdc.org
Website: http://www.prsbdc.org
Carmen Marti, Executive Director

Rhode Island

Rhode Island SBDC

UNIVERSITY OF RHODE ISLAND
75 Lower College Road, 2nd Floor
Kingston, RI 02881
Phone: 401-874-4576
E-mail: gsonnenfeld@uri.edu
Website: http://www.risbdc.org
Gerald Sonnenfeld, State Director

South Carolina

South Carolina SBDC

UNIVERSITY OF SOUTH CAROLINA

Moore School of Business
1014 Greene Street
Columbia, SC 29208
Phone: 803-777-0749
Fax: 803-777-6876
E-mail: michele.abraham@moore.sc.edu
Website: http://www.scsbdc.com
Michele Abraham, State Director

South Dakota

South Dakota SBDC

UNIVERSITY OF SOUTH DAKOTA
414 East Clark Street, Patterson Hall
Vermillion, SD 57069
Phone: 605-677-5103
Fax: 605-677-5427
E-mail: jeff.eckhoff@usd.edu
Website: http://www.usd.edu/sbdc
Jeff Eckhoff, State Director

Tennessee

Tennessee SBDC

MIDDLE TENNESSEE STATE UNIVERSITY
3050 Medical Center Parkway, Ste. 200
Nashville, TN 37129
Phone: 615-849-9999
Fax: 615-893-7089
E-mail: pgeho@tsbdc.org
Website: http://www.tsbdc.org
Patrick Geho, State Director

Texas

Texas-North SBDC

DALLAS COUNTY COMMUNITY COLLEGE
1402 Corinth Street
Dallas, TX 75215
Phone: 214-860-5832
Fax: 214-860-5813
E-mail: m.langford@dcccd.edu
Website: http://www.ntsbdc.org
Mark Langford, Region Director

Texas Gulf Coast SBDC

UNIVERSITY OF HOUSTON
2302 Fannin, Suite 200
Houston, TX 77002
Phone: 713-752-8444
Fax: 713-756-1500
E-mail: fyoung@uh.edu
Website: http://sbdcnetwork.uh.edu
Mike Young, Executive Director

Texas-NW SBDC

TEXAS TECH UNIVERSITY
2579 South Loop 289, Suite 114
Lubbock, TX 79423
Phone: 806-745-3973
Fax: 806-745-6207
E-mail: c.bean@nwtsbdc.org
Website: http://www.nwtsbdc.org
Craig Bean, Executive Director

Texas-South-West Texas Border Region SBDC

UNIVERSITY OF TEXAS - SAN ANTONIO
501 West Durango Boulevard
San Antonio, TX 78207-4415
Phone: 210-458-2480
Fax: 210-458-2425
E-mail: albert.salgado@utsa.edu
Website: https://www.txsbdc.org
Alberto Salgado, Region Director

Utah

Utah SBDC

SALT LAKE COMMUNITY COLLEGE
9750 South 300 West
Salt Lake City, UT 84070
Phone: 801-957-5384
Fax: 801-985-5300
E-mail: Sherm.Wilkinson@slcc.edu
Website: http://www.utahsbdc.org
Sherm Wilkinson, State Director

Vermont

Vermont SBDC

VERMONT TECHNICAL COLLEGE
PO Box 188, 1 Main Street
Randolph Center, VT 05061-0188
Phone: 802-728-9101
Fax: 802-728-3026
E-mail: lrossi@vtsbdc.org
Website: http://www.vtsbdc.org
Linda Rossi, State Director

Virgin Islands

Virgin Islands SBDC

UNIVERSITY OF THE VIRGIN ISLANDS
8000 Nisky Center, Suite 720
St. Thomas, VI 00802
Phone: 340-776-3206
Fax: 340-775-3756
E-mail: ldottin@uvi.edu
Website: http://www.sbdcvi.org
Leonor Dottin, State Director

Virginia

Virginia SBDC

GEORGE MASON UNIVERSITY
4031 University Drive, Suite100
Fairfax, VA 22030
Phone: 703-277-7727
Fax: 703-352-8518
E-mail: jkeenan@gmu.edu
Website: http://www.virginiasbdc.org
Jody Keenan, Director

Washington

Washington SBDC

WASHINGTON STATE UNIVERSITY
1235 N. Post Street, Suite 201
Spokane, WA 99201
Phone: 509-358-7765
Fax: 509-358-7764
E-mail: duane.fladland@wsbdc.org
Website: http://www.wsbdc.org
Duane Fladland, State Director

West Virginia

West Virginia SBDC

WEST VIRGINIA DEVELOPMENT OFFICE
Capital Complex, Building 6, Room 652
1900 Kanawha Boulevard
Charleston, WV 25305
Phone: 304-957-2087
Fax: 304-558-0127
E-mail: Kristina.J.Oliver@wv.gov
Website: http://www.wvsbdc.org
Mr. Conley Salyor, State Director

Wisconsin

Wisconsin SBDC

UNIVERSITY OF WISCONSIN
432 North Lake Street, Room 423
Madison, WI 53706
Phone: 608-263-7794
Fax: 608-263-7830
E-mail: bon.wikenheiser@uwex.edu
Website: http://www.uwex.edu/sbdc
Bon Wikenheiser, State Director

Wyoming

Wyoming SBDC

UNIVERSITY OF WYOMING
1000 E. University Ave., Dept. 3922
Laramie, WY 82071-3922
Phone: 307-766-3405
Fax: 307-766-3406
E-mail: jkline@uwyo.edu
Website: http://www.wyomingentre
preneur.biz
Jill Kline, Acting State Director

Service corps of retired executives (score) offices

This section contains a listing of all SCORE offices organized alphabetically by state/U.S. territory, then by city, then by agency name.

Alabama

SCORE Office (Northeast Alabama)
1400 Commerce Blvd., Northeast
Anniston, AL 36207
(256)241-6111

SCORE Office (North Alabama)
1731 1st Ave. North, Ste. 200
Birmingham, AL 35203
(205)264-8425
Fax: (205)934-0538

SCORE Office (Baldwin County)
327 Fairhope Avenue
Fairhope, AL 36532
(251)928-6387

SCORE Office (Mobile)
451 Government Street
Mobile, AL 36652
(251)431-8614
Fax: (251)431-8646

SCORE Office (Alabama Capitol City)
600 S. Court St.
Montgomery, AL 36104
(334)240-6868
Fax: (334)240-6869

SCORE Office (Tuscaloosa)
2200 University Blvd.
Tuscaloosa, AL 35402
(205)758-7588

Alaska

SCORE Office (Anchorage)
420 L St., Ste. 300
Anchorage, AK 99501
(907)271-4022
Fax: (907)271-4545

Arizona

SCORE Office (Greater Phoenix)
2828 N. Central Ave., Ste. 800
Phoenix, AZ 85004
(602)745-7250
Fax: (602)745-7210
E-mail: e-mail@SCORE-phoenix.org
Website: http://www.greaterphoenix
.score.org/

SCORE Office (Northern Arizona)
1228 Willow Creek Rd., Ste. 2
Prescott, AZ 86301
(928)778-7438
Fax: (928)778-0812
Website: http://www.northernarizona
.score.org/

SCORE Office (Southern Arizona)
1400 W Speedway Blvd.
Tucson, AZ 85745
(520)505-3636
Fax: (520)670-5011
Website: http://www.southernarizona
.score.org/

Arkansas

SCORE Office (South Central)
201 N. Jackson Ave.
El Dorado, AR 71730-5803
(870)863-6113
Fax: (870)863-6115

SCORE Office (Northwest Arkansas)
614 E. Emma St., Room M412
Springdale, AR 72764
(479)725-1809
Website: http://www.northwestarkansas
.score.org

SCORE Office (Little Rock)
2120 Riverfront Dr., Ste. 250
Little Rock, AR 72202-1747
(501)324-7379
Fax: (501)324-5199
Website: http://www.littlerock.score.org

SCORE Office (Southeast Arkansas)
P.O. Box 5069
Pine Bluff, AR 71611-5069
(870)535-0110
Fax: (870)535-1643

California

SCORE Office (Bakersfield)
P.O. Box 2426
Bakersfield, CA 93303
(661)861-9249
Fax: (661)395-4134
Website: http://www.bakersfield.score.org

SCORE Office (Santa Cruz County)
716 G Capitola Ave.
Capitola, CA 95010
(831)621-3735
Fax: (831)475-6530
Website: http://santacruzcounty
.score.org

SCORE Office (Greater Chico Area)
1324 Mangrove St., Ste. 114
Chico, CA 95926
(530)342-8932
Fax: (530)342-8932
Website: http://www.greaterchicoarea
.score.org

SCORE Office (El Centro)
1850 W. Main St, Ste. C
El Centro, CA 92243
(760)337-2692
Website: http://www.sandiego.score.org/

SCORE Office (Central Valley)
801 R St., Ste. 201
Fresno, CA 93721
(559)487-5605
Fax: (559)487-5636
Website: http://www.centralvalley.score
.org

SCORE Office (Los Angeles)
330 N. Brand Blvd., Ste. 190
Glendale, CA 91203-2304
(818)552-3206

Fax: (818)552-3323
Website: http://www.greaterlosangeles
.score.org

SCORE Office (Modesto Merced)
1880 W. Wardrobe Ave.
Merced, CA 95340
(209)725-2033
Fax: (209)577-2673
Website: http://www.modestomerced
.score.org

SCORE Office (Monterey Bay)
Monterey Chamber of Commerce
30 Ragsdale Dr.
Monterey, CA 93940
(831)648-5360
Website: http://
www.montereybay.score.org

SCORE Office (East Bay)
492 9th St., Ste. 350
Oakland, CA 94607
(510)273-6611
Fax: (510)273-6015
E-mail: webmaster@eastbayscore.org
Website: http://www.eastbay.score.org/

SCORE Office (Ventura County)
400 E. Esplanade Dr., Ste. 301
Oxnard, CA 93036
(805)204-6022
Fax: (805)650-1414
Website: http://www.ventura.score.org

SCORE Office (Coachella)
43100 Cook St., Ste. 104
Palm Desert, CA 92211
(760)773-6507
Fax: (760)773-6514
Website: http://www.coachellavalley
.score.org

SCORE Office (Antelope Valley)
1212 E. Avenue, S Ste. A3
Palmdale, CA 93550
(661)947-7679
Website: http://www.antelopevalley
.score.org/

SCORE Office (Inland Empire)
11801 Pierce St., 2nd Fl.
Riverside, CA 92505
(951)-652-4390
Fax: (951)929-8543
Website: http://www.inlandempire
.score.org/

SCORE Office (Sacramento)
4990 Stockton Blvd.
Sacramento, CA 95820
(916)635-9085

Fax: (916)635-9089
Website: http://www.sacramento
.score.org

SCORE Office (San Diego)
550 West C. St., Ste. 550
San Diego, CA 92101-3540
(619)557-7272
Website: http://www.sandiego
.score.org/

SCORE Office (San Francisco)
455 Market St., 6th Fl.
San Francisco, CA 94105
(415)744-6827
Fax: (415)744-6750
E-mail: sfscore@sfscore.
Website: http://www.sanfrancisco
.score.org/

SCORE Office (Silicon Valley)
234 E. Gish Rd., Ste. 100
San Jose, CA 95112
(408)453-6237
Fax: (408)494-0214
E-mail: info@svscore.org
Website: http://www.siliconvalley
.score.org/

SCORE Office (San Luis Obispo)
711 Tank Farm Rd., Ste. 210
San Luis Obispo, CA 93401
(805)547-0779
Website: http://www.sanluisobispo
.score.org

SCORE Office (Orange County)
200 W. Santa Anna Blvd., Ste. 700
Santa Ana, CA 92701
(714)550-7369
Fax: (714)550-0191
Website: http://www.orangecounty.score
.org

SCORE Office (Santa Barbara)
924 Anacapa St.
Santa Barbara, CA 93101
(805)563-0084
Website: http://www.santabarbara.score
.org/

SCORE Office (North Coast)
777 Sonoma Ave., Rm. 115E
Santa Rosa, CA 95404
(707)571-8342
Fax: (707)541-0331
Website: http://www.northcoast.score
.org

SCORE Office (Tuolumne County)
222 S. Shepherd St.
Sonora, CA 95370

(209)532-4316
Fax: (209)588-0673
Website: http://www.tuolumnecounty
.score.org/

Colorado

SCORE Office (Colorado Springs)
3595 E. Fountain Blvd., Ste. E-1
Colorado Springs, CO 80910
(719)636-3074
Fax: (719)635-1571
Website: http://www.coloradosprings
.score.org/

SCORE Office (Denver)
US Custom's House, 4th Fl.
721 19th St.
Denver, CO 80202
(303)844-3985
Fax: (303)844-6490
Website: http://www.denver.score.org/

SCORE Office (Tri-River)
1102 Grand Ave.
Glenwood Springs, CO 81601
(970)945-6589

SCORE Office (Grand Junction)
2591 B & 3/4 Rd.
Grand Junction, CO 81503
(970)243-5242

SCORE Office (Gunnison)
608 N. 11th
Gunnison, CO 81230
(303)641-4422

SCORE Office (Montrose)
1214 Peppertree Dr.
Montrose, CO 81401
(970)249-6080

SCORE Office (Pagosa Springs)
PO Box 4381
Pagosa Springs, CO 81157
(970)731-4890

SCORE Office (Rifle)
0854 W. Battlement Pky., Apt. C106
Parachute, CO 81635
(970)285-9390

SCORE Office (Pueblo)
302 N. Santa Fe
Pueblo, CO 81003
(719)542-1704
Fax: (719)542-1624
Website: http://www.pueblo.score.org

SCORE Office (Ridgway)
143 Poplar Pl.
Ridgway, CO 81432

SCORE Office (Silverton)
PO Box 480
Silverton, CO 81433
(303)387-5430

SCORE Office (Minturn)
PO Box 2066
Vail, CO 81658
(970)476-1224

Connecticut

SCORE Office (Greater Bridgeport)
230 Park Ave.
Bridgeport, CT 06604
(203)450-9484
Fax: (203)576-4388

SCORE Office (Western Connecticut)
155 Deer Hill Ave.
Danbury, CT 06010
(203)794-1404
Website: http://www.westernconnecticut
.score.org

SCORE Office (Greater Hartford County)
330 Main St., 2nd Fl.
Hartford, CT 06106
(860)240-4700
Fax: (860)240-4659
Website: http://www.greaterhartford.score.org

SCORE Office (Manchester)
20 Hartford Rd.
Manchester, CT 06040
(203)646-2223
Fax: (203)646-5871

SCORE Office (New Britain)
185 Main St., Ste. 431
New Britain, CT 06051
(203)827-4492
Fax: (203)827-4480

SCORE Office (New Haven)
60 Sargent Dr.
New Haven, CT 06511
(203)865-7645
Website: http://www.newhaven.score.org

SCORE Office (Fairfield County)
111 East Ave.
Norwalk, CT 06851
(203)847-7348
Fax: (203)849-9308
Website: http://www.fairfieldcounty
.score.org

SCORE Office (Southeastern Connecticut)
665 Boston Post Rd.
Old Saybrook, CT 06475

(860)388-9508
Website: http://www.southeastern
connecticut.score.org

SCORE Office (Northwest Connecticut)
333 Kennedy Dr.
Torrington, CT 06790
(560)482-6586
Website: http://www.northwest
connecticut.score.org

Delaware

SCORE Office (Dover)
Treadway Towers
PO Box 576
Dover, DE 19903
(302)678-0892
Fax: (302)678-0189

SCORE Office (Lewes)
PO Box 1
Lewes, DE 19958
(302)645-8073
Fax: (302)645-8412

SCORE Office (Milford)
204 NE Front St.
Milford, DE 19963
(302)422-3301

SCORE Office (Wilmington)
824 Market St., Ste. 610
Wilmington, DE 19801
(302)573-6652
Fax: (302)573-6092
Website: http://www.scoredelaware.com

District of Columbia

SCORE Office (George Mason University)
409 3rd St. SW, 4th Fl.
Washington, DC 20024
800-634-0245

SCORE Office (Washington DC)
1110 Vermont Ave. NW, 9th Fl.
Washington, DC 20043
(202)606-4000
Fax: (202)606-4225
E-mail: dcscore@hotmail.com
Website: http://www.scoredc.org/

Florida

SCORE Office (Desota County Chamber of Commerce)
16 South Velucia Ave.
Arcadia, FL 34266
(941)494-4033

SCORE Office (Suncoast/Pinellas)
Airport Business Ctr.
4707 - 140th Ave. N, No. 311
Clearwater, FL 33755
(813)532-6800
Fax: (813)532-6800

SCORE Office (DeLand)
336 N. Woodland Blvd.
DeLand, FL 32720
(904)734-4331
Fax: (904)734-4333

SCORE Office (South Palm Beach)
1050 S. Federal Hwy., Ste. 132
Delray Beach, FL 33483
(561)278-7752
Fax: (561)278-0288

SCORE Office (Ft. Lauderdale)
Federal Bldg., Ste. 123
299 E. Broward Blvd.
Ft. Lauderdale, FL 33301
(954)356-7263
Fax: (954)356-7145

SCORE Office (Southwest Florida)
The Renaissance
8695 College Pky., Ste. 345 & 346
Ft. Myers, FL 33919
(941)489-2935
Fax: (941)489-1170

SCORE Office (Treasure Coast)
Professional Center, Ste. 2
3220 S. US, No. 1
Ft. Pierce, FL 34982
(561)489-0548

SCORE Office (Gainesville)
101 SE 2nd Pl., Ste. 104
Gainesville, FL 32601
(904)375-8278

SCORE Office (Hialeah Dade Chamber)
59 W. 5th St.
Hialeah, FL 33010
(305)887-1515
Fax: (305)887-2453

SCORE Office (Daytona Beach)
921 Nova Rd., Ste. A
Holly Hills, FL 32117
(904)255-6889
Fax: (904)255-0229
E-mail: score87@dbeach.com

SCORE Office (South Broward)
3475 Sheridian St., Ste. 203
Hollywood, FL 33021
(305)966-8415

SCORE Office (Citrus County)
5 Poplar Ct.
Homosassa, FL 34446
(352)382-1037

SCORE Office (Jacksonville)
7825 Baymeadows Way, Ste. 100-B
Jacksonville, FL 32256
(904)443-1911
Fax: (904)443-1980
E-mail: scorejax@juno.com
Website: http://www.scorejax.org/

SCORE Office (Jacksonville Satellite)
3 Independent Dr.
Jacksonville, FL 32256
(904)366-6600
Fax: (904)632-0617

SCORE Office (Central Florida)
5410 S. Florida Ave., No. 3
Lakeland, FL 33801
(941)687-5783
Fax: (941)687-6225

SCORE Office (Lakeland)
100 Lake Morton Dr.
Lakeland, FL 33801
(941)686-2168

SCORE Office (St. Petersburg)
800 W. Bay Dr., Ste. 505
Largo, FL 33712
(813)585-4571

SCORE Office (Leesburg)
9501 US Hwy. 441
Leesburg, FL 34788-8751
(352)365-3556
Fax: (352)365-3501

SCORE Office (Cocoa)
1600 Farno Rd., Unit 205
Melbourne, FL 32935
(407)254-2288

SCORE Office (Melbourne)
Melbourne Professional Complex
1600 Sarno, Ste. 205
Melbourne, FL 32935
(407)254-2288
Fax: (407)245-2288

SCORE Office (Merritt Island)
1600 Sarno Rd., Ste. 205
Melbourne, FL 32935
(407)254-2288
Fax: (407)254-2288

SCORE Office (Space Coast)
Melbourn Professional Complex
1600 Sarno, Ste. 205
Melbourne, FL 32935
(407)254-2288
Fax: (407)254-2288

SCORE Office (Dade)
49 NW 5th St.
Miami, FL 33128
(305)371-6889
Fax: (305)374-1882
E-mail: score@netrox.net
Website: http://www.netrox.net/~score/

SCORE Office (Naples of Collier)
International College
2654 Tamiami Trl. E
Naples, FL 34112
(941)417-1280
Fax: (941)417-1281
E-mail: score@naples.net
Website: http://www.naples.net/clubs/
score/index.htm

SCORE Office (Pasco County)
6014 US Hwy. 19, Ste. 302
New Port Richey, FL 34652
(813)842-4638

SCORE Office (Southeast Volusia)
115 Canal St.
New Smyrna Beach, FL 32168
(904)428-2449
Fax: (904)423-3512

SCORE Office (Ocala)
110 E. Silver Springs Blvd.
Ocala, FL 34470
(352)629-5959

Clay County SCORE Office
Clay County Chamber of Commerce
1734 Kingsdey Ave.
PO Box 1441
Orange Park, FL 32073
(904)264-2651
Fax: (904)269-0363

SCORE Office (Orlando)
80 N. Hughey Ave.
Rm. 445 Federal Bldg.
Orlando, FL 32801
(407)648-6476
Fax: (407)648-6425

SCORE Office (Emerald Coast)
19 W. Garden St., No. 325
Pensacola, FL 32501
(904)444-2060
Fax: (904)444-2070

SCORE Office (Charlotte County)
201 W. Marion Ave., Ste. 211
Punta Gorda, FL 33950
(941)575-1818
E-mail: score@gls3c.com
Website: http://www.charlotte-florida
.com/business/scorepg01.htm

SCORE Office (St. Augustine)
1 Riberia St.
St. Augustine, FL 32084
(904)829-5681
Fax: (904)829-6477

SCORE Office (Bradenton)
2801 Fruitville, Ste. 280
Sarasota, FL 34237
(813)955-1029

SCORE Office (Manasota)
2801 Fruitville Rd., Ste. 280
Sarasota, FL 34237
(941)955-1029
Fax: (941)955-5581
E-mail: score116@gte.net
Website: http://www.score-suncoast.org/

SCORE Office (Tallahassee)
200 W. Park Ave.
Tallahassee, FL 32302
(850)487-2665

SCORE Office (Hillsborough)
4732 Dale Mabry Hwy. N, Ste. 400
Tampa, FL 33614-6509
(813)870-0125

SCORE Office (Lake Sumter)
122 E. Main St.
Tavares, FL 32778-3810
(352)365-3556

SCORE Office (Titusville)
2000 S. Washington Ave.
Titusville, FL 32780
(407)267-3036
Fax: (407)264-0127

SCORE Office (Venice)
257 N. Tamiami Trl.
Venice, FL 34285
(941)488-2236
Fax: (941)484-5903

SCORE Office (Palm Beach)
500 Australian Ave. S, Ste. 100
West Palm Beach, FL 33401
(561)833-1672
Fax: (561)833-1712

SCORE Office (Wildwood)
103 N. Webster St.
Wildwood, FL 34785

Georgia

SCORE Office (Atlanta)
Harris Tower, Suite 1900
233 Peachtree Rd., NE
Atlanta, GA 30309
(404)347-2442
Fax: (404)347-1227

SCORE Office (Augusta)
3126 Oxford Rd.
Augusta, GA 30909
(706)869-9100

SCORE Office (Columbus)
School Bldg.
PO Box 40
Columbus, GA 31901
(706)327-3654

SCORE Office (Dalton-Whitfield)
305 S. Thorton Ave.
Dalton, GA 30720
(706)279-3383

SCORE Office (Gainesville)
PO Box 374
Gainesville, GA 30503
(770)532-6206
Fax: (770)535-8419

SCORE Office (Macon)
711 Grand Bldg.
Macon, GA 31201
(912)751-6160

SCORE Office (Brunswick)
4 Glen Ave.
St. Simons Island, GA 31520
(912)265-0620
Fax: (912)265-0629

SCORE Office (Savannah)
111 E. Liberty St., Ste. 103
Savannah, GA 31401
(912)652-4335
Fax: (912)652-4184
E-mail: info@scoresav.org
Website: http://www.coastalempire.com/
score/index.htm

Guam

SCORE Office (Guam)
Pacific News Bldg., Rm. 103
238 Archbishop Flores St.
Agana, GU 96910-5100
(671)472-7308

Hawaii

SCORE Office (Hawaii, Inc.)
1111 Bishop St., Ste. 204
PO Box 50207
Honolulu, HI 96813
(808)522-8132
Fax: (808)522-8135
E-mail: hnlscore@juno.com

SCORE Office (Kahului)
250 Alamaha, Unit N16A
Kahului, HI 96732
(808)871-7711

SCORE Office (Maui, Inc.)
590 E. Lipoa Pkwy., Ste. 227
Kihei, HI 96753
(808)875-2380

Idaho

SCORE Office (Treasure Valley)
1020 Main St., No. 290
Boise, ID 83702
(208)334-1696
Fax: (208)334-9353

SCORE Office (Eastern Idaho)
2300 N. Yellowstone, Ste. 119
Idaho Falls, ID 83401
(208)523-1022
Fax: (208)528-7127

Illinois

SCORE Office (Fox Valley)
40 W. Downer Pl.
PO Box 277
Aurora, IL 60506
(630)897-9214
Fax: (630)897-7002

SCORE Office (Greater Belvidere)
419 S. State St.
Belvidere, IL 61008
(815)544-4357
Fax: (815)547-7654

SCORE Office (Bensenville)
1050 Busse Hwy. Suite 100
Bensenville, IL 60106
(708)350-2944
Fax: (708)350-2979

SCORE Office (Central Illinois)
402 N. Hershey Rd.
Bloomington, IL 61704
(309)644-0549
Fax: (309)663-8270
E-mail: webmaster@central-illinois-score
.org
Website: http://www.central-illinois-score
.org/

SCORE Office (Southern Illinois)
150 E. Pleasant Hill Rd.
Box 1
Carbondale, IL 62901
(618)453-6654
Fax: (618)453-5040

SCORE Office (Chicago)
Northwest Atrium Ctr.
500 W. Madison St., No. 1250
Chicago, IL 60661
(312)353-7724
Fax: (312)886-5688
Website: http://www.mcs.net/~bic/

SCORE Office (Chicago–Oliver Harvey College)
Pullman Bldg.
1000 E. 11th St., 7th Fl.
Chicago, IL 60628
Fax: (312)468-8086

SCORE Office (Danville)
28 W. N. Street
Danville, IL 61832
(217)442-7232
Fax: (217)442-6228

SCORE Office (Decatur)
Milliken University
1184 W. Main St.
Decatur, IL 62522
(217)424-6297
Fax: (217)424-3993
E-mail: charding@mail.millikin.edu
Website: http://www.millikin.edu/
academics/Tabor/score.html

SCORE Office (Downers Grove)
925 Curtis
Downers Grove, IL 60515
(708)968-4050
Fax: (708)968-8368

SCORE Office (Elgin)
24 E. Chicago, 3rd Fl.
PO Box 648
Elgin, IL 60120
(847)741-5660
Fax: (847)741-5677

SCORE Office (Freeport Area)
26 S. Galena Ave.
Freeport, IL 61032
(815)233-1350
Fax: (815)235-4038

SCORE Office (Galesburg)
292 E. Simmons St.
PO Box 749
Galesburg, IL 61401
(309)343-1194
Fax: (309)343-1195

SCORE Office (Glen Ellyn)
500 Pennsylvania
Glen Ellyn, IL 60137
(708)469-0907
Fax: (708)469-0426

SCORE Office (Greater Alton)
Alden Hall
5800 Godfrey Rd.
Godfrey, IL 62035-2466
(618)467-2280

Fax: (618)466-8289
Website: http://www.altonweb.com/score/

SCORE Office (Grayslake)
19351 W. Washington St.
Grayslake, IL 60030
(708)223-3633
Fax: (708)223-9371

SCORE Office (Harrisburg)
303 S. Commercial
Harrisburg, IL 62946-1528
(618)252-8528
Fax: (618)252-0210

SCORE Office (Joliet)
100 N. Chicago
Joliet, IL 60432
(815)727-5371
Fax: (815)727-5374

SCORE Office (Kankakee)
101 S. Schuyler Ave.
Kankakee, IL 60901
(815)933-0376
Fax: (815)933-0380

SCORE Office (Macomb)
216 Seal Hall, Rm. 214
Macomb, IL 61455
(309)298-1128
Fax: (309)298-2520

SCORE Office (Matteson)
210 Lincoln Mall
Matteson, IL 60443
(708)709-3750
Fax: (708)503-9322

SCORE Office (Mattoon)
1701 Wabash Ave.
Mattoon, IL 61938
(217)235-5661
Fax: (217)234-6544

SCORE Office (Quad Cities)
622 19th St.
Moline, IL 61265
(309)797-0082
Fax: (309)757-5435
E-mail: score@qconline.com
Website: http://www.qconline.com/
business/score/

SCORE Office (Naperville)
131 W. Jefferson Ave.
Naperville, IL 60540
(708)355-4141
Fax: (708)355-8355

SCORE Office (Northbrook)
2002 Walters Ave.
Northbrook, IL 60062

(847)498-5555
Fax: (847)498-5510

SCORE Office (Palos Hills)
10900 S. 88th Ave.
Palos Hills, IL 60465
(847)974-5468
Fax: (847)974-0078

SCORE Office (Peoria)
124 SW Adams, Ste. 300
Peoria, IL 61602
(309)676-0755
Fax: (309)676-7534

SCORE Office (Prospect Heights)
1375 Wolf Rd.
Prospect Heights, IL 60070
(847)537-8660
Fax: (847)537-7138

SCORE Office (Quincy Tri-State)
300 Civic Center Plz., Ste. 245
Quincy, IL 62301
(217)222-8093
Fax: (217)222-3033

SCORE Office (River Grove)
2000 5th Ave.
River Grove, IL 60171
(708)456-0300
Fax: (708)583-3121

SCORE Office (Northern Illinois)
515 N. Court St.
Rockford, IL 61103
(815)962-0122
Fax: (815)962-0122

SCORE Office (St. Charles)
103 N. 1st Ave.
St. Charles, IL 60174-1982
(847)584-8384
Fax: (847)584-6065

SCORE Office (Springfield)
511 W. Capitol Ave., Ste. 302
Springfield, IL 62704
(217)492-4416
Fax: (217)492-4867

SCORE Office (Sycamore)
112 Somunak St.
Sycamore, IL 60178
(815)895-3456
Fax: (815)895-0125

SCORE Office (University)
Hwy. 50 & Stuenkel Rd. Ste. C3305
University Park, IL 60466
(708)534-5000
Fax: (708)534-8457

Indiana

SCORE Office (Anderson)
205 W. 11th St.
Anderson, IN 46015
(317)642-0264

SCORE Office (Bloomington)
Star Center
216 W. Allen
Bloomington, IN 47403
(812)335-7334
E-mail: wtfische@indiana.edu
Website: http://www.brainfreezemedia
.com/score527/

SCORE Office (South East Indiana)
500 Franklin St.
Box 29
Columbus, IN 47201
(812)379-4457

SCORE Office (Corydon)
310 N. Elm St.
Corydon, IN 47112
(812)738-2137
Fax: (812)738-6438

SCORE Office (Crown Point)
Old Courthouse Sq. Ste. 206
PO Box 43
Crown Point, IN 46307
(219)663-1800

SCORE Office (Elkhart)
418 S. Main St.
Elkhart, IN 46515
(219)293-1531
Fax: (219)294-1859

SCORE Office (Evansville)
1100 W. Lloyd Expy., Ste. 105
Evansville, IN 47708
(812)426-6144

SCORE Office (Fort Wayne)
1300 S. Harrison St.
Ft. Wayne, IN 46802
(219)422-2601
Fax: (219)422-2601

SCORE Office (Gary)
973 W. 6th Ave., Rm. 326
Gary, IN 46402
(219)882-3918

SCORE Office (Hammond)
7034 Indianapolis Blvd.
Hammond, IN 46324
(219)931-1000
Fax: (219)845-9548

SCORE Office (Indianapolis)
429 N. Pennsylvania St., Ste. 100
Indianapolis, IN 46204-1873

(317)226-7264
Fax: (317)226-7259
E-mail: inscore@indy.net
Website: http://www.score-indianapolis
.org/

SCORE Office (Jasper)
PO Box 307
Jasper, IN 47547-0307
(812)482-6866

**SCORE Office (Kokomo/Howard
Counties)**
106 N. Washington St.
Kokomo, IN 46901
(765)457-5301
Fax: (765)452-4564

SCORE Office (Logansport)
300 E. Broadway, Ste. 103
Logansport, IN 46947
(219)753-6388

SCORE Office (Madison)
301 E. Main St.
Madison, IN 47250
(812)265-3135
Fax: (812)265-2923

SCORE Office (Marengo)
Rt. 1 Box 224D
Marengo, IN 47140
Fax: (812)365-2793

**SCORE Office (Marion/Grant
Counties)**
215 S. Adams
Marion, IN 46952
(765)664-5107

SCORE Office (Merrillville)
255 W. 80th Pl.
Merrillville, IN 46410
(219)769-8180
Fax: (219)736-6223

SCORE Office (Michigan City)
200 E. Michigan Blvd.
Michigan City, IN 46360
(219)874-6221
Fax: (219)873-1204

SCORE Office (South Central Indiana)
4100 Charleston Rd.
New Albany, IN 47150-9538
(812)945-0066

SCORE Office (Rensselaer)
104 W. Washington
Rensselaer, IN 47978

SCORE Office (Salem)
210 N. Main St.
Salem, IN 47167

(812)883-4303
Fax: (812)883-1467

SCORE Office (South Bend)
300 N. Michigan St.
South Bend, IN 46601
(219)282-4350
E-mail: chair@southbend-score.org
Website: http://www.southbend-score.org/

SCORE Office (Valparaiso)
150 Lincolnway
Valparaiso, IN 46383
(219)462-1105
Fax: (219)469-5710

SCORE Office (Vincennes)
27 N. 3rd
PO Box 553
Vincennes, IN 47591
(812)882-6440
Fax: (812)882-6441

SCORE Office (Wabash)
PO Box 371
Wabash, IN 46992
(219)563-1168
Fax: (219)563-6920

Iowa

SCORE Office (Burlington)
Federal Bldg.
300 N. Main St.
Burlington, IA 52601
(319)752-2967

SCORE Office (Cedar Rapids)
2750 1st Ave. NE, Ste 350
Cedar Rapids, IA 52401-1806
(319)362-6405
Fax: (319)362-7861
E:mail: score@scorecr.org
Website: http://www.scorecr.org

SCORE Office (Illowa)
333 4th Ave. S
Clinton, IA 52732
(319)242-5702

SCORE Office (Council Bluffs)
7 N. 6th St.
Council Bluffs, IA 51502
(712)325-1000

SCORE Office (Northeast Iowa)
3404 285th St.
Cresco, IA 52136
(319)547-3377

SCORE Office (Des Moines)
Federal Bldg., Rm. 749
210 Walnut St.

Des Moines, IA 50309-2186
(515)284-4760

SCORE Office (Ft. Dodge)
Federal Bldg., Rm. 436
205 S. 8th St.
Ft. Dodge, IA 50501
(515)955-2622

SCORE Office (Independence)
110 1st. St. east
Independence, IA 50644
(319)334-7178
Fax: (319)334-7179

SCORE Office (Iowa City)
210 Federal Bldg.
PO Box 1853
Iowa City, IA 52240-1853
(319)338-1662

SCORE Office (Keokuk)
401 Main St.
Pierce Bldg., No. 1
Keokuk, IA 52632
(319)524-5055

SCORE Office (Central Iowa)
Fisher Community College
709 S. Center
Marshalltown, IA 50158
(515)753-6645

SCORE Office (River City)
15 West State St.
Mason City, IA 50401
(515)423-5724

SCORE Office (South Central)
SBDC, Indian Hills Community College
525 Grandview Ave.
Ottumwa, IA 52501
(515)683-5127
Fax: (515)683-5263

SCORE Office (Dubuque)
10250 Sundown Rd.
Peosta, IA 52068
(319)556-5110

SCORE Office (Southwest Iowa)
614 W. Sheridan
Shenandoah, IA 51601
(712)246-3260

SCORE Office (Sioux City)
Federal Bldg.
320 6th St.
Sioux City, IA 51101
(712)277-2324
Fax: (712)277-2325

SCORE Office (Iowa Lakes)
122 W. 5th St.
Spencer, IA 51301
(712)262-3059

SCORE Office (Vista)
119 W. 6th St.
Storm Lake, IA 50588
(712)732-3780

SCORE Office (Waterloo)
215 E. 4th
Waterloo, IA 50703
(319)233-8431

Kansas

SCORE Office (Southwest Kansas)
501 W. Spruce
Dodge City, KS 67801
(316)227-3119

SCORE Office (Emporia)
811 Homewood
Emporia, KS 66801
(316)342-1600

SCORE Office (Golden Belt)
1307 Williams
Great Bend, KS 67530
(316)792-2401

SCORE Office (Hays)
PO Box 400
Hays, KS 67601
(913)625-6595

SCORE Office (Hutchinson)
1 E. 9th St.
Hutchinson, KS 67501
(316)665-8468
Fax: (316)665-7619

SCORE Office (Southeast Kansas)
404 Westminster Pl.
PO Box 886
Independence, KS 67301
(316)331-4741

SCORE Office (McPherson)
306 N. Main
PO Box 616
McPherson, KS 67460
(316)241-3303

SCORE Office (Salina)
120 Ash St.
Salina, KS 67401
(785)243-4290
Fax: (785)243-1833

SCORE Office (Topeka)
1700 College
Topeka, KS 66621
(785)231-1010

SCORE Office (Wichita)
100 E. English, Ste. 510
Wichita, KS 67202

(316)269-6273
Fax: (316)269-6499

SCORE Office (Ark Valley)
205 E. 9th St.
Winfield, KS 67156
(316)221-1617

Kentucky

SCORE Office (Ashland)
PO Box 830
Ashland, KY 41105
(606)329-8011
Fax: (606)325-4607

SCORE Office (Bowling Green)
812 State St.
PO Box 51
Bowling Green, KY 42101
(502)781-3200
Fax: (502)843-0458

SCORE Office (Tri-Lakes)
508 Barbee Way
Danville, KY 40422-1548
(606)231-9902

SCORE Office (Glasgow)
301 W. Main St.
Glasgow, KY 42141
(502)651-3161
Fax: (502)651-3122

SCORE Office (Hazard)
B & I Technical Center
100 Airport Gardens Rd.
Hazard, KY 41701
(606)439-5856
Fax: (606)439-1808

SCORE Office (Lexington)
410 W. Vine St., Ste. 290, Civic C
Lexington, KY 40507
(606)231-9902
Fax: (606)253-3190
E-mail: scorelex@uky.campus.mci.net

SCORE Office (Louisville)
188 Federal Office Bldg.
600 Dr. Martin L. King Jr. Pl.
Louisville, KY 40202
(502)582-5976

SCORE Office (Madisonville)
257 N. Main
Madisonville, KY 42431
(502)825-1399
Fax: (502)825-1396

SCORE Office (Paducah)
Federal Office Bldg.
501 Broadway, Rm. B-36

Paducah, KY 42001
(502)442-5685

Louisiana

SCORE Office (Central Louisiana)
802 3rd St.
Alexandria, LA 71309
(318)442-6671

SCORE Office (Baton Rouge)
564 Laurel St.
PO Box 3217
Baton Rouge, LA 70801
(504)381-7130
Fax: (504)336-4306

SCORE Office (North Shore)
2 W. Thomas
Hammond, LA 70401
(504)345-4457
Fax: (504)345-4749

SCORE Office (Lafayette)
804 St. Mary Blvd.
Lafayette, LA 70505-1307
(318)233-2705
Fax: (318)234-8671
E-mail: score302@aol.com

SCORE Office (Lake Charles)
120 W. Pujo St.
Lake Charles, LA 70601
(318)433-3632

SCORE Office (New Orleans)
365 Canal St., Ste. 3100
New Orleans, LA 70130
(504)589-2356
Fax: (504)589-2339

SCORE Office (Shreveport)
400 Edwards St.
Shreveport, LA 71101
(318)677-2536
Fax: (318)677-2541

Maine

SCORE Office (Augusta)
40 Western Ave.
Augusta, ME 04330
(207)622-8509

SCORE Office (Bangor)
Peabody Hall, Rm. 229
One College Cir.
Bangor, ME 04401
(207)941-9707

SCORE Office (Central & Northern Arroostock)
111 High St.
Caribou, ME 04736

(207)492-8010
Fax: (207)492-8010

SCORE Office (Penquis)
South St.
Dover Foxcroft, ME 04426
(207)564-7021

SCORE Office (Maine Coastal)
Mill Mall
Box 1105
Ellsworth, ME 04605-1105
(207)667-5800
E-mail: score@arcadia.net

SCORE Office (Lewiston-Auburn)
BIC of Maine-Bates Mill Complex
35 Canal St.
Lewiston, ME 04240-7764
(207)782-3708
Fax: (207)783-7745

SCORE Office (Portland)
66 Pearl St., Rm. 210
Portland, ME 04101
(207)772-1147
Fax: (207)772-5581
E-mail: Score53@score.maine.org
Website: http://www.score.maine.org/
chapter53/

SCORE Office (Western Mountains)
255 River St.
PO Box 252
Rumford, ME 04257-0252
(207)369-9976

SCORE Office (Oxford Hills)
166 Main St.
South Paris, ME 04281
(207)743-0499

Maryland

SCORE Office (Southern Maryland)
2525 Riva Rd., Ste. 110
Annapolis, MD 21401
(410)266-9553
Fax: (410)573-0981
E-mail: score390@aol.com
Website: http://members.aol.com/
score390/index.htm

SCORE Office (Baltimore)
The City Crescent Bldg., 6th Fl.
10 S. Howard St.
Baltimore, MD 21201
(410)962-2233
Fax: (410)962-1805

SCORE Office (Bel Air)
108 S. Bond St.
Bel Air, MD 21014

(410)838-2020
Fax: (410)893-4715

SCORE Office (Bethesda)
7910 Woodmont Ave., Ste. 1204
Bethesda, MD 20814
(301)652-4900
Fax: (301)657-1973

SCORE Office (Bowie)
6670 Race Track Rd.
Bowie, MD 20715
(301)262-0920
Fax: (301)262-0921

SCORE Office (Dorchester County)
203 Sunburst Hwy.
Cambridge, MD 21613
(410)228-3575

SCORE Office (Upper Shore)
210 Marlboro Ave.
Easton, MD 21601
(410)822-4606
Fax: (410)822-7922

SCORE Office (Frederick County)
43A S. Market St.
Frederick, MD 21701
(301)662-8723
Fax: (301)846-4427

SCORE Office (Gaithersburg)
9 Park Ave.
Gaithersburg, MD 20877
(301)840-1400
Fax: (301)963-3918

SCORE Office (Glen Burnie)
103 Crain Hwy. SE
Glen Burnie, MD 21061
(410)766-8282
Fax: (410)766-9722

SCORE Office (Hagerstown)
111 W. Washington St.
Hagerstown, MD 21740
(301)739-2015
Fax: (301)739-1278

SCORE Office (Laurel)
7901 Sandy Spring Rd. Ste. 501
Laurel, MD 20707
(301)725-4000
Fax: (301)725-0776

SCORE Office (Salisbury)
300 E. Main St.
Salisbury, MD 21801
(410)749-0185
Fax: (410)860-9925

Massachusetts

SCORE Office (NE Massachusetts)
100 Cummings Ctr., Ste. 101 K
Beverly, MA 01923
(978)922-9441
Website: http://www1.shore.net/~score/

SCORE Office (Boston)
10 Causeway St., Rm. 265
Boston, MA 02222-1093
(617)565-5591
Fax: (617)565-5598
E-mail: boston-score-
20@worldnet.att.net
Website: http://www.scoreboston.org/

**SCORE office (Bristol/Plymouth
County)**
53 N. 6th St., Federal Bldg.
Bristol, MA 02740
(508)994-5093

SCORE Office (SE Massachusetts)
60 School St.
Brockton, MA 02401
(508)587-2673
Fax: (508)587-1340
Website: http://www.metrosouth
chamber.com/score.html

SCORE Office (North Adams)
820 N. State Rd.
Cheshire, MA 01225
(413)743-5100

SCORE Office (Clinton Satellite)
1 Green St.
Clinton, MA 01510
Fax: (508)368-7689

SCORE Office (Greenfield)
PO Box 898
Greenfield, MA 01302
(413)773-5463
Fax: (413)773-7008

SCORE Office (Haverhill)
87 Winter St.
Haverhill, MA 01830
(508)373-5663
Fax: (508)373-8060

SCORE Office (Hudson Satellite)
PO Box 578
Hudson, MA 01749
(508)568-0360
Fax: (508)568-0360

SCORE Office (Cape Cod)
Independence Pk., Ste. 5B
270 Communications Way
Hyannis, MA 02601

(508)775-4884
Fax: (508)790-2540

SCORE Office (Lawrence)
264 Essex St.
Lawrence, MA 01840
(508)686-0900
Fax: (508)794-9953

SCORE Office (Leominster Satellite)
110 Erdman Way
Leominster, MA 01453
(508)840-4300
Fax: (508)840-4896

SCORE Office (Bristol/Plymouth Counties)
53 N. 6th St., Federal Bldg.
New Bedford, MA 02740
(508)994-5093

SCORE Office (Newburyport)
29 State St.
Newburyport, MA 01950
(617)462-6680

SCORE Office (Pittsfield)
66 West St.
Pittsfield, MA 01201
(413)499-2485

SCORE Office (Haverhill-Salem)
32 Derby Sq.
Salem, MA 01970
(508)745-0330
Fax: (508)745-3855

SCORE Office (Springfield)
1350 Main St.
Federal Bldg.
Springfield, MA 01103
(413)785-0314

SCORE Office (Carver)
12 Taunton Green, Ste. 201
Taunton, MA 02780
(508)824-4068
Fax: (508)824-4069

SCORE Office (Worcester)
33 Waldo St.
Worcester, MA 01608
(508)753-2929
Fax: (508)754-8560

Michigan

SCORE Office (Allegan)
PO Box 338
Allegan, MI 49010
(616)673-2479

SCORE Office (Ann Arbor)
425 S. Main St., Ste. 103
Ann Arbor, MI 48104
(313)665-4433

SCORE Office (Battle Creek)
34 W. Jackson Ste. 4A
Battle Creek, MI 49017-3505
(616)962-4076
Fax: (616)962-6309

SCORE Office (Cadillac)
222 Lake St.
Cadillac, MI 49601
(616)775-9776
Fax: (616)768-4255

SCORE Office (Detroit)
477 Michigan Ave., Rm. 515
Detroit, MI 48226
(313)226-7947
Fax: (313)226-3448

SCORE Office (Flint)
708 Root Rd., Rm. 308
Flint, MI 48503
(810)233-6846

SCORE Office (Grand Rapids)
111 Pearl St. NW
Grand Rapids, MI 49503-2831
(616)771-0305
Fax: (616)771-0328
E-mail: scoreone@iserv.net
Website: http://www.iserv.net/
~scoreone/

SCORE Office (Holland)
480 State St.
Holland, MI 49423
(616)396-9472

SCORE Office (Jackson)
209 East Washington
PO Box 80
Jackson, MI 49204
(517)782-8221
Fax: (517)782-0061

SCORE Office (Kalamazoo)
345 W. Michigan Ave.
Kalamazoo, MI 49007
(616)381-5382
Fax: (616)384-0096
E-mail: score@nucleus.net

SCORE Office (Lansing)
117 E. Allegan
PO Box 14030
Lansing, MI 48901
(517)487-6340
Fax: (517)484-6910

SCORE Office (Livonia)
15401 Farmington Rd.
Livonia, MI 48154
(313)427-2122
Fax: (313)427-6055

SCORE Office (Madison Heights)
26345 John R
Madison Heights, MI 48071
(810)542-5010
Fax: (810)542-6821

SCORE Office (Monroe)
111 E. 1st
Monroe, MI 48161
(313)242-3366
Fax: (313)242-7253

SCORE Office (Mt. Clemens)
58 S/B Gratiot
Mt. Clemens, MI 48043
(810)463-1528
Fax: (810)463-6541

SCORE Office (Muskegon)
PO Box 1087
230 Terrace Plz.
Muskegon, MI 49443
(616)722-3751
Fax: (616)728-7251

SCORE Office (Petoskey)
401 E. Mitchell St.
Petoskey, MI 49770
(616)347-4150

SCORE Office (Pontiac)
Executive Office Bldg.
1200 N. Telegraph Rd.
Pontiac, MI 48341
(810)975-9555

SCORE Office (Pontiac)
PO Box 430025
Pontiac, MI 48343
(810)335-9600

SCORE Office (Port Huron)
920 Pinegrove Ave.
Port Huron, MI 48060
(810)985-7101

SCORE Office (Rochester)
71 Walnut Ste. 110
Rochester, MI 48307
(810)651-6700
Fax: (810)651-5270

SCORE Office (Saginaw)
901 S. Washington Ave.
Saginaw, MI 48601
(517)752-7161
Fax: (517)752-9055

SCORE Office (Upper Peninsula)
2581 I-75 Business Spur
Sault Ste. Marie, MI 49783
(906)632-3301

SCORE Office (Southfield)
21000 W. 10 Mile Rd.
Southfield, MI 48075
(810)204-3050
Fax: (810)204-3099

SCORE Office (Traverse City)
202 E. Grandview Pkwy.
PO Box 387
Traverse City, MI 49685
(616)947-5075
Fax: (616)946-2565

SCORE Office (Warren)
30500 Van Dyke, Ste. 118
Warren, MI 48093
(810)751-3939

Minnesota

SCORE Office (Aitkin)
Aitkin, MN 56431
(218)741-3906

SCORE Office (Albert Lea)
202 N. Broadway Ave.
Albert Lea, MN 56007
(507)373-7487

SCORE Office (Austin)
PO Box 864
Austin, MN 55912
(507)437-4561
Fax: (507)437-4869

SCORE Office (South Metro)
Ames Business Ctr.
2500 W. County Rd., No. 42
Burnsville, MN 55337
(612)898-5645
Fax: (612)435-6972
E-mail: southmetro@scoreminn.org
Website: http://www.scoreminn.org/
southmetro/

SCORE Office (Duluth)
1717 Minnesota Ave.
Duluth, MN 55802
(218)727-8286
Fax: (218)727-3113
E-mail: duluth@scoreminn.org
Website: http://www.scoreminn.org

SCORE Office (Fairmont)
PO Box 826
Fairmont, MN 56031
(507)235-5547
Fax: (507)235-8411

SCORE Office (Southwest Minnesota)
112 Riverfront St.
Box 999
Mankato, MN 56001

(507)345-4519
Fax: (507)345-4451
Website: http://www.scoreminn.org/

SCORE Office (Minneapolis)
North Plaza Bldg., Ste. 51
5217 Wayzata Blvd.
Minneapolis, MN 55416
(612)591-0539
Fax: (612)544-0436
Website: http://www.scoreminn.org/

SCORE Office (Owatonna)
PO Box 331
Owatonna, MN 55060
(507)451-7970
Fax: (507)451-7972

SCORE Office (Red Wing)
2000 W. Main St., Ste. 324
Red Wing, MN 55066
(612)388-4079

SCORE Office (Southeastern Minnesota)
220 S. Broadway, Ste. 100
Rochester, MN 55901
(507)288-1122
Fax: (507)282-8960
Website: http://www.scoreminn.org/

SCORE Office (Brainerd)
St. Cloud, MN 56301

SCORE Office (Central Area)
1527 Northway Dr.
St. Cloud, MN 56301
(320)240-1332
Fax: (320)255-9050
Website: http://www.scoreminn.org/

SCORE Office (St. Paul)
350 St. Peter St., No. 295
Lowry Professional Bldg.
St. Paul, MN 55102
(651)223-5010
Fax: (651)223-5048
Website: http://www.scoreminn.org/

SCORE Office (Winona)
Box 870
Winona, MN 55987
(507)452-2272
Fax: (507)454-8814

SCORE Office (Worthington)
1121 3rd Ave.
Worthington, MN 56187
(507)372-2919
Fax: (507)372-2827

Mississippi

SCORE Office (Delta)
915 Washington Ave.
PO Box 933
Greenville, MS 38701
(601)378-3141

SCORE Office (Gulfcoast)
1 Government Plaza
2909 13th St., Ste. 203
Gulfport, MS 39501
(228)863-0054

SCORE Office (Jackson)
1st Jackson Center, Ste. 400
101 W. Capitol St.
Jackson, MS 39201
(601)965-5533

SCORE Office (Meridian)
5220 16th Ave.
Meridian, MS 39305
(601)482-4412

Missouri

SCORE Office (Lake of the Ozark)
University Extension
113 Kansas St.
PO Box 1405
Camdenton, MO 65020
(573)346-2644
Fax: (573)346-2694
E-mail: score@cdoc.net
Website: http://sites.cdoc.net/score/

Chamber of Commerce (Cape Girardeau)
PO Box 98
Cape Girardeau, MO 63702-0098
(314)335-3312

SCORE Office (Mid-Missouri)
1705 Halstead Ct.
Columbia, MO 65203
(573)874-1132

SCORE Office (Ozark-Gateway)
1486 Glassy Rd.
Cuba, MO 65453-1640
(573)885-4954

SCORE Office (Kansas City)
323 W. 8th St., Ste. 104
Kansas City, MO 64105
(816)374-6675
Fax: (816)374-6692
E-mail: SCOREBIC@AOL.COM
Website: http://www.crn.org/score/

SCORE Office (Sedalia)
Lucas Place
323 W. 8th St., Ste.104

Kansas City, MO 64105
(816)374-6675

SCORE office (Tri-Lakes)
PO Box 1148
Kimberling, MO 65686
(417)739-3041

SCORE Office (Tri-Lakes)
HCRI Box 85
Lampe, MO 65681
(417)858-6798

SCORE Office (Mexico)
111 N. Washington St.
Mexico, MO 65265
(314)581-2765

SCORE Office (Southeast Missouri)
Rte. 1, Box 280
Neelyville, MO 63954
(573)989-3577

SCORE office (Poplar Bluff Area)
806 Emma St.
Poplar Bluff, MO 63901
(573)686-8892

SCORE Office (St. Joseph)
3003 Frederick Ave.
St. Joseph, MO 64506
(816)232-4461

SCORE Office (St. Louis)
815 Olive St., Rm. 242
St. Louis, MO 63101-1569
(314)539-6970
Fax: (314)539-3785
E-mail: info@stlscore.org
Website: http://www.stlscore.org/

SCORE Office (Lewis & Clark)
425 Spencer Rd.
St. Peters, MO 63376
(314)928-2900
Fax: (314)928-2900
E-mail: score01@mail.win.org

SCORE Office (Springfield)
620 S. Glenstone, Ste. 110
Springfield, MO 65802-3200
(417)864-7670
Fax: (417)864-4108

SCORE office (Southeast Kansas)
1206 W. First St.
Webb City, MO 64870
(417)673-3984

Montana

SCORE Office (Billings)
815 S. 27th St.
Billings, MT 59101
(406)245-4111

SCORE Office (Bozeman)
1205 E. Main St.
Bozeman, MT 59715
(406)586-5421

SCORE Office (Butte)
1000 George St.
Butte, MT 59701
(406)723-3177

SCORE Office (Great Falls)
710 First Ave. N
Great Falls, MT 59401
(406)761-4434
E-mail: scoregtf@in.tch.com

SCORE Office (Havre, Montana)
518 First St.
Havre, MT 59501
(406)265-4383

SCORE Office (Helena)
Federal Bldg.
301 S. Park
Helena, MT 59626-0054
(406)441-1081

SCORE Office (Kalispell)
2 Main St.
Kalispell, MT 59901
(406)756-5271
Fax: (406)752-6665

SCORE Office (Missoula)
723 Ronan
Missoula, MT 59806
(406)327-8806
E-mail: score@safeshop.com
Website: http://missoula.bigsky.net/score/

Nebraska

SCORE Office (Columbus)
Columbus, NE 68601
(402)564-2769

SCORE Office (Fremont)
92 W. 5th St.
Fremont, NE 68025
(402)721-2641

SCORE Office (Hastings)
Hastings, NE 68901
(402)463-3447

SCORE Office (Lincoln)
8800 O St.
Lincoln, NE 68520
(402)437-2409

SCORE Office (Panhandle)
150549 CR 30
Minatare, NE 69356

(308)632-2133
Website: http://www.tandt.com/SCORE

SCORE Office (Norfolk)
3209 S. 48th Ave.
Norfolk, NE 68106
(402)564-2769

SCORE Office (North Platte)
3301 W. 2nd St.
North Platte, NE 69101
(308)532-4466

SCORE Office (Omaha)
11145 Mill Valley Rd.
Omaha, NE 68154
(402)221-3606
Fax: (402)221-3680
E-mail: infoctr@ne.uswest.net
Website: http://www.tandt.com/score/

Nevada

SCORE Office (Incline Village)
969 Tahoe Blvd.
Incline Village, NV 89451
(702)831-7327
Fax: (702)832-1605

SCORE Office (Carson City)
301 E. Stewart
PO Box 7527
Las Vegas, NV 89125
(702)388-6104

SCORE Office (Las Vegas)
300 Las Vegas Blvd. S, Ste. 1100
Las Vegas, NV 89101
(702)388-6104

SCORE Office (Northern Nevada)
SBDC, College of Business
Administration
Univ. of Nevada
Reno, NV 89557-0100
(702)784-4436
Fax: (702)784-4337

New Hampshire

SCORE Office (North Country)
PO Box 34
Berlin, NH 03570
(603)752-1090

SCORE Office (Concord)
143 N. Main St., Rm. 202A
PO Box 1258
Concord, NH 03301
(603)225-1400
Fax: (603)225-1409

SCORE Office (Dover)
299 Central Ave.
Dover, NH 03820

(603)742-2218
Fax: (603)749-6317

SCORE Office (Monadnock)
34 Mechanic St.
Keene, NH 03431-3421
(603)352-0320

SCORE Office (Lakes Region)
67 Water St., Ste. 105
Laconia, NH 03246
(603)524-9168

SCORE Office (Upper Valley)
Citizens Bank Bldg., Rm. 310
20 W. Park St.
Lebanon, NH 03766
(603)448-3491
Fax: (603)448-1908
E-mail: billt@valley.net
Website: http://www.valley.net/~score/

SCORE Office (Merrimack Valley)
275 Chestnut St., Rm. 618
Manchester, NH 03103
(603)666-7561
Fax: (603)666-7925

SCORE Office (Mt. Washington Valley)
PO Box 1066
North Conway, NH 03818
(603)383-0800

SCORE Office (Seacoast)
195 Commerce Way, Unit-A
Portsmouth, NH 03801-3251
(603)433-0575

New Jersey

SCORE Office (Somerset)
Paritan Valley Community College,
Rte. 28
Branchburg, NJ 08807
(908)218-8874
E-mail: nj-score@grizbiz.com.
Website: http://www.nj-score.org/

SCORE Office (Chester)
5 Old Mill Rd.
Chester, NJ 07930
(908)879-7080

SCORE Office (Greater Princeton)
4 A George Washington Dr.
Cranbury, NJ 08512
(609)520-1776

SCORE Office (Freehold)
36 W. Main St.
Freehold, NJ 07728
(908)462-3030
Fax: (908)462-2123

SCORE Office (North West)
Picantinny Innovation Ctr.
3159 Schrader Rd.
Hamburg, NJ 07419
(973)209-8525
Fax: (973)209-7252
E-mail: nj-score@grizbiz.com
Website: http://www.nj-score.org/

SCORE Office (Monmouth)
765 Newman Springs Rd.
Lincroft, NJ 07738
(908)224-2573
E-mail: nj-score@grizbiz.com
Website: http://www.nj-score.org/

SCORE Office (Manalapan)
125 Symmes Dr.
Manalapan, NJ 07726
(908)431-7220

SCORE Office (Jersey City)
2 Gateway Ctr., 4th Fl.
Newark, NJ 07102
(973)645-3982
Fax: (973)645-2375

SCORE Office (Newark)
2 Gateway Center, 15th Fl.
Newark, NJ 07102-5553
(973)645-3982
Fax: (973)645-2375
E-mail: nj-score@grizbiz.com
Website: http://www.nj-score.org

SCORE Office (Bergen County)
327 E. Ridgewood Ave.
Paramus, NJ 07652
(201)599-6090
E-mail: nj-score@grizbiz.com
Website: http://www.nj-score.org/

SCORE Office (Pennsauken)
4900 Rte. 70
Pennsauken, NJ 08109
(609)486-3421

SCORE Office (Southern New Jersey)
4900 Rte. 70
Pennsauken, NJ 08109
(609)486-3421
E-mail: nj-score@grizbiz.com
Website: http://www.nj-score.org/

SCORE Office (Greater Princeton)
216 Rockingham Row
Princeton Forrestal Village
Princeton, NJ 08540
(609)520-1776
Fax: (609)520-9107
E-mail: nj-score@grizbiz.com
Website: http://www.nj-score.org/

SCORE Office (Shrewsbury)
Hwy. 35
Shrewsbury, NJ 07702
(908)842-5995
Fax: (908)219-6140

SCORE Office (Ocean County)
33 Washington St.
Toms River, NJ 08754
(732)505-6033
E-mail: nj-score@grizbiz.com
Website: http://www.nj-score.org/

SCORE Office (Wall)
2700 Allaire Rd.
Wall, NJ 07719
(908)449-8877

SCORE Office (Wayne)
2055 Hamburg Tpke.
Wayne, NJ 07470
(201)831-7788
Fax: (201)831-9112

New Mexico

SCORE Office (Albuquerque)
525 Buena Vista, SE
Albuquerque, NM 87106
(505)272-7999
Fax: (505)272-7963

SCORE Office (Las Cruces)
Loretto Towne Center
505 S. Main St., Ste. 125
Las Cruces, NM 88001
(505)523-5627
Fax: (505)524-2101
E-mail: score.397@zianet.com

SCORE Office (Roswell)
Federal Bldg., Rm. 237
Roswell, NM 88201
(505)625-2112
Fax: (505)623-2545

SCORE Office (Santa Fe)
Montoya Federal Bldg.
120 Federal Place, Rm. 307
Santa Fe, NM 87501
(505)988-6302
Fax: (505)988-6300

New York

SCORE Office (Northeast)
1 Computer Dr. S
Albany, NY 12205
(518)446-1118
Fax: (518)446-1228

SCORE Office (Auburn)
30 South St.
PO Box 675

Auburn, NY 13021
(315)252-7291

SCORE Office (South Tier Binghamton)
Metro Center, 2nd Fl.
49 Court St.
PO Box 995
Binghamton, NY 13902
(607)772-8860

SCORE Office (Queens County City)
12055 Queens Blvd., Rm. 333
Borough Hall, NY 11424
(718)263-8961

SCORE Office (Buffalo)
Federal Bldg., Rm. 1311
111 W. Huron St.
Buffalo, NY 14202
(716)551-4301
Website: http://www2.pcom.net/score/
buf45.html

SCORE Office (Canandaigua)
Chamber of Commerce Bldg.
113 S. Main St.
Canandaigua, NY 14424
(716)394-4400
Fax: (716)394-4546

SCORE Office (Chemung)
333 E. Water St., 4th Fl.
Elmira, NY 14901
(607)734-3358

SCORE Office (Geneva)
Chamber of Commerce Bldg.
PO Box 587
Geneva, NY 14456
(315)789-1776
Fax: (315)789-3993

SCORE Office (Glens Falls)
84 Broad St.
Glens Falls, NY 12801
(518)798-8463
Fax: (518)745-1433

SCORE Office (Orange County)
40 Matthews St.
Goshen, NY 10924
(914)294-8080
Fax: (914)294-6121

SCORE Office (Huntington Area)
151 W. Carver St.
Huntington, NY 11743
(516)423-6100

SCORE Office (Tompkins County)
904 E. Shore Dr.
Ithaca, NY 14850
(607)273-7080

SCORE Office (Long Island City)
120-55 Queens Blvd.
Jamaica, NY 11424
(718)263-8961
Fax: (718)263-9032

SCORE Office (Chatauqua)
101 W. 5th St.
Jamestown, NY 14701
(716)484-1103

SCORE Office (Westchester)
2 Caradon Ln.
Katonah, NY 10536
(914)948-3907
Fax: (914)948-4645
E-mail: score@w-w-w.com
Website: http://w-w-w.com/score/

SCORE Office (Queens County)
Queens Borough Hall
120-55 Queens Blvd. Rm. 333
Kew Gardens, NY 11424
(718)263-8961
Fax: (718)263-9032

SCORE Office (Brookhaven)
3233 Rte. 112
Medford, NY 11763
(516)451-6563
Fax: (516)451-6925

SCORE Office (Melville)
35 Pinelawn Rd., Rm. 207-W
Melville, NY 11747
(516)454-0771

SCORE Office (Nassau County)
400 County Seat Dr., No. 140
Mineola, NY 11501
(516)571-3303
E-mail: Counse1998@aol.com
Website: http://members.aol.com/
Counse1998/Default.htm

SCORE Office (Mt. Vernon)
4 N. 7th Ave.
Mt. Vernon, NY 10550
(914)667-7500

SCORE Office (New York)
26 Federal Plz., Rm. 3100
New York, NY 10278
(212)264-4507
Fax: (212)264-4963
E-mail: score1000@erols.com
Website: http://users.erols.com/
score-nyc/

SCORE Office (Newburgh)
47 Grand St.
Newburgh, NY 12550
(914)562-5100

SCORE Office (Owego)
188 Front St.
Owego, NY 13827
(607)687-2020

SCORE Office (Peekskill)
1 S. Division St.
Peekskill, NY 10566
(914)737-3600
Fax: (914)737-0541

SCORE Office (Penn Yan)
2375 Rte. 14A
Penn Yan, NY 14527
(315)536-3111

SCORE Office (Dutchess)
110 Main St.
Poughkeepsie, NY 12601
(914)454-1700

SCORE Office (Rochester)
601 Keating Federal Bldg., Rm. 410
100 State St.
Rochester, NY 14614
(716)263-6473
Fax: (716)263-3146
Website: http://www.ggw.org/score/

SCORE Office (Saranac Lake)
30 Main St.
Saranac Lake, NY 12983
(315)448-0415

SCORE Office (Suffolk)
286 Main St.
Setauket, NY 11733
(516)751-3886

SCORE Office (Staten Island)
130 Bay St.
Staten Island, NY 10301
(718)727-1221

SCORE Office (Ulster)
Clinton Bldg., Rm. 107
Stone Ridge, NY 12484
(914)687-5035
Fax: (914)687-5015
Website: http://www.scoreulster.org/

SCORE Office (Syracuse)
401 S. Salina, 5th Fl.
Syracuse, NY 13202
(315)471-9393

SCORE Office (Utica)
SUNY Institute of Technology, Route 12
Utica, NY 13504-3050
(315)792-7553

SCORE Office (Watertown)
518 Davidson St.
Watertown, NY 13601

(315)788-1200

Fax: (315)788-8251

North Carolina

SCORE office (Asheboro)

317 E. Dixie Dr.

Asheboro, NC 27203

(336)626-2626

Fax: (336)626-7077

SCORE Office (Asheville)

Federal Bldg., Rm. 259

151 Patton

Asheville, NC 28801-5770

(828)271-4786

Fax: (828)271-4009

SCORE Office (Chapel Hill)

104 S. Estes Dr.

PO Box 2897

Chapel Hill, NC 27514

(919)967-7075

SCORE Office (Coastal Plains)

PO Box 2897

Chapel Hill, NC 27515

(919)967-7075

Fax: (919)968-6874

SCORE Office (Charlotte)

200 N. College St., Ste. A-2015

Charlotte, NC 28202

(704)344-6576

Fax: (704)344-6769

E-mail: CharlotteSCORE47@AOL.com

Website: http://www.charweb.org/

business/score/

SCORE Office (Durham)

411 W. Chapel Hill St.

Durham, NC 27707

(919)541-2171

SCORE Office (Gastonia)

PO Box 2168

Gastonia, NC 28053

(704)864-2621

Fax: (704)854-8723

SCORE Office (Greensboro)

400 W. Market St., Ste. 103

Greensboro, NC 27401-2241

(910)333-5399

SCORE Office (Henderson)

PO Box 917

Henderson, NC 27536

(919)492-2061

Fax: (919)430-0460

SCORE Office (Hendersonville)

Federal Bldg., Rm. 108

W. 4th Ave. & Church St.

Hendersonville, NC 28792

(828)693-8702

E-mail: score@circle.net

Website: http://www.wncguide.com/

score/Welcome.html

SCORE Office (Unifour)

PO Box 1828

Hickory, NC 28603

(704)328-6111

SCORE Office (High Point)

1101 N. Main St.

High Point, NC 27262

(336)882-8625

Fax: (336)889-9499

SCORE Office (Outer Banks)

Collington Rd. and Mustain

Kill Devil Hills, NC 27948

(252)441-8144

SCORE Office (Down East)

312 S. Front St., Ste. 6

New Bern, NC 28560

(252)633-6688

Fax: (252)633-9608

SCORE Office (Kinston)

PO Box 95

New Bern, NC 28561

(919)633-6688

SCORE Office (Raleigh)

Century Post Office Bldg., Ste. 306

300 Federal St. Mall

Raleigh, NC 27601

(919)856-4739

E-mail: jendres@ibm.net

Website: http://www.intrex.net/score96/

score96.htm

SCORE Office (Sanford)

1801 Nash St.

Sanford, NC 27330

(919)774-6442

Fax: (919)776-8739

SCORE Office (Sandhills Area)

1480 Hwy. 15-501

PO Box 458

Southern Pines, NC 28387

(910)692-3926

SCORE Office (Wilmington)

Corps of Engineers Bldg.

96 Darlington Ave., Ste. 207

Wilmington, NC 28403

(910)815-4576

Fax: (910)815-4658

North Dakota

SCORE Office (Bismarck-Mandan)

700 E. Main Ave., 2nd Fl.

PO Box 5509

Bismarck, ND 58506-5509

(701)250-4303

SCORE Office (Fargo)

657 2nd Ave., Rm. 225

Fargo, ND 58108-3083

(701)239-5677

SCORE Office (Upper Red River)

4275 Technology Dr., Rm. 156

Grand Forks, ND 58202-8372

(701)777-3051

SCORE Office (Minot)

100 1st St. SW

Minot, ND 58701-3846

(701)852-6883

Fax: (701)852-6905

Ohio

SCORE Office (Akron)

1 Cascade Plz., 7th Fl.

Akron, OH 44308

(330)379-3163

Fax: (330)379-3164

SCORE Office (Ashland)

Gill Center

47 W. Main St.

Ashland, OH 44805

(419)281-4584

SCORE Office (Canton)

116 Cleveland Ave. NW, Ste. 601

Canton, OH 44702-1720

(330)453-6047

SCORE Office (Chillicothe)

165 S. Paint St.

Chillicothe, OH 45601

(614)772-4530

SCORE Office (Cincinnati)

Ameritrust Bldg., Rm. 850

525 Vine St.

Cincinnati, OH 45202

(513)684-2812

Fax: (513)684-3251

Website: http://

www.score.chapter34.org/

SCORE Office (Cleveland)

Eaton Center, Ste. 620

1100 Superior Ave.

Cleveland, OH 44114-2507

(216)522-4194

Fax: (216)522-4844

SCORE Office (Columbus)
2 Nationwide Plz., Ste. 1400
Columbus, OH 43215-2542
(614)469-2357
Fax: (614)469-2391
E-mail: info@scorecolumbus.org
Website: http://www.scorecolumbus.org/

SCORE Office (Dayton)
Dayton Federal Bldg., Rm. 505
200 W. Second St.
Dayton, OH 45402-1430
(513)225-2887
Fax: (513)225-7667

SCORE Office (Defiance)
615 W. 3rd St.
PO Box 130
Defiance, OH 43512
(419)782-7946

SCORE Office (Findlay)
123 E. Main Cross St.
PO Box 923
Findlay, OH 45840
(419)422-3314

SCORE Office (Lima)
147 N. Main St.
Lima, OH 45801
(419)222-6045
Fax: (419)229-0266

SCORE Office (Mansfield)
55 N. Mulberry St.
Mansfield, OH 44902
(419)522-3211

SCORE Office (Marietta)
Thomas Hall
Marietta, OH 45750
(614)373-0268

SCORE Office (Medina)
County Administrative Bldg.
144 N. Broadway
Medina, OH 44256
(216)764-8650

SCORE Office (Licking County)
50 W. Locust St.
Newark, OH 43055
(614)345-7458

SCORE Office (Salem)
2491 State Rte. 45 S
Salem, OH 44460
(216)332-0361

SCORE Office (Tiffin)
62 S. Washington St.
Tiffin, OH 44883
(419)447-4141
Fax: (419)447-5141

SCORE Office (Toledo)
608 Madison Ave, Ste. 910
Toledo, OH 43624
(419)259-7598
Fax: (419)259-6460

SCORE Office (Heart of Ohio)
377 W. Liberty St.
Wooster, OH 44691
(330)262-5735
Fax: (330)262-5745

SCORE Office (Youngstown)
306 Williamson Hall
Youngstown, OH 44555
(330)746-2687

Oklahoma

SCORE Office (Anadarko)
PO Box 366
Anadarko, OK 73005
(405)247-6651

SCORE Office (Ardmore)
410 W. Main
Ardmore, OK 73401
(580)226-2620

SCORE Office (Northeast Oklahoma)
210 S. Main
Grove, OK 74344
(918)787-2796
Fax: (918)787-2796
E-mail: Score595@greencis.net

SCORE Office (Lawton)
4500 W. Lee Blvd., Bldg. 100, Ste. 107
Lawton, OK 73505
(580)353-8727
Fax: (580)250-5677

SCORE Office (Oklahoma City)
210 Park Ave., No. 1300
Oklahoma City, OK 73102
(405)231-5163
Fax: (405)231-4876
E-mail: score212@usa.net

SCORE Office (Stillwater)
439 S. Main
Stillwater, OK 74074
(405)372-5573
Fax: (405)372-4316

SCORE Office (Tulsa)
616 S. Boston, Ste. 406
Tulsa, OK 74119
(918)581-7462
Fax: (918)581-6908
Website: http://www.ionet.net/~tulscore/

Oregon

SCORE Office (Bend)
63085 N. Hwy. 97
Bend, OR 97701
(541)923-2849
Fax: (541)330-6900

SCORE Office (Willamette)
1401 Willamette St.
PO Box 1107
Eugene, OR 97401-4003
(541)465-6600
Fax: (541)484-4942

SCORE Office (Florence)
3149 Oak St.
Florence, OR 97439
(503)997-8444
Fax: (503)997-8448

SCORE Office (Southern Oregon)
33 N. Central Ave., Ste. 216
Medford, OR 97501
(541)776-4220
E-mail: pgr134f@prodigy.com

SCORE Office (Portland)
1515 SW 5th Ave., Ste. 1050
Portland, OR 97201
(503)326-3441
Fax: (503)326-2808
E-mail: gr134@prodigy.com

SCORE Office (Salem)
416 State St. (corner of Liberty)
Salem, OR 97301
(503)370-2896

Pennsylvania

SCORE Office (Altoona-Blair)
1212 12th Ave.
Altoona, PA 16601-3493
(814)943-8151

SCORE Office (Lehigh Valley)
Rauch Bldg. 37
Lehigh University
621 Taylor St.
Bethlehem, PA 18015
(610)758-4496
Fax: (610)758-5205

SCORE Office (Butler County)
100 N. Main St.
PO Box 1082
Butler, PA 16003
(412)283-2222
Fax: (412)283-0224

SCORE Office (Harrisburg)
4211 Trindle Rd.
Camp Hill, PA 17011

(717)761-4304
Fax: (717)761-4315

SCORE Office (Cumberland Valley)
75 S. 2nd St.
Chambersburg, PA 17201
(717)264-2935

SCORE Office (Monroe County-Stroudsburg)
556 Main St.
East Stroudsburg, PA 18301
(717)421-4433

SCORE Office (Erie)
120 W. 9th St.
Erie, PA 16501
(814)871-5650
Fax: (814)871-7530

SCORE Office (Bucks County)
409 Hood Blvd.
Fairless Hills, PA 19030
(215)943-8850
Fax: (215)943-7404

SCORE Office (Hanover)
146 Broadway
Hanover, PA 17331
(717)637-6130
Fax: (717)637-9127

SCORE Office (Harrisburg)
100 Chestnut, Ste. 309
Harrisburg, PA 17101
(717)782-3874

SCORE Office (East Montgomery County)
Baederwood Shopping Center
1653 The Fairways, Ste. 204
Jenkintown, PA 19046
(215)885-3027

SCORE Office (Kittanning)
2 Butler Rd.
Kittanning, PA 16201
(412)543-1305
Fax: (412)543-6206

SCORE Office (Lancaster)
118 W. Chestnut St.
Lancaster, PA 17603
(717)397-3092

SCORE Office (Westmoreland County)
300 Fraser Purchase Rd.
Latrobe, PA 15650-2690
(412)539-7505
Fax: (412)539-1850

SCORE Office (Lebanon)
252 N. 8th St.
PO Box 899

Lebanon, PA 17042-0899
(717)273-3727
Fax: (717)273-7940

SCORE Office (Lewistown)
3 W. Monument Sq., Ste. 204
Lewistown, PA 17044
(717)248-6713
Fax: (717)248-6714

SCORE Office (Delaware County)
602 E. Baltimore Pike
Media, PA 19063
(610)565-3677
Fax: (610)565-1606

SCORE Office (Milton Area)
112 S. Front St.
Milton, PA 17847
(717)742-7341
Fax: (717)792-2008

SCORE Office (Mon-Valley)
435 Donner Ave.
Monessen, PA 15062
(412)684-4277
Fax: (412)684-7688

SCORE Office (Monroeville)
William Penn Plaza
2790 Mosside Blvd., Ste. 295
Monroeville, PA 15146
(412)856-0622
Fax: (412)856-1030

SCORE Office (Airport Area)
986 Brodhead Rd.
Moon Township, PA 15108-2398
(412)264-6270
Fax: (412)264-1575

SCORE Office (Northeast)
8601 E. Roosevelt Blvd.
Philadelphia, PA 19152
(215)332-3400
Fax: (215)332-6050

SCORE Office (Philadelphia)
1315 Walnut St., Ste. 500
Philadelphia, PA 19107
(215)790-5050
Fax: (215)790-5057
E-mail: score46@bellatlantic.net
Website: http://www.pgweb.net/score46/

SCORE Office (Pittsburgh)
1000 Liberty Ave., Rm. 1122
Pittsburgh, PA 15222
(412)395-6560
Fax: (412)395-6562

SCORE Office (Tri-County)
801 N. Charlotte St.
Pottstown, PA 19464
(610)327-2673

SCORE Office (Reading)
601 Penn St.
Reading, PA 19601
(610)376-3497

SCORE Office (Scranton)
Oppenheim Bldg.
116 N. Washington Ave., Ste. 650
Scranton, PA 18503
(717)347-4611
Fax: (717)347-4611

SCORE Office (Central Pennsylvania)
200 Innovation Blvd., Ste. 242-B
State College, PA 16803
(814)234-9415
Fax: (814)238-9686
Website: http://countrystore.org/business/score.htm

SCORE Office (Monroe-Stroudsburg)
556 Main St.
Stroudsburg, PA 18360
(717)421-4433

SCORE Office (Uniontown)
Federal Bldg.
Pittsburg St.
PO Box 2065 DTS
Uniontown, PA 15401
(412)437-4222
E-mail: uniontownscore@lcsys.net

SCORE Office (Warren County)
315 2nd Ave.
Warren, PA 16365
(814)723-9017

SCORE Office (Waynesboro)
323 E. Main St.
Waynesboro, PA 17268
(717)762-7123
Fax: (717)962-7124

SCORE Office (Chester County)
Government Service Center, Ste. 281
601 Westtown Rd.
West Chester, PA 19382-4538
(610)344-6910
Fax: (610)344-6919
E-mail: score@locke.ccil.org

SCORE Office (Wilkes-Barre)
7 N. Wilkes-Barre Blvd.
Wilkes Barre, PA 18702-5241
(717)826-6502
Fax: (717)826-6287

SCORE Office (North Central Pennsylvania)
240 W. 3rd St., Rm. 227
PO Box 725
Williamsport, PA 17703

(717)322-3720
Fax: (717)322-1607
E-mail: score234@mail.csrlink.net
Website: http://www.lycoming.org/score/

SCORE Office (York)
Cyber Center
2101 Pennsylvania Ave.
York, PA 17404
(717)845-8830
Fax: (717)854-9333

Puerto Rico

SCORE Office (Puerto Rico & Virgin Islands)
PO Box 12383-96
San Juan, PR 00914-0383
(787)726-8040
Fax: (787)726-8135

Rhode Island

SCORE Office (Barrington)
281 County Rd.
Barrington, RI 02806
(401)247-1920
Fax: (401)247-3763

SCORE Office (Woonsocket)
640 Washington Hwy.
Lincoln, RI 02865
(401)334-1000
Fax: (401)334-1009

SCORE Office (Wickford)
8045 Post Rd.
North Kingstown, RI 02852
(401)295-5566
Fax: (401)295-8987

SCORE Office (J.G.E. Knight)
380 Westminster St.
Providence, RI 02903
(401)528-4571
Fax: (401)528-4539
Website: http://www.riscore.org

SCORE Office (Warwick)
3288 Post Rd.
Warwick, RI 02886
(401)732-1100
Fax: (401)732-1101

SCORE Office (Westerly)
74 Post Rd.
Westerly, RI 02891
(401)596-7761
800-732-7636
Fax: (401)596-2190

South Carolina

SCORE Office (Aiken)
PO Box 892
Aiken, SC 29802
(803)641-1111
800-542-4536
Fax: (803)641-4174

SCORE Office (Anderson)
Anderson Mall
3130 N. Main St.
Anderson, SC 29621
(864)224-0453

SCORE Office (Coastal)
284 King St.
Charleston, SC 29401
(803)727-4778
Fax: (803)853-2529

SCORE Office (Midlands)
Strom Thurmond Bldg., Rm. 358
1835 Assembly St., Rm 358
Columbia, SC 29201
(803)765-5131
Fax: (803)765-5962
Website: http://www.scoremidlands.org/

SCORE Office (Piedmont)
Federal Bldg., Rm. B-02
300 E. Washington St.
Greenville, SC 29601
(864)271-3638

SCORE Office (Greenwood)
PO Drawer 1467
Greenwood, SC 29648
(864)223-8357

SCORE Office (Hilton Head Island)
52 Savannah Trail
Hilton Head, SC 29926
(803)785-7107
Fax: (803)785-7110

SCORE Office (Grand Strand)
937 Broadway
Myrtle Beach, SC 29577
(803)918-1079
Fax: (803)918-1083
E-mail: score381@aol.com

SCORE Office (Spartanburg)
PO Box 1636
Spartanburg, SC 29304
(864)594-5000
Fax: (864)594-5055

South Dakota

SCORE Office (West River)
Rushmore Plz. Civic Ctr.
444 Mount Rushmore Rd., No. 209

Rapid City, SD 57701
(605)394-5311
E-mail: score@gwtc.net

SCORE Office (Sioux Falls)
First Financial Center
110 S. Phillips Ave., Ste. 200
Sioux Falls, SD 57104-6727
(605)330-4231
Fax: (605)330-4231

Tennessee

SCORE Office (Chattanooga)
Federal Bldg., Rm. 26
900 Georgia Ave.
Chattanooga, TN 37402
(423)752-5190
Fax: (423)752-5335

SCORE Office (Cleveland)
PO Box 2275
Cleveland, TN 37320
(423)472-6587
Fax: (423)472-2019

SCORE Office (Upper Cumberland Center)
1225 S. Willow Ave.
Cookeville, TN 38501
(615)432-4111
Fax: (615)432-6010

SCORE Office (Unicoi County)
PO Box 713
Erwin, TN 37650
(423)743-3000
Fax: (423)743-0942

SCORE Office (Greeneville)
115 Academy St.
Greeneville, TN 37743
(423)638-4111
Fax: (423)638-5345

SCORE Office (Jackson)
194 Auditorium St.
Jackson, TN 38301
(901)423-2200

SCORE Office (Northeast Tennessee)
1st Tennessee Bank Bldg.
2710 S. Roan St., Ste. 584
Johnson City, TN 37601
(423)929-7686
Fax: (423)461-8052

SCORE Office (Kingsport)
151 E. Main St.
Kingsport, TN 37662
(423)392-8805

SCORE Office (Greater Knoxville)
Farragot Bldg., Ste. 224
530 S. Gay St.
Knoxville, TN 37902
(423)545-4203
E-mail: scoreknox@ntown.com
Website: http://www.scoreknox.org/

SCORE Office (Maryville)
201 S. Washington St.
Maryville, TN 37804-5728
(423)983-2241
800-525-6834
Fax: (423)984-1386

SCORE Office (Memphis)
Federal Bldg., Ste. 390
167 N. Main St.
Memphis, TN 38103
(901)544-3588

SCORE Office (Nashville)
50 Vantage Way, Ste. 201
Nashville, TN 37228-1500
(615)736-7621

Texas

SCORE Office (Abilene)
2106 Federal Post Office and Court Bldg.
Abilene, TX 79601
(915)677-1857

SCORE Office (Austin)
2501 S. Congress
Austin, TX 78701
(512)442-7235
Fax: (512)442-7528

SCORE Office (Golden Triangle)
450 Boyd St.
Beaumont, TX 77704
(409)838-6581
Fax: (409)833-6718

SCORE Office (Brownsville)
3505 Boca Chica Blvd., Ste. 305
Brownsville, TX 78521
(210)541-4508

SCORE Office (Brazos Valley)
3000 Briarcrest, Ste. 302
Bryan, TX 77802
(409)776-8876
E-mail: 102633.2612@compuserve.com

SCORE Office (Cleburne)
Watergarden Pl., 9th Fl., Ste. 400
Cleburne, TX 76031
(817)871-6002

SCORE Office (Corpus Christi)
651 Upper North Broadway, Ste. 654
Corpus Christi, TX 78477

(512)888-4322
Fax: (512)888-3418

SCORE Office (Dallas)
6260 E. Mockingbird
Dallas, TX 75214-2619
(214)828-2471
Fax: (214)821-8033

SCORE Office (El Paso)
10 Civic Center Plaza
El Paso, TX 79901
(915)534-0541
Fax: (915)534-0513

SCORE Office (Bedford)
100 E. 15th St., Ste. 400
Ft. Worth, TX 76102
(817)871-6002

SCORE Office (Ft. Worth)
100 E. 15th St., No. 24
Ft. Worth, TX 76102
(817)871-6002
Fax: (817)871-6031
E-mail: fwbac@onramp.net

SCORE Office (Garland)
2734 W. Kingsley Rd.
Garland, TX 75041
(214)271-9224

SCORE Office (Granbury Chamber of Commerce)
416 S. Morgan
Granbury, TX 76048
(817)573-1622
Fax: (817)573-0805

SCORE Office (Lower Rio Grande Valley)
222 E. Van Buren, Ste. 500
Harlingen, TX 78550
(956)427-8533
Fax: (956)427-8537

SCORE Office (Houston)
9301 Southwest Fwy., Ste. 550
Houston, TX 77074
(713)773-6565
Fax: (713)773-6550

SCORE Office (Irving)
3333 N. MacArthur Blvd., Ste. 100
Irving, TX 75062
(214)252-8484
Fax: (214)252-6710

SCORE Office (Lubbock)
1205 Texas Ave., Rm. 411D
Lubbock, TX 79401
(806)472-7462
Fax: (806)472-7487

SCORE Office (Midland)
Post Office Annex
200 E. Wall St., Rm. P121
Midland, TX 79701
(915)687-2649

SCORE Office (Orange)
1012 Green Ave.
Orange, TX 77630-5620
(409)883-3536
800-528-4906
Fax: (409)886-3247

SCORE Office (Plano)
1200 E. 15th St.
PO Drawer 940287
Plano, TX 75094-0287
(214)424-7547
Fax: (214)422-5182

SCORE Office (Port Arthur)
4749 Twin City Hwy., Ste. 300
Port Arthur, TX 77642
(409)963-1107
Fax: (409)963-3322

SCORE Office (Richardson)
411 Belle Grove
Richardson, TX 75080
(214)234-4141
800-777-8001
Fax: (214)680-9103

SCORE Office (San Antonio)
Federal Bldg., Rm. A527
727 E. Durango
San Antonio, TX 78206
(210)472-5931
Fax: (210)472-5935

SCORE Office (Texarkana State College)
819 State Line Ave.
Texarkana, TX 75501
(903)792-7191
Fax: (903)793-4304

SCORE Office (East Texas)
RTDC
1530 SSW Loop 323, Ste. 100
Tyler, TX 75701
(903)510-2975
Fax: (903)510-2978

SCORE Office (Waco)
401 Franklin Ave.
Waco, TX 76701
(817)754-8898
Fax: (817)756-0776
Website: http://www.brc-waco.com/

SCORE Office (Wichita Falls)
Hamilton Bldg.
900 8th St.

Wichita Falls, TX 76307
(940)723-2741
Fax: (940)723-8773

Utah

SCORE Office (Northern Utah)
160 N. Main
Logan, UT 84321
(435)746-2269

SCORE Office (Ogden)
1701 E. Windsor Dr.
Ogden, UT 84604
(801)629-8613
E-mail: score158@netscape.net

SCORE Office (Central Utah)
1071 E. Windsor Dr.
Provo, UT 84604
(801)373-8660

SCORE Office (Southern Utah)
225 South 700 East
St. George, UT 84770
(435)652-7751

SCORE Office (Salt Lake)
310 S Main St.
Salt Lake City, UT 84101
(801)746-2269
Fax: (801)746-2273

Vermont

SCORE Office (Champlain Valley)
Winston Prouty Federal Bldg.
11 Lincoln St., Rm. 106
Essex Junction, VT 05452
(802)951-6762

SCORE Office (Montpelier)
87 State St., Rm. 205
PO Box 605
Montpelier, VT 05601
(802)828-4422
Fax: (802)828-4485

SCORE Office (Marble Valley)
256 N. Main St.
Rutland, VT 05701-2413
(802)773-9147

SCORE Office (Northeast Kingdom)
20 Main St.
PO Box 904
St. Johnsbury, VT 05819
(802)748-5101

Virgin Islands

SCORE Office (St. Croix)
United Plaza Shopping Center
PO Box 4010, Christiansted

St. Croix, VI 00822
(809)778-5380

SCORE Office (St. Thomas-St. John)
Federal Bldg., Rm. 21
Veterans Dr.
St. Thomas, VI 00801
(809)774-8530

Virginia

SCORE Office (Arlington)
2009 N. 14th St., Ste. 111
Arlington, VA 22201
(703)525-2400

SCORE Office (Blacksburg)
141 Jackson St.
Blacksburg, VA 24060
(540)552-4061

SCORE Office (Bristol)
20 Volunteer Pkwy.
Bristol, VA 24203
(540)989-4850

SCORE Office (Central Virginia)
1001 E. Market St., Ste. 101
Charlottesville, VA 22902
(804)295-6712
Fax: (804)295-7066

SCORE Office (Alleghany Satellite)
241 W. Main St.
Covington, VA 24426
(540)962-2178
Fax: (540)962-2179

SCORE Office (Central Fairfax)
3975 University Dr., Ste. 350
Fairfax, VA 22030
(703)591-2450

SCORE Office (Falls Church)
PO Box 491
Falls Church, VA 22040
(703)532-1050
Fax: (703)237-7904

SCORE Office (Glenns)
Glenns Campus
Box 287
Glenns, VA 23149
(804)693-9650

SCORE Office (Peninsula)
6 Manhattan Sq.
PO Box 7269
Hampton, VA 23666
(757)766-2000
Fax: (757)865-0339
E-mail: score100@seva.net

SCORE Office (Tri-Cities)
108 N. Main St.
Hopewell, VA 23860
(804)458-5536

SCORE Office (Lynchburg)
Federal Bldg.
1100 Main St.
Lynchburg, VA 24504-1714
(804)846-3235

SCORE Office (Greater Prince William)
8963 Center St
Manassas, VA 20110
(703)368-4813
Fax: (703)368-4733

SCORE Office (Martinsvile)
115 Broad St.
Martinsville, VA 24112-0709
(540)632-6401
Fax: (540)632-5059

SCORE Office (Hampton Roads)
Federal Bldg., Rm. 737
200 Grandby St.
Norfolk, VA 23510
(757)441-3733
Fax: (757)441-3733
E-mail: scorehr60@juno.com

SCORE Office (Norfolk)
Federal Bldg., Rm. 737
200 Granby St.
Norfolk, VA 23510
(757)441-3733
Fax: (757)441-3733

SCORE Office (Virginia Beach)
Chamber of Commerce
200 Grandby St., Rm 737
Norfolk, VA 23510
(804)441-3733

SCORE Office (Radford)
1126 Norwood St.
Radford, VA 24141
(540)639-2202

SCORE Office (Richmond)
Federal Bldg.
400 N. 8th St., Ste. 1150
PO Box 10126
Richmond, VA 23240-0126
(804)771-2400
Fax: (804)771-8018
E-mail: scorechapter12@yahoo.com
Website: http://www.cvco.org/score/

SCORE Office (Roanoke)
Federal Bldg., Rm. 716
250 Franklin Rd.
Roanoke, VA 24011

(540)857-2834
Fax: (540)857-2043
E-mail: scorerva@juno.com
Website: http://hometown.aol.com/
scorerv/Index.html

SCORE Office (Fairfax)
8391 Old Courthouse Rd., Ste. 300
Vienna, VA 22182
(703)749-0400

SCORE Office (Greater Vienna)
513 Maple Ave. West
Vienna, VA 22180
(703)281-1333
Fax: (703)242-1482

SCORE Office (Shenandoah Valley)
301 W. Main St.
Waynesboro, VA 22980
(540)949-8203
Fax: (540)949-7740
E-mail: score427@intelos.net

SCORE Office (Williamsburg)
201 Penniman Rd.
Williamsburg, VA 23185
(757)229-6511
E-mail: wacc@williamsburgcc.com

SCORE Office (Northern Virginia)
1360 S. Pleasant Valley Rd.
Winchester, VA 22601
(540)662-4118

Washington

SCORE Office (Gray's Harbor)
506 Duffy St.
Aberdeen, WA 98520
(360)532-1924
Fax: (360)533-7945

SCORE Office (Bellingham)
101 E. Holly St.
Bellingham, WA 98225
(360)676-3307

SCORE Office (Everett)
2702 Hoyt Ave.
Everett, WA 98201-3556
(206)259-8000

SCORE Office (Gig Harbor)
3125 Judson St.
Gig Harbor, WA 98335
(206)851-6865

SCORE Office (Kennewick)
PO Box 6986
Kennewick, WA 99336
(509)736-0510

SCORE Office (Puyallup)
322 2nd St. SW
PO Box 1298
Puyallup, WA 98371
(206)845-6755
Fax: (206)848-6164

SCORE Office (Seattle)
1200 6th Ave., Ste. 1700
Seattle, WA 98101
(206)553-7320
Fax: (206)553-7044
E-mail: score55@aol.com
Website: http://www.scn.org/civic/score-
online/index55.html

SCORE Office (Spokane)
801 W. Riverside Ave., No. 240
Spokane, WA 99201
(509)353-2820
Fax: (509)353-2600
E-mail: score@dmi.net
Website: http://www.dmi.net/score/

SCORE Office (Clover Park)
PO Box 1933
Tacoma, WA 98401-1933
(206)627-2175

SCORE Office (Tacoma)
1101 Pacific Ave.
Tacoma, WA 98402
(253)274-1288
Fax: (253)274-1289

SCORE Office (Fort Vancouver)
1701 Broadway, S-1
Vancouver, WA 98663
(360)699-1079

SCORE Office (Walla Walla)
500 Tausick Way
Walla Walla, WA 99362
(509)527-4681

SCORE Office (Mid-Columbia)
1113 S. 14th Ave.
Yakima, WA 98907
(509)574-4944
Fax: (509)574-2943
Website: http://www.ellensburg.com/
~score/

West Virginia

SCORE Office (Charleston)
1116 Smith St.
Charleston, WV 25301
(304)347-5463
E-mail: score256@juno.com

SCORE Office (Virginia Street)
1116 Smith St., Ste. 302
Charleston, WV 25301
(304)347-5463

SCORE Office (Marion County)
PO Box 208
Fairmont, WV 26555-0208
(304)363-0486

SCORE Office (Upper Monongahela Valley)
1000 Technology Dr., Ste. 1111
Fairmont, WV 26555
(304)363-0486
E-mail: score537@hotmail.com

SCORE Office (Huntington)
1101 6th Ave., Ste. 220
Huntington, WV 25701-2309
(304)523-4092

SCORE Office (Wheeling)
1310 Market St.
Wheeling, WV 26003
(304)233-2575
Fax: (304)233-1320

Wisconsin

SCORE Office (Fox Cities)
227 S. Walnut St.
Appleton, WI 54913
(920)734-7101
Fax: (920)734-7161

SCORE Office (Beloit)
136 W. Grand Ave., Ste. 100
PO Box 717
Beloit, WI 53511
(608)365-8835
Fax: (608)365-9170

SCORE Office (Eau Claire)
Federal Bldg., Rm. B11
510 S. Barstow St.
Eau Claire, WI 54701
(715)834-1573
E-mail: score@ecol.net
Website: http://www.ecol.net/~score/

SCORE Office (Fond du Lac)
207 N. Main St.
Fond du Lac, WI 54935
(414)921-9500
Fax: (414)921-9559

SCORE Office (Green Bay)
835 Potts Ave.
Green Bay, WI 54304
(414)496-8930
Fax: (414)496-6009

SCORE Office (Janesville)
20 S. Main St., Ste. 11
PO Box 8008
Janesville, WI 53547
(608)757-3160
Fax: (608)757-3170

SCORE Office (La Crosse)
712 Main St.
La Crosse, WI 54602-0219
(608)784-4880

SCORE Office (Madison)
505 S. Rosa Rd.
Madison, WI 53719
(608)441-2820

SCORE Office (Manitowoc)
1515 Memorial Dr.
PO Box 903
Manitowoc, WI 54221-0903
(414)684-5575
Fax: (414)684-1915

**SCORE Office
(Milwaukee)**
310 W. Wisconsin Ave., Ste. 425
Milwaukee, WI 53203
(414)297-3942
Fax: (414)297-1377

**SCORE Office
(Central Wisconsin)**
1224 Lindbergh Ave.
Stevens Point, WI 54481
(715)344-7729

SCORE Office (Superior)
Superior Business Center Inc.
1423 N. 8th St.
Superior, WI 54880
(715)394-7388
Fax: (715)393-7414

SCORE Office (Waukesha)
223 Wisconsin Ave.
Waukesha, WI 53186-4926
(414)542-4249

SCORE Office (Wausau)
300 3rd St., Ste. 200
Wausau, WI 54402-6190
(715)845-6231

**SCORE Office
(Wisconsin Rapids)**
2240 Kingston Rd.
Wisconsin Rapids, WI 54494
(715)423-1830

Wyoming

SCORE Office (Casper)
Federal Bldg., No. 2215
100 East B St.
Casper, WY 82602
(307)261-6529
Fax: (307)261-6530

Venture capital & financing companies

This section contains a listing of financing and loan companies in the United States and Canada. These listing are arranged alphabetically by country, then by state or province, then by city, then by organization name.

Canada

Alberta

Launchworks Inc.
1902J 11th St., S.E.
Calgary, AB, Canada T2G 3G2
(403)269-1119
Fax: (403)269-1141
Website: http://www.launchworks.com

Native Venture Capital Company, Inc.
21 Artist View Point, Box 7
Site 25, RR 12
Calgary, AB, Canada T3E 6W3
(903)208-5380

Miralta Capital Inc.
4445 Calgary Trail South
888 Terrace Plaza Alberta
Edmonton, AB, Canada T6H 5R7
(780)438-3535
Fax: (780)438-3129

Vencap Equities Alberta Ltd.
10180-101st St., Ste. 1980
Edmonton, AB, Canada T5J 3S4
(403)420-1171
Fax: (403)429-2541

British Columbia

Discovery Capital
5th Fl., 1199 West Hastings
Vancouver, BC, Canada V6E 3T5
(604)683-3000
Fax: (604)662-3457
E-mail: info@discoverycapital.com
Website: http://www.discoverycapital.com

Greenstone Venture Partners
1177 West Hastings St.
Ste. 400
Vancouver, BC, Canada V6E 2K3
(604)717-1977
Fax: (604)717-1976
Website: http://www.greenstonevc.com

Growthworks Capital
2600-1055 West Georgia St.
Box 11170 Royal Centre

Vancouver, BC, Canada V6E 3R5
(604)895-7259
Fax: (604)669-7605
Website: http://www.wofund.com

MDS Discovery Venture Management, Inc.
555 W. Eighth Ave., Ste. 305
Vancouver, BC, Canada V5Z 1C6
(604)872-8464
Fax: (604)872-2977
E-mail: info@mds-ventures.com

Ventures West Management Inc.
1285 W. Pender St., Ste. 280
Vancouver, BC, Canada V6E 4B1
(604)688-9495
Fax: (604)687-2145
Website: http://www.ventureswest.com

Nova Scotia

ACF Equity Atlantic Inc.
Purdy's Wharf Tower II
Ste. 2106
Halifax, NS, Canada B3J 3R7
(902)421-1965
Fax: (902)421-1808

Montgomerie, Huck & Co.
146 Bluenose Dr.
PO Box 538
Lunenburg, NS, Canada B0J 2C0
(902)634-7125
Fax: (902)634-7130

Ontario

IPS Industrial Promotion Services Ltd.
60 Columbia Way, Ste. 720
Markham, ON, Canada L3R 0C9
(905)475-9400
Fax: (905)475-5003

Betwin Investments Inc.
Box 23110
Sault Ste. Marie, ON, Canada P6A 6W6
(705)253-0744
Fax: (705)253-0744

Bailey & Company, Inc.
594 Spadina Ave.
Toronto, ON, Canada M5S 2H4
(416)921-6930
Fax: (416)925-4670

BCE Capital
200 Bay St.
South Tower, Ste. 3120
Toronto, ON, Canada M5J 2J2
(416)815-0078
Fax: (416)941-1073
Website: http://www.bcecapital.com

Castlehill Ventures

55 University Ave., Ste. 500
Toronto, ON, Canada M5J 2H7
(416)862-8574
Fax: (416)862-8875

CCFL Mezzanine Partners of Canada

70 University Ave.
Ste. 1450
Toronto, ON, Canada M5J 2M4
(416)977-1450
Fax: (416)977-6764
E-mail: info@ccfl.com
Website: http://www.ccfl.com

Celtic House International

100 Simcoe St., Ste. 100
Toronto, ON, Canada M5H 3G2
(416)542-2436
Fax: (416)542-2435
Website: http://www.celtic-house.com

Clairvest Group Inc.

22 St. Clair Ave. East
Ste. 1700
Toronto, ON, Canada M4T 2S3
(416)925-9270
Fax: (416)925-5753

Crosbie & Co., Inc.

One First Canadian Place
9th Fl.
PO Box 116
Toronto, ON, Canada M5X 1A4
(416)362-7726
Fax: (416)362-3447
E-mail: info@crosbieco.com
Website: http://www.crosbieco.com

Drug Royalty Corp.

Eight King St. East
Ste. 202
Toronto, ON, Canada M5C 1B5
(416)863-1865
Fax: (416)863-5161

Grieve, Horner, Brown & Asculai

8 King St. E, Ste. 1704
Toronto, ON, Canada M5C 1B5
(416)362-7668
Fax: (416)362-7660

Jefferson Partners

77 King St. West
Ste. 4010
PO Box 136
Toronto, ON, Canada M5K 1H1
(416)367-1533
Fax: (416)367-5827
Website: http://www.jefferson.com

J.L. Albright Venture Partners

Canada Trust Tower, 161 Bay St.
Ste. 4440
PO Box 215
Toronto, ON, Canada M5J 2S1
(416)367-2440
Fax: (416)367-4604
Website: http://www.jlaventures.com

McLean Watson Capital Inc.

One First Canadian Place
Ste. 1410
PO Box 129
Toronto, ON, Canada M5X 1A4
(416)363-2000
Fax: (416)363-2010
Website: http://www.mcleanwatson.com

Middlefield Capital Fund

One First Canadian Place
85th Fl.
PO Box 192
Toronto, ON, Canada M5X 1A6
(416)362-0714
Fax: (416)362-7925
Website: http://www.middlefield.com

Mosaic Venture Partners

24 Duncan St.
Ste. 300
Toronto, ON, Canada M5V 3M6
(416)597-8889
Fax: (416)597-2345

Onex Corp.

161 Bay St.
PO Box 700
Toronto, ON, Canada M5J 2S1
(416)362-7711
Fax: (416)362-5765

Penfund Partners Inc.

145 King St. West
Ste. 1920
Toronto, ON, Canada M5H 1J8
(416)865-0300
Fax: (416)364-6912
Website: http://www.penfund.com

Primaxis Technology Ventures Inc.

1 Richmond St. West, 8th Fl.
Toronto, ON, Canada M5H 3W4
(416)313-5210
Fax: (416)313-5218
Website: http://www.primaxis.com

Priveq Capital Funds

240 Duncan Mill Rd., Ste. 602
Toronto, ON, Canada M3B 3P1
(416)447-3330
Fax: (416)447-3331
E-mail: priveq@sympatico.ca

Roynat Ventures

40 King St. West, 26th Fl.
Toronto, ON, Canada M5H 1H1
(416)933-2667
Fax: (416)933-2783
Website: http://www.roynatcapital.com

Tera Capital Corp.

366 Adelaide St. East, Ste. 337
Toronto, ON, Canada M5A 3X9
(416)368-1024
Fax: (416)368-1427

Working Ventures Canadian Fund Inc.

250 Bloor St. East, Ste. 1600
Toronto, ON, Canada M4W 1E6
(416)934-7718
Fax: (416)929-0901
Website: http://www.workingventures.ca

Quebec

Altamira Capital Corp.

202 University
Niveau de Maisoneuve, Bur. 201
Montreal, QC, Canada H3A 2A5
(514)499-1656
Fax: (514)499-9570

Federal Business Development Bank

Venture Capital Division
Five Place Ville Marie, Ste. 600
Montreal, QC, Canada H3B 5E7
(514)283-1896
Fax: (514)283-5455

Hydro-Quebec Capitech Inc.

75 Boul, Rene Levesque Quest
Montreal, QC, Canada H2Z 1A4
(514)289-4783
Fax: (514)289-5420
Website: http://www.hqcapitech.com

Investissement Desjardins

2 complexe Desjardins
C.P. 760
Montreal, QC, Canada H5B 1B8
(514)281-7131
Fax: (514)281-7808
Website: http://www.desjardins.com/id

Marleau Lemire Inc.

One Place Ville-Marie, Ste. 3601
Montreal, QC, Canada H3B 3P2
(514)877-3800
Fax: (514)875-6415

Speirs Consultants Inc.

365 Stanstead
Montreal, QC, Canada H3R 1X5
(514)342-3858
Fax: (514)342-1977

Tecnocap Inc.
4028 Marlowe
Montreal, QC, Canada H4A 3M2
(514)483-6009
Fax: (514)483-6045
Website: http://www.technocap.com

Telsoft Ventures
1000, Rue de la Gauchetiere
Quest, 25eme Etage
Montreal, QC, Canada H3B 4W5
(514)397-8450
Fax: (514)397-8451

Saskatchewan

Saskatchewan Government Growth Fund
1801 Hamilton St., Ste. 1210
Canada Trust Tower
Regina, SK, Canada S4P 4B4
(306)787-2994
Fax: (306)787-2086

United states

Alabama

FHL Capital Corp.
600 20th Street North
Suite 350
Birmingham, AL 35203
(205)328-3098
Fax: (205)323-0001

Harbert Management Corp.
One Riverchase Pkwy. South
Birmingham, AL 35244
(205)987-5500
Fax: (205)987-5707
Website: http://www.harbert.net

Jefferson Capital Fund
PO Box 13129
Birmingham, AL 35213
(205)324-7709

Private Capital Corp.
100 Brookwood Pl., 4th Fl.
Birmingham, AL 35209
(205)879-2722
Fax: (205)879-5121

21st Century Health Ventures
One Health South Pkwy.
Birmingham, AL 35243
(256)268-6250
Fax: (256)970-8928

FJC Growth Capital Corp.
200 W. Side Sq., Ste. 340
Huntsville, AL 35801
(256)922-2918
Fax: (256)922-2909

Hickory Venture Capital Corp.
301 Washington St. NW
Suite 301
Huntsville, AL 35801
(256)539-1931
Fax: (256)539-5130
E-mail: hvcc@hvcc.com
Website: http://www.hvcc.com

Southeastern Technology Fund
7910 South Memorial Pkwy., Ste. F
Huntsville, AL 35802
(256)883-8711
Fax: (256)883-8558

Cordova Ventures
4121 Carmichael Rd., Ste. 301
Montgomery, AL 36106
(334)271-6011
Fax: (334)260-0120
Website: http://
www.cordovaventures.com

Small Business Clinic of Alabama/AG Bartholomew & Associates
PO Box 231074
Montgomery, AL 36123-1074
(334)284-3640

Arizona

Miller Capital Corp.
4909 E. McDowell Rd.
Phoenix, AZ 85008
(602)225-0504
Fax: (602)225-9024
Website: http://www.themillergroup.com

The Columbine Venture Funds
9449 North 90th St., Ste. 200
Scottsdale, AZ 85258
(602)661-9222
Fax: (602)661-6262

Koch Ventures
17767 N. Perimeter Dr., Ste. 101
Scottsdale, AZ 85255
(480)419-3600
Fax: (480)419-3606
Website: http://www.kochventures.com

McKee & Co.
7702 E. Doubletree Ranch Rd.
Suite 230
Scottsdale, AZ 85258
(480)368-0333
Fax: (480)607-7446

Merita Capital Ltd.
7350 E. Stetson Dr., Ste. 108-A
Scottsdale, AZ 85251
(480)947-8700
Fax: (480)947-8766

Valley Ventures / Arizona Growth Partners L.P.
6720 N. Scottsdale Rd., Ste. 208
Scottsdale, AZ 85253
(480)661-6600
Fax: (480)661-6262

Estreetcapital.com
660 South Mill Ave., Ste. 315
Tempe, AZ 85281
(480)968-8400
Fax: (480)968-8480
Website: http://www.estreetcapital.com

Coronado Venture Fund
PO Box 65420
Tucson, AZ 85728-5420
(520)577-3764
Fax: (520)299-8491

Arkansas

Arkansas Capital Corp.
225 South Pulaski St.
Little Rock, AR 72201
(501)374-9247
Fax: (501)374-9425
Website: http://www.arcapital.com

California

Sundance Venture Partners, L.P.
100 Clocktower Place, Ste. 130
Carmel, CA 93923
(831)625-6500
Fax: (831)625-6590

Westar Capital (Costa Mesa)
949 South Coast Dr., Ste. 650
Costa Mesa, CA 92626
(714)481-5160
Fax: (714)481-5166
E-mail: mailbox@westarcapital.com
Website: http://www.westarcapital.com

Alpine Technology Ventures
20300 Stevens Creek Boulevard, Ste. 495
Cupertino, CA 95014
(408)725-1810
Fax: (408)725-1207
Website: http://www.alpineventures.com

Bay Partners
10600 N. De Anza Blvd.
Cupertino, CA 95014-2031
(408)725-2444
Fax: (408)446-4502
Website: http://www.baypartners.com

Novus Ventures
20111 Stevens Creek Blvd., Ste. 130
Cupertino, CA 95014
(408)252-3900

Fax: (408)252-1713
Website: http://www.novusventures.com

Triune Capital
19925 Stevens Creek Blvd., Ste. 200
Cupertino, CA 95014
(310)284-6800
Fax: (310)284-3290

Acorn Ventures
268 Bush St., Ste. 2829
Daly City, CA 94014
(650)994-7801
Fax: (650)994-3305
Website: http://www.acornventures.com

Digital Media Campus
2221 Park Place
El Segundo, CA 90245
(310)426-8000
Fax: (310)426-8010
E-mail: info@thecampus.com
Website: http://
www.digitalmediacampus.com

BankAmerica Ventures / BA Venture Partners
950 Tower Ln., Ste. 700
Foster City, CA 94404
(650)378-6000
Fax: (650)378-6040
Website: http://www.baventurepartners.com

Starting Point Partners
666 Portofino Lane
Foster City, CA 94404
(650)722-1035
Website: http://
www.startingpointpartners.com

Opportunity Capital Partners
2201 Walnut Ave., Ste. 210
Fremont, CA 94538
(510)795-7000
Fax: (510)494-5439
Website: http://www.ocpcapital.com

Imperial Ventures Inc.
9920 S. La Cienega Boulevar, 14th Fl.
Inglewood, CA 90301
(310)417-5409
Fax: (310)338-6115

Ventana Global (Irvine)
18881 Von Karman Ave., Ste. 1150
Irvine, CA 92612
(949)476-2204
Fax: (949)752-0223
Website: http://www.ventanaglobal.com

Integrated Consortium Inc.
50 Ridgecrest Rd.
Kentfield, CA 94904

(415)925-0386
Fax: (415)461-2726

Enterprise Partners
979 Ivanhoe Ave., Ste. 550
La Jolla, CA 92037
(858)454-8833
Fax: (858)454-2489
Website: http://www.epvc.com

Domain Associates
28202 Cabot Rd., Ste. 200
Laguna Niguel, CA 92677
(949)347-2446
Fax: (949)347-9720
Website: http://www.domainvc.com

Cascade Communications Ventures
60 E. Sir Francis Drake Blvd., Ste. 300
Larkspur, CA 94939
(415)925-6500
Fax: (415)925-6501

Allegis Capital
One First St., Ste. Two
Los Altos, CA 94022
(650)917-5900
Fax: (650)917-5901
Website: http://www.allegiscapital.com

Aspen Ventures
1000 Fremont Ave., Ste. 200
Los Altos, CA 94024
(650)917-5670
Fax: (650)917-5677
Website: http://www.aspenventures.com

AVI Capital L.P.
1 First St., Ste. 2
Los Altos, CA 94022
(650)949-9862
Fax: (650)949-8510
Website: http://www.avicapital.com

Bastion Capital Corp.
1999 Avenue of the Stars, Ste. 2960
Los Angeles, CA 90067
(310)788-5700
Fax: (310)277-7582
E-mail: ga@bastioncapital.com
Website: http://www.bastioncapital.com

Davis Group
PO Box 69953
Los Angeles, CA 90069-0953
(310)659-6327
Fax: (310)659-6337

Developers Equity Corp.
1880 Century Park East, Ste. 211
Los Angeles, CA 90067
(213)277-0300

Far East Capital Corp.
350 S. Grand Ave., Ste. 4100
Los Angeles, CA 90071
(213)687-1361
Fax: (213)617-7939
E-mail: free@fareastnationalbank.com

Kline Hawkes & Co.
11726 San Vicente Blvd., Ste. 300
Los Angeles, CA 90049
(310)442-4700
Fax: (310)442-4707
Website: http://www.klinehawkes.com

Lawrence Financial Group
701 Teakwood
PO Box 491773
Los Angeles, CA 90049
(310)471-4060
Fax: (310)472-3155

Riordan Lewis & Haden
300 S. Grand Ave., 29th Fl.
Los Angeles, CA 90071
(213)229-8500
Fax: (213)229-8597

Union Venture Corp.
445 S. Figueroa St., 9th Fl.
Los Angeles, CA 90071
(213)236-4092
Fax: (213)236-6329

Wedbush Capital Partners
1000 Wilshire Blvd.
Los Angeles, CA 90017
(213)688-4545
Fax: (213)688-6642
Website: http://www.wedbush.com

Advent International Corp.
2180 Sand Hill Rd., Ste. 420
Menlo Park, CA 94025
(650)233-7500
Fax: (650)233-7515
Website: http://www.adventinternational
.com

Altos Ventures
2882 Sand Hill Rd., Ste. 100
Menlo Park, CA 94025
(650)234-9771
Fax: (650)233-9821
Website: http://www.altosvc.com

Applied Technology
1010 El Camino Real, Ste. 300
Menlo Park, CA 94025
(415)326-8622
Fax: (415)326-8163

APV Technology Partners
535 Middlefield, Ste. 150
Menlo Park, CA 94025

(650)327-7871
Fax: (650)327-7631
Website: http://www.apvtp.com

August Capital Management
2480 Sand Hill Rd., Ste. 101
Menlo Park, CA 94025
(650)234-9900
Fax: (650)234-9910
Website: http://www.augustcap.com

Baccharis Capital Inc.
2420 Sand Hill Rd., Ste. 100
Menlo Park, CA 94025
(650)324-6844
Fax: (650)854-3025

Benchmark Capital
2480 Sand Hill Rd., Ste. 200
Menlo Park, CA 94025
(650)854-8180
Fax: (650)854-8183
E-mail: info@benchmark.com
Website: http://www.benchmark.com

Bessemer Venture Partners (Menlo Park)
535 Middlefield Rd., Ste. 245
Menlo Park, CA 94025
(650)853-7000
Fax: (650)853-7001
Website: http://www.bvp.com

The Cambria Group
1600 El Camino Real Rd., Ste. 155
Menlo Park, CA 94025
(650)329-8600
Fax: (650)329-8601
Website: http://www.cambriagroup.com

Canaan Partners
2884 Sand Hill Rd., Ste. 115
Menlo Park, CA 94025
(650)854-8092
Fax: (650)854-8127
Website: http://www.canaan.com

Capstone Ventures
3000 Sand Hill Rd., Bldg. One, Ste. 290
Menlo Park, CA 94025
(650)854-2523
Fax: (650)854-9010
Website: http://www.capstonevc.com

Comdisco Venture Group (Silicon Valley)
3000 Sand Hill Rd., Bldg. 1, Ste. 155
Menlo Park, CA 94025
(650)854-9484
Fax: (650)854-4026

Commtech International
535 Middlefield Rd., Ste. 200
Menlo Park, CA 94025

(650)328-0190
Fax: (650)328-6442

Compass Technology Partners
1550 El Camino Real, Ste. 275
Menlo Park, CA 94025-4111
(650)322-7595
Fax: (650)322-0588
Website: http://www.compasstechpartners.com

Convergence Partners
3000 Sand Hill Rd., Ste. 235
Menlo Park, CA 94025
(650)854-3010
Fax: (650)854-3015
Website: http://www.convergencepartners.com

The Dakota Group
PO Box 1025
Menlo Park, CA 94025
(650)853-0600
Fax: (650)851-4899
E-mail: info@dakota.com

Delphi Ventures
3000 Sand Hill Rd.
Bldg. One, Ste. 135
Menlo Park, CA 94025
(650)854-9650
Fax: (650)854-2961
Website: http://www.delphiventures.com

El Dorado Ventures
2884 Sand Hill Rd., Ste. 121
Menlo Park, CA 94025
(650)854-1200
Fax: (650)854-1202
Website: http://www.eldoradoventures.com

Glynn Ventures
3000 Sand Hill Rd., Bldg. 4, Ste. 235
Menlo Park, CA 94025
(650)854-2215

Indosuez Ventures
2180 Sand Hill Rd., Ste. 450
Menlo Park, CA 94025
(650)854-0587
Fax: (650)323-5561
Website: http://www.indosuezventures.com

Institutional Venture Partners
3000 Sand Hill Rd., Bldg. 2, Ste. 290
Menlo Park, CA 94025
(650)854-0132
Fax: (650)854-5762
Website: http://www.ivp.com

Interwest Partners (Menlo Park)
3000 Sand Hill Rd., Bldg. 3, Ste. 255
Menlo Park, CA 94025-7112
(650)854-8585
Fax: (650)854-4706
Website: http://www.interwest.com

Kleiner Perkins Caufield & Byers (Menlo Park)
2750 Sand Hill Rd.
Menlo Park, CA 94025
(650)233-2750
Fax: (650)233-0300
Website: http://www.kpcb.com

Magic Venture Capital LLC
1010 El Camino Real, Ste. 300
Menlo Park, CA 94025
(650)325-4149

Matrix Partners
2500 Sand Hill Rd., Ste. 113
Menlo Park, CA 94025
(650)854-3131
Fax: (650)854-3296
Website: http://www.matrixpartners.com

Mayfield Fund
2800 Sand Hill Rd.
Menlo Park, CA 94025
(650)854-5560
Fax: (650)854-5712
Website: http://www.mayfield.com

McCown De Leeuw and Co. (Menlo Park)
3000 Sand Hill Rd., Bldg. 3, Ste. 290
Menlo Park, CA 94025-7111
(650)854-6000
Fax: (650)854-0853
Website: http://www.mdcpartners.com

Menlo Ventures
3000 Sand Hill Rd., Bldg. 4, Ste. 100
Menlo Park, CA 94025
(650)854-8540
Fax: (650)854-7059
Website: http://www.menloventures.com

Merrill Pickard Anderson & Eyre
2480 Sand Hill Rd., Ste. 200
Menlo Park, CA 94025
(650)854-8600
Fax: (650)854-0345

New Enterprise Associates (Menlo Park)
2490 Sand Hill Rd.
Menlo Park, CA 94025
(650)854-9499
Fax: (650)854-9397
Website: http://www.nea.com

Onset Ventures
2400 Sand Hill Rd., Ste. 150
Menlo Park, CA 94025
(650)529-0700
Fax: (650)529-0777
Website: http://www.onset.com

Paragon Venture Partners
3000 Sand Hill Rd., Bldg. 1, Ste. 275
Menlo Park, CA 94025
(650)854-8000
Fax: (650)854-7260

**Pathfinder Venture Capital Funds
(Menlo Park)**
3000 Sand Hill Rd., Bldg. 3, Ste. 255
Menlo Park, CA 94025
(650)854-0650
Fax: (650)854-4706

Rocket Ventures
3000 Sandhill Rd., Bldg. 1, Ste. 170
Menlo Park, CA 94025
(650)561-9100
Fax: (650)561-9183
Website: http://www.rocketventures.com

Sequoia Capital
3000 Sand Hill Rd., Bldg. 4, Ste. 280
Menlo Park, CA 94025
(650)854-3927
Fax: (650)854-2977
E-mail: sequoia@sequoiacap.com
Website: http://www.sequoiacap.com

Sierra Ventures
3000 Sand Hill Rd., Bldg. 4, Ste. 210
Menlo Park, CA 94025
(650)854-1000
Fax: (650)854-5593
Website: http://www.sierraventures.com

Sigma Partners
2884 Sand Hill Rd., Ste. 121
Menlo Park, CA 94025-7022
(650)853-1700
Fax: (650)853-1717
E-mail: info@sigmapartners.com
Website: http://www.sigmapartners.com

Sprout Group (Menlo Park)
3000 Sand Hill Rd.
Bldg. 3, Ste. 170
Menlo Park, CA 94025
(650)234-2700
Fax: (650)234-2779
Website: http://www.sproutgroup.com

TA Associates (Menlo Park)
70 Willow Rd., Ste. 100
Menlo Park, CA 94025
(650)328-1210

Fax: (650)326-4933
Website: http://www.ta.com

Thompson Clive & Partners Ltd.
3000 Sand Hill Rd., Bldg. 1, Ste. 185
Menlo Park, CA 94025-7102
(650)854-0314
Fax: (650)854-0670
E-mail: mail@tcvc.com
Website: http://www.tcvc.com

Trinity Ventures Ltd.
3000 Sand Hill Rd., Bldg. 1, Ste. 240
Menlo Park, CA 94025
(650)854-9500
Fax: (650)854-9501
Website: http://www.trinityventures.com

U.S. Venture Partners
2180 Sand Hill Rd., Ste. 300
Menlo Park, CA 94025
(650)854-9080
Fax: (650)854-3018
Website: http://www.usvp.com

USVP-Schlein Marketing Fund
2180 Sand Hill Rd., Ste. 300
Menlo Park, CA 94025
(415)854-9080
Fax: (415)854-3018
Website: http://www.usvp.com

Venrock Associates
2494 Sand Hill Rd., Ste. 200
Menlo Park, CA 94025
(650)561-9580
Fax: (650)561-9180
Website: http://www.venrock.com

Brad Peery Capital Inc.
145 Chapel Pkwy.
Mill Valley, CA 94941
(415)389-0625
Fax: (415)389-1336

Dot Edu Ventures
650 Castro St., Ste. 270
Mountain View, CA 94041
(650)575-5638
Fax: (650)325-5247
Website: http://www.doteduventures.com

Forrest, Binkley & Brown
840 Newport Ctr. Dr., Ste. 480
Newport Beach, CA 92660
(949)729-3222
Fax: (949)729-3226
Website: http://www.fbbvc.com

Marwit Capital LLC
180 Newport Center Dr., Ste. 200
Newport Beach, CA 92660
(949)640-6234

Fax: (949)720-8077
Website: http://www.marwit.com

**Kaiser Permanente / National Venture
Development**
1800 Harrison St., 22nd Fl.
Oakland, CA 94612
(510)267-4010
Fax: (510)267-4036
Website: http://www.kpventures.com

Nu Capital Access Group, Ltd.
7677 Oakport St., Ste. 105
Oakland, CA 94621
(510)635-7345
Fax: (510)635-7068

Inman and Bowman
4 Orinda Way, Bldg. D, Ste. 150
Orinda, CA 94563
(510)253-1611
Fax: (510)253-9037

Accel Partners (San Francisco)
428 University Ave.
Palo Alto, CA 94301
(650)614-4800
Fax: (650)614-4880
Website: http://www.accel.com

Advanced Technology Ventures
485 Ramona St., Ste. 200
Palo Alto, CA 94301
(650)321-8601
Fax: (650)321-0934
Website: http://www.atvcapital.com

Anila Fund
400 Channing Ave.
Palo Alto, CA 94301
(650)833-5790
Fax: (650)833-0590
Website: http://www.anila.com

**Asset Management Company Venture
Capital**
2275 E. Bayshore, Ste. 150
Palo Alto, CA 94303
(650)494-7400
Fax: (650)856-1826
E-mail: postmaster@assetman.com
Website: http://www.assetman.com

**BancBoston Capital / BancBoston
Ventures**
435 Tasso St., Ste. 250
Palo Alto, CA 94305
(650)470-4100
Fax: (650)853-1425
Website: http://www.bancbostoncapital
.com

Charter Ventures
525 University Ave., Ste. 1400
Palo Alto, CA 94301
(650)325-6953
Fax: (650)325-4762
Website: http://
www.charterventures.com

Communications Ventures
505 Hamilton Avenue, Ste. 305
Palo Alto, CA 94301
(650)325-9600
Fax: (650)325-9608
Website: http://www.comven.com

HMS Group
2468 Embarcadero Way
Palo Alto, CA 94303-3313
(650)856-9862
Fax: (650)856-9864

Jafco America Ventures, Inc.
505 Hamilton Ste. 310
Palto Alto, CA 94301
(650)463-8800
Fax: (650)463-8801
Website: http://www.jafco.com

New Vista Capital
540 Cowper St., Ste. 200
Palo Alto, CA 94301
(650)329-9333
Fax: (650)328-9434
E-mail: fgreene@nvcap.com
Website: http://www.nvcap.com

Norwest Equity Partners (Palo Alto)
245 Lytton Ave., Ste. 250
Palo Alto, CA 94301-1426
(650)321-8000
Fax: (650)321-8010
Website: http://www.norwestvp.com

Oak Investment Partners
525 University Ave., Ste. 1300
Palo Alto, CA 94301
(650)614-3700
Fax: (650)328-6345
Website: http://www.oakinv.com

Patricof & Co. Ventures, Inc. (Palo Alto)
2100 Geng Rd., Ste. 150
Palo Alto, CA 94303
(650)494-9944
Fax: (650)494-6751
Website: http://www.patricof.com

RWI Group
835 Page Mill Rd.
Palo Alto, CA 94304
(650)251-1800

Fax: (650)213-8660
Website: http://www.rwigroup.com

Summit Partners (Palo Alto)
499 Hamilton Ave., Ste. 200
Palo Alto, CA 94301
(650)321-1166
Fax: (650)321-1188
Website: http://www.summitpartners.com

Sutter Hill Ventures
755 Page Mill Rd., Ste. A-200
Palo Alto, CA 94304
(650)493-5600
Fax: (650)858-1854
E-mail: shv@shv.com

Vanguard Venture Partners
525 University Ave., Ste. 600
Palo Alto, CA 94301
(650)321-2900
Fax: (650)321-2902
Website: http://
www.vanguardventures.com

Venture Growth Associates
2479 East Bayshore St., Ste. 710
Palo Alto, CA 94303
(650)855-9100
Fax: (650)855-9104

Worldview Technology Partners
435 Tasso St., Ste. 120
Palo Alto, CA 94301
(650)322-3800
Fax: (650)322-3880
Website: http://www.worldview.com

Draper, Fisher, Jurvetson / Draper Associates
400 Seaport Ct., Ste.250
Redwood City, CA 94063
(415)599-9000
Fax: (415)599-9726
Website: http://www.dfj.com

Gabriel Venture Partners
350 Marine Pkwy., Ste. 200
Redwood Shores, CA 94065
(650)551-5000
Fax: (650)551-5001
Website: http://www.gabrielvp.com

Hallador Venture Partners, L.L.C.
740 University Ave., Ste. 110
Sacramento, CA 95825-6710
(916)920-0191
Fax: (916)920-5188
E-mail: chris@hallador.com

Emerald Venture Group
12396 World Trade Dr., Ste. 116
San Diego, CA 92128

(858)451-1001
Fax: (858)451-1003
Website: http://
www.emeraldventure.com

Forward Ventures
9255 Towne Centre Dr.
San Diego, CA 92121
(858)677-6077
Fax: (858)452-8799
E-mail: info@forwardventure.com
Website: http://
www.forwardventure.com

Idanta Partners Ltd.
4660 La Jolla Village Dr., Ste. 850
San Diego, CA 92122
(619)452-9690
Fax: (619)452-2013
Website: http://www.idanta.com

Kingsbury Associates
3655 Nobel Dr., Ste. 490
San Diego, CA 92122
(858)677-0600
Fax: (858)677-0800

Kyocera International Inc.
Corporate Development
8611 Balboa Ave.
San Diego, CA 92123
(858)576-2600
Fax: (858)492-1456

Sorrento Associates, Inc.
4370 LaJolla Village Dr., Ste. 1040
San Diego, CA 92122
(619)452-3100
Fax: (619)452-7607
Website: http://www.sorrentoventures
.com

Western States Investment Group
9191 Towne Ctr. Dr., Ste. 310
San Diego, CA 92122
(619)678-0800
Fax: (619)678-0900

Aberdare Ventures
One Embarcadero Center, Ste. 4000
San Francisco, CA 94111
(415)392-7442
Fax: (415)392-4264
Website: http://www.aberdare.com

Acacia Venture Partners
101 California St., Ste. 3160
San Francisco, CA 94111
(415)433-4200
Fax: (415)433-4250
Website: http://www.acaciavp.com

Access Venture Partners
319 Laidley St.
San Francisco, CA 94131
(415)586-0132
Fax: (415)392-6310
Website: http://
www.accessventurepartners.com

Alta Partners
One Embarcadero Center, Ste. 4050
San Francisco, CA 94111
(415)362-4022
Fax: (415)362-6178
E-mail: alta@altapartners.com
Website: http://www.altapartners.com

Bangert Dawes Reade Davis & Thom
220 Montgomery St., Ste. 424
San Francisco, CA 94104
(415)954-9900
Fax: (415)954-9901
E-mail: bdrdt@pacbell.net

Berkeley International Capital Corp.
650 California St., Ste. 2800
San Francisco, CA 94108-2609
(415)249-0450
Fax: (415)392-3929
Website: http://www.berkeleyvc.com

Blueprint Ventures LLC
456 Montgomery St., 22nd Fl.
San Francisco, CA 94104
(415)901-4000
Fax: (415)901-4035
Website: http://www.blueprintventures.com

Blumberg Capital Ventures
580 Howard St., Ste. 401
San Francisco, CA 94105
(415)905-5007
Fax: (415)357-5027
Website: http://www.blumberg-capital.com

Burr, Egan, Deleage, and Co. (San Francisco)
1 Embarcadero Center, Ste. 4050
San Francisco, CA 94111
(415)362-4022
Fax: (415)362-6178

Burrill & Company
120 Montgomery St., Ste. 1370
San Francisco, CA 94104
(415)743-3160
Fax: (415)743-3161
Website: http://www.burrillandco.com

CMEA Ventures
235 Montgomery St., Ste. 920
San Francisco, CA 94401

(415)352-1520
Fax: (415)352-1524
Website: http://www.cmeaventures.com

Crocker Capital
1 Post St., Ste. 2500
San Francisco, CA 94101
(415)956-5250
Fax: (415)959-5710

Dominion Ventures, Inc.
44 Montgomery St., Ste. 4200
San Francisco, CA 94104
(415)362-4890
Fax: (415)394-9245

Dorset Capital
Pier 1
Bay 2
San Francisco, CA 94111
(415)398-7101
Fax: (415)398-7141
Website: http://www.dorsetcapital
.com

Gatx Capital
Four Embarcadero Center, Ste. 2200
San Francisco, CA 94904
(415)955-3200
Fax: (415)955-3449

IMinds
135 Main St., Ste. 1350
San Francisco, CA 94105
(415)547-0000
Fax: (415)227-0300
Website: http://www.iminds.com

LF International Inc.
360 Post St., Ste. 705
San Francisco, CA 94108
(415)399-0110
Fax: (415)399-9222
Website: http://www.lfvc.com

Newbury Ventures
535 Pacific Ave., 2nd Fl.
San Francisco, CA 94133
(415)296-7408
Fax: (415)296-7416
Website: http://www.newburyven
.com

Quest Ventures (San Francisco)
333 Bush St., Ste. 1750
San Francisco, CA 94104
(415)782-1414
Fax: (415)782-1415

Robertson-Stephens Co.
555 California St., Ste. 2600
San Francisco, CA 94104
(415)781-9700

Fax: (415)781-2556
Website: http://
www.omegaadventures.com

Rosewood Capital, L.P.
One Maritime Plaza, Ste. 1330
San Francisco, CA 94111-3503
(415)362-5526
Fax: (415)362-1192
Website: http://www.rosewoodvc.com

Ticonderoga Capital Inc.
555 California St., No. 4950
San Francisco, CA 94104
(415)296-7900
Fax: (415)296-8956

21st Century Internet Venture Partners
Two South Park
2nd Floor
San Francisco, CA 94107
(415)512-1221
Fax: (415)512-2650
Website: http://www.21vc.com

VK Ventures
600 California St., Ste.1700
San Francisco, CA 94111
(415)391-5600
Fax: (415)397-2744

Walden Group of Venture Capital Funds
750 Battery St., Seventh Floor
San Francisco, CA 94111
(415)391-7225
Fax: (415)391-7262

Acer Technology Ventures
2641 Orchard Pkwy.
San Jose, CA 95134
(408)433-4945
Fax: (408)433-5230

Authosis
226 Airport Pkwy., Ste. 405
San Jose, CA 95110
(650)814-3603
Website: http://www.authosis.com

Western Technology Investment
2010 N. First St., Ste. 310
San Jose, CA 95131
(408)436-8577
Fax: (408)436-8625
E-mail: mktg@westerntech.com

Drysdale Enterprises
177 Bovet Rd., Ste. 600
San Mateo, CA 94402
(650)341-6336
Fax: (650)341-1329
E-mail: drysdale@aol.com

Greylock
2929 Campus Dr., Ste. 400
San Mateo, CA 94401
(650)493-5525
Fax: (650)493-5575
Website: http://www.greylock.com

Technology Funding
2000 Alameda de las Pulgas, Ste. 250
San Mateo, CA 94403
(415)345-2200
Fax: (415)345-1797

2M Invest Inc.
1875 S. Grant St.
Suite 750
San Mateo, CA 94402
(650)655-3765
Fax: (650)372-9107
E-mail: 2minfo@2minvest.com
Website: http://www.2minvest.com

Phoenix Growth Capital Corp.
2401 Kerner Blvd.
San Rafael, CA 94901
(415)485-4569
Fax: (415)485-4663

NextGen Partners LLC
1705 East Valley Rd.
Santa Barbara, CA 93108
(805)969-8540
Fax: (805)969-8542
Website: http://
www.nextgenpartners.com

Denali Venture Capital
1925 Woodland Ave.
Santa Clara, CA 95050
(408)690-4838
Fax: (408)247-6979
E-mail: wael@denaliventurecapital.com
Website: http://www.denaliventurecapital
.com

Dotcom Ventures LP
3945 Freedom Circle, Ste. 740
Santa Clara, CA 95045
(408)919-9855
Fax: (408)919-9857
Website: http://
www.dotcomventuresatl.com

Silicon Valley Bank
3003 Tasman
Santa Clara, CA 95054
(408)654-7400
Fax: (408)727-8728

Al Shugart International
920 41st Ave.
Santa Cruz, CA 95062

(831)479-7852
Fax: (831)479-7852
Website: http://www.alshugart.com

Leonard Mautner Associates
1434 Sixth St.
Santa Monica, CA 90401
(213)393-9788
Fax: (310)459-9918

Palomar Ventures
100 Wilshire Blvd., Ste. 450
Santa Monica, CA 90401
(310)260-6050
Fax: (310)656-4150
Website: http://
www.palomarventures.com

Medicus Venture Partners
12930 Saratoga Ave., Ste. D8
Saratoga, CA 95070
(408)447-8600
Fax: (408)447-8599
Website: http://www.medicusvc.com

Redleaf Venture Management
14395 Saratoga Ave., Ste. 130
Saratoga, CA 95070
(408)868-0800
Fax: (408)868-0810
E-mail: nancy@redleaf.com
Website: http://www.redleaf.com

Artemis Ventures
207 Second St., Ste. E
3rd Fl.
Sausalito, CA 94965
(415)289-2500
Fax: (415)289-1789
Website: http://
www.artemisventures.com

Deucalion Venture Partners
19501 Brooklime
Sonoma, CA 95476
(707)938-4974
Fax: (707)938-8921

Windward Ventures
PO Box 7688
Thousand Oaks, CA 91359-7688
(805)497-3332
Fax: (805)497-9331

National Investment Management, Inc.
2601 Airport Dr., Ste.210
Torrance, CA 90505
(310)784-7600
Fax: (310)784-7605

Southern California Ventures
406 Amapola Ave. Ste. 125
Torrance, CA 90501

(310)787-4381
Fax: (310)787-4382

Sandton Financial Group
21550 Oxnard St., Ste. 300
Woodland Hills, CA 91367
(818)702-9283

Woodside Fund
850 Woodside Dr.
Woodside, CA 94062
(650)368-5545
Fax: (650)368-2416
Website: http://www.woodsidefund.com

Colorado

Colorado Venture Management
Ste. 300
Boulder, CO 80301
(303)440-4055
Fax: (303)440-4636

Dean & Associates
4362 Apple Way
Boulder, CO 80301
Fax: (303)473-9900

Roser Ventures LLC
1105 Spruce St.
Boulder, CO 80302
(303)443-6436
Fax: (303)443-1885
Website: http://www.roserventures.com

Sequel Venture Partners
4430 Arapahoe Ave., Ste. 220
Boulder, CO 80303
(303)546-0400
Fax: (303)546-9728
E-mail: tom@sequelvc.com
Website: http://www.sequelvc.com

New Venture Resources
445C E. Cheyenne Mtn. Blvd.
Colorado Springs, CO 80906-4570
(719)598-9272
Fax: (719)598-9272

The Centennial Funds
1428 15th St.
Denver, CO 80202-1318
(303)405-7500
Fax: (303)405-7575
Website: http://www.centennial.com

Rocky Mountain Capital Partners
1125 17th St., Ste. 2260
Denver, CO 80202
(303)291-5200
Fax: (303)291-5327

Sandlot Capital LLC
600 South Cherry St., Ste. 525
Denver, CO 80246
(303)893-3400
Fax: (303)893-3403
Website: http://www.sandlotcapital.com

Wolf Ventures
50 South Steele St., Ste. 777
Denver, CO 80209
(303)321-4800
Fax: (303)321-4848
E-mail: businessplan@wolfventures.com
Website: http://www.wolfventures.com

The Columbine Venture Funds
5460 S. Quebec St., Ste. 270
Englewood, CO 80111
(303)694-3222
Fax: (303)694-9007

Investment Securities of Colorado, Inc.
4605 Denice Dr.
Englewood, CO 80111
(303)796-9192

Kinship Partners
6300 S. Syracuse Way, Ste. 484
Englewood, CO 80111
(303)694-0268
Fax: (303)694-1707
E-mail: block@vailsys.com

Boranco Management, L.L.C.
1528 Hillside Dr.
Fort Collins, CO 80524-1969
(970)221-2297
Fax: (970)221-4787

Aweida Ventures
890 West Cherry St., Ste. 220
Louisville, CO 80027
(303)664-9520
Fax: (303)664-9530
Website: http://www.aweida.com

Access Venture Partners
8787 Turnpike Dr., Ste. 260
Westminster, CO 80030
(303)426-8899
Fax: (303)426-8828

Connecticut

Medmax Ventures, LP
1 Northwestern Dr., Ste. 203
Bloomfield, CT 06002
(860)286-2960
Fax: (860)286-9960

James B. Kobak & Co.
Four Mansfield Place
Darien, CT 06820

(203)656-3471
Fax: (203)655-2905

Orien Ventures
1 Post Rd.
Fairfield, CT 06430
(203)259-9933
Fax: (203)259-5288

ABP Acquisition Corporation
115 Maple Ave.
Greenwich, CT 06830
(203)625-8287
Fax: (203)447-6187

Catterton Partners
9 Greenwich Office Park
Greenwich, CT 06830
(203)629-4901
Fax: (203)629-4903
Website: http://www.cpequity.com

Consumer Venture Partners
3 Pickwick Plz.
Greenwich, CT 06830
(203)629-8800
Fax: (203)629-2019

Insurance Venture Partners
31 Brookside Dr., Ste. 211
Greenwich, CT 06830
(203)861-0030
Fax: (203)861-2745

The NTC Group
Three Pickwick Plaza
Ste. 200
Greenwich, CT 06830
(203)862-2800
Fax: (203)622-6538

Regulus International Capital Co., Inc.
140 Greenwich Ave.
Greenwich, CT 06830
(203)625-9700
Fax: (203)625-9706

Axiom Venture Partners
City Place II
185 Asylum St., 17th Fl.
Hartford, CT 06103
(860)548-7799
Fax: (860)548-7797
Website: http://www.axiomventures.com

Conning Capital Partners
City Place II
185 Asylum St.
Hartford, CT 06103-4105
(860)520-1289
Fax: (860)520-1299
E-mail: pe@conning.com
Website: http://www.conning.com

First New England Capital L.P.
100 Pearl St.
Hartford, CT 06103
(860)293-3333
Fax: (860)293-3338
E-mail: info@firstnewenglandcapital.com
Website: http://www.firstnewenglandcapital
.com

Northeast Ventures
One State St., Ste. 1720
Hartford, CT 06103
(860)547-1414
Fax: (860)246-8755

Windward Holdings
38 Sylvan Rd.
Madison, CT 06443
(203)245-6870
Fax: (203)245-6865

Advanced Materials Partners, Inc.
45 Pine St.
PO Box 1022
New Canaan, CT 06840
(203)966-6415
Fax: (203)966-8448
E-mail: wkb@amplink.com

RFE Investment Partners
36 Grove St.
New Canaan, CT 06840
(203)966-2800
Fax: (203)966-3109
Website: http://www.rfeip.com

Connecticut Innovations, Inc.
999 West St.
Rocky Hill, CT 06067
(860)563-5851
Fax: (860)563-4877
E-mail: pamela.hartley@ctinnovations.com
Website: http://www.ctinnovations.com

Canaan Partners
105 Rowayton Ave.
Rowayton, CT 06853
(203)855-0400
Fax: (203)854-9117
Website: http://www.canaan.com

Landmark Partners, Inc.
10 Mill Pond Ln.
Simsbury, CT 06070
(860)651-9760
Fax: (860)651-8890
Website: http://www.landmarkpartners.com

Sweeney & Company
PO Box 567
Southport, CT 06490
(203)255-0220
Fax: (203)255-0220
E-mail: sweeney@connix.com

Baxter Associates, Inc.
PO Box 1333
Stamford, CT 06904
(203)323-3143
Fax: (203)348-0622

Beacon Partners Inc.
6 Landmark Sq., 4th Fl.
Stamford, CT 06901-2792
(203)359-5776
Fax: (203)359-5876

Collinson, Howe, and Lennox, LLC
1055 Washington Blvd., 5th Fl.
Stamford, CT 06901
(203)324-7700
Fax: (203)324-3636
E-mail: info@chlmedical.com
Website: http://www.chlmedical.com

Prime Capital Management Co.
550 West Ave.
Stamford, CT 06902
(203)964-0642
Fax: (203)964-0862

Saugatuck Capital Co.
1 Canterbury Green
Stamford, CT 06901
(203)348-6669
Fax: (203)324-6995
Website: http://www.saugatuckcapital
.com

Soundview Financial Group Inc.
22 Gatehouse Rd.
Stamford, CT 06902
(203)462-7200
Fax: (203)462-7350
Website: http://www.sndv.com

TSG Ventures, L.L.C.
177 Broad St., 12th Fl.
Stamford, CT 06901
(203)406-1500
Fax: (203)406-1590

Whitney & Company
177 Broad St.
Stamford, CT 06901
(203)973-1400
Fax: (203)973-1422
Website: http://www.jhwhitney.com

Cullinane & Donnelly Venture Partners L.P.
970 Farmington Ave.
West Hartford, CT 06107
(860)521-7811

The Crestview Investment and Financial Group
431 Post Rd. E, Ste. 1

Westport, CT 06880-4403
(203)222-0333
Fax: (203)222-0000

Marketcorp Venture Associates, L.P. (MCV)
274 Riverside Ave.
Westport, CT 06880
(203)222-3030
Fax: (203)222-3033

Oak Investment Partners (Westport)
1 Gorham Island
Westport, CT 06880
(203)226-8346
Fax: (203)227-0372
Website: http://www.oakinv.com

Oxford Bioscience Partners
315 Post Rd. W
Westport, CT 06880-5200
(203)341-3300
Fax: (203)341-3309
Website: http://www.oxbio.com

Prince Ventures (Westport)
25 Ford Rd.
Westport, CT 06880
(203)227-8332
Fax: (203)226-5302

LTI Venture Leasing Corp.
221 Danbury Rd.
Wilton, CT 06897
(203)563-1100
Fax: (203)563-1111
Website: http://www.ltileasing.com

Delaware

Blue Rock Capital
5803 Kennett Pike, Ste. A
Wilmington, DE 19807
(302)426-0981
Fax: (302)426-0982
Website: http://
www.bluerockcapital.com

District of Columbia

Allied Capital Corp.
1919 Pennsylvania Ave. NW
Washington, DC 20006-3434
(202)331-2444
Fax: (202)659-2053
Website: http://www.alliedcapital.com

Atlantic Coastal Ventures, L.P.
3101 South St. NW
Washington, DC 20007
(202)293-1166
Fax: (202)293-1181
Website: http://www.atlanticcv.com

Columbia Capital Group, Inc.
1660 L St. NW, Ste. 308
Washington, DC 20036
(202)775-8815
Fax: (202)223-0544

Core Capital Partners
901 15th St., NW
9th Fl.
Washington, DC 20005
(202)589-0090
Fax: (202)589-0091
Website: http://www.core-capital.com

Next Point Partners
701 Pennsylvania Ave. NW, Ste. 900
Washington, DC 20004
(202)661-8703
Fax: (202)434-7400
E-mail: mf@nextpoint.vc
Website: http://www.nextpointvc.com

Telecommunications Development Fund
2020 K. St. NW
Ste. 375
Washington, DC 20006
(202)293-8840
Fax: (202)293-8850
Website: http://www.tdfund.com

Wachtel & Co., Inc.
1101 4th St. NW
Washington, DC 20005-5680
(202)898-1144

Winslow Partners LLC
1300 Connecticut Ave. NW
Washington, DC 20036-1703
(202)530-5000
Fax: (202)530-5010
E-mail: winslow@winslowpartners.com

Women's Growth Capital Fund
1054 31st St., NW
Ste. 110
Washington, DC 20007
(202)342-1431
Fax: (202)341-1203
Website: http://www.wgcf.com

Florida

Sigma Capital Corp.
22668 Caravelle Circle
Boca Raton, FL 33433
(561)368-9783

North American Business Development Co., L.L.C.
111 East Las Olas Blvd.
Ft. Lauderdale, FL 33301
(305)463-0681

Fax: (305)527-0904
Website: http://
www.northamericanfund.com

Chartwell Capital Management Co. Inc.
1 Independent Dr., Ste. 3120
Jacksonville, FL 32202
(904)355-3519
Fax: (904)353-5833
E-mail: info@chartwellcap.com

CEO Advisors
1061 Maitland Center Commons
Ste. 209
Maitland, FL 32751
(407)660-9327
Fax: (407)660-2109

Henry & Co.
8201 Peters Rd., Ste. 1000
Plantation, FL 33324
(954)797-7400

Avery Business Development Services
2506 St. Michel Ct.
Ponte Vedra, FL 32082
(904)285-6033

New South Ventures
5053 Ocean Blvd.
Sarasota, FL 34242
(941)358-6000
Fax: (941)358-6078
Website: http://
www.newsouthventures.com

Venture Capital Management Corp.
PO Box 2626
Satellite Beach, FL 32937
(407)777-1969

Florida Capital Venture Ltd.
325 Florida Bank Plaza
100 W. Kennedy Blvd.
Tampa, FL 33602
(813)229-2294
Fax: (813)229-2028

Quantum Capital Partners
339 South Plant Ave.
Tampa, FL 33606
(813)250-1999
Fax: (813)250-1998
Website: http://
www.quantumcapitalpartners.com

South Atlantic Venture Fund
614 W. Bay St.
Tampa, FL 33606-2704
(813)253-2500
Fax: (813)253-2360
E-mail: venture@southatlantic.com
Website: http://www.southatlantic.com

LM Capital Corp.
120 S. Olive, Ste. 400
West Palm Beach, FL 33401
(561)833-9700
Fax: (561)655-6587
Website: http://www.lmcapitalsecurities
.com

Georgia

Venture First Associates
4811 Thornwood Dr.
Acworth, GA 30102
(770)928-3733
Fax: (770)928-6455

Alliance Technology Ventures
8995 Westside Pkwy., Ste. 200
Alpharetta, GA 30004
(678)336-2000
Fax: (678)336-2001
E-mail: info@atv.com
Website: http://www.atv.com

Cordova Ventures
2500 North Winds Pkwy., Ste. 475
Alpharetta, GA 30004
(678)942-0300
Fax: (678)942-0301
Website: http://www.cordovaventures
.com

Advanced Technology Development Fund
1000 Abernathy, Ste. 1420
Atlanta, GA 30328-5614
(404)668-2333
Fax: (404)668-2333

CGW Southeast Partners
12 Piedmont Center, Ste. 210
Atlanta, GA 30305
(404)816-3255
Fax: (404)816-3258
Website: http://www.cgwlp.com

Cyberstarts
1900 Emery St., NW
3rd Fl.
Atlanta, GA 30318
(404)267-5000
Fax: (404)267-5200
Website: http://www.cyberstarts.com

EGL Holdings, Inc.
10 Piedmont Center, Ste. 412
Atlanta, GA 30305
(404)949-8300
Fax: (404)949-8311

Equity South
1790 The Lenox Bldg.
3399 Peachtree Rd. NE

Atlanta, GA 30326
(404)237-6222
Fax: (404)261-1578

Five Paces
3400 Peachtree Rd., Ste. 200
Atlanta, GA 30326
(404)439-8300
Fax: (404)439-8301
Website: http://www.fivepaces.com

Frontline Capital, Inc.
3475 Lenox Rd., Ste. 400
Atlanta, GA 30326
(404)240-7280
Fax: (404)240-7281

Fuqua Ventures LLC
1201 W. Peachtree St. NW, Ste. 5000
Atlanta, GA 30309
(404)815-4500
Fax: (404)815-4528
Website: http://www.fuquaventures.com

Noro-Moseley Partners
4200 Northside Pkwy., Bldg. 9
Atlanta, GA 30327
(404)233-1966
Fax: (404)239-9280
Website: http://www.noro-moseley.com

Renaissance Capital Corp.
34 Peachtree St. NW, Ste. 2230
Atlanta, GA 30303
(404)658-9061
Fax: (404)658-9064

River Capital, Inc.
Two Midtown Plaza
1360 Peachtree St. NE, Ste. 1430
Atlanta, GA 30309
(404)873-2166
Fax: (404)873-2158

State Street Bank & Trust Co.
3414 Peachtree Rd. NE, Ste. 1010
Atlanta, GA 30326
(404)364-9500
Fax: (404)261-4469

UPS Strategic Enterprise Fund
55 Glenlake Pkwy. NE
Atlanta, GA 30328
(404)828-8814
Fax: (404)828-8088
E-mail: jcacyce@ups.com
Website: http://www.ups.com/sef/
sef_home

Wachovia
191 Peachtree St. NE, 26th Fl.
Atlanta, GA 30303
(404)332-1000

Fax: (404)332-1392
Website: http://www.wachovia.com/wca

Brainworks Ventures
4243 Dunwoody Club Dr.
Chamblee, GA 30341
(770)239-7447

First Growth Capital Inc.
Best Western Plaza, Ste. 105
PO Box 815
Forsyth, GA 31029
(912)781-7131

Financial Capital Resources, Inc.
21 Eastbrook Bend, Ste. 116
Peachtree City, GA 30269
(404)487-6650

Hawaii

HMS Hawaii Management Partners
Davies Pacific Center
841 Bishop St., Ste. 860
Honolulu, HI 96813
(808)545-3755
Fax: (808)531-2611

Idaho

Sun Valley Ventures
160 Second St.
Ketchum, ID 83340
(208)726-5005
Fax: (208)726-5094

Illinois

Open Prairie Ventures
115 N. Neil St., Ste. 209
Champaign, IL 61820
(217)351-7000
Fax: (217)351-7051
E-mail: inquire@openprairie.com
Website: http://www.openprairie.com

ABN AMRO Private Equity
208 S. La Salle St., 10th Fl.
Chicago, IL 60604
(312)855-7079
Fax: (312)553-6648
Website: http://www.abnequity.com

Alpha Capital Partners, Ltd.
122 S. Michigan Ave., Ste. 1700
Chicago, IL 60603
(312)322-9800
Fax: (312)322-9808
E-mail: acp@alphacapital.com

Ameritech Development Corp.
30 S. Wacker Dr., 37th Fl.
Chicago, IL 60606

(312)750-5083
Fax: (312)609-0244

Apex Investment Partners
225 W. Washington, Ste. 1450
Chicago, IL 60606
(312)857-2800
Fax: (312)857-1800
E-mail: apex@apexvc.com
Website: http://www.apexvc.com

Arch Venture Partners
8725 W. Higgins Rd., Ste. 290
Chicago, IL 60631
(773)380-6600
Fax: (773)380-6606
Website: http://www.archventure.com

The Bank Funds
208 South LaSalle St., Ste. 1680
Chicago, IL 60604
(312)855-6020
Fax: (312)855-8910

Batterson Venture Partners
303 W. Madison St., Ste. 1110
Chicago, IL 60606-3309
(312)269-0300
Fax: (312)269-0021
Website: http://www.battersonvp.com

William Blair Capital Partners, L.L.C.
222 W. Adams St., Ste. 1300
Chicago, IL 60606
(312)364-8250
Fax: (312)236-1042
E-mail: privateequity@wmblair.com
Website: http://www.wmblair.com

Bluestar Ventures
208 South LaSalle St., Ste. 1020
Chicago, IL 60604
(312)384-5000
Fax: (312)384-5005
Website: http://
www.bluestarventures.com

The Capital Strategy Management Co.
233 S. Wacker Dr.
Box 06334
Chicago, IL 60606
(312)444-1170

DN Partners
77 West Wacker Dr., Ste. 4550
Chicago, IL 60601
(312)332-7960
Fax: (312)332-7979

Dresner Capital Inc.
29 South LaSalle St., Ste. 310
Chicago, IL 60603
(312)726-3600
Fax: (312)726-7448

Eblast Ventures LLC
11 South LaSalle St., 5th Fl.
Chicago, IL 60603
(312)372-2600
Fax: (312)372-5621
Website: http://www.eblastventures.com

Essex Woodlands Health Ventures, L.P.
190 S. LaSalle St., Ste. 2800
Chicago, IL 60603
(312)444-6040
Fax: (312)444-6034
Website: http://
www.essexwoodlands.com

First Analysis Venture Capital
233 S. Wacker Dr., Ste. 9500
Chicago, IL 60606
(312)258-1400
Fax: (312)258-0334
Website: http://www.firstanalysis.com

Frontenac Co.
135 S. LaSalle St., Ste.3800
Chicago, IL 60603
(312)368-0044
Fax: (312)368-9520
Website: http://www.frontenac.com

GTCR Golder Rauner, LLC
6100 Sears Tower
Chicago, IL 60606
(312)382-2200
Fax: (312)382-2201
Website: http://www.gtcr.com

High Street Capital LLC
311 South Wacker Dr., Ste. 4550
Chicago, IL 60606
(312)697-4990
Fax: (312)697-4994
Website: http://www.highstr.com

IEG Venture Management, Inc.
70 West Madison
Chicago, IL 60602
(312)644-0890
Fax: (312)454-0369
Website: http://www.iegventure.com

JK&B Capital
180 North Stetson, Ste. 4500
Chicago, IL 60601
(312)946-1200
Fax: (312)946-1103
E-mail: gspencer@jkbcapital.com
Website: http://www.jkbcapital.com

Kettle Partners L.P.
350 W. Hubbard, Ste. 350
Chicago, IL 60610
(312)329-9300

Fax: (312)527-4519
Website: http://www.kettlevc.com

Lake Shore Capital Partners
20 N. Wacker Dr., Ste. 2807
Chicago, IL 60606
(312)803-3536
Fax: (312)803-3534

LaSalle Capital Group Inc.
70 W. Madison St., Ste. 5710
Chicago, IL 60602
(312)236-7041
Fax: (312)236-0720

Linc Capital, Inc.
303 E. Wacker Pkwy., Ste. 1000
Chicago, IL 60601
(312)946-2670
Fax: (312)938-4290
E-mail: bdemars@linccap.com

Madison Dearborn Partners, Inc.
3 First National Plz., Ste. 3800
Chicago, IL 60602
(312)895-1000
Fax: (312)895-1001
E-mail: invest@mdcp.com
Website: http://www.mdcp.com

Mesirow Private Equity Investments Inc.
350 N. Clark St.
Chicago, IL 60610
(312)595-6950
Fax: (312)595-6211
Website: http://
www.meisrowfinancial.com

Mosaix Ventures LLC
1822 North Mohawk
Chicago, IL 60614
(312)274-0988
Fax: (312)274-0989
Website: http://www.mosaixventures
.com

Nesbitt Burns
111 West Monroe St.
Chicago, IL 60603
(312)416-3855
Fax: (312)765-8000
Website: http://www.harrisbank.com

Polestar Capital, Inc.
180 N. Michigan Ave., Ste. 1905
Chicago, IL 60601
(312)984-9090
Fax: (312)984-9877
E-mail: wl@polestarvc.com
Website: http://www.polestarvc.com

Prince Ventures (Chicago)
10 S. Wacker Dr., Ste. 2575
Chicago, IL 60606-7407
(312)454-1408
Fax: (312)454-9125

Prism Capital
444 N. Michigan Ave.
Chicago, IL 60611
(312)464-7900
Fax: (312)464-7915
Website: http://www.prismfund.com

Third Coast Capital
900 N. Franklin St., Ste. 700
Chicago, IL 60610
(312)337-3303
Fax: (312)337-2567
E-mail: manic@earthlink.com
Website: http://
www.thirdcoastcapital.com

Thoma Cressey Equity Partners
4460 Sears Tower, 92nd Fl.
233 S. Wacker Dr.
Chicago, IL 60606
(312)777-4444
Fax: (312)777-4445
Website: http://www.thomacressey.com

Tribune Ventures
435 N. Michigan Ave., Ste. 600
Chicago, IL 60611
(312)527-8797
Fax: (312)222-5993
Website: http://
www.tribuneventures.com

Wind Point Partners (Chicago)
676 N. Michigan Ave., Ste. 330
Chicago, IL 60611
(312)649-4000
Website: http://www.wppartners.com

Marquette Venture Partners
520 Lake Cook Rd., Ste. 450
Deerfield, IL 60015
(847)940-1700
Fax: (847)940-1724
Website: http://
www.marquetteventures.com

Duchossois Investments Limited, LLC
845 Larch Ave.
Elmhurst, IL 60126
(630)530-6105
Fax: (630)993-8644
Website: http://www.duchtec.com

Evanston Business Investment Corp.
1840 Oak Ave.
Evanston, IL 60201

(847)866-1840
Fax: (847)866-1808
E-mail: t-parkinson@nwu.com
Website: http://www.ebic.com

Inroads Capital Partners L.P.
1603 Orrington Ave., Ste. 2050
Evanston, IL 60201-3841
(847)864-2000
Fax: (847)864-9692

The Cerulean Fund/WGC Enterprises
1701 E. Lake Ave., Ste. 170
Glenview, IL 60025
(847)657-8002
Fax: (847)657-8168

Ventana Financial Resources, Inc.
249 Market Sq.
Lake Forest, IL 60045
(847)234-3434

Beecken, Petty & Co.
901 Warrenville Rd., Ste. 205
Lisle, IL 60532
(630)435-0300
Fax: (630)435-0370
E-mail: hep@bpcompany.com
Website: http://www.bpcompany.com

Allstate Private Equity
3075 Sanders Rd., Ste. G5D
Northbrook, IL 60062-7127
(847)402-8247
Fax: (847)402-0880

KB Partners
1101 Skokie Blvd., Ste. 260
Northbrook, IL 60062-2856
(847)714-0444
Fax: (847)714-0445
E-mail: keith@kbpartners.com
Website: http://www.kbpartners.com

Transcap Associates Inc.
900 Skokie Blvd., Ste. 210
Northbrook, IL 60062
(847)753-9600
Fax: (847)753-9090

Graystone Venture Partners, L.L.C. / Portage Venture Partners
One Northfield Plaza, Ste. 530
Northfield, IL 60093
(847)446-9460
Fax: (847)446-9470
Website: http://
www.portageventures.com

Motorola Inc.
1303 E. Algonquin Rd.
Schaumburg, IL 60196-1065
(847)576-4929

Fax: (847)538-2250
Website: http://www.mot.com/mne

Indiana

Irwin Ventures LLC
500 Washington St.
Columbus, IN 47202
(812)373-1434
Fax: (812)376-1709
Website: http://www.irwinventures.com

Cambridge Venture Partners
4181 East 96th St., Ste. 200
Indianapolis, IN 46240
(317)814-6192
Fax: (317)944-9815

CID Equity Partners
One American Square, Ste. 2850
Box 82074
Indianapolis, IN 46282
(317)269-2350
Fax: (317)269-2355
Website: http://www.cidequity.com

Gazelle Techventures
6325 Digital Way, Ste. 460
Indianapolis, IN 46278
(317)275-6800
Fax: (317)275-1101
Website: http://www.gazellevc.com

Monument Advisors Inc.
Bank One Center/Circle
111 Monument Circle, Ste. 600
Indianapolis, IN 46204-5172
(317)656-5065
Fax: (317)656-5060
Website: http://www.monumentadv.com

MWV Capital Partners
201 N. Illinois St., Ste. 300
Indianapolis, IN 46204
(317)237-2323
Fax: (317)237-2325
Website: http://www.mwvcapital.com

First Source Capital Corp.
100 North Michigan St.
PO Box 1602
South Bend, IN 46601
(219)235-2180
Fax: (219)235-2227

Iowa

Allsop Venture Partners
118 Third Ave. SE, Ste. 837
Cedar Rapids, IA 52401
(319)368-6675
Fax: (319)363-9515

InvestAmerica Investment Advisors, Inc.
101 2nd St. SE, Ste. 800
Cedar Rapids, IA 52401
(319)363-8249
Fax: (319)363-9683

Pappajohn Capital Resources
2116 Financial Center
Des Moines, IA 50309
(515)244-5746
Fax: (515)244-2346
Website: http://www.pappajohn.com

Berthel Fisher & Company Planning Inc.
701 Tama St.
PO Box 609
Marion, IA 52302
(319)497-5700
Fax: (319)497-4244

Kansas

Enterprise Merchant Bank
7400 West 110th St., Ste. 560
Overland Park, KS 66210
(913)327-8500
Fax: (913)327-8505

Kansas Venture Capital, Inc. (Overland Park)
6700 Antioch Plz., Ste. 460
Overland Park, KS 66204
(913)262-7117
Fax: (913)262-3509
E-mail: jdalton@kvci.com

Child Health Investment Corp.
6803 W. 64th St., Ste. 208
Shawnee Mission, KS 66202
(913)262-1436
Fax: (913)262-1575
Website: http://www.chca.com

Kansas Technology Enterprise Corp.
214 SW 6th, 1st Fl.
Topeka, KS 66603-3719
(785)296-5272
Fax: (785)296-1160
E-mail: ktec@ktec.com
Website: http://www.ktec.com

Kentucky

Kentucky Highlands Investment Corp.
362 Old Whitley Rd.
London, KY 40741
(606)864-5175
Fax: (606)864-5194
Website: http://www.khic.org

Chrysalis Ventures, L.L.C.
1850 National City Tower
Louisville, KY 40202
(502)583-7644
Fax: (502)583-7648
E-mail: bobsany@chrysalisventures.com
Website: http://www.chrysalisventures
.com

Humana Venture Capital
500 West Main St.
Louisville, KY 40202
(502)580-3922
Fax: (502)580-2051
E-mail: gemont@humana.com
George Emont, Director

Summit Capital Group, Inc.
6510 Glenridge Park Pl., Ste. 8
Louisville, KY 40222
(502)332-2700

Louisiana

Bank One Equity Investors, Inc.
451 Florida St.
Baton Rouge, LA 70801
(504)332-4421
Fax: (504)332-7377

Advantage Capital Partners
LLE Tower
909 Poydras St., Ste. 2230
New Orleans, LA 70112
(504)522-4850
Fax: (504)522-4950
Website: http://www.advantagecap.com

Maine

CEI Ventures / Coastal Ventures LP
2 Portland Fish Pier, Ste. 201
Portland, ME 04101
(207)772-5356
Fax: (207)772-5503
Website: http://www.ceiventures.com

Commwealth Bioventures, Inc.
4 Milk St.
Portland, ME 04101
(207)780-0904
Fax: (207)780-0913

Maryland

Annapolis Ventures LLC
151 West St., Ste. 302
Annapolis, MD 21401
(443)482-9555
Fax: (443)482-9565
Website: http://www.annapolisventures
.com

Delmag Ventures
220 Wardour Dr.
Annapolis, MD 21401
(410)267-8196
Fax: (410)267-8017
Website: http://www.delmagventures.com

Abell Venture Fund
111 S. Calvert St., Ste. 2300
Baltimore, MD 21202
(410)547-1300
Fax: (410)539-6579
Website: http://www.abell.org

ABS Ventures (Baltimore)
1 South St., Ste. 2150
Baltimore, MD 21202
(410)895-3895
Fax: (410)895-3899
Website: http://www.absventures.com

Anthem Capital, L.P.
16 S. Calvert St., Ste. 800
Baltimore, MD 21202-1305
(410)625-1510
Fax: (410)625-1735
Website: http://www.anthemcapital.com

Catalyst Ventures
1119 St. Paul St.
Baltimore, MD 21202
(410)244-0123
Fax: (410)752-7721

Maryland Venture Capital Trust
217 E. Redwood St., Ste. 2200
Baltimore, MD 21202
(410)767-6361
Fax: (410)333-6931

New Enterprise Associates (Baltimore)
1119 St. Paul St.
Baltimore, MD 21202
(410)244-0115
Fax: (410)752-7721
Website: http://www.nea.com

T. Rowe Price Threshold Partnerships
100 E. Pratt St., 8th Fl.
Baltimore, MD 21202
(410)345-2000
Fax: (410)345-2800

Spring Capital Partners
16 W. Madison St.
Baltimore, MD 21201
(410)685-8000
Fax: (410)727-1436
E-mail: mailbox@springcap.com

Arete Corporation
3 Bethesda Metro Ctr., Ste. 770
Bethesda, MD 20814

(301)657-6268
Fax: (301)657-6254
Website: http://www.arete-microgen.com

Embryon Capital
7903 Sleaford Place
Bethesda, MD 20814
(301)656-6837
Fax: (301)656-8056

Potomac Ventures
7920 Norfolk Ave., Ste. 1100
Bethesda, MD 20814
(301)215-9240
Website: http://
www.potomacventures.com

Toucan Capital Corp.
3 Bethesda Metro Center, Ste. 700
Bethesda, MD 20814
(301)961-1970
Fax: (301)961-1969
Website: http://www.toucancapital.com

Kinetic Ventures LLC
2 Wisconsin Cir., Ste. 620
Chevy Chase, MD 20815
(301)652-8066
Fax: (301)652-8310
Website: http://
www.kineticventures.com

Boulder Ventures Ltd.
4750 Owings Mills Blvd.
Owings Mills, MD 21117
(410)998-3114
Fax: (410)356-5492
Website: http://
www.boulderventures.com

Grotech Capital Group
9690 Deereco Rd., Ste. 800
Timonium, MD 21093
(410)560-2000
Fax: (410)560-1910
Website: http://www.grotech.com

Massachusetts

Adams, Harkness & Hill, Inc.
60 State St.
Boston, MA 02109
(617)371-3900

Advent International
75 State St., 29th Fl.
Boston, MA 02109
(617)951-9400
Fax: (617)951-0566
Website: http://www.adventinernational
.com

American Research and Development
30 Federal St.
Boston, MA 02110-2508
(617)423-7500
Fax: (617)423-9655

Ascent Venture Partners
255 State St., 5th Fl.
Boston, MA 02109
(617)270-9400
Fax: (617)270-9401
E-mail: info@ascentvp.com
Website: http://www.ascentvp.com

Atlas Venture
222 Berkeley St.
Boston, MA 02116
(617)488-2200
Fax: (617)859-9292
Website: http://www.atlasventure.com

Axxon Capital
28 State St., 37th Fl.
Boston, MA 02109
(617)722-0980
Fax: (617)557-6014
Website: http://www.axxoncapital.com

BancBoston Capital/BancBoston Ventures
175 Federal St., 10th Fl.
Boston, MA 02110
(617)434-2509
Fax: (617)434-6175
Website: http://
www.bancbostoncapital.com

Boston Capital Ventures
Old City Hall
45 School St.
Boston, MA 02108
(617)227-6550
Fax: (617)227-3847
E-mail: info@bcv.com
Website: http://www.bcv.com

Boston Financial & Equity Corp.
20 Overland St.
PO Box 15071
Boston, MA 02215
(617)267-2900
Fax: (617)437-7601
E-mail: debbie@bfec.com

Boston Millennia Partners
30 Rowes Wharf
Boston, MA 02110
(617)428-5150
Fax: (617)428-5160
Website: http://www.millenniapartners
.com

Bristol Investment Trust
842A Beacon St.
Boston, MA 02215-3199
(617)566-5212
Fax: (617)267-0932

Brook Venture Management LLC
50 Federal St., 5th Fl.
Boston, MA 02110
(617)451-8989
Fax: (617)451-2369
Website: http://www.brookventure.com

Burr, Egan, Deleage, and Co. (Boston)
200 Clarendon St., Ste. 3800
Boston, MA 02116
(617)262-7770
Fax: (617)262-9779

Cambridge/Samsung Partners
One Exeter Plaza
Ninth Fl.
Boston, MA 02116
(617)262-4440
Fax: (617)262-5562

Chestnut Street Partners, Inc.
75 State St., Ste. 2500
Boston, MA 02109
(617)345-7220
Fax: (617)345-7201
E-mail: chestnut@chestnutp.com

Claflin Capital Management, Inc.
10 Liberty Sq., Ste. 300
Boston, MA 02109
(617)426-6505
Fax: (617)482-0016
Website: http://www.claflincapital.com

Copley Venture Partners
99 Summer St., Ste. 1720
Boston, MA 02110
(617)737-1253
Fax: (617)439-0699

Corning Capital / Corning Technology Ventures
121 High Street, Ste. 400
Boston, MA 02110
(617)338-2656
Fax: (617)261-3864
Website: http://www.corningventures.com

Downer & Co.
211 Congress St.
Boston, MA 02110
(617)482-6200
Fax: (617)482-6201
E-mail: cdowner@downer.com
Website: http://www.downer.com

Fidelity Ventures
82 Devonshire St.
Boston, MA 02109
(617)563-6370
Fax: (617)476-9023
Website: http://www.fidelityventures.com

Greylock Management Corp. (Boston)
1 Federal St.
Boston, MA 02110-2065
(617)423-5525
Fax: (617)482-0059

Gryphon Ventures
222 Berkeley St., Ste.1600
Boston, MA 02116
(617)267-9191
Fax: (617)267-4293
E-mail: all@gryphoninc.com

Halpern, Denny & Co.
500 Boylston St.
Boston, MA 02116
(617)536-6602
Fax: (617)536-8535

Harbourvest Partners, LLC
1 Financial Center, 44th Fl.
Boston, MA 02111
(617)348-3707
Fax: (617)350-0305
Website: http://www.hvpllc.com

Highland Capital Partners
2 International Pl.
Boston, MA 02110
(617)981-1500
Fax: (617)531-1550
E-mail: info@hcp.com
Website: http://www.hcp.com

Lee Munder Venture Partners
John Hancock Tower T-53
200 Clarendon St.
Boston, MA 02103
(617)380-5600
Fax: (617)380-5601
Website: http://www.leemunder.com

M/C Venture Partners
75 State St., Ste. 2500
Boston, MA 02109
(617)345-7200
Fax: (617)345-7201
Website: http://www.mcventurepartners.com

Massachusetts Capital Resources Co.
420 Boylston St.
Boston, MA 02116
(617)536-3900
Fax: (617)536-7930

Massachusetts Technology Development Corp. (MTDC)
148 State St.
Boston, MA 02109
(617)723-4920
Fax: (617)723-5983
E-mail: jhodgman@mtdc.com
Website: http://www.mtdc.com

New England Partners
One Boston Place, Ste. 2100
Boston, MA 02108
(617)624-8400
Fax: (617)624-8999
Website: http://www.nepartners.com

North Hill Ventures
Ten Post Office Square
11th Fl.
Boston, MA 02109
(617)788-2112
Fax: (617)788-2152
Website: http://www.northhillventures.com

OneLiberty Ventures
150 Cambridge Park Dr.
Boston, MA 02140
(617)492-7280
Fax: (617)492-7290
Website: http://www.oneliberty.com

Schroder Ventures
Life Sciences
60 State St., Ste. 3650
Boston, MA 02109
(617)367-8100
Fax: (617)367-1590
Website: http://www.shroderventures.com

Shawmut Capital Partners
75 Federal St., 18th Fl.
Boston, MA 02110
(617)368-4900
Fax: (617)368-4910
Website: http://www.shawmutcapital.com

Solstice Capital LLC
15 Broad St., 3rd Fl.
Boston, MA 02109
(617)523-7733
Fax: (617)523-5827
E-mail: solticecapital@solcap.com

Spectrum Equity Investors
One International Pl., 29th Fl.
Boston, MA 02110
(617)464-4600
Fax: (617)464-4601
Website: http://www.spectrumequity.com

Spray Venture Partners
One Walnut St.
Boston, MA 02108
(617)305-4140
Fax: (617)305-4144
Website: http://www.sprayventure.com

The Still River Fund
100 Federal St., 29th Fl.
Boston, MA 02110
(617)348-2327
Fax: (617)348-2371
Website: http://www.stillriverfund.com

Summit Partners
600 Atlantic Ave., Ste. 2800
Boston, MA 02210-2227
(617)824-1000
Fax: (617)824-1159
Website: http://www.summitpartners.com

TA Associates, Inc. (Boston)
High Street Tower
125 High St., Ste. 2500
Boston, MA 02110
(617)574-6700
Fax: (617)574-6728
Website: http://www.ta.com

TVM Techno Venture Management
101 Arch St., Ste. 1950
Boston, MA 02110
(617)345-9320
Fax: (617)345-9377
E-mail: info@tvmvc.com
Website: http://www.tvmvc.com

UNC Ventures
64 Burough St.
Boston, MA 02130-4017
(617)482-7070
Fax: (617)522-2176

Venture Investment Management Company (VIMAC)
177 Milk St.
Boston, MA 02190-3410
(617)292-3300
Fax: (617)292-7979
E-mail: bzeisig@vimac.com
Website: http://www.vimac.com

MDT Advisers, Inc.
125 Cambridge Park Dr.
Cambridge, MA 02140-2314
(617)234-2200
Fax: (617)234-2210
Website: http://www.mdtai.com

TTC Ventures
One Main St., 6th Fl.
Cambridge, MA 02142

(617)528-3137
Fax: (617)577-1715
E-mail: info@ttcventures.com

Zero Stage Capital Co. Inc.
101 Main St., 17th Fl.
Cambridge, MA 02142
(617)876-5355
Fax: (617)876-1248
Website: http://www.zerostage.com

Atlantic Capital
164 Cushing Hwy.
Cohasset, MA 02025
(617)383-9449
Fax: (617)383-6040
E-mail: info@atlanticcap.com
Website: http://www.atlanticcap.com

Seacoast Capital Partners
55 Ferncroft Rd.
Danvers, MA 01923
(978)750-1300
Fax: (978)750-1301
E-mail: gdeli@seacoastcapital.com
Website: http://www.seacoastcapital.com

Sage Management Group
44 South Street
PO Box 2026
East Dennis, MA 02641
(508)385-7172
Fax: (508)385-7272
E-mail: sagemgt@capecod.net

Applied Technology
1 Cranberry Hill
Lexington, MA 02421-7397
(617)862-8622
Fax: (617)862-8367

Royalty Capital Management
5 Downing Rd.
Lexington, MA 02421-6918
(781)861-8490

Argo Global Capital
210 Broadway, Ste. 101
Lynnfield, MA 01940
(781)592-5250
Fax: (781)592-5230
Website: http://www.gsmcapital.com

Industry Ventures
6 Bayne Lane
Newburyport, MA 01950
(978)499-7606
Fax: (978)499-0686
Website: http://www.industryventures.com

Softbank Capital Partners
10 Langley Rd., Ste. 202
Newton Center, MA 02459

(617)928-9300
Fax: (617)928-9305
E-mail: clax@bvc.com

Advanced Technology Ventures (Boston)
281 Winter St., Ste. 350
Waltham, MA 02451
(781)290-0707
Fax: (781)684-0045
E-mail: info@atvcapital.com
Website: http://www.atvcapital.com

Castile Ventures
890 Winter St., Ste. 140
Waltham, MA 02451
(781)890-0060
Fax: (781)890-0065
Website: http://www.castileventures.com

Charles River Ventures
1000 Winter St., Ste. 3300
Waltham, MA 02451
(781)487-7060
Fax: (781)487-7065
Website: http://www.crv.com

Comdisco Venture Group (Waltham)
Totton Pond Office Center
400-1 Totten Pond Rd.
Waltham, MA 02451
(617)672-0250
Fax: (617)398-8099

Marconi Ventures
890 Winter St., Ste. 310
Waltham, MA 02451
(781)839-7177
Fax: (781)522-7477
Website: http://www.marconi.com

Matrix Partners
Bay Colony Corporate Center
1000 Winter St., Ste.4500
Waltham, MA 02451
(781)890-2244
Fax: (781)890-2288
Website: http://www.matrixpartners.com

North Bridge Venture Partners
950 Winter St. Ste. 4600
Waltham, MA 02451
(781)290-0004
Fax: (781)290-0999
E-mail: eta@nbvp.com

Polaris Venture Partners
Bay Colony Corporate Ctr.
1000 Winter St., Ste. 3500
Waltham, MA 02451
(781)290-0770
Fax: (781)290-0880

E-mail: partners@polarisventures.com
Website: http://www.polarisventures.com

Seaflower Ventures
Bay Colony Corporate Ctr.
1000 Winter St. Ste. 1000
Waltham, MA 02451
(781)466-9552
Fax: (781)466-9553
E-mail: moot@seaflower.com
Website: http://www.seaflower.com

Ampersand Ventures
55 William St., Ste. 240
Wellesley, MA 02481
(617)239-0700
Fax: (617)239-0824
E-mail: info@ampersandventures.com
Website: http://www.ampersandventures
.com

Battery Ventures (Boston)
20 William St., Ste. 200
Wellesley, MA 02481
(781)577-1000
Fax: (781)577-1001
Website: http://www.battery.com

Commonwealth Capital Ventures, L.P.
20 William St., Ste.225
Wellesley, MA 02481
(781)237-7373
Fax: (781)235-8627
Website: http://www.ccvlp.com

Fowler, Anthony & Company
20 Walnut St.
Wellesley, MA 02481
(781)237-4201
Fax: (781)237-7718

Gemini Investors
20 William St.
Wellesley, MA 02481
(781)237-7001
Fax: (781)237-7233

Grove Street Advisors Inc.
20 William St., Ste. 230
Wellesley, MA 02481
(781)263-6100
Fax: (781)263-6101
Website: http://
www.grovestreetadvisors.com

Mees Pierson Investeringsmaat B.V.
20 William St., Ste. 210
Wellesley, MA 02482
(781)239-7600
Fax: (781)239-0377

Norwest Equity Partners
40 William St., Ste. 305

Wellesley, MA 02481-3902
(781)237-5870
Fax: (781)237-6270
Website: http://www.norwestvp.com

Bessemer Venture Partners (Wellesley Hills)
83 Walnut St.
Wellesley Hills, MA 02481
(781)237-6050
Fax: (781)235-7576
E-mail: travis@bvpny.com
Website: http://www.bvp.com

Venture Capital Fund of New England
20 Walnut St., Ste. 120
Wellesley Hills, MA 02481-2175
(781)239-8262
Fax: (781)239-8263

Prism Venture Partners
100 Lowder Brook Dr., Ste. 2500
Westwood, MA 02090
(781)302-4000
Fax: (781)302-4040
E-mail: dwbaum@prismventure.com

Palmer Partners LP
200 Unicorn Park Dr.
Woburn, MA 01801
(781)933-5445
Fax: (781)933-0698

Michigan

Arbor Partners, L.L.C.
130 South First St.
Ann Arbor, MI 48104
(734)668-9000
Fax: (734)669-4195
Website: http://www.arborpartners.com

EDF Ventures
425 N. Main St.
Ann Arbor, MI 48104
(734)663-3213
Fax: (734)663-7358
E-mail: edf@edfvc.com
Website: http://www.edfvc.com

White Pines Management, L.L.C.
2401 Plymouth Rd., Ste. B
Ann Arbor, MI 48105
(734)747-9401
Fax: (734)747-9704
E-mail: ibund@whitepines.com
Website: http://www.whitepines.com

Wellmax, Inc.
3541 Bendway Blvd., Ste. 100
Bloomfield Hills, MI 48301
(248)646-3554
Fax: (248)646-6220

Venture Funding, Ltd.
Fisher Bldg.
3011 West Grand Blvd., Ste. 321
Detroit, MI 48202
(313)871-3606
Fax: (313)873-4935

Investcare Partners L.P. / GMA Capital LLC
32330 W. Twelve Mile Rd.
Farmington Hills, MI 48334
(248)489-9000
Fax: (248)489-8819
E-mail: gma@gmacapital.com
Website: http://www.gmacapital.com

Liberty Bidco Investment Corp.
30833 Northwestern Highway, Ste. 211
Farmington Hills, MI 48334
(248)626-6070
Fax: (248)626-6072

Seaflower Ventures
5170 Nicholson Rd.
PO Box 474
Fowlerville, MI 48836
(517)223-3335
Fax: (517)223-3337
E-mail: gibbons@seaflower.com
Website: http://www.seaflower.com

Ralph Wilson Equity Fund LLC
15400 E. Jefferson Ave.
Gross Pointe Park, MI 48230
(313)821-9122
Fax: (313)821-9101
Website: http://www.RalphWilsonEquity
Fund.com
J. Skip Simms, President

Minnesota

Development Corp. of Austin
1900 Eighth Ave., NW
Austin, MN 55912
(507)433-0346
Fax: (507)433-0361
E-mail: dca@smig.net
Website: http://www.spamtownusa.com

Northeast Ventures Corp.
802 Alworth Bldg.
Duluth, MN 55802
(218)722-9915
Fax: (218)722-9871

Medical Innovation Partners, Inc.
6450 City West Pkwy.
Eden Prairie, MN 55344-3245
(612)828-9616
Fax: (612)828-9596

St. Paul Venture Capital, Inc.
10400 Vicking Dr., Ste. 550
Eden Prairie, MN 55344
(612)995-7474
Fax: (612)995-7475
Website: http://www.stpaulvc.com

Cherry Tree Investments, Inc.
7601 France Ave. S, Ste. 150
Edina, MN 55435
(612)893-9012
Fax: (612)893-9036
Website: http://www.cherrytree.com

Shared Ventures, Inc.
6550 York Ave. S
Edina, MN 55435
(612)925-3411

Sherpa Partners LLC
5050 Lincoln Dr., Ste. 490
Edina, MN 55436
(952)942-1070
Fax: (952)942-1071
Website: http://www.sherpapartners.com

Affinity Capital Management
901 Marquette Ave., Ste. 1810
Minneapolis, MN 55402
(612)252-9900
Fax: (612)252-9911
Website: http://www.affinitycapital.com

Artesian Capital
1700 Foshay Tower
821 Marquette Ave.
Minneapolis, MN 55402
(612)334-5600
Fax: (612)334-5601
E-mail: artesian@artesian.com

Coral Ventures
60 S. 6th St., Ste. 3510
Minneapolis, MN 55402
(612)335-8666
Fax: (612)335-8668
Website: http://www.coralventures.com

Crescendo Venture Management, L.L.C.
800 LaSalle Ave., Ste. 2250
Minneapolis, MN 55402
(612)607-2800
Fax: (612)607-2801
Website: http://www.crescendoventures
.com

Gideon Hixon Venture
1900 Foshay Tower
821 Marquette Ave.
Minneapolis, MN 55402
(612)904-2314
Fax: (612)204-0913

Norwest Equity Partners
3600 IDS Center
80 S. 8th St.
Minneapolis, MN 55402
(612)215-1600
Fax: (612)215-1601
Website: http://www.norwestvp.com

Oak Investment Partners (Minneapolis)
4550 Norwest Center
90 S. 7th St.
Minneapolis, MN 55402
(612)339-9322
Fax: (612)337-8017
Website: http://www.oakinv.com

Pathfinder Venture Capital Funds (Minneapolis)
7300 Metro Blvd., Ste. 585
Minneapolis, MN 55439
(612)835-1121
Fax: (612)835-8389
E-mail: jahrens620@aol.com

U.S. Bancorp Piper Jaffray Ventures, Inc.
800 Nicollet Mall, Ste. 800
Minneapolis, MN 55402
(612)303-5686
Fax: (612)303-1350
Website: http://www.paperjaffrey
ventures.com

The Food Fund, Ltd. Partnership
5720 Smatana Dr., Ste. 300
Minnetonka, MN 55343
(612)939-3950
Fax: (612)939-8106

Mayo Medical Ventures
200 First St. SW
Rochester, MN 55905
(507)266-4586
Fax: (507)284-5410
Website: http://www.mayo.edu

Missouri

Bankers Capital Corp.
3100 Gillham Rd.
Kansas City, MO 64109
(816)531-1600
Fax: (816)531-1334

Capital for Business, Inc. (Kansas City)
1000 Walnut St., 18th Fl.
Kansas City, MO 64106
(816)234-2357
Fax: (816)234-2952
Website: http://www.capitalforbusiness
.com

De Vries & Co. Inc.
800 West 47th St.
Kansas City, MO 64112
(816)756-0055
Fax: (816)756-0061

InvestAmerica Venture Group Inc. (Kansas City)
Commerce Tower
911 Main St., Ste. 2424
Kansas City, MO 64105
(816)842-0114
Fax: (816)471-7339

Kansas City Equity Partners
233 W. 47th St.
Kansas City, MO 64112
(816)960-1771
Fax: (816)960-1777
Website: http://www.kcep.com

Bome Investors, Inc.
8000 Maryland Ave., Ste. 1190
St. Louis, MO 63105
(314)721-5707
Fax: (314)721-5135
Website: http://www.gatewayventures.com

Capital for Business, Inc. (St. Louis)
11 S. Meramac St., Ste. 1430
St. Louis, MO 63105
(314)746-7427
Fax: (314)746-8739
Website: http://www.capitalforbusiness.com

Crown Capital Corp.
540 Maryville Centre Dr., Ste. 120
Saint Louis, MO 63141
(314)576-1201
Fax: (314)576-1525
Website: http://www.crown-cap.com

Gateway Associates L.P.
8000 Maryland Ave., Ste. 1190
St. Louis, MO 63105
(314)721-5707
Fax: (314)721-5135

Harbison Corp.
8112 Maryland Ave., Ste. 250
Saint Louis, MO 63105
(314)727-8200
Fax: (314)727-0249

Nebraska

Heartland Capital Fund, Ltd.
PO Box 642117
Omaha, NE 68154
(402)778-5124
Fax: (402)445-2370
Website: http://www.heartlandcapitalfund
.com

Odin Capital Group
1625 Farnam St., Ste. 700
Omaha, NE 68102
(402)346-6200
Fax: (402)342-9311
Website: http://www.odincapital.com

Nevada

Edge Capital Investment Co. LLC
1350 E. Flamingo Rd., Ste. 3000
Las Vegas, NV 89119
(702)438-3343
E-mail: info@edgecapital.net
Website: http://www.edgecapital.net

The Benefit Capital Companies Inc.
PO Box 542
Logandale, NV 89021
(702)398-3222
Fax: (702)398-3700

Millennium Three Venture Group LLC
6880 South McCarran Blvd., Ste. A-11
Reno, NV 89509
(775)954-2020
Fax: (775)954-2023
Website: http://www.m3vg.com

New Jersey

Alan I. Goldman & Associates
497 Ridgewood Ave.
Glen Ridge, NJ 07028
(973)857-5680
Fax: (973)509-8856

CS Capital Partners LLC
328 Second St., Ste. 200
Lakewood, NJ 08701
(732)901-1111
Fax: (212)202-5071
Website: http://www.cs-capital.com

Edison Venture Fund
1009 Lenox Dr., Ste. 4
Lawrenceville, NJ 08648
(609)896-1900
Fax: (609)896-0066
E-mail: info@edisonventure.com
Website: http://www.edisonventure.com

Tappan Zee Capital Corp. (New Jersey)
201 Lower Notch Rd.
PO Box 416
Little Falls, NJ 07424
(973)256-8280
Fax: (973)256-2841

The CIT Group/Venture Capital, Inc.
650 CIT Dr.
Livingston, NJ 07039
(973)740-5429

Fax: (973)740-5555
Website: http://www.cit.com

Capital Express, L.L.C.
1100 Valleybrook Ave.
Lyndhurst, NJ 07071
(201)438-8228
Fax: (201)438-5131
E-mail: niles@capitalexpress.com
Website: http://www.capitalexpress.com

Westford Technology Ventures, L.P.
17 Academy St.
Newark, NJ 07102
(973)624-2131
Fax: (973)624-2008

Accel Partners
1 Palmer Sq.
Princeton, NJ 08542
(609)683-4500
Fax: (609)683-4880
Website: http://www.accel.com

Cardinal Partners
221 Nassau St.
Princeton, NJ 08542
(609)924-6452
Fax: (609)683-0174
Website: http://www.cardinalhealth
partners.com

Domain Associates L.L.C.
One Palmer Sq., Ste. 515
Princeton, NJ 08542
(609)683-5656
Fax: (609)683-9789
Website: http://www.domainvc.com

Johnston Associates, Inc.
181 Cherry Valley Rd.
Princeton, NJ 08540
(609)924-3131
Fax: (609)683-7524
E-mail: jaincorp@aol.com

Kemper Ventures
Princeton Forrestal Village
155 Village Blvd.
Princeton, NJ 08540
(609)936-3035
Fax: (609)936-3051

Penny Lane Parnters
One Palmer Sq., Ste. 309
Princeton, NJ 08542
(609)497-4646
Fax: (609)497-0611

Early Stage Enterprises L.P.
995 Route 518
Skillman, NJ 08558
(609)921-8896

Fax: (609)921-8703
Website: http://www.esevc.com

MBW Management Inc.
1 Springfield Ave.
Summit, NJ 07901
(908)273-4060
Fax: (908)273-4430

BCI Advisors, Inc.
Glenpointe Center W.
Teaneck, NJ 07666
(201)836-3900
Fax: (201)836-6368
E-mail: info@bciadvisors.com
Website: http://www.bcipartners.com

**Demuth, Folger & Wetherill / DFW
Capital Partners**
Glenpointe Center E., 5th Fl.
300 Frank W. Burr Blvd.
Teaneck, NJ 07666
(201)836-2233
Fax: (201)836-5666
Website: http://www.dfwcapital.com

First Princeton Capital Corp.
189 Berdan Ave., No. 131
Wayne, NJ 07470-3233
(973)278-3233
Fax: (973)278-4290
Website: http://www.lytellcatt.net

Edelson Technology Partners
300 Tice Blvd.
Woodcliff Lake, NJ 07675
(201)930-9898
Fax: (201)930-8899
Website: http://www.edelsontech.com

New Mexico

Bruce F. Glaspell & Associates
10400 Academy Rd. NE, Ste. 313
Albuquerque, NM 87111
(505)292-4505
Fax: (505)292-4258

High Desert Ventures, Inc.
6101 Imparata St. NE, Ste. 1721
Albuquerque, NM 87111
(505)797-3330
Fax: (505)338-5147

New Business Capital Fund, Ltd.
5805 Torreon NE
Albuquerque, NM 87109
(505)822-8445

SBC Ventures
10400 Academy Rd. NE, Ste. 313
Albuquerque, NM 87111

(505)292-4505
Fax: (505)292-4528

Technology Ventures Corp.
1155 University Blvd. SE
Albuquerque, NM 87106
(505)246-2882
Fax: (505)246-2891

New York

Small Business Technology Investment Fund
99 Washington Ave., Ste. 1731
Albany, NY 12210
(518)473-9741
Fax: (518)473-6876

Rand Capital Corp.
2200 Rand Bldg.
Buffalo, NY 14203
(716)853-0802
Fax: (716)854-8480
Website: http://www.randcapital.com

Seed Capital Partners
620 Main St.
Buffalo, NY 14202
(716)845-7520
Fax: (716)845-7539
Website: http://www.seedcp.com

Coleman Venture Group
5909 Northern Blvd.
PO Box 224
East Norwich, NY 11732
(516)626-3642
Fax: (516)626-9722

Vega Capital Corp.
45 Knollwood Rd.
Elmsford, NY 10523
(914)345-9500
Fax: (914)345-9505

Herbert Young Securities, Inc.
98 Cuttermill Rd.
Great Neck, NY 11021
(516)487-8300
Fax: (516)487-8319

Sterling/Carl Marks Capital, Inc.
175 Great Neck Rd., Ste. 408
Great Neck, NY 11021
(516)482-7374
Fax: (516)487-0781
E-mail: stercrlmar@aol.com
Website: http://www.serlingcarlmarks.com

Impex Venture Management Co.
PO Box 1570
Green Island, NY 12183
(518)271-8008
Fax: (518)271-9101

Corporate Venture Partners L.P.
200 Sunset Park
Ithaca, NY 14850
(607)257-6323
Fax: (607)257-6128

Arthur P. Gould & Co.
One Wilshire Dr.
Lake Success, NY 11020
(516)773-3000
Fax: (516)773-3289

Dauphin Capital Partners
108 Forest Ave.
Locust Valley, NY 11560
(516)759-3339
Fax: (516)759-3322
Website: http://www.dauphincapital.com

550 Digital Media Ventures
555 Madison Ave., 10th Fl.
New York, NY 10022
Website: http://www.550dmv.com

Aberlyn Capital Management Co., Inc.
500 Fifth Ave.
New York, NY 10110
(212)391-7750
Fax: (212)391-7762

Adler & Company
342 Madison Ave., Ste. 807
New York, NY 10173
(212)599-2535
Fax: (212)599-2526

Alimansky Capital Group, Inc.
605 Madison Ave., Ste. 300
New York, NY 10022-1901
(212)832-7300
Fax: (212)832-7338

Allegra Partners
515 Madison Ave., 29th Fl.
New York, NY 10022
(212)826-9080
Fax: (212)759-2561

The Argentum Group
The Chyrsler Bldg.
405 Lexington Ave.
New York, NY 10174
(212)949-6262
Fax: (212)949-8294
Website: http://www.argentumgroup.com

Axavision Inc.
14 Wall St., 26th Fl.
New York, NY 10005
(212)619-4000
Fax: (212)619-7202

Bedford Capital Corp.
18 East 48th St., Ste. 1800
New York, NY 10017
(212)688-5700
Fax: (212)754-4699
E-mail: info@bedfordnyc.com
Website: http://www.bedfordnyc.com

Bloom & Co.
950 Third Ave.
New York, NY 10022
(212)838-1858
Fax: (212)838-1843

Bristol Capital Management
300 Park Ave., 17th Fl.
New York, NY 10022
(212)572-6306
Fax: (212)705-4292

Citicorp Venture Capital Ltd. (New York City)
399 Park Ave., 14th Fl.
Zone 4
New York, NY 10043
(212)559-1127
Fax: (212)888-2940

CM Equity Partners
135 E. 57th St.
New York, NY 10022
(212)909-8428
Fax: (212)980-2630

Cohen & Co., L.L.C.
800 Third Ave.
New York, NY 10022
(212)317-2250
Fax: (212)317-2255
E-mail: nlcohen@aol.com

Cornerstone Equity Investors, L.L.C.
717 5th Ave., Ste. 1100
New York, NY 10022
(212)753-0901
Fax: (212)826-6798
Website: http://www.cornerstone-equity.com

CW Group, Inc.
1041 3rd Ave., 2nd fl.
New York, NY 10021
(212)308-5266
Fax: (212)644-0354
Website: http://www.cwventures.com

DH Blair Investment Banking Corp.
44 Wall St., 2nd Fl.
New York, NY 10005
(212)495-5000
Fax: (212)269-1438

Dresdner Kleinwort Capital
75 Wall St.
New York, NY 10005
(212)429-3131
Fax: (212)429-3139
Website: http://www.dresdnerkb.com

East River Ventures, L.P.
645 Madison Ave., 22nd Fl.
New York, NY 10022
(212)644-2322
Fax: (212)644-5498

Easton Hunt Capital Partners
641 Lexington Ave., 21st Fl.
New York, NY 10017
(212)702-0950
Fax: (212)702-0952
Website: http://www.eastoncapital.com

Elk Associates Funding Corp.
747 3rd Ave., Ste. 4C
New York, NY 10017
(212)355-2449
Fax: (212)759-3338

EOS Partners, L.P.
320 Park Ave., 22nd Fl.
New York, NY 10022
(212)832-5800
Fax: (212)832-5815
E-mail: mfirst@eospartners.com
Website: http://www.eospartners.com

Euclid Partners
45 Rockefeller Plaza, Ste. 3240
New York, NY 10111
(212)218-6880
Fax: (212)218-6877
E-mail: graham@euclidpartners.com
Website: http://www.euclidpartners.com

Evergreen Capital Partners, Inc.
150 East 58th St.
New York, NY 10155
(212)813-0758
Fax: (212)813-0754

Exeter Capital L.P.
10 E. 53rd St.
New York, NY 10022
(212)872-1172
Fax: (212)872-1198
E-mail: exeter@usa.net

Financial Technology Research Corp.
518 Broadway
Penthouse
New York, NY 10012
(212)625-9100
Fax: (212)431-0300
E-mail: fintek@financier.com

4C Ventures
237 Park Ave., Ste. 801
New York, NY 10017
(212)692-3680
Fax: (212)692-3685
Website: http://www.4cventures.com

Fusient Ventures
99 Park Ave., 20th Fl.
New York, NY 10016
(212)972-8999
Fax: (212)972-9876
E-mail: info@fusient.com
Website: http://www.fusient.com

Generation Capital Partners
551 Fifth Ave., Ste. 3100
New York, NY 10176
(212)450-8507
Fax: (212)450-8550
Website: http://www.genpartners.com

Golub Associates, Inc.
555 Madison Ave.
New York, NY 10022
(212)750-6060
Fax: (212)750-5505

Hambro America Biosciences Inc.
650 Madison Ave., 21st Floor
New York, NY 10022
(212)223-7400
Fax: (212)223-0305

Hanover Capital Corp.
505 Park Ave., 15th Fl.
New York, NY 10022
(212)755-1222
Fax: (212)935-1787

Harvest Partners, Inc.
280 Park Ave, 33rd Fl.
New York, NY 10017
(212)559-6300
Fax: (212)812-0100
Website: http://www.harvpart.com

Holding Capital Group, Inc.
10 E. 53rd St., 30th Fl.
New York, NY 10022
(212)486-6670
Fax: (212)486-0843

Hudson Venture Partners
660 Madison Ave., 14th Fl.
New York, NY 10021-8405
(212)644-9797
Fax: (212)644-7430
Website: http://www.hudsonptr.com

IBJS Capital Corp.
1 State St., 9th Fl.
New York, NY 10004

(212)858-2018
Fax: (212)858-2768

InterEquity Capital Partners, L.P.
220 5th Ave.
New York, NY 10001
(212)779-2022
Fax: (212)779-2103
Website: http://www.interequity-capital.com

The Jordan Edmiston Group Inc.
150 East 52nd St., 18th Fl.
New York, NY 10022
(212)754-0710
Fax: (212)754-0337

Josephberg, Grosz and Co., Inc.
633 3rd Ave., 13th Fl.
New York, NY 10017
(212)974-9926
Fax: (212)397-5832

J.P. Morgan Capital Corp.
60 Wall St.
New York, NY 10260-0060
(212)648-9000
Fax: (212)648-5002
Website: http://www.jpmorgan.com

The Lambda Funds
380 Lexington Ave., 54th Fl.
New York, NY 10168
(212)682-3454
Fax: (212)682-9231

Lepercq Capital Management Inc.
1675 Broadway
New York, NY 10019
(212)698-0795
Fax: (212)262-0155

Loeb Partners Corp.
61 Broadway, Ste. 2400
New York, NY 10006
(212)483-7000
Fax: (212)574-2001

Madison Investment Partners
660 Madison Ave.
New York, NY 10021
(212)223-2600
Fax: (212)223-8208

MC Capital Inc.
520 Madison Ave., 16th Fl.
New York, NY 10022
(212)644-0841
Fax: (212)644-2926

McCown, De Leeuw and Co. (New York)
65 E. 55th St., 36th Fl.
New York, NY 10022

(212)355-5500
Fax: (212)355-6283
Website: http://www.mdcpartners.com

Morgan Stanley Venture Partners
1221 Avenue of the Americas, 33rd Fl.
New York, NY 10020
(212)762-7900
Fax: (212)762-8424
E-mail: msventures@ms.com
Website: http://www.msvp.com

Nazem and Co.
645 Madison Ave., 12th Fl.
New York, NY 10022
(212)371-7900
Fax: (212)371-2150

Needham Capital Management, L.L.C.
445 Park Ave.
New York, NY 10022
(212)371-8300
Fax: (212)705-0299
Website: http://www.needhamco.com

Norwood Venture Corp.
1430 Broadway, Ste. 1607
New York, NY 10018
(212)869-5075
Fax: (212)869-5331
E-mail: nvc@mail.idt.net
Website: http://www.norven.com

Noveltek Venture Corp.
521 Fifth Ave., Ste. 1700
New York, NY 10175
(212)286-1963

Paribas Principal, Inc.
787 7th Ave.
New York, NY 10019
(212)841-2005
Fax: (212)841-3558

Patricof & Co. Ventures, Inc.
(New York)
445 Park Ave.
New York, NY 10022
(212)753-6300
Fax: (212)319-6155
Website: http://www.patricof.com

The Platinum Group, Inc.
350 Fifth Ave, Ste. 7113
New York, NY 10118
(212)736-4300
Fax: (212)736-6086
Website: http://www.platinumgroup.com

Pomona Capital
780 Third Ave., 28th Fl.
New York, NY 10017
(212)593-3639

Fax: (212)593-3987
Website: http://www.pomonacapital.com

Prospect Street Ventures
10 East 40th St., 44th Fl.
New York, NY 10016
(212)448-0702
Fax: (212)448-9652
E-mail: wkohler@prospectstreet.com
Website: http://www.prospectstreet.com

Regent Capital Management
505 Park Ave., Ste. 1700
New York, NY 10022
(212)735-9900
Fax: (212)735-9908

Rothschild Ventures, Inc.
1251 Avenue of the Americas, 51st Fl.
New York, NY 10020
(212)403-3500
Fax: (212)403-3652
Website: http://www.nmrothschild.com

Sandler Capital Management
767 Fifth Ave., 45th Fl.
New York, NY 10153
(212)754-8100
Fax: (212)826-0280

Siguler Guff & Company
630 Fifth Ave., 16th Fl.
New York, NY 10111
(212)332-5100
Fax: (212)332-5120

Spencer Trask Ventures Inc.
535 Madison Ave.
New York, NY 10022
(212)355-5565
Fax: (212)751-3362
Website: http://www.spencertrask.com

Sprout Group (New York City)
277 Park Ave.
New York, NY 10172
(212)892-3600
Fax: (212)892-3444
E-mail: info@sproutgroup.com
Website: http://www.sproutgroup.com

US Trust Private Equity
114 W.47th St.
New York, NY 10036
(212)852-3949
Fax: (212)852-3759
Website: http://www.ustrust.com/
privateequity

Vencon Management Inc.
301 West 53rd St., Ste. 10F
New York, NY 10019
(212)581-8787

Fax: (212)397-4126
Website: http://www.venconinc.com

Venrock Associates
30 Rockefeller Plaza, Ste. 5508
New York, NY 10112
(212)649-5600
Fax: (212)649-5788
Website: http://www.venrock.com

Venture Capital Fund of America, Inc.
509 Madison Ave., Ste. 812
New York, NY 10022
(212)838-5577
Fax: (212)838-7614
E-mail: mail@vcfa.com
Website: http://www.vcfa.com

Venture Opportunities Corp.
150 E. 58th St.
New York, NY 10155
(212)832-3737
Fax: (212)980-6603

Warburg Pincus Ventures, Inc.
466 Lexington Ave., 11th Fl.
New York, NY 10017
(212)878-9309
Fax: (212)878-9200
Website: http://www.warburgpincus.com

Wasserstein, Perella & Co. Inc.
31 W. 52nd St., 27th Fl.
New York, NY 10019
(212)702-5691
Fax: (212)969-7879

Welsh, Carson, Anderson, & Stowe
320 Park Ave., Ste. 2500
New York, NY 10022-6815
(212)893-9500
Fax: (212)893-9575

Whitney and Co. (New York)
630 Fifth Ave. Ste. 3225
New York, NY 10111
(212)332-2400
Fax: (212)332-2422
Website: http://www.jhwitney.com

Winthrop Ventures
74 Trinity Place, Ste. 600
New York, NY 10006
(212)422-0100

The Pittsford Group
8 Lodge Pole Rd.
Pittsford, NY 14534
(716)223-3523

Genesee Funding
70 Linden Oaks, 3rd Fl.
Rochester, NY 14625

(716)383-5550
Fax: (716)383-5305

Gabelli Multimedia Partners
One Corporate Center
Rye, NY 10580
(914)921-5395
Fax: (914)921-5031

Stamford Financial
108 Main St.
Stamford, NY 12167
(607)652-3311
Fax: (607)652-6301
Website: http://www.stamfordfinancial.com

Northwood Ventures LLC
485 Underhill Blvd., Ste. 205
Syosset, NY 11791
(516)364-5544
Fax: (516)364-0879
E-mail: northwood@northwood.com
Website: http://www.northwood
ventures.com

Exponential Business Development Co.
216 Walton St.
Syracuse, NY 13202-1227
(315)474-4500
Fax: (315)474-4682
E-mail: dirksonn@aol.com
Website: http://www.exponential-ny.com

Onondaga Venture Capital Fund Inc.
714 State Tower Bldg.
Syracuse, NY 13202
(315)478-0157
Fax: (315)478-0158

Bessemer Venture Partners (Westbury)
1400 Old Country Rd., Ste. 109
Westbury, NY 11590
(516)997-2300
Fax: (516)997-2371
E-mail: bob@bvpny.com
Website: http://www.bvp.com

Ovation Capital Partners
120 Bloomingdale Rd., 4th Fl.
White Plains, NY 10605
(914)258-0011
Fax: (914)684-0848
Website: http://www.ovationcapital.com

North Carolina

Carolinas Capital Investment Corp.
1408 Biltmore Dr.
Charlotte, NC 28207
(704)375-3888
Fax: (704)375-6226

First Union Capital Partners
1st Union Center, 12th Fl.
301 S. College St.
Charlotte, NC 28288-0732
(704)383-0000
Fax: (704)374-6711
Website: http://www.fucp.com

Frontier Capital LLC
525 North Tryon St., Ste. 1700
Charlotte, NC 28202
(704)414-2880
Fax: (704)414-2881
Website: http://www.frontierfunds.com

Kitty Hawk Capital
2700 Coltsgate Rd., Ste. 202
Charlotte, NC 28211
(704)362-3909
Fax: (704)362-2774
Website: http://www.kittyhawk
capital.com

Piedmont Venture Partners
One Morrocroft Centre
6805 Morisson Blvd., Ste. 380
Charlotte, NC 28211
(704)731-5200
Fax: (704)365-9733
Website: http://www.piedmontvp.com

Ruddick Investment Co.
1800 Two First Union Center
Charlotte, NC 28282
(704)372-5404
Fax: (704)372-6409

The Shelton Companies Inc.
3600 One First Union Center
301 S. College St.
Charlotte, NC 28202
(704)348-2200
Fax: (704)348-2260

Wakefield Group
1110 E. Morehead St.
PO Box 36329
Charlotte, NC 28236
(704)372-0355
Fax: (704)372-8216
Website: http://www.wakefieldgroup.com

Aurora Funds, Inc.
2525 Meridian Pkwy., Ste. 220
Durham, NC 27713
(919)484-0400
Fax: (919)484-0444
Website: http://www.aurorafunds.com

Intersouth Partners
3211 Shannon Rd., Ste. 610
Durham, NC 27707

(919)493-6640
Fax: (919)493-6649
E-mail: info@intersouth.com
Website: http://www.intersouth.com

Geneva Merchant Banking Partners
PO Box 21962
Greensboro, NC 27420
(336)275-7002
Fax: (336)275-9155
Website: http://www.genevamer
chantbank.com

The North Carolina Enterprise Fund, L.P.
3600 Glenwood Ave., Ste. 107
Raleigh, NC 27612
(919)781-2691
Fax: (919)783-9195
Website: http://www.ncef.com

Ohio

Senmend Medical Ventures
4445 Lake Forest Dr., Ste. 600
Cincinnati, OH 45242
(513)563-3264
Fax: (513)563-3261

The Walnut Group
312 Walnut St., Ste. 1151
Cincinnati, OH 45202
(513)651-3300
Fax: (513)929-4441
Website: http://www.thewalnutgroup.com

Brantley Venture Partners
20600 Chagrin Blvd., Ste. 1150
Cleveland, OH 44122
(216)283-4800
Fax: (216)283-5324

Clarion Capital Corp.
1801 E. 9th St., Ste. 1120
Cleveland, OH 44114
(216)687-1096
Fax: (216)694-3545

Crystal Internet Venture Fund, L.P.
1120 Chester Ave., Ste. 418
Cleveland, OH 44114
(216)263-5515
Fax: (216)263-5518
E-mail: jf@crystalventure.com
Website: http://www.crystalventure.com

Key Equity Capital Corp.
127 Public Sq., 28th Fl.
Cleveland, OH 44114
(216)689-3000
Fax: (216)689-3204
Website: http://www.keybank.com

Morgenthaler Ventures
Terminal Tower
50 Public Square, Ste. 2700
Cleveland, OH 44113
(216)416-7500
Fax: (216)416-7501
Website: http://www.morgenthaler.com

National City Equity Partners Inc.
1965 E. 6th St.
Cleveland, OH 44114
(216)575-2491
Fax: (216)575-9965
E-mail: nccap@aol.com
Website: http://www.nccapital.com

Primus Venture Partners, Inc.
5900 LanderBrook Dr., Ste. 2000
Cleveland, OH 44124-4020
(440)684-7300
Fax: (440)684-7342
E-mail: info@primusventure.com
Website: http://www.primusventure.com

Banc One Capital Partners (Columbus)
150 East Gay St., 24th Fl.
Columbus, OH 43215
(614)217-1100
Fax: (614)217-1217

Battelle Venture Partners
505 King Ave.
Columbus, OH 43201
(614)424-7005
Fax: (614)424-4874

Ohio Partners
62 E. Board St., 3rd Fl.
Columbus, OH 43215
(614)621-1210
Fax: (614)621-1240

Capital Technology Group, L.L.C.
400 Metro Place North, Ste. 300
Dublin, OH 43017
(614)792-6066
Fax: (614)792-6036
E-mail: info@capitaltech.com
Website: http://www.capitaltech.com

Northwest Ohio Venture Fund
4159 Holland-Sylvania R., Ste. 202
Toledo, OH 43623
(419)824-8144
Fax: (419)882-2035
E-mail: bwalsh@novf.com

Oklahoma

Moore & Associates
1000 W. Wilshire Blvd., Ste. 370
Oklahoma City, OK 73116
(405)842-3660
Fax: (405)842-3763

Chisholm Private Capital Partners
100 West 5th St., Ste. 805
Tulsa, OK 74103
(918)584-0440
Fax: (918)584-0441
Website: http://www.chisholmvc.com

Davis, Tuttle Venture Partners (Tulsa)
320 S. Boston, Ste. 1000
Tulsa, OK 74103-3703
(918)584-7272
Fax: (918)582-3404
Website: http://www.davistuttle.com

RBC Ventures
2627 E. 21st St.
Tulsa, OK 74114
(918)744-5607
Fax: (918)743-8630

Oregon

Utah Ventures II LP
10700 SW Beaverton-Hillsdale Hwy.,
Ste. 548
Beaverton, OR 97005
(503)574-4125
E-mail: adishlip@uven.com
Website: http://www.uven.com

Orien Ventures
14523 SW Westlake Dr.
Lake Oswego, OR 97035
(503)699-1680
Fax: (503)699-1681

OVP Venture Partners (Lake Oswego)
340 Oswego Pointe Dr., Ste. 200
Lake Oswego, OR 97034
(503)697-8766
Fax: (503)697-8863
E-mail: info@ovp.com
Website: http://www.ovp.com

Oregon Resource and Technology Development Fund
4370 NE Halsey St., Ste. 233
Portland, OR 97213-1566
(503)282-4462
Fax: (503)282-2976

Shaw Venture Partners
400 SW 6th Ave., Ste. 1100
Portland, OR 97204-1636
(503)228-4884
Fax: (503)227-2471
Website: http://www.shawventures.com

Pennsylvania

Mid-Atlantic Venture Funds
125 Goodman Dr.
Bethlehem, PA 18015

(610)865-6550
Fax: (610)865-6427
Website: http://www.mavf.com

Newspring Ventures
100 W. Elm St., Ste. 101
Conshohocken, PA 19428
(610)567-2380
Fax: (610)567-2388
Website: http://www.newsprintventures.
com

Patricof & Co. Ventures, Inc.
455 S. Gulph Rd., Ste. 410
King of Prussia, PA 19406
(610)265-0286
Fax: (610)265-4959
Website: http://www.patricof.com

Loyalhanna Venture Fund
527 Cedar Way, Ste. 104
Oakmont, PA 15139
(412)820-7035
Fax: (412)820-7036

Innovest Group Inc.
2000 Market St., Ste. 1400
Philadelphia, PA 19103
(215)564-3960
Fax: (215)569-3272

Keystone Venture Capital Management Co.
1601 Market St., Ste. 2500
Philadelphia, PA 19103
(215)241-1200
Fax: (215)241-1211
Website: http://www.keystonevc.com

Liberty Venture Partners
2005 Market St., Ste. 200
Philadelphia, PA 19103
(215)282-4484
Fax: (215)282-4485
E-mail: info@libertyvp.com
Website: http://www.libertyvp.com

Penn Janney Fund, Inc.
1801 Market St., 11th Fl.
Philadelphia, PA 19103
(215)665-4447
Fax: (215)557-0820

Philadelphia Ventures, Inc.
The Bellevue
200 S. Broad St.
Philadelphia, PA 19102
(215)732-4445
Fax: (215)732-4644

Birchmere Ventures Inc.
2000 Technology Dr.
Pittsburgh, PA 15219-3109

(412)803-8000
Fax: (412)687-8139
Website: http://www.birchmerevc.com

CEO Venture Fund
2000 Technology Dr., Ste. 160
Pittsburgh, PA 15219-3109
(412)687-3451
Fax: (412)687-8139
E-mail: ceofund@aol.com
Website: http://
www.ceoventurefund.com

Innovation Works Inc.
2000 Technology Dr., Ste. 250
Pittsburgh, PA 15219
(412)681-1520
Fax: (412)681-2625
Website: http://www.innovationworks.org

Keystone Minority Capital Fund L.P.
1801 Centre Ave., Ste. 201
Williams Sq.
Pittsburgh, PA 15219
(412)338-2230
Fax: (412)338-2224

Mellon Ventures, Inc.
One Mellon Bank Ctr., Rm. 3500
Pittsburgh, PA 15258
(412)236-3594
Fax: (412)236-3593
Website: http://www.mellonventures.com

Pennsylvania Growth Fund
5850 Ellsworth Ave., Ste. 303
Pittsburgh, PA 15232
(412)661-1000
Fax: (412)361-0676

Point Venture Partners
The Century Bldg.
130 Seventh St., 7th Fl.
Pittsburgh, PA 15222
(412)261-1966
Fax: (412)261-1718

Cross Atlantic Capital Partners
5 Radnor Corporate Center, Ste. 555
Radnor, PA 19087
(610)995-2650
Fax: (610)971-2062
Website: http://www.xacp.com

Meridian Venture Partners (Radnor)
The Radnor Court Bldg., Ste. 140
259 Radnor-Chester Rd.
Radnor, PA 19087
(610)254-2999
Fax: (610)254-2996
E-mail: mvpart@ix.netcom.com

TDH
919 Conestoga Rd., Bldg. 1, Ste. 301
Rosemont, PA 19010
(610)526-9970
Fax: (610)526-9971

Adams Capital Management
500 Blackburn Ave.
Sewickley, PA 15143
(412)749-9454
Fax: (412)749-9459
Website: http://www.acm.com

S.R. One, Ltd.
Four Tower Bridge
200 Barr Harbor Dr., Ste. 250
W. Conshohocken, PA 19428
(610)567-1000
Fax: (610)567-1039

Greater Philadelphia Venture Capital Corp.
351 East Conestoga Rd.
Wayne, PA 19087
(610)688-6829
Fax: (610)254-8958

PA Early Stage
435 Devon Park Dr., Bldg. 500, Ste. 510
Wayne, PA 19087
(610)293-4075
Fax: (610)254-4240
Website: http://www.paearlystage.com

The Sandhurst Venture Fund, L.P.
351 E. Constoga Rd.
Wayne, PA 19087
(610)254-8900
Fax: (610)254-8958

TL Ventures
700 Bldg.
435 Devon Park Dr.
Wayne, PA 19087-1990
(610)975-3765
Fax: (610)254-4210
Website: http://www.tlventures.com

Rockhill Ventures, Inc.
100 Front St., Ste. 1350
West Conshohocken, PA 19428
(610)940-0300
Fax: (610)940-0301

Puerto Rico

Advent-Morro Equity Partners
Banco Popular Bldg.
206 Tetuan St., Ste. 903
San Juan, PR 00902
(787)725-5285
Fax: (787)721-1735

North America Investment Corp.
Mercantil Plaza, Ste. 813
PO Box 191831
San Juan, PR 00919
(787)754-6178
Fax: (787)754-6181

Rhode Island

Manchester Humphreys, Inc.
40 Westminster St., Ste. 900
Providence, RI 02903
(401)454-0400
Fax: (401)454-0403

Navis Partners
50 Kennedy Plaza, 12th Fl.
Providence, RI 02903
(401)278-6770
Fax: (401)278-6387
Website: http://www.navispartners.com

South Carolina

Capital Insights, L.L.C.
PO Box 27162
Greenville, SC 29616-2162
(864)242-6832
Fax: (864)242-6755
E-mail: jwarner@capitalinsights.com
Website: http://www.capitalinsights.com

Transamerica Mezzanine Financing
7 N. Laurens St., Ste. 603
Greenville, SC 29601
(864)232-6198
Fax: (864)241-4444

Tennessee

Valley Capital Corp.
Krystal Bldg.
100 W. Martin Luther King Blvd., Ste. 212
Chattanooga, TN 37402
(423)265-1557
Fax: (423)265-1588

Coleman Swenson Booth Inc.
237 2nd Ave. S
Franklin, TN 37064-2649
(615)791-9462
Fax: (615)791-9636
Website: http://www.colemanswenson.com

Capital Services & Resources, Inc.
5159 Wheelis Dr., Ste. 106
Memphis, TN 38117
(901)761-2156
Fax: (907)767-0060

Paradigm Capital Partners LLC
6410 Poplar Ave., Ste. 395
Memphis, TN 38119

(901)682-6060
Fax: (901)328-3061

SSM Ventures
845 Crossover Ln., Ste. 140
Memphis, TN 38117
(901)767-1131
Fax: (901)767-1135
Website: http://www.ssmventures.com

Capital Across America L.P.
501 Union St., Ste. 201
Nashville, TN 37219
(615)254-1414
Fax: (615)254-1856
Website: http://www.capitalacrossamerica.
com

Equitas L.P.
2000 Glen Echo Rd., Ste. 101
PO Box 158838
Nashville, TN 37215-8838
(615)383-8673
Fax: (615)383-8693

Massey Burch Capital Corp.
One Burton Hills Blvd., Ste. 350
Nashville, TN 37215
(615)665-3221
Fax: (615)665-3240
E-mail: tcalton@masseyburch.com
Website: http://www.masseyburch.com

Nelson Capital Corp.
3401 West End Ave., Ste. 300
Nashville, TN 37203
(615)292-8787
Fax: (615)385-3150

Texas

Phillips-Smith Specialty Retail Group
5080 Spectrum Dr., Ste. 805 W
Addison, TX 75001
(972)387-0725
Fax: (972)458-2560
E-mail: pssrg@aol.com
Website: http://www.phillips-smith.com

Austin Ventures, L.P.
701 Brazos St., Ste. 1400
Austin, TX 78701
(512)485-1900
Fax: (512)476-3952
E-mail: info@ausven.com
Website: http://www.austinventures.com

The Capital Network
3925 West Braker Lane, Ste. 406
Austin, TX 78759-5321
(512)305-0826
Fax: (512)305-0836

Techxas Ventures LLC
5000 Plaza on the Lake
Austin, TX 78746
(512)343-0118
Fax: (512)343-1879
E-mail: bruce@techxas.com
Website: http://www.techxas.com

Alliance Financial of Houston
218 Heather Ln.
Conroe, TX 77385-9013
(936)447-3300
Fax: (936)447-4222

Amerimark Capital Corp.
1111 W. Mockingbird, Ste. 1111
Dallas, TX 75247
(214)638-7878
Fax: (214)638-7612
E-mail: amerimark@amcapital.com
Website: http://www.amcapital.com

**AMT Venture Partners / AMT
Capital Ltd.**
5220 Spring Valley Rd., Ste. 600
Dallas, TX 75240
(214)905-9757
Fax: (214)905-9761
Website: http://www.amtcapital.com

Arkoma Venture Partners
5950 Berkshire Lane, Ste. 1400
Dallas, TX 75225
(214)739-3515
Fax: (214)739-3572
E-mail: joelf@arkomavp.com

Capital Southwest Corp.
12900 Preston Rd., Ste. 700
Dallas, TX 75230
(972)233-8242
Fax: (972)233-7362
Website: http://www.capitalsouthwest.com

Dali, Hook Partners
One Lincoln Center, Ste. 1550
5400 LBJ Freeway
Dallas, TX 75240
(972)991-5457
Fax: (972)991-5458
E-mail: dhook@hookpartners.com
Website: http://www.hookpartners.com

HO2 Partners
Two Galleria Tower
13455 Noel Rd., Ste. 1670
Dallas, TX 75240
(972)702-1144
Fax: (972)702-8234
Website: http://www.ho2.com

Interwest Partners (Dallas)
2 Galleria Tower
13455 Noel Rd., Ste. 1670
Dallas, TX 75240
(972)392-7279
Fax: (972)490-6348
Website: http://www.interwest.com

Kahala Investments, Inc.
8214 Westchester Dr., Ste. 715
Dallas, TX 75225
(214)987-0077
Fax: (214)987-2332

MESBIC Ventures Holding Co.
2435 North Central Expressway, Ste. 200
Dallas, TX 75080
(972)991-1597
Fax: (972)991-4770
Website: http://www.mvhc.com

North Texas MESBIC, Inc.
9500 Forest Lane, Ste. 430
Dallas, TX 75243
(214)221-3565
Fax: (214)221-3566

Richard Jaffe & Company, Inc,
7318 Royal Cir.
Dallas, TX 75230
(214)265-9397
Fax: (214)739-1845

Sevin Rosen Management Co.
13455 Noel Rd., Ste. 1670
Dallas, TX 75240
(972)702-1100
Fax: (972)702-1103
E-mail: info@srfunds.com
Website: http://www.srfunds.com

Stratford Capital Partners, L.P.
300 Crescent Ct., Ste. 500
Dallas, TX 75201
(214)740-7377
Fax: (214)720-7393
E-mail: stratcap@hmtf.com

Sunwestern Investment Group
12221 Merit Dr., Ste. 935
Dallas, TX 75251
(972)239-5650
Fax: (972)701-0024

Wingate Partners
750 N. St. Paul St., Ste. 1200
Dallas, TX 75201
(214)720-1313
Fax: (214)871-8799

Buena Venture Associates
201 Main St., 32nd Fl.
Fort Worth, TX 76102

(817)339-7400
Fax: (817)390-8408
Website: http://www.buenaventure.com

The Catalyst Group
3 Riverway, Ste. 770
Houston, TX 77056
(713)623-8133
Fax: (713)623-0473
E-mail: herman@thecatalystgroup.net
Website: http://www.thecatalystgroup.net

Cureton & Co., Inc.
1100 Louisiana, Ste. 3250
Houston, TX 77002
(713)658-9806
Fax: (713)658-0476

Davis, Tuttle Venture Partners (Dallas)
8 Greenway Plaza, Ste. 1020
Houston, TX 77046
(713)993-0440
Fax: (713)621-2297
Website: http://www.davistuttle.com

Houston Partners
401 Louisiana, 8th Fl.
Houston, TX 77002
(713)222-8600
Fax: (713)222-8932

Southwest Venture Group
10878 Westheimer, Ste. 178
Houston, TX 77042
(713)827-8947
(713)461-1470

AM Fund
4600 Post Oak Place, Ste. 100
Houston, TX 77027
(713)627-9111
Fax: (713)627-9119

Ventex Management, Inc.
3417 Milam St.
Houston, TX 77002-9531
(713)659-7870
Fax: (713)659-7855

MBA Venture Group
1004 Olde Town Rd., Ste. 102
Irving, TX 75061
(972)986-6703

First Capital Group Management Co.
750 East Mulberry St., Ste. 305
PO Box 15616
San Antonio, TX 78212
(210)736-4233
Fax: (210)736-5449

The Southwest Venture Partnerships
16414 San Pedro, Ste. 345
San Antonio, TX 78232

(210)402-1200
Fax: (210)402-1221
E-mail: swvp@aol.com

Medtech International Inc.
1742 Carriageway
Sugarland, TX 77478
(713)980-8474
Fax: (713)980-6343

Utah

First Security Business Investment Corp.
15 East 100 South, Ste. 100
Salt Lake City, UT 84111
(801)246-5737
Fax: (801)246-5740

Utah Ventures II, L.P.
423 Wakara Way, Ste. 206
Salt Lake City, UT 84108
(801)583-5922
Fax: (801)583-4105
Website: http://www.uven.com

Wasatch Venture Corp.
1 S. Main St., Ste. 1400
Salt Lake City, UT 84133
(801)524-8939
Fax: (801)524-8941
E-mail: mail@wasatchvc.com

Vermont

North Atlantic Capital Corp.
76 Saint Paul St., Ste. 600
Burlington, VT 05401
(802)658-7820
Fax: (802)658-5757
Website: http://
www.northatlanticcapital.com

Green Mountain Advisors Inc.
PO Box 1230
Quechee, VT 05059
(802)296-7800
Fax: (802)296-6012
Website: http://www.gmtcap.com

Virginia

Oxford Financial Services Corp.
Alexandria, VA 22314
(703)519-4900
Fax: (703)519-4910
E-mail: oxford133@aol.com

Continental SBIC
4141 N. Henderson Rd.
Arlington, VA 22203
(703)527-5200
Fax: (703)527-3700

Novak Biddle Venture Partners
1750 Tysons Blvd., Ste. 1190
McLean, VA 22102
(703)847-3770
Fax: (703)847-3771
E-mail: roger@novakbiddle.com
Website: http://www.novakbiddle.com

Spacevest
11911 Freedom Dr., Ste. 500
Reston, VA 20190
(703)904-9800
Fax: (703)904-0571
E-mail: spacevest@spacevest.com
Website: http://www.spacevest.com

Virginia Capital
1801 Libbie Ave., Ste. 201
Richmond, VA 23226
(804)648-4802
Fax: (804)648-4809
E-mail: webmaster@vacapital.com
Website: http://www.vacapital.com

Calvert Social Venture Partners
402 Maple Ave. W
Vienna, VA 22180
(703)255-4930
Fax: (703)255-4931
E-mail: calven2000@aol.com

Fairfax Partners
8000 Towers Crescent Dr., Ste. 940
Vienna, VA 22182
(703)847-9486
Fax: (703)847-0911

Global Internet Ventures
8150 Leesburg Pike, Ste. 1210
Vienna, VA 22182
(703)442-3300
Fax: (703)442-3388
Website: http://www.givinc.com

Walnut Capital Corp. (Vienna)
8000 Towers Crescent Dr., Ste. 1070
Vienna, VA 22182
(703)448-3771
Fax: (703)448-7751

Washington

Encompass Ventures
777 108th Ave. NE, Ste. 2300
Bellevue, WA 98004
(425)486-3900
Fax: (425)486-3901
E-mail: info@evpartners.com
Website: http://www.encompass
ventures.com

Fluke Venture Partners
11400 SE Sixth St., Ste. 230

Bellevue, WA 98004
(425)453-4590
Fax: (425)453-4675
E-mail: gabelein@flukeventures.com
Website: http://www.flukeventures.com

Pacific Northwest Partners SBIC, L.P.
15352 SE 53rd St.
Bellevue, WA 98006
(425)455-9967
Fax: (425)455-9404

Materia Venture Associates, L.P.
3435 Carillon Pointe
Kirkland, WA 98033-7354
(425)822-4100
Fax: (425)827-4086

OVP Venture Partners (Kirkland)
2420 Carillon Pt.
Kirkland, WA 98033
(425)889-9192
Fax: (425)889-0152
E-mail: info@ovp.com
Website: http://www.ovp.com

Digital Partners
999 3rd Ave., Ste. 1610
Seattle, WA 98104
(206)405-3607
Fax: (206)405-3617
Website: http://www.digitalpartners.com

Frazier & Company
601 Union St., Ste. 3300
Seattle, WA 98101

(206)621-7200
Fax: (206)621-1848
E-mail: jon@frazierco.com

Kirlan Venture Capital, Inc.
221 First Ave. W, Ste. 108
Seattle, WA 98119-4223
(206)281-8610
Fax: (206)285-3451
Website: http://www.kirlanventure.com

Phoenix Partners
1000 2nd Ave., Ste. 3600
Seattle, WA 98104
(206)624-8968
Fax: (206)624-1907

Voyager Capital
800 5th St., Ste. 4100
Seattle, WA 98103
(206)470-1180
Fax: (206)470-1185
E-mail: info@voyagercap.com
Website: http://www.voyagercap.com

Northwest Venture Associates
221 N. Wall St., Ste. 628
Spokane, WA 99201
(509)747-0728
Fax: (509)747-0758
Website: http://www.nwva.com

Wisconsin

Venture Investors Management, L.L.C.
University Research Park

505 S. Rosa Rd.
Madison, WI 53719
(608)441-2700
Fax: (608)441-2727
E-mail: roger@ventureinvestors.com
Website: http://www.ventureinvesters.com

Capital Investments, Inc.
1009 West Glen Oaks Lane,
Ste. 103
Mequon, WI 53092
(414)241-0303
Fax: (414)241-8451
Website: http://www.capitalinvest
mentsinc.com

Future Value Venture, Inc.
2745 N. Martin Luther King Dr.,
Ste. 204
Milwaukee, WI 53212-2300
(414)264-2252
Fax: (414)264-2253
E-mail: fvvventures@aol.com
William Beckett, President

Lubar and Co., Inc.
700 N. Water St., Ste. 1200
Milwaukee, WI 53202
(414)291-9000
Fax: (414)291-9061

GCI
20875 Crossroads Cir., Ste. 100
Waukesha, WI 53186
(262)798-5080
Fax: (262)798-5087

Glossary of Small Business Terms

Absolute liability
Liability that is incurred due to product defects or negligent actions. Manufacturers or retail establishments are held responsible, even though the defect or action may not have been intentional or negligent.

ACE
See Active Corps of Executives

Accident and health benefits
Benefits offered to employees and their families in order to offset the costs associated with accidental death, accidental injury, or sickness.

Account statement
A record of transactions, including payments, new debt, and deposits, incurred during a defined period of time.

Accounting system
System capturing the costs of all employees and/or machinery included in business expenses.

Accounts payable
See Trade credit

Accounts receivable
Unpaid accounts which arise from unsettled claims and transactions from the sale of a company's products or services to its customers.

Active Corps of Executives (ACE)
A group of volunteers for a management assistance program of the U.S. Small Business Administration; volunteers provide one-on-one counseling and teach workshops and seminars for small firms.

ADA
See Americans with Disabilities Act

Adaptation
The process whereby an invention is modified to meet the needs of users.

Adaptive engineering
The process whereby an invention is modified to meet the manufacturing and commercial requirements of a targeted market.

Adverse selection
The tendency for higher-risk individuals to purchase health care and more comprehensive plans, resulting in increased costs.

Advertising
A marketing tool used to capture public attention and influence purchasing decisions for a product or service. Utilizes various forms of media to generate consumer response, such as flyers, magazines, newspapers, radio, and television.

Age discrimination
The denial of the rights and privileges of employment based solely on the age of an individual.

Agency costs
Costs incurred to insure that the lender or investor maintains control over assets while allowing the borrower or entrepreneur to use them. Monitoring and information costs are the two major types of agency costs.

Agribusiness
The production and sale of commodities and products from the commercial farming industry.

Americans with Disabilities Act (ADA)
Law designed to ensure equal access and opportunity to handicapped persons.

Annual report
Yearly financial report prepared by a business that adheres to the requirements set forth by the Securities and Exchange Commission (SEC).

Antitrust immunity
Exemption from prosecution under antitrust laws. In the transportation industry, firms with antitrust immunity are permitted under certain conditions to set schedules and sometimes prices for the public benefit.

Applied research
Scientific study targeted for use in a product or process.

Assets
Anything of value owned by a company.

Audit
The verification of accounting records and business procedures conducted by an outside accounting service.

Average cost
Total production costs divided by the quantity produced.

Balance Sheet
A financial statement listing the total assets and liabilities of a company at a given time.

Bankruptcy
The condition in which a business cannot meet its debt obligations and petitions a federal district court either for reorganization of its debts (Chapter 11) or for liquidation of its assets (Chapter 7).

Basket clause
A provision specifying the amount of public pension funds that may be placed in investments not included on a state's legal list (see separate citation).

BDC
See Business development corporation

Benefit
Various services, such as health care, flextime, day care, insurance, and vacation, offered to employees as part of a hiring package. Typically subsidized in whole or in part by the business.

BIDCO
See Business and industrial development company

Billing cycle
A system designed to evenly distribute customer billing throughout the month, preventing clerical backlogs.

Blue chip security
A low-risk, low-yield security representing an interest in a very stable company.

Blue sky laws
A general term that denotes various states' laws regulating securities.

Bond
A written instrument executed by a bidder or contractor (the principal) and a second party (the surety or sureties) to assure fulfillment of the principal's obligations to a third party (the obligee or government) identified in the bond. If the principal's obligations are not met, the bond assures payment to the extent stipulated of any loss sustained by the obligee.

Bonding requirements
Terms contained in a bond (see separate citation).

Bonus
An amount of money paid to an employee as a reward for achieving certain business goals or objectives.

Brainstorming
A group session where employees contribute their ideas for solving a problem or meeting a company objective without fear of retribution or ridicule.

Brand name
The part of a brand, trademark, or service mark that can be spoken. It can be a word, letter, or group of words or letters.

Bridge financing
A short-term loan made in expectation of intermediateterm or long-term financing. Can be used when a company plans to go public in the near future.

Broker
One who matches resources available for innovation with those who need them.

Budget
An estimate of the spending necessary to complete a project or offer a service in comparison to cash-on-hand and expected earnings for the coming year, with an emphasis on cost control.

Business and industrial development company (BIDCO)
A private, for-profit financing corporation chartered by the state to provide both equity and long-term debt

capital to small business owners (see separate citations for equity and debt capital).

Business birth
The formation of a new establishment or enterprise. The appearance of a new establishment or enterprise in the Small Business Data Base (see separate citation).

Business conditions
Outside factors that can affect the financial performance of a business.

Business contractions
The number of establishments that have decreased in employment during a specified time.

Business cycle
A period of economic recession and recovery. These cycles vary in duration.

Business death
The voluntary or involuntary closure of a firm or establishment. The disappearance of an establishment or enterprise from the Small Business Data Base (see separate citation).

Business development corporation (BDC)
A business financing agency, usually composed of the financial institutions in an area or state, organized to assist in financing businesses unable to obtain assistance through normal channels; the risk is spread among various members of the business development corporation, and interest rates may vary somewhat from those charged by member institutions. A venture capital firm in which shares of ownership are publicly held and to which the Investment Act of 1940 applies.

Business dissolution
For enumeration purposes, the absence of a business that was present in the prior time period from any current record.

Business entry
See Business birth

Business ethics
Moral values and principles espoused by members of the business community as a guide to fair and honest business practices.

Business exit
See Business death

Business expansions
The number of establishments that added employees during a specified time.

Business failure
Closure of a business causing a loss to at least one creditor.

Business format franchising
The purchase of the name, trademark, and an ongoing business plan of the parent corporation or franchisor by the franchisee.

Business license
A legal authorization issued by municipal and state governments and required for business operations.

Business name
Enterprises must register their business names with local governments usually on a "doing business as" (DBA) form. (This name is sometimes referred to as a "fictional name.") The procedure is part of the business licensing process and prevents any other business from using that same name for a similar business in the same locality.

Business norms
See Financial ratios

Business permit
See Business license

Business plan
A document that spells out a company's expected course of action for a specified period, usually including a detailed listing and analysis of risks and uncertainties. For the small business, it should examine the proposed products, the market, the industry, the management policies, the marketing policies, production needs, and financial needs. Frequently, it is used as a prospectus for potential investors and lenders.

Business proposal
See Business plan

Business service firm
An establishment primarily engaged in rendering services to other business organizations on a fee or contract basis.

Business start
For enumeration purposes, a business with a name or similar designation that did not exist in a prior time period.

Cafeteria plan
See Flexible benefit plan

Capacity
Level of a firm's, industry's, or nation's output corresponding to full practical utilization of available resources.

Capital
Assets less liabilities, representing the ownership interest in a business. A stock of accumulated goods, especially at a specified time and in contrast to income received during a specified time period. Accumulated goods devoted to production. Accumulated possessions calculated to bring income.

Capital expenditure
Expenses incurred by a business for improvements that will depreciate over time.

Capital gain
The monetary difference between the purchase price and the selling price of capital. Capital gains are taxed at a rate of 28% by the federal government.

Capital intensity
The relative importance of capital in the production process, usually expressed as the ratio of capital to labor but also sometimes as the ratio of capital to output.

Capital resource
The equipment, facilities and labor used to create products and services.

Catastrophic care
Medical and other services for acute and long-term illnesses that cost more than insurance coverage limits or that cost the amount most families may be expected to pay with their own resources.

CDC
See Certified development corporation

Certified development corporation (CDC)
A local area or statewide corporation or authority (for profit or nonprofit) that packages U.S. Small Business

Administration (SBA), bank, state, and/or private money into financial assistance for existing business capital improvements. The SBA holds the second lien on its maximum share of 40 percent involvement. Each state has at least one certified development corporation. This program is called the SBA 504 Program.

Certified lenders
Banks that participate in the SBA guaranteed loan program (see separate citation). Such banks must have a good track record with the U.S. Small Business Administration (SBA) and must agree to certain conditions set forth by the agency. In return, the SBA agrees to process any guaranteed loan application within three business days.

Channel of distribution
The means used to transport merchandise from the manufacturer to the consumer.

Chapter 7 of the 1978 Bankruptcy Act
Provides for a court-appointed trustee who is responsible for liquidating a company's assets in order to settle outstanding debts.

Chapter 11 of the 1978 Bankruptcy Act
Allows the business owners to retain control of the company while working with their creditors to reorganize their finances and establish better business practices to prevent liquidation of assets.

Closely held corporation
A corporation in which the shares are held by a few persons, usually officers, employees, or others close to the management; these shares are rarely offered to the public.

Code of Federal Regulations
Codification of general and permanent rules of the federal government published in the Federal Register.

Code sharing
See Computer code sharing

Coinsurance
Upon meeting the deductible payment, health insurance participants may be required to make additional health care cost-sharing payments. Coinsurance is a payment of a fixed percentage of the

cost of each service; copayment is usually a fixed amount to be paid with each service.

Collateral
Securities, evidence of deposit, or other property pledged by a borrower to secure repayment of a loan.

Collective ratemaking
The establishment of uniform charges for services by a group of businesses in the same industry.

Commercial insurance plan
See Underwriting

Commercial loans
Short-term renewable loans used to finance specific capital needs of a business.

Commercialization
The final stage of the innovation process, including production and distribution.

Common stock
The most frequently used instrument for purchasing ownership in private or public companies. Common stock generally carries the right to vote on certain corporate actions and may pay dividends, although it rarely does in venture investments. In liquidation, common stockholders are the last to share in the proceeds from the sale of a corporation's assets; bondholders and preferred shareholders have priority. Common stock is often used in firstround start-up financing.

Community development corporation
A corporation established to develop economic programs for a community and, in most cases, to provide financial support for such development.

Competitor
A business whose product or service is marketed for the same purpose/use and to the same consumer group as the product or service of another.

Consignment
A merchandising agreement, usually referring to secondhand shops, where the dealer pays the owner of an item a percentage of the profit when the item is sold.

Consortium
A coalition of organizations such as banks and corporations for ventures requiring large capital resources.

Consultant
An individual that is paid by a business to provide advice and expertise in a particular area.

Consumer price index
A measure of the fluctuation in prices between two points in time.

Consumer research
Research conducted by a business to obtain information about existing or potential consumer markets.

Continuation coverage
Health coverage offered for a specified period of time to employees who leave their jobs and to their widows, divorced spouses, or dependents.

Contractions
See Business contractions

Convertible preferred stock
A class of stock that pays a reasonable dividend and is convertible into common stock (see separate citation). Generally the convertible feature may only be exercised after being held for a stated period of time. This arrangement is usually considered second-round financing when a company needs equity to maintain its cash flow.

Convertible securities
A feature of certain bonds, debentures, or preferred stocks that allows them to be exchanged by the owner for another class of securities at a future date and in accordance with any other terms of the issue.

Copayment
See Coinsurance

Copyright
A legal form of protection available to creators and authors to safeguard their works from unlawful use or claim of ownership by others. Copyrights may be acquired for works of art, sculpture, music, and published or unpublished manuscripts. All copyrights should be registered at the Copyright Office of the Library of Congress.

Corporate financial ratios
The relationship between key figures found in a company's financial statement expressed as a numeric

value. Used to evaluate risk and company performance. Also known as Financial averages, Operating ratios, and Business ratios.

Corporation
A legal entity, chartered by a state or the federal government, recognized as a separate entity having its own rights, privileges, and liabilities distinct from those of its members.

Cost containment
Actions taken by employers and insurers to curtail rising health care costs; for example, increasing employee cost sharing (see separate citation), requiring second opinions, or preadmission screening.

Cost sharing
The requirement that health care consumers contribute to their own medical care costs through deductibles and coinsurance (see separate citations). Cost sharing does not include the amounts paid in premiums. It is used to control utilization of services; for example, requiring a fixed amount to be paid with each health care service.

Cottage industry
Businesses based in the home in which the family members are the labor force and family-owned equipment is used to process the goods.

Credit Rating
A letter or number calculated by an organization (such as Dun & Bradstreet) to represent the ability and disposition of a business to meet its financial obligations.

Customer service
Various techniques used to ensure the satisfaction of a customer.

Cyclical peak
The upper turning point in a business cycle.

Cyclical trough
The lower turning point in a business cycle.

DBA (Doing business as)
See Business name

Death
See Business death

Debenture
A certificate given as acknowledgment of a debt (see separate citation) secured by the general credit of the issuing corporation. A bond, usually without security, issued by a corporation and sometimes convertible to common stock.

Debt
Something owed by one person to another. Financing in which a company receives capital that must be repaid; no ownership is transferred.

Debt capital
Business financing that normally requires periodic interest payments and repayment of the principal within a specified time.

Debt financing
See Debt capital

Debt securities
Loans such as bonds and notes that provide a specified rate of return for a specified period of time.

Deductible
A set amount that an individual must pay before any benefits are received.

Demand shock absorbers
A term used to describe the role that some small firms play by expanding their output levels to accommodate a transient surge in demand.

Demographics
Statistics on various markets, including age, income, and education, used to target specific products or services to appropriate consumer groups.

Demonstration
Showing that a product or process has been modified sufficiently to meet the needs of users.

Deregulation
The lifting of government restrictions; for example, the lifting of government restrictions on the entry of new businesses, the expansion of services, and the setting of prices in particular industries.

Disaster loans
Various types of physical and economic assistance available to individuals and businesses through the

U.S. Small Business Administration (SBA). This is the only SBA loan program available for residential purposes.

Discrimination
The denial of the rights and privileges of employment based on factors such as age, race, religion, or gender.

Diseconomies of scale
The condition in which the costs of production increase faster than the volume of production.

Dissolution
See Business dissolution

Distribution
Delivering a product or process to the user.

Distributor
One who delivers merchandise to the user.

Diversified company
A company whose products and services are used by several different markets.

Doing business as (DBA)
See Business name

Dow Jones
An information services company that publishes the Wall Street Journal and other sources of financial information.

Dow Jones Industrial Average
An indicator of stock market performance.

Earned income
A tax term that refers to wages and salaries earned by the recipient, as opposed to monies earned through interest and dividends.

Economic efficiency
The use of productive resources to the fullest practical extent in the provision of the set of goods and services that is most preferred by purchasers in the economy.

Economic indicators
Statistics used to express the state of the economy. These include the length of the average work week, the rate of unemployment, and stock prices.

Economically disadvantaged
See Socially and economically disadvantaged

Economies of scale
See Scale economies

EEOC
See Equal Employment Opportunity Commission

8(a) Program
A program authorized by the Small Business Act that directs federal contracts to small businesses owned and operated by socially and economically disadvantaged individuals.

Electronic mail (e-mail)
The electronic transmission of mail via phone lines.

E-mail
See Electronic mail

Employee leasing
A contract by which employers arrange to have their workers hired by a leasing company and then leased back to them for a management fee. The leasing company typically assumes the administrative burden of payroll and provides a benefit package to the workers.

Employee tenure
The length of time an employee works for a particular employer.

Employer identification number
The business equivalent of a social security number. Assigned by the U.S. Internal Revenue Service.

Enterprise
An aggregation of all establishments owned by a parent company. An enterprise may consist of a single, independent establishment or include subsidiaries and other branches under the same ownership and control.

Enterprise zone
A designated area, usually found in inner cities and other areas with significant unemployment, where businesses receive tax credits and other incentives to entice them to establish operations there.

Entrepreneur
A person who takes the risk of organizing and operating a new business venture.

Entry
See Business entry

Glossary

Equal Employment Opportunity Commission (EEOC)
A federal agency that ensures nondiscrimination in the hiring and firing practices of a business.

Equal opportunity employer
An employer who adheres to the standards set by the Equal Employment Opportunity Commission (see separate citation).

Equity
The ownership interest. Financing in which partial or total ownership of a company is surrendered in exchange for capital. An investor's financial return comes from dividend payments and from growth in the net worth of the business.

Equity capital
See Equity; Equity midrisk venture capital

Equity financing
See Equity; Equity midrisk venture capital

Equity midrisk venture capital
An unsecured investment in a company. Usually a purchase of ownership interest in a company that occurs in the later stages of a company's development.

Equity partnership
A limited partnership arrangement for providing start-up and seed capital to businesses.

Equity securities
See Equity

Equity-type
Debt financing subordinated to conventional debt.

Establishment
A single-location business unit that may be independent (a single-establishment enterprise) or owned by a parent enterprise.

Establishment and Enterprise Microdata File
See U.S. Establishment and Enterprise Microdata File

Establishment birth
See Business birth

Establishment Longitudinal Microdata File
See U.S. Establishment Longitudinal Microdata File

Ethics
See Business ethics

Evaluation
Determining the potential success of translating an invention into a product or process.

Exit
See Business exit

Experience rating
See Underwriting

Export
A product sold outside of the country.

Export license
A general or specific license granted by the U.S. Department of Commerce required of anyone wishing to export goods. Some restricted articles need approval from the U.S. Departments of State, Defense, or Energy.

Failure
See Business failure

Fair share agreement
An agreement reached between a franchisor and a minority business organization to extend business ownership to minorities by either reducing the amount of capital required or by setting aside certain marketing areas for minority business owners.

Feasibility study
A study to determine the likelihood that a proposed product or development will fulfill the objectives of a particular investor.

Federal Trade Commission (FTC)
Federal agency that promotes free enterprise and competition within the U.S.

Federal Trade Mark Act of 1946
See Lanham Act

Fictional name
See Business name

Fiduciary
An individual or group that hold assets in trust for a beneficiary.

Financial analysis
The techniques used to determine money needs in a business. Techniques include ratio analysis, calculation of return on investment, guides for measuring

profitability, and break-even analysis to determine ultimate success.

Financial intermediary

A financial institution that acts as the intermediary between borrowers and lenders. Banks, savings and loan associations, finance companies, and venture capital companies are major financial intermediaries in the United States.

Financial ratios

See Corporate financial ratios; Industry financial ratios

Financial statement

A written record of business finances, including balance sheets and profit and loss statements.

Financing

See First-stage financing; Second-stage financing; Thirdstage financing

First-stage financing

Financing provided to companies that have expended their initial capital, and require funds to start full-scale manufacturing and sales. Also known as First-round financing.

Fiscal year

Any twelve-month period used by businesses for accounting purposes.

504 Program

See Certified development corporation

Flexible benefit plan

A plan that offers a choice among cash and/or qualified benefits such as group term life insurance, accident and health insurance, group legal services, dependent care assistance, and vacations.

FOB

See Free on board

Format franchising

See Business format franchising; Franchising

401(k) plan

A financial plan where employees contribute a percentage of their earnings to a fund that is invested in stocks, bonds, or money markets for the purpose of saving money for retirement.

Four Ps

Marketing terms referring to Product, Price, Place, and Promotion.

Franchising

A form of licensing by which the owner-the franchisor- distributes or markets a product, method, or service through affiliated dealers called franchisees. The product, method, or service being marketed is identified by a brand name, and the franchisor maintains control over the marketing methods employed. The franchisee is often given exclusive access to a defined geographic area.

Free on board (FOB)

A pricing term indicating that the quoted price includes the cost of loading goods into transport vessels at a specified place.

Frictional unemployment

See Unemployment

FTC

See Federal Trade Commission

Fulfillment

The systems necessary for accurate delivery of an ordered item, including subscriptions and direct marketing.

Full-time workers

Generally, those who work a regular schedule of more than 35 hours per week.

Garment registration number

A number that must appear on every garment sold in the U.S. to indicate the manufacturer of the garment, which may or may not be the same as the label under which the garment is sold. The U.S. Federal Trade Commission assigns and regulates garment registration numbers.

Gatekeeper

A key contact point for entry into a network.

GDP

See Gross domestic product

General obligation bond

A municipal bond secured by the taxing power of the municipality. The Tax Reform Act of 1986 limits the purposes for which such bonds may be issued and establishes volume limits on the extent of their issuance.

GNP
See Gross national product

Good Housekeeping Seal
Seal appearing on products that signifies the fulfillment of the standards set by the Good Housekeeping Institute to protect consumer interests.

Goods sector
All businesses producing tangible goods, including agriculture, mining, construction, and manufacturing businesses.

GPO
See Gross product originating

Gross domestic product (GDP)
The part of the nation's gross national product (see separate citation) generated by private business using resources from within the country.

Gross national product (GNP)
The most comprehensive single measure of aggregate economic output. Represents the market value of the total output of goods and services produced by a nation's economy.

Gross product originating (GPO)
A measure of business output estimated from the income or production side using employee compensation, profit income, net interest, capital consumption, and indirect business taxes.

HAL
See Handicapped assistance loan program

Handicapped assistance loan program (HAL)
Low-interest direct loan program through the U.S. Small Business Administration (SBA) for handicapped persons. The SBA requires that these persons demonstrate that their disability is such that it is impossible for them to secure employment, thus making it necessary to go into their own business to make a living.

Health maintenance organization (HMO)
Organization of physicians and other health care professionals that provides health services to subscribers and their dependents on a prepaid basis.

Health provider
An individual or institution that gives medical care. Under Medicare, an institutional provider is a hospital, skilled nursing facility, home health agency, or provider of certain physical therapy services.

Hispanic
A person of Cuban, Mexican, Puerto Rican, Latin American (Central or South American), European Spanish, or other Spanish-speaking origin or ancestry.

HMO
See Health maintenance organization

Home-based business
A business with an operating address that is also a residential address (usually the residential address of the proprietor).

Hub-and-spoke system
A system in which flights of an airline from many different cities (the spokes) converge at a single airport (the hub). After allowing passengers sufficient time to make connections, planes then depart for different cities.

Human Resources Management
A business program designed to oversee recruiting, pay, benefits, and other issues related to the company's work force, including planning to determine the optimal use of labor to increase production, thereby increasing profit.

Idea
An original concept for a new product or process.

Import
Products produced outside the country in which they are consumed.

Income
Money or its equivalent, earned or accrued, resulting from the sale of goods and services.

Income statement
A financial statement that lists the profits and losses of a company at a given time.

Incorporation
The filing of a certificate of incorporation with a state's secretary of state, thereby limiting the business owner's liability.

Incubator

A facility designed to encourage entrepreneurship and minimize obstacles to new business formation and growth, particularly for high-technology firms, by housing a number of fledgling enterprises that share an array of services, such as meeting areas, secretarial services, accounting, research library, on-site financial and management counseling, and word processing facilities.

Independent contractor

An individual considered self-employed (see separate citation) and responsible for paying Social Security taxes and income taxes on earnings.

Indirect health coverage

Health insurance obtained through another individual's health care plan; for example, a spouse's employersponsored plan.

Industrial development authority

The financial arm of a state or other political subdivision established for the purpose of financing economic development in an area, usually through loans to nonprofit organizations, which in turn provide facilities for manufacturing and other industrial operations.

Industry financial ratios

Corporate financial ratios averaged for a specified industry. These are used for comparison purposes and reveal industry trends and identify differences between the performance of a specific company and the performance of its industry. Also known as Industrial averages, Industry ratios, Financial averages, and Business or Industrial norms.

Inflation

Increases in volume of currency and credit, generally resulting in a sharp and continuing rise in price levels.

Informal capital

Financing from informal, unorganized sources; includes informal debt capital such as trade credit or loans from friends and relatives and equity capital from informal investors.

Initial public offering (IPO)

A corporation's first offering of stock to the public.

Innovation

The introduction of a new idea into the marketplace in the form of a new product or service or an improvement in organization or process.

Intellectual property

Any idea or work that can be considered proprietary in nature and is thus protected from infringement by others.

Internal capital

Debt or equity financing obtained from the owner or through retained business earnings.

Internet

A government-designed computer network that contains large amounts of information and is accessible through various vendors for a fee.

Intrapreneurship

The state of employing entrepreneurial principles to nonentrepreneurial situations.

Invention

The tangible form of a technological idea, which could include a laboratory prototype, drawings, formulas, etc.

IPO

See Initial public offering

Job description

The duties and responsibilities required in a particular position.

Job tenure

A period of time during which an individual is continuously employed in the same job.

Joint marketing agreements

Agreements between regional and major airlines, often involving the coordination of flight schedules, fares, and baggage transfer. These agreements help regional carriers operate at lower cost.

Joint venture

Venture in which two or more people combine efforts in a particular business enterprise, usually a single transaction or a limited activity, and agree to share the profits and losses jointly or in proportion to their contributions.

Keogh plan

Designed for self-employed persons and unincorporated businesses as a tax-deferred pension account.

Labor force
Civilians considered eligible for employment who are also willing and able to work.

Labor force participation rate
The civilian labor force as a percentage of the civilian population.

Labor intensity
The relative importance of labor in the production process, usually measured as the capital-labor ratio; i.e., the ratio of units of capital (typically, dollars of tangible assets) to the number of employees. The higher the capital-labor ratio exhibited by a firm or industry, the lower the capital intensity of that firm or industry is said to be.

Labor surplus area
An area in which there exists a high unemployment rate. In procurement (see separate citation), extra points are given to firms in counties that are designated a labor surplus area; this information is requested on procurement bid sheets.

Labor union
An organization of similarly-skilled workers who collectively bargain with management over the conditions of employment.

Laboratory prototype
See Prototype

LAN
See Local Area Network

Lanham Act
Refers to the Federal Trade Mark Act of 1946. Protects registered trademarks, trade names, and other service marks used in commerce.

Large business-dominated industry
Industry in which a minimum of 60 percent of employment or sales is in firms with more than 500 workers.

LBO
See Leveraged buy-out

Leader pricing
A reduction in the price of a good or service in order to generate more sales of that good or service.

Legal list
A list of securities selected by a state in which certain institutions and fiduciaries (such as pension funds, insurance companies, and banks) may invest. Securities not on the list are not eligible for investment. Legal lists typically restrict investments to high quality securities meeting certain specifications. Generally, investment is limited to U.S. securities and investment-grade blue chip securities (see separate citation).

Leveraged buy-out (LBO)
The purchase of a business or a division of a corporation through a highly leveraged financing package.

Liability
An obligation or duty to perform a service or an act. Also defined as money owed.

License
A legal agreement granting to another the right to use a technological innovation.

Limited Liability Company
A hybrid type of legal structure that provides the limited liability features of a corporation and the tax efficiencies and operational flexibility of a partnership. Depending on the state, the members can consist of a single individual (one owner), two or more individuals, corporations or other LLCs.

Limited liability partnerships
A business organization that allows limited partners to enjoy limited personal liability while general partners have unlimited personal liability

Liquidity
The ability to convert a security into cash promptly.

Loans
See Commercial loans; Disaster loans; SBA direct loans; SBA guaranteed loans; SBA special lending institution categories Local Area Network (LAN) Computer networks contained within a single building or small area; used to facilitate the sharing of information.

Local development corporation
An organization, usually made up of local citizens of a community, designed to improve the economy of the

area by inducing business and industry to locate and expand there. A local development corporation establishes a capability to finance local growth.

Long-haul rates
Rates charged by a transporter in which the distance traveled is more than 800 miles.

Long-term debt
An obligation that matures in a period that exceeds five years.

Low-grade bond
A corporate bond that is rated below investment grade by the major rating agencies (Standard and Poor's, Moody's).

Macro-efficiency
Efficiency as it pertains to the operation of markets and market systems.

Managed care
A cost-effective health care program initiated by employers whereby low-cost health care is made available to the employees in return for exclusive patronage to program doctors.

Management Assistance Programs
See SBA Management Assistance Programs

Management and technical assistance
A term used by many programs to mean business (as opposed to technological) assistance.

Mandated benefits
Specific treatments, providers, or individuals required by law to be included in commercial health plans.

Market evaluation
The use of market information to determine the sales potential of a specific product or process.

Market failure
The situation in which the workings of a competitive market do not produce the best results from the point of view of the entire society.

Market information
Data of any type that can be used for market evaluation, which could include demographic data, technology forecasting, regulatory changes, etc.

Market research
A systematic collection, analysis, and reporting of data about the market and its preferences, opinions, trends, and plans; used for corporate decision-making.

Market share
In a particular market, the percentage of sales of a specific product.

Marketing
Promotion of goods or services through various media.

Master Establishment List (MEL)
A list of firms in the United States developed by the U.S. Small Business Administration; firms can be selected by industry, region, state, standard metropolitan statistical area (see separate citation), county, and zip code.

Maturity
The date upon which the principal or stated value of a bond or other indebtedness becomes due and payable.

Medicaid (Title XIX)
A federally aided, state-operated and administered program that provides medical benefits for certain low income persons in need of health and medical care who are eligible for one of the government's welfare cash payment programs, including the aged, the blind, the disabled, and members of families with dependent children where one parent is absent, incapacitated, or unemployed.

Medicare (Title XVIII)
A nationwide health insurance program for disabled and aged persons. Health insurance is available to insured persons without regard to income. Monies from payroll taxes cover hospital insurance and monies from general revenues and beneficiary premiums pay for supplementary medical insurance.

MEL
See Master Establishment List

Merchant Status
The relationship between a company and a bank or credit card company allowing the company to accept credit card payments

MESBIC
See Minority enterprise small business investment corporation

MET
See Multiple employer trust

Metropolitan statistical area (MSA)
A means used by the government to define large population centers that may transverse different governmental jurisdictions. For example, the Washington, D.C. MSA includes the District of Columbia and contiguous parts of Maryland and Virginia because all of these geopolitical areas comprise one population and economic operating unit.

Mezzanine financing
See Third-stage financing

Micro-efficiency
Efficiency as it pertains to the operation of individual firms.

Microdata
Information on the characteristics of an individual business firm.

Microloan
An SBA loan program that helps entrepreneurs obtain loans from less than $100 to $25,000.

Mid-term debt
An obligation that matures within one to five years.

Midrisk venture capital
See Equity midrisk venture capital

Minimum premium plan
A combination approach to funding an insurance plan aimed primarily at premium tax savings. The employer self-funds a fixed percentage of estimated monthly claims and the insurance company insures the excess.

Minimum wage
The lowest hourly wage allowed by the federal government.

Minority Business Development Agency
Contracts with private firms throughout the nation to sponsor Minority Business Development Centers which provide minority firms with advice and technical assistance on a fee basis.

Minority Enterprise Small Business Investment Corporation (MESBIC)
A federally funded private venture capital firm licensed by the U.S. Small Business Administration to provide capital to minority-owned businesses (see separate citation).

Minority-owned business
Businesses owned by those who are socially or economically disadvantaged (see separate citation).

Mission statement
A short statement describing a company's function, markets and competitive advantages.

Mom and Pop business
A small store or enterprise having limited capital, principally employing family members.

Multi-employer plan
A health plan to which more than one employer is required to contribute and that may be maintained through a collective bargaining agreement and required to meet standards prescribed by the U.S. Department of Labor.

Multi-level marketing
A system of selling in which you sign up other people to assist you and they, in turn, recruit others to help them. Some entrepreneurs have built successful companies on this concept because the main focus of their activities is their product and product sales.

Multiple employer trust (MET)
A self-funded benefit plan generally geared toward small employers sharing a common interest.

NASDAQ
See National Association of Securities Dealers Automated Quotations

National Association of Securities Dealers Automated Quotations
Provides price quotes on over-the-counter securities as well as securities listed on the New York Stock Exchange.

National income
Aggregate earnings of labor and property arising from the production of goods and services in a nation's economy.

Net assets
See Net worth

Net income
The amount remaining from earnings and profits after all expenses and costs have been met or deducted. Also known as Net earnings.

Net profit
Money earned after production and overhead expenses (see separate citations) have been deducted.

Net worth
The difference between a company's total assets and its total liabilities.

Network
A chain of interconnected individuals or organizations sharing information and/or services.

New York Stock Exchange (NYSE)
The oldest stock exchange in the U.S. Allows for trading in stocks, bonds, warrants, options, and rights that meet listing requirements.

Niche
A career or business for which a person is well-suited. Also, a product which fulfills one need of a particular market segment, often with little or no competition.

Nodes
One workstation in a network, either local area or wide area (see separate citations).

Nonbank bank
A bank that either accepts deposits or makes loans, but not both. Used to create many new branch banks.

Noncompetitive awards
A method of contracting whereby the federal government negotiates with only one contractor to supply a product or service.

Nonmember bank
A state-regulated bank that does not belong to the federal bank system.

Nonprofit
An organization that has no shareholders, does not distribute profits, and is without federal and state tax liabilities.

Norms
See Financial ratios

North American Free Trade Agreement (NAFTA)
Passed in 1993, NAFTA eliminates trade barriers among businesses in the U.S., Canada, and Mexico.

NYSE
See New York Stock Exchange

Occupational Safety & Health Administration (OSHA)
Federal agency that regulates health and safety standards within the workplace.

Operating Expenses
Business expenditures not directly associated with the production of goods or services.

Optimal firm size
The business size at which the production cost per unit of output (average cost) is, in the long run, at its minimum.

Organizational chart
A hierarchical chart tracking the chain of command within an organization.

OSHA
See Occupational Safety & Health Administration

Overhead
Expenses, such as employee benefits and building utilities, incurred by a business that are unrelated to the actual product or service sold.

Owner's capital
Debt or equity funds provided by the owner(s) of a business; sources of owner's capital are personal savings, sales of assets, or loans from financial institutions.

P & L
See Profit and loss statement

Part-time workers
Normally, those who work less than 35 hours per week. The Tax Reform Act indicated that part-time workers who work less than 17.5 hours per week may be excluded from health plans for purposes of complying with federal nondiscrimination rules.

Part-year workers
Those who work less than 50 weeks per year.

Partnership
Two or more parties who enter into a legal relationship to conduct business for profit. Defined by the U.S. Internal Revenue Code as joint ventures, syndicates, groups, pools, and other associations of two or more persons organized for profit that are not specifically classified in the IRS code as corporations or proprietorships.

Patent
A grant made by the government assuring an inventor the sole right to make, use, and sell an invention for a period of 17 years.

PC
See Professional corporation

Peak
See Cyclical peak

Pension
A series of payments made monthly, semiannually, annually, or at other specified intervals during the lifetime of the pensioner for distribution upon retirement. The term is sometimes used to denote the portion of the retirement allowance financed by the employer's contributions.

Pension fund
A fund established to provide for the payment of pension benefits; the collective contributions made by all of the parties to the pension plan.

Performance appraisal
An established set of objective criteria, based on job description and requirements, that is used to evaluate the performance of an employee in a specific job.

Permit
See Business license

Plan
See Business plan

Pooling
An arrangement for employers to achieve efficiencies and lower health costs by joining together to purchase group health insurance or self-insurance.

PPO
See Preferred provider organization

Preferred lenders program
See SBA special lending institution categories

Preferred provider organization (PPO)
A contractual arrangement with a health care services organization that agrees to discount its health care rates in return for faster payment and/or a patient base.

Premiums
The amount of money paid to an insurer for health insurance under a policy. The premium is generally paid periodically (e.g., monthly), and often is split between the employer and the employee. Unlike deductibles and coinsurance or copayments, premiums are paid for coverage whether or not benefits are actually used.

Prime-age workers
Employees 25 to 54 years of age.

Prime contract
A contract awarded directly by the U.S. Federal Government.

Private company
See Closely held corporation

Private placement
A method of raising capital by offering for sale an investment or business to a small group of investors (generally avoiding registration with the Securities and Exchange Commission or state securities registration agencies). Also known as Private financing or Private offering.

Pro forma
The use of hypothetical figures in financial statements to represent future expenditures, debts, and other potential financial expenses.

Proactive
Taking the initiative to solve problems and anticipate future events before they happen, instead of reacting to an already existing problem or waiting for a difficult situation to occur.

Procurement
A contract from an agency of the federal government for goods or services from a small business.

Product development
The stage of the innovation process where research is translated into a product or process through evaluation, adaptation, and demonstration.

Product franchising
An arrangement for a franchisee to use the name and to produce the product line of the franchisor or parent corporation.

Production
The manufacture of a product.

Production prototype
See Prototype

Productivity
A measurement of the number of goods produced during a specific amount of time.

Professional corporation (PC)
Organized by members of a profession such as medicine, dentistry, or law for the purpose of conducting their professional activities as a corporation. Liability of a member or shareholder is limited in the same manner as in a business corporation.

Profit and loss statement (P & L)
The summary of the incomes (total revenues) and costs of a company's operation during a specific period of time. Also known as Income and expense statement.

Proposal
See Business plan

Proprietorship
The most common legal form of business ownership; about 85 percent of all small businesses are proprietorships. The liability of the owner is unlimited in this form of ownership.

Prospective payment system
A cost-containment measure included in the Social Security Amendments of 1983 whereby Medicare payments to hospitals are based on established prices, rather than on cost reimbursement.

Prototype
A model that demonstrates the validity of the concept of an invention (laboratory prototype); a model that

meets the needs of the manufacturing process and the user (production prototype).

Prudent investor rule or standard
A legal doctrine that requires fiduciaries to make investments using the prudence, diligence, and intelligence that would be used by a prudent person in making similar investments. Because fiduciaries make investments on behalf of third-party beneficiaries, the standard results in very conservative investments. Until recently, most state regulations required the fiduciary to apply this standard to each investment. Newer, more progressive regulations permit fiduciaries to apply this standard to the portfolio taken as a whole, thereby allowing a fiduciary to balance a portfolio with higher-yield, higher-risk investments. In states with more progressive regulations, practically every type of security is eligible for inclusion in the portfolio of investments made by a fiduciary, provided that the portfolio investments, in their totality, are those of a prudent person.

Public equity markets
Organized markets for trading in equity shares such as common stocks, preferred stocks, and warrants. Includes markets for both regularly traded and nonregularly traded securities.

Public offering
General solicitation for participation in an investment opportunity. Interstate public offerings are supervised by the U.S. Securities and Exchange Commission (see separate citation).

Quality control
The process by which a product is checked and tested to ensure consistent standards of high quality.

Rate of return
The yield obtained on a security or other investment based on its purchase price or its current market price. The total rate of return is current income plus or minus capital appreciation or depreciation.

Real property
Includes the land and all that is contained on it.

Realignment
See Resource realignment

Recession
Contraction of economic activity occurring between the peak and trough (see separate citations) of a business cycle.

Regulated market
A market in which the government controls the forces of supply and demand, such as who may enter and what price may be charged.

Regulation D
A vehicle by which small businesses make small offerings and private placements of securities with limited disclosure requirements. It was designed to ease the burdens imposed on small businesses utilizing this method of capital formation.

Regulatory Flexibility Act
An act requiring federal agencies to evaluate the impact of their regulations on small businesses before the regulations are issued and to consider less burdensome alternatives.

Research
The initial stage of the innovation process, which includes idea generation and invention.

Research and development financing
A tax-advantaged partnership set up to finance product development for start-ups as well as more mature companies.

Resource mobility
The ease with which labor and capital move from firm to firm or from industry to industry.

Resource realignment
The adjustment of productive resources to interindustry changes in demand.

Resources
The sources of support or help in the innovation process, including sources of financing, technical evaluation, market evaluation, management and business assistance, etc.

Retained business earnings
Business profits that are retained by the business rather than being distributed to the shareholders as dividends.

Return on investment
A profitability measure that evaluates the performance of a business by dividing net profit by net worth.

Revolving credit
An agreement with a lending institution for an amount of money, which cannot exceed a set maximum, over a specified period of time. Each time the borrower repays a portion of the loan, the amount of the repayment may be borrowed yet again.

Risk capital
See Venture capital

Risk management
The act of identifying potential sources of financial loss and taking action to minimize their negative impact.

Routing
The sequence of steps necessary to complete a product during production.

S corporations
See Sub chapter S corporations

SBA
See Small Business Administration

SBA direct loans
Loans made directly by the U.S. Small Business Administration (SBA); monies come from funds appropriated specifically for this purpose. In general, SBA direct loans carry interest rates slightly lower than those in the private financial markets and are available only to applicants unable to secure private financing or an SBA guaranteed loan.

SBA 504 Program
See Certified development corporation

SBA guaranteed loans
Loans made by lending institutions in which the U.S. Small Business Administration (SBA) will pay a prior agreed-upon percentage of the outstanding principal in the event the borrower of the loan defaults. The terms of the loan and the interest rate are negotiated between theborrower and the lending institution, within set parameters.

SBA loans
See Disaster loans; SBA direct loans; SBA guaranteed loans; SBA special lending institution categories

SBA Management Assistance Programs
Classes, workshops, counseling, and publications offered by the U.S. Small Business Administration.

SBA special lending institution categories
U.S. Small Business Administration (SBA) loan program in which the SBA promises certified banks a 72-hour turnaround period in giving its approval for a loan, and in which preferred lenders in a pilot program are allowed to write SBA loans without seeking prior SBA approval.

SBDB
See Small Business Data Base

SBDC
See Small business development centers

SBI
See Small business institutes program

SBIC
See Small business investment corporation

SBIR Program
See Small Business Innovation Development Act of 1982

Scale economies
The decline of the production cost per unit of output (average cost) as the volume of output increases.

Scale efficiency
The reduction in unit cost available to a firm when producing at a higher output volume.

SCORE
See Service Corps of Retired Executives

SEC
See Securities and Exchange Commission

SECA
See Self-Employment Contributions Act

Second-stage financing
Working capital for the initial expansion of a company that is producing, shipping, and has growing accounts receivable and inventories. Also known as Second-round financing.

Secondary market
A market established for the purchase and sale of outstanding securities following their initial distribution.

Secondary worker
Any worker in a family other than the person who is the primary source of income for the family.

Secondhand capital
Previously used and subsequently resold capital equipment (e.g., buildings and machinery).

Securities and Exchange Commission (SEC)
Federal agency charged with regulating the trade of securities to prevent unethical practices in the investor market.

Securitized debt
A marketing technique that converts long-term loans to marketable securities.

Seed capital
Venture financing provided in the early stages of the innovation process, usually during product development.

Self-employed person
One who works for a profit or fees in his or her own business, profession, or trade, or who operates a farm.

Self-Employment Contributions Act (SECA)
Federal law that governs the self-employment tax (see separate citation).

Self-employment income
Income covered by Social Security if a business earns a net income of at least $400.00 during the year. Taxes are paid on earnings that exceed $400.00.

Self-employment retirement plan
See Keogh plan

Self-employment tax
Required tax imposed on self-employed individuals for the provision of Social Security and Medicare. The tax must be paid quarterly with estimated income tax statements.

Self-funding
A health benefit plan in which a firm uses its own funds to pay claims, rather than transferring the

financial risks of paying claims to an outside insurer in exchange for premium payments.

Service Corps of Retired Executives (SCORE)
Volunteers for the SBA Management Assistance Program who provide one-on-one counseling and teach workshops and seminars for small firms.

Service firm
See Business service firm

Service sector
Broadly defined, all U.S. industries that produce intangibles, including the five major industry divisions of transportation, communications, and utilities; wholesale trade; retail trade; finance, insurance, and real estate; and services.

Set asides
See Small business set asides

Short-haul service
A type of transportation service in which the transporter supplies service between cities where the maximum distance is no more than 200 miles.

Short-term debt
An obligation that matures in one year.

SIC codes
See Standard Industrial Classification codes

Single-establishment enterprise
See Establishment

Small business
An enterprise that is independently owned and operated, is not dominant in its field, and employs fewer than 500 people. For SBA purposes, the U.S. Small Business Administration (SBA) considers various other factors (such as gross annual sales) in determining size of a business.

Small Business Administration (SBA)
An independent federal agency that provides assistance with loans, management, and advocating interests before other federal agencies.

Small Business Data Base
A collection of microdata (see separate citation) files on individual firms developed and maintained by the U.S. Small Business Administration.

Small business development centers (SBDC)
Centers that provide support services to small businesses, such as individual counseling, SBA advice, seminars and conferences, and other learning center activities. Most services are free of charge, or available at minimal cost.

Small business development corporation
See Certified development corporation

Small business-dominated industry
Industry in which a minimum of 60 percent of employment or sales is in firms with fewer than 500 employees.

Small Business Innovation Development Act of 1982
Federal statute requiring federal agencies with large extramural research and development budgets to allocate a certain percentage of these funds to small research and development firms. The program, called the Small Business Innovation Research (SBIR) Program, is designed to stimulate technological innovation and make greater use of small businesses in meeting national innovation needs.

Small business institutes (SBI) program
Cooperative arrangements made by U.S. Small Business Administration district offices and local colleges and universities to provide small business firms with graduate students to counsel them without charge.

Small business investment corporation (SBIC)
A privately owned company licensed and funded through the U.S. Small Business Administration and private sector sources to provide equity or debt capital to small businesses.

Small business set asides
Procurement (see separate citation) opportunities required by law to be on all contracts under $10,000 or a certain percentage of an agency's total procurement expenditure.

Smaller firms
For U.S. Department of Commerce purposes, those firms not included in the Fortune 1000.

SMSA
See Metropolitan statistical area

Socially and economically disadvantaged
Individuals who have been subjected to racial or ethnic prejudice or cultural bias without regard to their qualities as individuals, and whose abilities to compete are impaired because of diminished opportunities to obtain capital and credit.

Sole proprietorship
An unincorporated, one-owner business, farm, or professional practice.

Special lending institution categories
See SBA special lending institution categories

Standard Industrial Classification (SIC) codes
Four-digit codes established by the U.S. Federal Government to categorize businesses by type of economic activity; the first two digits correspond to major groups such as construction and manufacturing, while the last two digits correspond to subgroups such as home construction or highway construction.

Start-up
A new business, at the earliest stages of development and financing.

Start-up costs
Costs incurred before a business can commence operations.

Start-up financing
Financing provided to companies that have either completed product development and initial marketing or have been in business for less than one year but have not yet sold their product commercially.

Stock
A certificate of equity ownership in a business.

Stop-loss coverage
Insurance for a self-insured plan that reimburses the company for any losses it might incur in its health claims beyond a specified amount.

Strategic planning
Projected growth and development of a business to establish a guiding direction for the future. Also used to determine which market segments to explore for optimal sales of products or services.

Structural unemployment
See Unemployment

Sub chapter S corporations
Corporations that are considered noncorporate for tax purposes but legally remain corporations.

Subcontract
A contract between a prime contractor and a subcontractor, or between subcontractors, to furnish supplies or services for performance of a prime contract (see separate citation) or a subcontract.

Surety bonds
Bonds providing reimbursement to an individual, company, or the government if a firm fails to complete a contract. The U.S. Small Business Administration guarantees surety bonds in a program much like the SBA guaranteed loan program (see separate citation).

Swing loan
See Bridge financing

Target market
The clients or customers sought for a business' product or service.

Targeted Jobs Tax Credit
Federal legislation enacted in 1978 that provides a tax credit to an employer who hires structurally unemployed individuals.

Tax number
A number assigned to a business by a state revenue department that enables the business to buy goods without paying sales tax.

Taxable bonds
An interest-bearing certificate of public or private indebtedness. Bonds are issued by public agencies to finance economic development.

Technical assistance
See Management and technical assistance

Technical evaluation
Assessment of technological feasibility.

Technology
The method in which a firm combines and utilizes labor and capital resources to produce goods or

services; the application of science for commercial or industrial purposes.

Technology transfer
The movement of information about a technology or intellectual property from one party to another for use.

Tenure
See Employee tenure

Term
The length of time for which a loan is made.

Terms of a note
The conditions or limits of a note; includes the interest rate per annum, the due date, and transferability and convertibility features, if any.

Third-party administrator
An outside company responsible for handling claims and performing administrative tasks associated with health insurance plan maintenance.

Third-stage financing
Financing provided for the major expansion of a company whose sales volume is increasing and that is breaking even or profitable. These funds are used for further plant expansion, marketing, working capital, or development of an improved product. Also known as Third-round or Mezzanine financing.

Time management
Skills and scheduling techniques used to maximize productivity.

Trade credit
Credit extended by suppliers of raw materials or finished products. In an accounting statement, trade credit is referred to as "accounts payable."

Trade name
The name under which a company conducts business, or by which its business, goods, or services are identified. It may or may not be registered as a trademark.

Trade periodical
A publication with a specific focus on one or more aspects of business and industry.

Trade secret
Competitive advantage gained by a business through the use of a unique manufacturing process or formula.

Trade show
An exhibition of goods or services used in a particular industry. Typically held in exhibition centers where exhibitors rent space to display their merchandise.

Trademark
A graphic symbol, device, or slogan that identifies a business. A business has property rights to its trademark from the inception of its use, but it is still prudent to register all trademarks with the Trademark Office of the U.S. Department of Commerce.

Trend
A statistical measurement used to track changes that occur over time.

Trough
See Cyclical trough

UCC
See Uniform Commercial Code

UL
See Underwriters Laboratories

Underwriters Laboratories (UL)
One of several private firms that tests products and processes to determine their safety. Although various firms can provide this kind of testing service, many local and insurance codes specify UL certification.

Underwriting
A process by which an insurer determines whether or not and on what basis it will accept an application for insurance. In an experience-rated plan, premiums are based on a firm's or group's past claims; factors other than prior claims are used for community-rated or manually rated plans.

Unfair competition
Refers to business practices, usually unethical, such as using unlicensed products, pirating merchandise, or misleading the public through false advertising, which give the offending business an unequitable advantage over others.

Unfunded accrued liability
The excess of total liabilities, both present and prospective, over present and prospective assets.

Unemployment
The joblessness of individuals who are willing to work, who are legally and physically able to work, and who are seeking work. Unemployment may represent the temporary joblessness of a worker between jobs (frictional unemployment) or the joblessness of a worker whose skills are not suitable for jobs available in the labor market (structural unemployment).

Uniform Commercial Code (UCC)
A code of laws governing commercial transactions across the U.S., except Louisiana. Their purpose is to bring uniformity to financial transactions.

Uniform product code (UPC symbol)
A computer-readable label comprised of ten digits and stripes that encodes what a product is and how much it costs. The first five digits are assigned by the Uniform Product Code Council, and the last five digits by the individual manufacturer.

Unit cost
See Average cost

UPC symbol
See Uniform product code

U.S. Establishment and Enterprise Microdata (USEEM) File
A cross-sectional database containing information on employment, sales, and location for individual enterprises and establishments with employees that have a Dun & Bradstreet credit rating.

U.S. Establishment Longitudinal Microdata (USELM) File
A database containing longitudinally linked sample microdata on establishments drawn from the U.S. Establishment and Enterprise Microdata file (see separate citation).

U.S. Small Business Administration 504 Program
See Certified development corporation

USEEM
See U.S. Establishment and Enterprise Microdata File

USELM
See U.S. Establishment Longitudinal Microdata File

VCN
See Venture capital network

Venture capital
Money used to support new or unusual business ventures that exhibit above-average growth rates, significant potential for market expansion, and are in need of additional financing to sustain growth or further research and development; equity or equity-type financing traditionally provided at the commercialization stage, increasingly available prior to commercialization.

Venture capital company
A company organized to provide seed capital to a business in its formation stage, or in its first or second stage of expansion. Funding is obtained through public or private pension funds, commercial banks and bank holding companies, small business investment corporations licensed by the U.S. Small Business Administration, private venture capital firms, insurance companies, investment management companies, bank trust departments, industrial companies seeking to diversify their investment, and investment bankers acting as intermediaries for other investors or directly investing on their own behalf.

Venture capital limited partnerships
Designed for business development, these partnerships are an institutional mechanism for providing capital for young, technology-oriented businesses. The investors' money is pooled and invested in money market assets until venture investments have been selected. The general partners are experienced investment managers who select and invest the equity and debt securities of firms with high growth potential and the ability to go public in the near future.

Venture capital network (VCN)
A computer database that matches investors with entrepreneurs.

WAN
See Wide Area Network

Wide Area Network (WAN)
Computer networks linking systems throughout a state or around the world in order to facilitate the sharing of information.

Withholding

Federal, state, social security, and unemployment taxes withheld by the employer from employees' wages; employers are liable for these taxes and the corporate umbrella and bankruptcy will not exonerate an employer from paying back payroll withholding. Employers should escrow these funds in a separate account and disperse them quarterly to withholding authorities.

Workers' compensation

A state-mandated form of insurance covering workers injured in job-related accidents. In some states, the state is the insurer; in other states, insurance must be acquired from commercial insurance firms. Insurance rates are based on a number of factors, including salaries, firm history, and risk of occupation.

Working capital

Refers to a firm's short-term investment of current assets, including cash, short-term securities, accounts receivable, and inventories.

Yield

The rate of income returned on an investment, expressed as a percentage. Income yield is obtained by dividing the current dollar income by the current market price of the security. Net yield or yield to maturity is the current income yield minus any premium above par or plus any discount from par in purchase price, with the adjustment spread over the period from the date of purchase to the date of maturity.

Index

Listings in this index are arranged alphabetically by business plan type, then alphabetically by business plan name. Users are provided with the volume number in which the plan appears.

Index

Index